PMP® IN DEPTH, SECOND EDITION:

PROJECT MANAGEMENT PROFESSIONAL STUDY GU~~IDE FOR THE PMP® EXAM~~

D0507184

Dr. Paul Sanghera, PMP

Course Technology PTR

A part of Cengage Learning

COURSE TECHNOLOGY
CENGAGE Learning™

Australia, Brazil, Japan, Korea, Mexico, Singapore, Spain, United Kingdom, United States

COURSE TECHNOLOGY
CENGAGE Learning™

PMP® In Depth, Second Edition: Project Management Professional Study Guide for the PMP® Exam
Dr. Paul Sanghera, PMP

Publisher and General Manager, Course Technology PTR:
Stacy L. Hiquet

Associate Director of Marketing:
Sarah Panella

Manager of Editorial Services:
Heather Talbot

Marketing Manager:
Mark Hughes

Acquisitions Editor:
Mitzi Koontz

Project Editor/Copy Editor:
Cathleen D. Small

Technical Reviewer:
Paul Gneco

Editorial Services Coordinator:
Jen Blaney

Interior Layout Tech:
Bill Hartman

Cover Designer:
Mike Tanamachi

Indexer:
Kelly Talbot

Proofreader:
Sandy Doell

For product information and technology assistance, contact us at
Cengage Learning Customer & Sales Support, 1-800-354-9706

For permission to use material from this text or product, submit all requests online at **cengage.com/permissions**. Further permissions questions can be e-mailed to **permissionrequest@cengage.com**.

PMI, PMP, and PMBOK are registered trademarks of Project Management Institute, Inc. in the United States and/or other countries. All other trademarks are the property of their respective owners.

Library of Congress Control Number: 2009927807

ISBN-13: 978-1-59863-996-4

ISBN-10: 1-59863-996-X

Course Technology, a part of Cengage Learning
20 Channel Center Street
Boston, MA 02210
USA

Cengage Learning is a leading provider of customized learning solutions with office locations around the globe, including Singapore, the United Kingdom, Australia, Mexico, Brazil, and Japan. Locate your local office at: **international.cengage.com/region**.

Cengage Learning products are represented in Canada by Nelson Education, Ltd.

For your lifelong learning solutions, visit **courseptr.com**.

Visit our corporate Web site at **cengage.com**.

Printed in the United States of America
1 2 3 4 5 6 7 11 10 09

To life

Whose every day is a project

That I run from time's shoulders.

To my friends,

the key stakeholders:

Gurmail Kandola, John Serri, and Kulwinder

Baldev Khullar, Ruth Gordon, and Bhupinder

Stanley Wong and Srilatha are a few to name.

With friends, I can see clearly

Through storm and rain.

Friends without whom

Every path is just a trail of dust.

With whom I'm like the first man

Walking on the planet Earth.

Acknowledgments

Each time I get a book published, I re-learn a lesson that transforming an idea into a finished book takes a project (it produces a unique product—that is, the book—and it has a beginning and an end) and a project team. As they say (well, if they don't anymore, they should), first things first. Let me begin by thanking Mitzi Koontz for initiating this project. With two thumbs up, thanks to Cathleen Small for managing this project from the planning stage through the executing stage, the monitoring/controlling stage, and all the way to the closing stage.

It's my pleasure to acknowledge the hard work of other members of the team as well: Bill Hartman for layout, Sandy Doell for proofreading, and Kelly Talbot for indexing. My special thanks to Paul Gneco, the technical editor of this book, for carefully reviewing a number of chapters and offering valuable feedback.

In some ways, writing this book is an expression of the project manager and educator inside me. I thank some great minds from whom I directly or indirectly learned about management during my journey in the computer industry from Novell to Dream Logic: Chuck Castleton at Novell, Delon Dotson at Netscape and MP3.com, Kate Peterson at Weborder, and Dr. John Serri at Dream Logic. I also thank my colleagues and seniors in the field of education for helping me in so many ways to become a better educator. Here are a few to mention: Dr. Gerald Pauler (Brooks College), Professor David Hayes (San Jose State University), Professor Michael Burke (San Jose State University), and Dr. John Serri (University of Phoenix).

Last, but not least, my appreciation (along with my heart) goes to my wife, Renee, and my son, Adam, for not only peacefully coexisting with my projects, but also for supporting them.

About the Author

One of the world's leading experts in project management, **Dr. Paul Sanghera** is a manager, an educator, a technologist, and an entrepreneur and has more than 15 years of diverse project management experience in the computer industry from Netscape to MP3 and at research labs from Cornell to CERN. Having worked in various roles, including director of project management, director of software development, software developer, trainer, and scientist, he has a broad view of project management. Expertise in multiple application areas, including physics, computer science, RFID, biotechnology, and nanotechnology, has helped him to master the global principles of project management that apply to all application areas. Dr. Sanghera has several industry certifications, including PMP, CAPM, Project+, Network+, Linux+, SCJP, and SCBCD, and he has contributed to building world-class technologies, such as Netscape Communicator and Novell's NDS. As an engineering manager, he has been at the ground floor of several startups and has been a lecturer at San Jose State University and Brooks College. He has authored or co-authored more than 100 technical papers published in well-reputed European and American research journals. Dr. Sanghera is the best-selling author of several books on science, technology, and project management. He has a master's degree in Computer Science from Cornell University and a Ph.D. in Physics from Carleton University. He lives in Silicon Valley, where he runs an information company, Infonential Inc., that specializes in project management and emerging technologies.

Contents

PART III: EXECUTING THE PROJECT

PART VI: APPENDIXES

Introduction

"Begin at the beginning, and go on till you come to the end: then stop."

—*Alice in Wonderland* by Lewis Carroll

The primary purpose of this book is to help you pass the Project Management Professional (PMP) exam administered by the Project Management Institute (PMI). Because the book has a laser-sharp focus on the exam objectives, expert project managers who want to pass the PMP exam can use this book to ensure that they do not miss any objective. Yet this is not an exam-cram book. The chapters and the sections within each chapter are presented in a logical learning sequence: A topic and a chapter only depend upon the previously covered topics and chapters, and there is no hopping from topic to topic. The concepts and topics, both simple and complex, are clearly explained when they appear for the first time. No prior knowledge of project management is assumed. This facilitates stepwise learning, prevents confusion, and makes this book useful also for beginners who want to get up to speed quickly to pass the PMP exam, even if they are new to the discipline of project management.

Who This Book Is For

With a focus on the PMP exam topics, this book is designed to serve the following audiences:

- ◆ Project management practitioners who want to prepare for the PMP exam.
- ◆ Entry-level project managers and project team members who want to prepare for the PMP exam.
- ◆ Beginners who want to join the field of project management.
- ◆ Project managers who want a book to use as a quick and easy reference to the discipline of project management.
- ◆ Instructors and trainers who want a textbook for a course on project management.

How This Book Is Organized

This book tells the story of project management in a cohesive, concise, yet comprehensive fashion. The book is written to the most current version of the PMP exam based on the Fourth Edition of *A Guide to the Project Management Body of Knowledge* (PMBOK Guide) by PMI. The discipline of project management, according to the PMBOK Guide, contains nine knowledge areas, such as cost management and quality management, and five process groups: initiating, planning, executing, monitoring and controlling, and closing. The PMBOK Guide and almost all project management exam books are organized along the knowledge areas. However, the exam objectives published by PMI, referred to as *tasks* in the exam specifications by PMI, are organized in order of the process groups. This poses a problem for the reader preparing for the exam based on exam objectives. For example, one of these books refers to 11 chapters for one exam objective in its exam readiness checklist. This book solves that problem by presenting the material in order of process groups: initiating, planning, executing, monitoring and controlling, and closing. This order of presentation is also consistent with the lifecycle of a project, and therefore facilitates natural learning by connecting to real-world experience.

How Each Chapter Is Organized

With the exception of Chapter 1, on project management framework, each chapter begins with a list of exam objectives on which the chapter is focused. These objectives are officially called *tasks* by PMI, and these tasks are organized into domains, which are essentially the process groups, except the last domain. I have exactly followed the order of the domains published by PMI, but I have shuffled around a few objectives to keep the topics and the subject matter in line with sequential learning and to avoid hopping from topic to topic.

The first section in each chapter is an introduction in which I establish three underlying concepts or topics that will be explored in the chapter. Each chapter has the following features:

- ◆ **Exam Objectives.** Each exam objective covered in the chapter is fully explained at the beginning of the chapter.
- ◆ **Big Picture**. Each chapter begins with introducing the big picture of the topics covered in the chapter. This prepares the reader for a smooth dive into the details.
- ◆ **Study Checkpoints**. Each chapter in its body presents Study Checkpoints, which are exercises to ensure that you get the crucial points in the covered material. The solution to Study Checkpoints are presented in Appendix A.
- ◆ **Notes and Tips.** As you read through a chapter, you will find *Notes* that present additional helpful material related to the topic being described and *Tips* that provide additional real-world insight into the topic being discussed.
- ◆ **Summary.** The Summary section of each chapter provides the big, unified picture while reviewing the important concepts in the chapter.

◆ **Exam's Eye View.** The Exam's Eye View section highlights the important points in the chapter from the perspective of the exam: the things that you must comprehend, the things that you should watch out for because they might not seem to fit in with the ordinary order of things, and the facts that you should memorize for the exam.

◆ **Key Terms and Definitions.** This section lists the important terms and concepts introduced in the chapter along with their definitions.

◆ **Review Questions.** Each chapter ends with a Review Questions section that has a two-pronged purpose: to help you test your knowledge about the material presented in the chapter and to help you evaluate your ability to answer the exam questions based on the exam objectives covered in the chapter. The answers to the review questions are presented in Appendix B.

About the PMP Exam

This book covers the material for the PMP exam. Passing this exam is necessary to obtain PMP certification.

To be eligible to take the PMP exam, you must meet a set of minimum requirements. A summary of these requirements and other details are listed in the following table.

The Details of the PMP Exam

Exam Detail	PMP Exam
Number of questions	Scoreable: 175
	Pretest: 25
Maximum time allowed	Four hours
Question types	Multiple choice
Minimum educational background	Category 1: Bachelor's degree
	Category 2: High school diploma
Minimum project management experience	Category 1: 4,500 hours
	Category 2: 7,500 hours
Minimum formal project management education	Category 1: 35 contact hours
	Category 2: 35 contact hours
Exam fee (given in U.S. dollars—may vary by country)	Member: $405
	Nonmember: $555
Sign code of professional conduct	Yes

As mentioned previously, the PMP exam objectives are organized along the process groups (stages of the project lifecycle, as we call them in this book). These process groups and the topics of professional and social responsibility are called the *domains*. The relative weight given to these domains in the PMP exam is listed in the following table.

Proportion of Questions from Each Domain

Domain #	Domain Name	Approximate Percentage Coverage in the Exam
1	Initiating the Project	11
2	Planning the Project	23
3	Executing the Project	27
4	Monitoring and Controlling the Project	21
5	Closing the Project	9
6	Professional and Social Responsibility	9
	Total	100

If you have already taken the CAPM exam, which is not a requirement for the PMP exam, you should know that the main differences between the questions in the two exams are the following:

◆ The PMP exam will have situational questions that assume you have been working in the project management field.

◆ The CAPM exam is entirely based on the PMBOK Guide, whereas the PMP exam can have questions on topics not covered in the PMBOK Guide or not covered in much detail. Some of these topics are management theories and professional and social responsibilities based on the Code of Ethics and Professional Conduct by the PMI. Of course, this book covers these topics.

The following points are common to both the PMP and CAPM exams:

◆ Pretest questions are randomly placed throughout the examination. Your score does not depend on these questions.

◆ Computer-based exams are preceded by a 15-minute computer tutorial, which is not part of the allotted exam time.

◆ The passing score is determined by an approach called the *Modified Angoff Technique*, which relies on the collective judgment of groups of CAPM certificants from around the globe. The final passing score for the examination is based on this pooled judgment and the calculation of the standard error on the mean. Finally, item analysis and reliability indices are calculated for each question.

These credential examinations are offered via computer at locations in North America and in other countries around the world. For a complete list of computer-based testing locations, please visit www.2test.com.

For the most up-to-date information regarding these examinations, please visit the certification section of PMI's website at www.pmi.org.

Following are a few tips that you can use during the exam:

◆ PMI has a very formal way of naming processes, process groups, knowledge areas, and some documents. However, just like in real life, do not expect that the exam will always refer to these names in a formal way. To help you on this issue, this book refers to these names in both formal and informal ways. For example, controlling quality (informal) means the Perform Quality Control process (formal), scope management (informal) means Project Scope Management (formal), and initiating (or initiation) means Initiating Process Group.

◆ The questions in the PMP exam can be wordy and might include unnecessary information to distract you from the relevant facts. So, you need to read the questions carefully and patiently and figure out what counts and what does not.

◆ Get comfortable with the idea that there will be some questions that you will not be able to answer correctly. In such a situation, just believe in yourself and your experience, and accordingly select the best answer. You may have the option to leave these questions for a possible review later if you have time. (Read the instructions before starting the exam to find out.) Key point: Move on without getting frustrated.

◆ There will be tricky questions to weed out candidates who might have project management experience, but who do not have an in-depth understanding of the discipline of project management from the perspective of PMI, as covered in this book.

◆ There will be questions for which you will need to choose between an innocent way of skipping the formal process to save time and following the formal project management process. In almost all cases, the correct answer will be to follow the process.

◆ There will be questions for which you will need to choose between facing the problem head on or taking an easy way out, such as dodging a thorny issue, ignoring a challenging problem, or postponing a difficult decision. Almost always, the correct answer is to meet the problem head on in a professional manner.

◆ To answer some questions correctly, understand that in the world of project management as seen from the perspective of PMI, project managers communicate directly and clearly and do not say things between the lines. For example, if you have a problem with a team member, you talk to the team member face to face rather than going to the member's manager, which you might need to do eventually if you can't solve the problem by directly dealing with the team member.

◆ Understand clearly the roles of the key stakeholders, such as the project manager, project sponsor, and customer. Especially understand your responsibilities as a project manager. You need to be proactive to make decisions and manage the project, influence the factors that contribute to changes rather than waiting for the changes to occur, and have up-to-date information about the project.

Best wishes for the exam; go for it!

Exam Readiness Checklist

Exam Objective	Chapter Number
1. Initiating the Project	
1.1 Conduct Project Selection Methods	2
1.2 Define Scope	2, 3
1.3 Document Project Risks, Assumptions, and Constraints	2, 6
1.4 Identify and Perform Stakeholder Analysis	2
1.5 Develop a Project Charter	2
1.6 Obtain Project Charter Approval	2
2. Planning the Project	
2.1 Define and Record Requirements, Constraints, and Assumptions	3
2.2 Identify Project Team and Define Roles and Responsibilities	4, 8
2.3 Create the WBS	3, 4, 5, 6
2.4 Develop Change Management Plan	3
2.5 Identify Risks and Define Risk Strategies	6
2.6 Obtain Plan Approval	3, 4
2.7 Conduct Kickoff Meeting	8
3. Executing the Project	
3.1 Execute Tasks Defined in the Project Plan	7
3.2 Ensure Common Understanding and Set Expectations	8, 9
3.3 Implement the Procurement of Project Resources	7
3.4 Manage Resource Allocation	5
3.5 Implement a Quality Management Plan	7
3.6 Implement Approved Changes	7
3.7 Implement Approved Actions and Workarounds	7
3.8 Improve Team Performance	8
4. Monitoring and Controlling the Project	
4.1 Measure Project Performance	10, 11, 12
4.2 Verify and Manage Changes to the Project	10, 12
4.3 Ensure Project Deliverables Conform to Quality Standards	11
4.4 Monitor All Risks	11

Exam Readiness Checklist (Continued)

Exam Objective	Chapter Number
5. Closing the Project	
5.1 Obtain Final Acceptance for the Project	13
5.2 Obtain Financial, Legal, and Administrative Closure	13
5.3 Release Project Resources	13
5.4 Identify, Document, and Communicate Lessons Learned	13
5.5 Create and Distribute Final Project Report	13
5.6 Archive and Retain Project Records	13
5.7 Measure Customer Satisfaction	13
6. Professional and Social Responsibility	
6.1 Ensure Individual Integrity	14
6.2 Contribute to the Project Management Knowledge Base	14
6.3 Enhance Personal Professional Competence	14
6.4 Promote Interaction among Stakeholders	14

PART

I

Initiating the Project

Welcome to the world of project management. Here is project management for you in five concepts: initiate, plan, execute, monitor and control, and close. The rest is the detail. In order to optimize your learning about initiating a project, you will want to know what a project is, and you will want to have an overview—a bird's-eye view—of the field of project management. This is presented in Chapter 1. In Chapter 2, you will learn where projects come from and how they are selected and initiated.

Chapter 1

Project Management Framework

Key Concepts Covered in This Chapter

- Basic concepts of project management

- Project, process, operation, program, and portfolio

- Progressive elaboration

- Project stakeholders

- Influence of project environment: organizational culture, organizational structure, enterprise environmental factors, and organizational process assets

- Project lifecycle, process groups, and knowledge areas

- Projects, programs, portfolios, and strategic business plans

- Probability

- Baseline

Introduction

What do the Taj Mahal, the Internet, and this book have in common? Projects! All three of them are products of projects. Even given all the required material and the knowledge, how do people really build immense and complex structures or systems, such as the Taj Mahal of Agra, the Eiffel Tower of Paris, or the World Wide Web of the Information Age? The answer is again projects. Through projects, it is possible to build small and big and simple and complex things in an effective and efficient manner. All projects need to be managed. A so-called unmanaged project is simply a poorly managed project that is destined to fail. Therefore, the importance of project management cannot be overstated.

Managing a project means managing the lifecycle of the project, starting from the beginning (initiating) and going to the end (closing); this is accomplished using processes, which constitute what are called *project management knowledge areas*. Although you use your knowledge in terms of processes to manage the projects, the management will be greatly influenced by the environment in which the project runs, such as the structure and culture of the performing organization.

The goal of this chapter is to walk you through the framework of project management. To that end, we will explore three avenues: the project lifecycle, project management knowledge areas, and the project environment.

Basic Concepts

Each discipline of knowledge builds upon some basic concepts. The terms that refer to or define these concepts make up the language of the discipline. The very basic terms in project management are described briefly in the following list:

◆ **Project.** A project is a work effort made over a finite period of time with a start and a finish to create a unique product, service, or result. Because a project has a start and an end, it is also called a *temporary effort or endeavor.*

◆ **Organization.** An organization is a group of individuals organized to work for some purpose or mission. Computer companies, energy companies (to whom you pay your electric bills), and cable companies are examples of organizations. An organization might offer products, such as books and donuts, or services, such as Internet access or online banking. A project is usually performed inside an organization. Organization is a very general concept that includes groups for profit and nonprofit, public and private, and government and nongovernment.

◆ **Project stakeholder.** A project stakeholder is an individual or an organization that can be positively or negatively affected by the project execution. A project can have a wide spectrum of stakeholders, from the project sponsor, to an environmental organization, to an ordinary citizen.

◆ **Process.** A process is a set of related tasks performed to manage a certain aspect of a project, such as cost. Each process belongs to a knowledge area and corresponds to a process group.

◆ **Knowledge area.** A knowledge area in project management is defined by its knowledge requirements related to managing a specific aspect of a project, such as cost, by using a set of processes. PMI recognizes a total of nine knowledge areas, such as cost management and human resource management.

◆ **Performing organization.** The performing organization is the organization that is performing the project.

◆ **Project management.** Project management is the usage of knowledge, skills, and tools to manage a project from start to finish with the goal of meeting the project requirements. It involves using the appropriate processes.

◆ **Program.** A program is a set of related projects managed in a coordinated fashion to improve overall efficiency and effectiveness and to obtain benefits and control that would not be obtained by managing them individually. For example, a program could be delivering a product (or service) that consists of sub-products (or service components) delivered by the constituent projects. Also, a program might include related work that is not included in the scope of any of the constituent projects.

◆ **Program management.** Program management is the centralized, coordinated management of a specific program to achieve its strategic goals, objectives, and benefits.

◆ **Program management office (PMO).** The program management office is an entity in an organization that is responsible for providing centralized, coordinated support to the program managers managing programs and unrelated projects.

◆ **Project management office.** Project management office (PMO) refers to an entity in an organization that is responsible for providing centralized coordinated management and support for projects in the organization.

 ALERT

Although both have the same abbreviation, PMO, the project management office and program management office are not identical. For example, only an organization that runs programs will have a program management office, whereas an organization that runs individual projects can have a project management office.

◆ **Portfolio.** A portfolio is a set of projects, programs, and related work that is managed in a coordinated fashion to obtain business objectives in the strategic plan of the organization.

◆ **Portfolio management.** Portfolio management is the centralized management of one or more portfolios that includes identifying, authorizing, prioritizing, managing, and controlling projects, programs, and other related work in order to obtain specific business objectives in the strategic plan of the organization.

This is a minimal set of terms that you need to understand before you can start exploring the world of project management. More terms will be introduced as you continue exploring the discipline of project management in this book.

Now that you understand these basic terms, you can ask a very basic question: What does it mean to manage a project? In other words, what's involved in managing a project?

Managing Projects

Before getting into project management, you need to understand what a project is. At any organization there are many activities being executed every day. Most of these activities are organized into groups of interrelated activities. These groups fall into two categories: projects and operations. An operation is an ongoing and repetitive set of tasks, whereas a project has a lifecycle—a beginning and an end.

Understanding a Project

A project is a work effort made over a finite period of time with a start and a finish to create a unique product, service, or result. Because a project has a start and a finish, it is also called a *temporary effort or endeavor*. In other words, a project is a temporary endeavor taken to create a unique product, service, or result. So, a project has two defining characteristics: It is temporary, and it creates a unique product. Let's explore further these two defining concepts: temporary and unique.

Temporary. The temporary nature of projects refers to the fact that each project has a definite beginning and a definite end. A project can reach its end in one of two possible ways:

◆ The project has met its objectives—that is, the planned unique product has been created.

◆ The project has been terminated before its successful completion for whatever reason.

The temporary nature of projects can also apply to two other aspects:

◆ The opportunity to market the product that the project will produce is temporary—that is, the product needs to be produced in a limited timeframe; otherwise, it will be too late.

◆ A project team is temporary—that is, the project team is disbanded after the project ends, and the team members may be individually assigned to other projects.

However, remember that the temporary nature of a project does not refer to the product it creates. The projects can create lasting products, such as the Taj Mahal, the Eiffel Tower, or the Internet. The second defining characteristic of a project is that it must create a unique product.

Unique product. The outcome of a project must be a unique product, service, or result. How do a product, a service, and a result differ from each other?

- ◆ **Product.** This is a tangible, quantifiable artifact that is either the end item or a component of it. The big-screen television set in your living room, the Swiss watch on your wrist, and the wine bottle on your table are some examples of products.
- ◆ **Service.** Actually, when we say a project can create a service, we really mean the capability to perform a service. For example, a project that creates a website for a bank to offer online banking has created the capability to offer the online banking service.
- ◆ **Result.** This is usually the knowledge-related outcome of a project—for example, the results of an analysis performed in a research project.

Quite often, I will refer to product, service, or result as just "product" for brevity.

Projects are organized to execute a set of activities that cannot be addressed within the limits of the organization's ongoing normal operations. To clearly identify whether an undertaking is a project, you must understand the difference between a project and an operation.

Distinguishing Projects from Operations

An organization executes a multitude of activities as part of the work to achieve objectives. Some of these activities are to support projects and others are to support what are called *operations*. An operation is a set of tasks that does not qualify to be a project. In other words, an operation is a function that performs ongoing tasks: It does not produce a unique (new) product or it does not have a beginning and an end—or both. For example, to put a data center together is a project, but after you put it together, keeping it up and running is an operation.

It is important to understand that projects and operations share some characteristics, such as the following:

- ◆ Both require resources, including human resources (people).
- ◆ Both are constrained to limited, as opposed to unlimited, resources.
- ◆ Both are managed—that is, planned, executed, and controlled.
- ◆ Both have objectives.

The distinctions between projects and operations can be made by sticking to the definition of a project—that it is temporary and unique. Operations are generally ongoing and repetitive. Although both projects and operations have objectives, a project ends when its objectives are met, whereas an operation continues toward attaining a new set of objectives when the current set of objectives has been attained.

Projects can be performed at various levels of an organization; they vary in size, and accordingly can involve just one person or a team. Table 1.1 presents some examples of projects.

Table 1.1 Examples of Projects

Project	Outcome (Product, Service, or Result)
Constructing Eiffel Tower	Product
Running presidential election campaign	Results: win or lose; Products: documents
Developing a website to offer online education	Service
Setting up a computer network in one building	Service
Moving a computer network from one building to another	Result: network is moved
Study the genes of members of Congress	Results (of the research); Product: research paper

---

STUDY CHECKPOINT 1.1

Identify each of the following items as a project or an operation.

A. Restaurant employees serving breakfast to the customers every day
B. A bookseller processing customer orders
C. A network administrator ensuring that the network stays up and running 24×7
D. Writing and publishing a book

A project can result in a product (or service) that is sustained by an operation. For example, constructing the Eiffel Tower is a project, whereas managing it for the tourists visiting it every day is an operation.

How do projects come into existence? In other words, how do you come up with a project? Sure, you have an idea, a concept of some final product, but how exactly do you write it down and declare it a project? A project is born and brought up through a procedure called *progressive elaboration*.

Understanding Progressive Elaboration

As the saying goes: Rome was not built in a day. Rest assured, the product of a project—even the project plan—is not built in a day, either. Usually there is a concept first and a broad vision for the end product—that is, the outcome of the project. The clearer vision you have of the unique product that you want from the project, the more accurate the project plan will be. So, you move toward the final project plan in incremental steps as the ideas about the final product are refined and as you get more and more information about the requirements in a progressive fashion. This procedure of defining (or planning) a project is called *progressive elaboration.*

Here is an example of progressive elaboration. You wake up one morning with an idea to close the digital gap in your community. Now, you have a concept of the final product (result) of your project: Close the digital gap in your community. But what do you really mean by that? It might include many things—building computers in an economical way and providing them at low prices to those who don't have them, raising awareness of the necessity of computer literacy, offering classes, and the like. Now you are really working to refine your idea of the final product. The second question is, how are you going to do this? Here you are referring to the project plan. You can see that the project plan and its accuracy and details depend upon how refined the idea of the final product is. The final product or objectives and the plan to achieve them will be elaborated further in steps.

 TIP

Uncontrolled changes that make it into the project without being properly processed are called *scope creep*. Do not confuse progressive elaboration with scope creep.

Progressive elaboration, in general, means developing something in incremental steps. The project plan will be broadly defined to start and will get more accurate, detailed, and explicit in an incremental fashion as better understanding about the project deliverables and objectives develops. It involves successive iterations of the planning process resulting in a more accurate and complete plan.

Even after you have an approved final project plan and the project starts executing, progressive elaboration continues to some extent. For example, you will see later in this chapter that execution and planning stages of the project interact with each other.

Each stage of a project is managed by performing a set of processes.

Understanding a Process

Processes are the heart of project management. If you want to think of project management like a project management professional, think in terms of processes. Almost everything in the world of project management is done through processes.

What is a process, anyway? Back up a little and look around you; you will see processes everywhere, not only in project management. For example, when you make coffee in the morning, you go through a process. The water, the coffee filter, and the roasted hazelnut coffee made by grinding golden-colored beans are the input items to this process. The coffeemaker is the tool, and how you made the coffee is the technique. A cup of freshly brewed hazelnut coffee is an output item from this process. So, a process is a set of interrelated activities performed to obtain a specified set of products, results, or services. A process, as explained in the example and in Figure 1.1, consists of three elements: input, tools and techniques, and output.

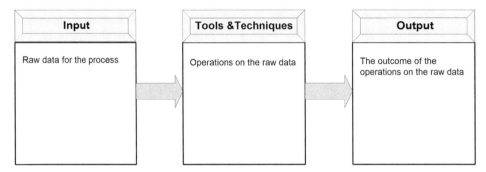

FIGURE 1.1 *Three elements of a process: input, tools and techniques, and output*

Of course, you can come up with other examples of processes that you have been using in your life without realizing it. In project management, you use processes to accomplish things, such as developing a project schedule, directing and managing the project execution, and developing and managing the project team.

As illustrated in Figure 1.1, each process consists of three elements, described in the following list:

◆ **Input.** The input to a process consists of the raw data that is needed to start the process. For example, the list of activities that need to be scheduled is one of several input items to the process that will be used to develop the schedule of a project.

◆ **Tools and techniques.** Tools and techniques are the methods used to operate on the input to transform it into output. For example, project management software that helps to develop a schedule is a tool used in the schedule development process.

◆ **Output.** The output is the outcome or the result of a process. Each process contains at least one output item; otherwise, there would be no point in performing a process. For example, an output item of the schedule development process is, well, the project schedule.

Now that you understand what a process is, you likely realize that you will be using different processes at the different stages of a project, such as planning and execution. Actually, the whole lifecycle of a project can be understood in terms of five stages, with each stage corresponding to a group of processes.

Understanding the Project Lifecycle

From initiation/authorization to completion/closure, a project goes through a whole lifecycle that includes defining the project objectives, planning the work to achieve those objectives, performing the work, monitoring and controlling the progress, and closing the project after receiving the product acceptance. Figure 1.2 shows the different stages of the project lifecycle; the arrows indicate the flow of information.

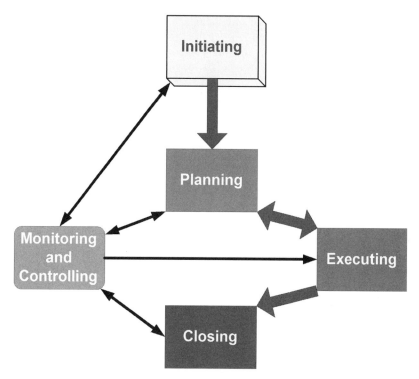

FIGURE 1.2 *Different stages in the lifecycle of a project. Each of these stages represents a process group.*

The five stages, called *process groups*, of a project lifecycle are described in the following list.

Initiating. This stage defines and authorizes the project. The project manager is named, and the project is officially launched through a signed document called the *project charter*, which contains items such as the purpose of the project, a high-level product description, a summary of the milestone schedule, and a business case for the project. Another outcome of this stage is a document called the *stakeholder register*, which identifies the project stakeholders and important information about them. The processes used to perform this stage fall into a group called the *initiating process group*.

 NOTE

In the discipline of project management, like in many other disciplines, the term *high-level* means lacking details or not referring to details. Keep this meaning in mind when you read the terms in this book, such as high-level product description, high-level plan, and the like. Details are usually worked out through a process called *progressive elaboration.*

Planning. In this stage, you, the project manager, along with the project management team, refine the project objectives and requirements and develop the project management plan, which is a collection of several plans that constitute a course of actions required to achieve the objectives and meet the requirements of the project. The project scope is finalized with the project scope statement. The project management plan, the outcome of this stage, contains subsidiary plans, such as a project scope management plan, a schedule management plan, and a quality management plan. The processes used to perform this stage fall into a group called the *planning process group*.

Executing. In this stage, you, the project manager, implement the project management plan, and the project team performs the work scheduled in the planning stage. You coordinate all the activities being performed to achieve the project objectives and meet the project requirements. Of course, the main output of this project is the project deliverables. Approved changes, recommendations, and defect repairs are also implemented in this stage. But where do these changes and recommendations come from? They arise from monitoring and controlling the project. The stakeholders can also suggest changes, which must go through an approval process before implementation. The project execution is performed using the processes that fall into a group called the *executing process group*.

Monitoring and controlling. You monitor and control the project through its lifecycle, including the executing stage. Monitoring and controlling includes defending the project against scope creep (unapproved changes to the project scope), monitoring the project progress and performance to identify variance from the plan, and recommending preventive and corrective actions to bring the project in line with the planned expectations in the approved project management plan. Requests for changes, such as change to the project scope, are also included in this stage; they can come from you or from any other project stakeholder. The changes must go through an approval process, and only the approved changes are implemented. The processes used in this stage fall into a group called the *monitoring and controlling process group*.

Closing. In this stage, you manage the formal acceptance of the project product, close any contracts involved, and bring the project to an end by disbanding the project team. Closing the project includes conducting a project review for lessons learned and possibly turning over the outcome of the project to another group, such as the maintenance or operations group. Don't forget the last, but not the least, task of the closing stage: celebration. Terminated projects (that is, projects cancelled before completion) should also go through the closing stage. The processes used to perform the closing stage fall into the group called the *closing process group*.

 NOTE

What we refer to as project stages here are not actually the project phases. A project phase is part of the whole project in which certain milestones or project deliverables are completed. All these stages, technically called *process groups*, can be applied to any phase of a project that is divided into multiple phases.

Table 1.2 presents a summary of the project lifecycle. The initiating stage authorizes a project by naming the project manager, the planning stage further defines the project objectives and plans the work to meet those objectives, the execution stage executes the work, the monitoring and controlling stage monitors the progress of the project and controls it to keep it in line with the plan, and the closing stage formally closes the project by obtaining the product acceptance. Each of these stages is performed by using a group of processes. Thereby, these stages are called *process groups*. In the table these process groups are mapped to another set of names for the project stages: starting the project, organizing and preparing, carrying out the work, and closing the project.

Table 1.2 The Stages of a Project Lifecycle: The Project Process Groups

Process Group	Corresponding Name for the Project Stage	Major Goal	Major Outcome
Initiating	Starting the project	Authorize the project	Project charter
Planning	Organizing and preparing	Plan and schedule the work to perform the project	Project management plan
Executing	Carrying out the work	Perform the project work	Project deliverables: product, service, results
Closing	Closing the project	Close the project formally	Product acceptance, contract closure, and archiving
Monitoring and controlling	Spans the project lifecycle	Monitor the progress of the project to identify the variance from the plan and to correct it	Change requests and recommendations for preventive and corrective actions

The stages of a project or process groups determine when a process is executed, whereas the processes themselves belong to certain knowledge areas of project management.

Understanding Project Management Knowledge Areas

Managing projects requires applying knowledge, skills, and tools and techniques to project activities in order to meet the project objectives. You do this by performing some processes at various stages of the project, discussed in the previous section. That means processes are part of the knowledge required to manage projects. Each aspect of a project is managed by using the corresponding knowledge area. For example, each project has a scope that needs to be managed, and the knowledge required to manage scope is in the knowledge area called *project scope management.* To perform the project work within the project scope, you need human resources, which need to be managed; the knowledge used to manage human resources is called *human resource management.* You get the idea. Each process belongs to one of the nine knowledge areas discussed in the following list.

Project scope management. The primary purpose of project scope management is to ensure that all the required work (and only the required work) is performed to complete the project successfully. This is accomplished by defining and controlling what is included in the project and what is not. To be specific, project scope management includes the following:

- ◆ **Collect requirements.** Collect the requirements for the project based on the stakeholders' needs, which will determine the project scope.

- ◆ **Define scope.** Develop the description for the project and its products, which is the basis for the project scope.

- ◆ **Create the work breakdown structure (WBS).** Decompose the project deliverables into smaller, more manageable work components. The outcome of this exercise is called the *work breakdown structure.*

- ◆ **Verify scope.** Plan how the completed deliverables of the project will be accepted.

- ◆ **Control scope.** Control changes to the project scope—only the approved changes to the scope should be implemented.

Obviously, these components are performed by using the corresponding processes. So, project scope management, in part, defines the work required to complete the project. It's a finite amount of work and will require a finite amount of time, which needs to be managed as well.

Project time management. The primary purpose of project time management is to develop and control the project schedule. This is accomplished by performing the following components:

- ◆ **Define activities.** Identify all the work activities that need to be scheduled to produce the project deliverables.

- ◆ **Sequence activities.** Identify the dependencies among the activities that need to be scheduled (that is, the schedule activities) so that they can be scheduled in the right order.

- ◆ **Estimate activity resources.** For each schedule activity, estimate the types of resources needed and the quantity for each type.

- ◆ **Estimate activity durations.** Estimate the time needed to complete each schedule activity.

- ◆ **Develop schedule.** Analyze the data created in the previous steps to develop the schedule.

- ◆ **Control schedule.** Control changes to the project schedule.

You perform these tasks by using the corresponding processes. It will cost you to get the activities in the schedule completed, and the cost needs to be managed, too.

Project cost management. The primary goal of project cost management is to estimate the cost and to complete the project within the approved budget. Accordingly, cost management includes the following components:

- **Estimate cost.** Develop the cost of the resources needed to complete the project, which includes schedule activities and outsourced (procured) work.
- **Determine budget.** Aggregate the costs of individual activities to establish a cost baseline that includes timing.
- **Control cost.** Monitor and control the cost variance in the project execution—that is, the difference between the planned cost and actual cost during execution, as well as changes to the project budget.

You will use the appropriate processes to accomplish these tasks. The resources needed to complete the project activities include human resources, which need to be managed as well.

 Project human resource management. The primary purpose of project human resource management is to obtain, develop, and manage the project team that will perform the project work. To be specific, project human resource management includes the following components:

- **Develop human resources plan.** Identify project roles, responsibilities for each role, and reporting relationships among the roles. Also, create the staff management plan that describes when and how the resource requirements will be met.
- **Acquire project team.** Obtain the human resources.
- **Develop project team.** Improve the competencies of the team members and the interaction among members to optimize the team performance.
- **Manage project team.** Track the performance of team members, provide them with feedback, and resolve issues and conflicts. This should all be done with the goal to enhance performance—that is, to complete the project on time and within the planned cost and scope.

These components are performed by using the corresponding processes. There will be situations in which your organization does not have the expertise to perform certain schedule activities in-house. For this or other reasons, you might want to acquire some items or services from an outside vendor. This kind of acquisition is called *procurement*, which also needs to be managed.

Project procurement management. The primary purpose of procurement management is to manage acquiring products (that is, products, services, or results) from outside the project team in order to complete the project. The external vendor who offers the service is called the *seller*. Procurement management includes the following:

- **Plan procurements**. Identify purchasing needs, specify the procurement approach, and identify potential sellers.
- **Conduct procurements**. Obtain seller responses, select sellers, and issue contracts.

- ◆ **Administer procurements**. Manage procurement relationships, monitor the procurement performance, and monitor and control changes in procurement.

- ◆ **Close procurements.** Complete each project procurement with proper closure, such as accepting products and closing contracts.

Be it the procured or the in-house work, there are always some uncertainties that give rise to project risks, which need to be managed.

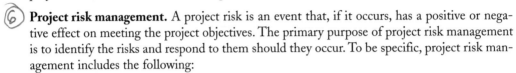 **Project risk management.** A project risk is an event that, if it occurs, has a positive or negative effect on meeting the project objectives. The primary purpose of project risk management is to identify the risks and respond to them should they occur. To be specific, project risk management includes the following:

- ◆ **Plan risk management.** Decide how to determine and execute the risk management tasks.

- ◆ **Identify risks.** Identify the potential risks relevant to the project at hand and determine the characteristics of those risks.

- ◆ **Perform qualitative risk analysis.** Assess the probability of occurrence and the impact for each risk in order to prioritize risks for an action or for further analysis.

- ◆ **Perform quantitative risk analysis.** Estimate the effects of identified risks on project objectives.

- ◆ **Plan risk responses.** Develop action options for risks to maximize opportunities for and minimize threats to satisfying project objectives.

- ◆ **Monitor and control risks.** Track identified risks, implement risk response plans, identify new risks, and evaluate the effectiveness of risk management processes throughout the project.

These tasks related to risk management are performed by using the corresponding processes. The goal of risk management is to help meet the project objectives. The degree to which the project objectives and requirements are met is called *quality*, which needs to be managed.

Project quality management. Project quality is defined as the degree to which a project satisfies its objectives and requirements. For example, a high-quality project is a project that is completed on time and with all the work in the project scope completed within the planned budget. Project quality management includes the following:

- ◆ **Plan quality.** Determine the quality requirements and standards that are relevant to the project at hand and how to apply them.

- ◆ **Perform quality assurance.** Ensure the planned quality requirements and standards are applied.

- ◆ **Perform quality control.** Monitor the quality activities and record the results of these activities in order to assess performance and make necessary recommendations for corrective actions and changes.

These tasks of project quality management are performed by using the corresponding processes. In order to unify different pieces into a whole project, the different project management activities need to be integrated.

 Project integration management. The project is initiated, planned, and executed in pieces, and all those pieces are related to each other and need to come together. That is where integration management comes in. For example, integrating different subsidiary plans into the project management plan needs to be managed. Project integration management includes developing the project charter, developing the project management plan, directing and managing project execution, monitoring and controlling project work, performing integrated change control, and closing the project or a phase of a project.

So, while managing all the aspects of the project, you, the project manager, will need to coordinate different activities and groups, and for that you need to communicate.

Project communication management. It is absolutely imperative for the success of the project that the project information is generated and distributed in a timely fashion. Some would say communication is the most important aspect of a project and the most important skill for a project manager to have. But without a doubt, it is certainly a critically important component of project management and a common thread that runs through the project lifecycle. Communication management includes the following:

- **Identify stakeholders**. Identify all individuals, groups, and organizations that will potentially be impacted by the project and find relevant information about them.

- **Plan communication**. Determine the information and communication needs of the project at hand and the communication approach to be used.

- **Distribute information**. Make the needed information available to the project stakeholders in a timely fashion as planned.

- **Manage stakeholder expectations**. Communicate and work with the stakeholders to understand and meet their needs, address the issues, and manage the expectations within the project scope and the project management plan.

- **Report performance.** Collect and distribute performance information to the stakeholders to stay on the same page.

As you have seen, managing a project largely means performing a set of processes at various stages of the project, such as initiating and planning. Accordingly, processes are grouped corresponding to these stages, and the groups are called *process groups*. Processes are part of the knowledge required to manage projects. Each of these processes belongs to one of the nine knowledge areas identified in the PMBOK Guide. So a process has a dual membership—one in a process group, indicating at what stage of the project the process is performed, and the other in a knowledge area, indicating what aspect of the project is managed by using the process. Table 1.3 shows this membership for all the processes identified in the PMBOK Guide.

Table 1.3 Mapping of the Project Management Processes to Process Groups and Knowledge Areas

Knowledge Areas IIV	Initiating Process Group	Planning Process Group	Executing Process Group	Monitoring and Controlling Process Group	Closing Process Group
Communications Management	Identify Stakeholders	Plan Communications	Distribute Information Manage Stakeholders' Expectations	Report Performance	n/a
Cost Management	n/a	1. Estimate Costs 2. Determine Budget	n/a	Control Cost	n/a
Human Resource Management	n/a	Develop Human Resource Plan	1. Acquire Project Team 2. Develop Project Team 3. Manage Project Team	n/a	n/a
Integration Management	Develop Project Charter	Develop Project Management Plan	Direct and Manage Project Execution	1. Monitor and Control Project Work 2. Perform Integrated Change Control	Close project or Phase
Procurement Management	n/a	Plan Procurements	Conduct Procurements	Administer Procurements	Close Procurements
Quality Management	n/a	Plan Quality	Perform Quality Assurance	Perform Quality Control	n/a
Risk Management	n/a	1. Plan Risk Management 2. Identify Risks 3. Perform Qualitative Risk Analysis 4. Perform Quantitative Risk Analysis 5. Plan Risk Responses	n/a	Monitor and Control Risks	n/a
Scope Management	n/a	1. Collect Requirements 2. Define Scope 3. Create Work Breakdown Structure	n/a	1. Verify Scope 2. Control Scope	n/a
Time Management	n/a	1. Define Activities 2. Sequence Activities 3. Estimate Activity Resources 4. Estimate Activity Durations 5. Develop Schedule	n/a	Control Schedule	n/a

Process Groups

Study Checkpoint 1.2

What is the core difference between knowledge areas and process groups? Try to answer this question in one sentence.

 NOTE

Not all the processes are used in all the projects. The project management team decides which processes needs to be used in a given project.

Study Checkpoint 1.3

In the following table, match each item in the first column with a corresponding item in the second column:

Knowledge Area

A. Scope 2

B. Cost 4

C. Time 3

D. Quality 5

E. Risk 8

F. Procurement 9

G. Human Resources 6

H. Communication 7

I. Integration 1

Action

1. Manage interdependencies among different processes belonging to different knowledge areas.

2. Ensure the project includes the work required to complete the project successfully and no extra work.

3. Plan the schedule and complete the project within the planned schedule.

4. Plan the budget, track what you are spending, and complete the project within budget.

5. Be sure to develop the right product that will satisfy the needs for which the project is undertaken.

6. Obtain the team to do the project work and lead and motivate the team to keep working in the right direction in an efficient and effective way.

7. Generate and distribute required project information to the right stakeholders at the right time by using the right method.

8. Plan for uncertain events that could happen and deal with them when they do happen in such a way that possible benefit is maximized and damage is minimized.

9. Identify the project work that needs to be contracted out of the performing organization and contract it out.

Each project is performed by individuals, and it can affect individuals or organizations even if they are not directly (officially) involved in the project. Now we are talking about the project stakeholders.

Introducing the Project Stakeholders

Right from the day you assume responsibility for managing a project, you start meeting a very special class of people called *project stakeholders*. It is very important for the success of the project that you identify these individuals and communicate with them effectively throughout the project.

Identifying Project Stakeholders

Project stakeholders are individuals and organizations whose interests are affected (positively or negatively) by the project execution and completion. In other words, a project stakeholder has something to gain from the project or lose to the project. Accordingly, the stakeholders fall into two categories—positive stakeholders, who will normally benefit from the success of the project, and negative stakeholders, who see some kind of disadvantage coming from the project. The implications obviously are that the positive stakeholders would like to see the project succeed and the negative stakeholders' interests would be better served if the project was delayed or cancelled altogether. For example, your city mayor might be a positive stakeholder in a project to open a Walmart store in your neighborhood because it brings business to the city, whereas some local business leaders might look at it as a threat to the local businesses and thereby may act as negative stakeholders.

Negative stakeholders are often overlooked by the project manager and the project team, which increases the project risk. Ignoring positive or negative project stakeholders will have a damaging impact on the project. Therefore, it's important that you, the project manager, start identifying the project stakeholders early on in the project. The different project stakeholders can have different and conflicting expectations, which you need to analyze and manage.

Identifying all the project stakeholders might be a difficult task, but the following are the obvious stakeholders, starting with you:

- ◆ **Project manager.** Include yourself, the project manager, in the list of the stakeholders to start with.
- ◆ **Project management office (PMO).** If your organization has a PMO, and it is directly or indirectly responsible for the outcome of a project, then the PMO is a stakeholder in that project.

◆ **Project team.** This team consists of the project manager, the project management team, and the individuals who perform the work of the project to produce the project outcome. This team may consist of individuals from different groups and departments with different subject matter expertise and skills.

◆ **Program manager.** If your project is part of a program, then the program manager is certainly a stakeholder of your project.

◆ **Portfolio managers and portfolio review board.** A portfolio manager is an individual who performs high-level management (governance) of a set of projects or programs and interfaces between the projects/programs and the business strategy of the organization for which the projects and programs are being run. A portfolio review board is a committee that selects and rejects the projects by reviewing them for factors such as the project value, return on investment, and risks involved in performing the project.

◆ **Functional managers.** These are the individuals who play the management roles within administrative or functional areas of the organization. For example, the VP of marketing is a functional manager and so is the director of engineering. The level of authority depends on their position in the hierarchy and also the organizational structure. For example, if you are using resources that are under a functional manager, that functional manager is a stakeholder of your project.

◆ **Operational management.** These are the individuals who are performing management roles in the operational areas of the organization. For example, the director of IT, who is responsible for maintaining the computer network that your team is using, is a stakeholder in your project. Depending on your project, you might be handing over the product of the project to an operations group that will be responsible for providing the long-term support for it.

◆ **Sellers and business partners.** Business partners are entities external to the performing organization, such as contractors and suppliers, that enter into a contractual agreement with the performing organization to provide certain components for the project. These components are the products, services, or results that you procure. Business partners are the external organizations that fill a specific role for the project, such as installing the product of the project, providing training and support for the product, or providing specialized expertise for the project. Business partners are different from vendors in that they have a special ongoing relationship with the organization, which sometimes is attained by satisfying some requirements, such as certifications.

◆ **Customer/user.** In general, customers are the entity that will acquire the project's outcome, such as product, and users are the entity that will use the product. In some cases the customers and users may be the same entity, and in other cases there may be a whole chain (with different layers) of customers and users. For example, a textbook produced by a project run by a publisher is recommended by the instructors, bought by the bookstores, and used by the students.

◆ **Project sponsor.** This is the individual or group that provides financial resources for the project. A sponsor has a major stake in the project and may perform an active role in the project team from time to time. Following are some of the functions of a sponsor:

   ◆ The sponsor champions the project when it's conceived. This includes gathering support for the project by performing actions such as acting as project spokesperson to the higher-level management and spelling out the benefits of the project.

   ◆ The sponsor leads the project through the selection process until the project is finally authorized, at which point the leadership role goes to the project manager.

   ◆ The sponsor plays an important role in developing the initial project scope and charter.

   ◆ The sponsor serves as an authority and a catalyst for issues beyond the control of project managers, such as authorizing some critical changes and other yes/no decisions.

In addition to these key stakeholders, who are easy to identify, there can be a number of other stakeholders, who might be more difficult to identify, inside and outside of your organization. Depending upon the project, these might include investors, sellers, contractors, family members of the project team members, government agencies, media outlets, lobbying organizations, individual citizens, and society at large. Have I left anyone out?

While dealing with the stakeholders, the keyword is *influence*. Watch out for influencers who are not direct customers or users of the product or service that will come from the project, but who can influence the course of the project due to their position in the customer organization or the performing organization. The influence can be positive or negative—that is, for or against the project.

 CAUTION

Do not confuse the project management team with the project team. The project management team consists of individuals involved in the project management tasks. It is a subset of the project team, which includes the members of the project management team and also other members, such as those who perform the actual work of the project.

So, not only are the stakeholders affected positively and negatively by the project, but the project can also be impacted positively or negatively by them. It is critical for the success of the project that you identify positive and negative stakeholders early on in the project, understand and analyze their varying and conflicting expectations, and manage those expectations throughout the project.

Identifying the Stakeholder Within: Project Manager

You, the project manager, are a very special project stakeholder yourself. The job (role) of a project manager is extremely challenging and thereby exciting. Depending on the organizational structure of your organization, you may be reporting to a functional manager, a program manager, a portfolio manager, or to some other manager or executive. Nevertheless, it is your responsibility to work with your team and other relevant individuals and groups, such as program managers and portfolio managers, to bring all the pieces together and make the project happen—that is, to achieve the project objectives. You do this by using a multitude of skills, described here.

Communication. The importance of communication in project management cannot be overemphasized. Even a well-scheduled and well-funded project can fail in the hands of a hard-working team of experts due to the lack of proper communication. As a project manager, you might be dealing with a wide functional variety of individuals, ranging from executives, to marketing personnel, to technologists. You should be able to wear different communication hats depending upon whom you are communicating with. For example, you will not be using technical jargon to talk to executives or marketing folks, and you will not speak marketing lingo to the software developers. You will be speaking to different stakeholders in their language, while filling the language gap between different functional groups and eliminating misunderstandings due to miscommunication. The key point is that you put on the appropriate communication hat depending on which individual you are communicating with. Be able to switch communication hats quickly and avoid technical jargon and acronyms that are not understood by the person or group with whom you are communicating. The goal is clarity of the language to convey the message accurately.

You will be communicating throughout the project. So, for a given project, you must develop a communication strategy that addresses the following issues:

- What needs to be communicated?
- With whom do you want to communicate? You might need to communicate different items to different individuals or groups.
- How do you want to communicate—that is, what is the medium of communication? Again, this might differ depending on whom you are communicating with.
- What is the outcome of your communication? You need to monitor your communication and its results to see what works and what does not, so you can improve communication.

Communication is an ingredient for many other skills, such as negotiation and problem-solving.

Negotiation. A negotiation is give and take, with the goal of generating a win-win outcome for both parties. You might need to negotiate at any stage of the project lifecycle. Here are some examples of negotiations:

- Negotiating with stakeholders regarding expectations during the project planning. For example, the suggested deadline for the project schedule might not be practical, or you might need a certain type or quantity of resources to make it happen.
- Negotiating with functional managers to obtain human resources, such as software developers.
- Negotiating with team members for specific job assignments and possibly during conflict resolution among the team members.
- Negotiating changes to the project schedule, budget, or both because a stakeholder proposed changes to the project objectives.
- Negotiating with external vendors in procurement. However, in contract negotiations, representatives from the legal department might be involved.

Sometimes you will be negotiating to solve a problem.

Problem-solving. Project-related problems might occur among the stakeholders (including team members) or with the projects. Either way, they are there to damage the project. Your task is twofold—to identify the problem early enough and to solve it. Here is the general technique for accomplishing this:

1. Look for early warning signs by paying close attention to formal progress reports and to what the team members say and do regarding the project.
2. Once you identify a potential problem, do your homework. Understand and identify the problem clearly by collecting more information without passing judgment.
3. Once the problem and its causes are clearly identified, work with the appropriate stakeholders, such as project team members, to explore multiple (alternative) solutions.
4. Evaluate the multiple solutions and choose the one you will implement.

The key point throughout the problem-solving process is to focus on the problem, not on the individuals, with the goal of finding the solution in order to help the project succeed. There should be no finger-pointing.

Sometimes, in choosing and implementing the correct solution, you will need to exercise your influencing skill.

Influencing. Influencing means getting individuals or groups to do what you want them to do without necessarily having formal authority to mandate an outcome from them. This is increasingly becoming an essential management skill in today's information economy. To exercise influence, you must understand the formal and informal structure of your organization. Again, you might need to use influencing when you are dealing with any aspect of the project—for example, controlling changes to the project, negotiating schedule or resource assignments, resolving conflicts, and the like.

Leadership. In the traditional organizational structure, project managers do not have formal authority over the project team members who perform the teamwork. So you have no other choice than to manage by leadership and not by authority (power). The good news is that managing by leadership is overall more effective and productive than managing by authority anyway. A project team is generally a group of individuals coming together for the lifetime of the project from different functional groups with different skills and experience. They need a leader to show them the vision and to excite, inspire, and motivate them toward the goals and the objectives of the project. You, the project manager, are that leader.

The Golden Triplet. PMI recommends that in addition to the skills related to application areas and management, an effective project manager must have the following three characteristics:

1. **Knowledge.** That is, knowledge of project management.
2. **Performance.** The ability to use the knowledge to perform the project—that is, to make accomplishments and get the job done.
3. **Personal.** This relates to the behavior of the project manager while performing the project and the related activities. This includes personal effectiveness, attitude, and leadership.

In other words, an effective project manager uses personal abilities, such as a positive attitude and leadership skills, to apply project management knowledge effectively in order to lead the project to success.

Different organizations have different attitudes and policies toward project management. The structure of the performing organization has a big influence on your job as a project manager.

Organizational Influences on Projects

A project is typically performed inside an organization called the *performing organization*, which creates an environment for the project called the *project environment*. The projects are influenced by the project environment, which is shaped by many elements, such as organizational culture, organizational structure, enterprise environmental factors, organizational process assets, and the maturity of the organization.

Understanding the Organizational Culture

Each organization often develops its own unique culture, which depends on many factors, such as the application area of the organization and the general management philosophy implemented in the organization. The organizational culture includes the following elements:

◆ **Work environment.** The organizational culture is reflected by work ethic and work hours. For example, do the employees work strictly from 8:00 AM to 5:00 PM, or do they work late into the night and on weekends?

◆ **Management style.** Organizational culture also reflects authority relationships. Do the managers manage by authority or by leadership? How much feedback is taken from the employees in making management decisions? How do the employees view the authority of the management?

◆ **Policies.** The organizational policies, methods, and procedures also reflect the organizational culture.

◆ **Values and vision.** A significant part of organizational culture lives in the set of values, norms, beliefs, and expectations shared within the organization. This may be impacted by the organization's mission and vision. For example, a nonprofit organization will have different values than a for-profit organization. Furthermore, one organization may encourage an entrepreneurial approach while another organization may be rigidly hierarchical and take an authoritarian approach to making decisions about what to do and what not to do.

Organizational culture influences multiple aspects of a project, including the following:

◆ **Project selection.** The organizational culture will creep into the selection criteria for projects and programs. For example, a rigidly hierarchical and authoritarian organization may not be very adaptive to programs and projects with high risk.

◆ **Project management style.** The project manager should adapt the management style to the organizational culture. For example, an authoritarian style may run into problems in an entrepreneurial organization with a participative culture.

◆ **Team performance assessments.** While making the team performance assessment, the project manager should keep in mind the established norms and expectations within the organization.

◆ **Project policies and procedures.** The project policies and procedures will be influenced by the organizational policies and procedures because both should be consistent with each other.

The culture of an organization is greatly influenced by its structure. From the perspective of a project, there are two kinds of organizations: project-based and non-project-based. The project-based organizations fall into two subcategories—those that derive their revenue primarily from performing projects for others and those that do in-house projects to deliver products or services for customers. Project-based organizations are well aware of the importance of project management and generally have systems to support project management. Non-project-based organizations generally have a low appreciation for and understanding of the importance of project management and often lack systems to support project management. By systems, I mean tools and facilities specialized or suitable for performing project management effectively, such as project management information systems.

The point here is that the type of organization and the organizational structure have a great influence on how the projects will be managed inside the organization.

Understanding the Organizational Structure

To do your job efficiently and effectively, you must figure out what kind of organizational structure you are in. From the perspective of structure, organizations fall into three categories—functional organizations, projectized organizations, and matrix organizations.

Functional Organizations

A functional organization has a traditional organizational structure in which each functional department, such as engineering, marketing, and sales, is a separate entity. As shown in Figure 1.3, the members of each department (staff) report to the functional manager of that department, and the functional manager in turn reports to an executive, such as the chief executive officer (CEO). Depending on the size of the organization, there could be a hierarchy within the functional managers—for example, directors of engineering, QA, and IT operations reporting to the vice president (VP) of engineering, who in turn reports to the CEO.

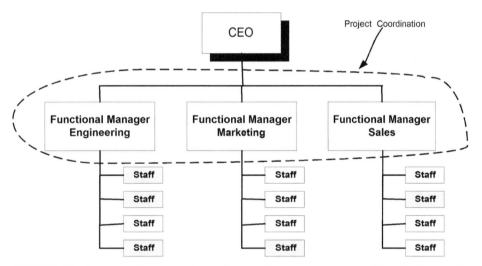

FIGURE 1.3 *Structure of a functional organization. Gray boxes represent staff involved in a project.*

The scope of a project in a functional organization is usually limited to the boundaries of the functional department. Therefore, each department runs its projects largely independent of other departments. When a communication needs to occur between two departments, it is carried through the hierarchy of functional managers.

All the managerial power (authority) in a functional organization is vested in the functional managers, who control the team members' performance evaluations, salaries, bonuses, hiring, and firing. Their role limited to coordinating the project activities, project managers are held responsible for the project results even though they have little say over resource assignments and holding team members accountable for their work. As a result, project managers in a functional organization are often frustrated. Their work is, at best, challenging. You, as a project manager in a functional organization, can benefit greatly from your good relationships with functional managers and team members. Networking and leadership are the key points to your success in a functional organization.

A project manager in a functional organization has the following attributes:

- ◆ The project manager's role and the project team are part-time.
- ◆ There is little or no authority over anything: resource assignments, team members, and the like.
- ◆ The project manager reports directly to a functional manager.
- ◆ There is little or no administrative staff to help with the project.

NOTE

In functional organizations, project management might be conducted under other names, such as project coordinator or team leader.

On the other end of the spectrum is the projectized organization.

Projectized Organization

A projectized organization's structure is organized around projects. Most of the organization's resources are devoted to the projects. As shown in Figure 1.4, the project team members report directly to the project manager, who has a great deal of independence and authority. Along with responsibility comes the high level of autonomy over the projects. The project managers are happy campers in a projectized organization. A functional organization and a projectized organization are on the opposite ends of the spectrum of a project manager's authority.

A project manager in a projectized organization has the following attributes:

- ◆ The project manager is full-time.
- ◆ The project manager has full authority over the project team.
- ◆ There is full-time administrative staff to help with the project.

In the middle of the spectrum are the matrix organizations.

Matrix Organization

A matrix organization is organized into functional departments, but a project is run by a project team, with members coming from different functional departments, as shown in Figure 1.5. On the spectrum of a project manager's authority, matrix organizations are in the middle of two extremes: functional and projectized organizations. The matrix organizations are generally categorized into a strong matrix, which is closer to projectized structure; a weak matrix, which is closer to functional structure; and a balanced matrix, which is in the middle of strong and weak.

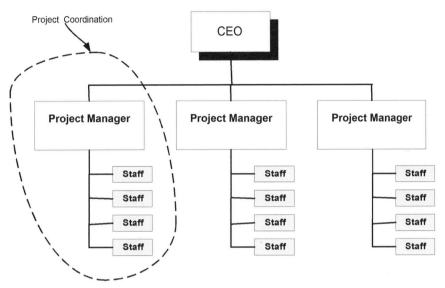

FIGURE 1.4 *Structure of a projectized organization. Gray boxes represent staff involved in a project under a given project manager.*

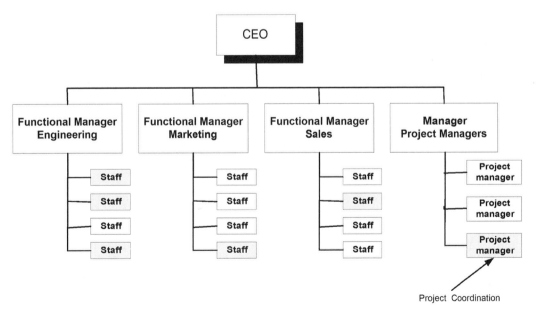

FIGURE 1.5 *Structure of a matrix organization. Gray boxes represent staff involved in a project.*

Tables 1.4 and 1.5 summarize the influences of the different organizational structures on the projects.

Table 1.4 Influences of Organizational Structures on Projects

Project Characteristic	Organization Structure		
	Functional	Matrix	Projectized
Project manager's authority	None to little	Limited to high	High to full
Project manager's role	Part-time	Part-time to full-time	Full-time
Project management administrative staff	None to part-time	Part-time to full-time	Full-time
Project budget controlled by	Functional manager	Functional manager, project manager, or both	Project manager
Resource availability	None to little	Limited to high	High to full

 NOTE

In a weak matrix, the role of a project manager is more of a coordinator or an expediter, and in a strong matrix, the project manager may have considerable authority and his or her role may be very close to a true project manager.

Table 1.5 Influences of Matrix Organizational Structures on Projects

Project Characteristic	Type of Matrix Structure		
	Weak	Balanced	Strong
Project manager's authority	Limited	Low to moderate	Moderate to high
Project manager's role	Part-time	Full-time	Full-time
Project management administrative staff	Part-time	Part-time	Full-time
Project budget controlled by	Functional manager	Functional manager, project manager, or both	Project manager
Resource availability	Limited	Low to moderate	Moderate to high

We have explored the three basic organizational structures. In the real world, some organizations use a hybrid (mix) of these structures to meet their varied needs. For example, a functional organization may run a specific project just like it would be run in a projectized organization. Such organizations are called *composite organizations*.

Obviously, organizational structure and organizational culture heavily determine the project environment. Two other important factors that influence the project environment are enterprise environmental factors and organizational process assets.

Identifying Environmental Factors and Process Assets

While exploring the environment of the performing organization, you should also identify the environmental factors and the process assets that will influence your project. Some of these assets and factors can be used to help the project; others may have a negative influence.

Enterprise Environmental Factors

The enterprise environmental factors are related to the environment internal or external to the performing organizations and can potentially impact the project. They may originate from within the performing organization, from any external organization participating in the project, or from both. These factors may have positive or negative influence on the project, and some of these factors may give rise to constraints for the project. Organizational environmental factors include the following:

- **Culture and structure.** These refer to the culture and type of structure of the performing organization.
- **Processes and standards.** Here are some examples:
  - The organization may have specific processes in place do certain things in certain ways.
  - There may be government and industry standards to follow, such as legal requirements, product standards, and quality standards relevant to the project.
  - Personnel administration information, such as guidelines for hiring, firing, and performance reviews.
- **Infrastructure and resources.** These may include the following:
  - Facilities and equipment to do the project
  - Project management information systems, such as software tools for scheduling tasks and meetings
  - Human resources currently available in the organization, such as skills and expertise
  - Commercial databases, such as standardized cost estimating data and risk databases
  - Work authorization system of the organization, because the project needs to be authorized
  - Communication channels and tools available in the organization, such as email systems

- ◆ **Internal and external conditions.** Examples include:
  - ◆ Risk tolerances of the project stakeholders
  - ◆ Marketplace conditions relevant to the project
  - ◆ Political climate

Note that the environmental factors can be internal to the performing organization, such as the organization's culture, or external to the organization, such as market conditions.

Organizational Process Assets

These are the processes or process-related assets from any of the organizations involved in the project that can be used to help the project succeed. The organizational process assets are typically grouped into two categories: processes and procedures for conducting work, and a corporate knowledge base for storing and retrieving information. For example, the performing organization might have its own guidelines, policies, and procedures, whose effect on the project must be considered while developing the project charter and other project documents that will follow. Another example of an organization's process assets are the knowledge and learning base acquired from previous projects. In the following list, I'll describe some items from both categories: processes and procedures and the knowledge database.

Processes and procedures. This category includes processes, procedures, guidelines, and requirements as described in the following:

- ◆ **Standardized processes and procedures.** Examples are organizational-level policies, such as health and safety policies, ethics policies, project management policies, and quality policies and procedures, such as quality checklists and auditing processes.
- ◆ **Standard guidelines and criteria.** Examples are:
  - ◆ Project closure guidelines, project acceptance criteria, proposal evaluation criteria, performance measurement criteria, and so on
  - ◆ Guidelines and criteria for tailoring the standardized organizational processes for the purposes of the project
- ◆ **Templates.** Examples are the templates to support some project management tasks, such as risk management, project schedule network diagrams, and work breakdown structure.
- ◆ **Requirements.** Examples are:
  - ◆ Communication requirements, hiring requirements, and safety and security requirements
  - ◆ Guidelines and requirements for project closures, such as final mandatory project audits and product acceptance criteria

You need to follow these guidelines and accommodate the requirements while working out the details of the project management processes that you will perform.

Knowledge base. This category includes databases, which allow you to store information and to retrieve the stored information when needed. Here are some items in this category:

- ◆ **Project files.** The documents and files related to the project, such as the project charter and the scope statement.

- ◆ **Measurement database.** Examples are the performance measurements.

- ◆ **Historical information and lessons learned.** Archives of files from previous projects and lessons learned from them.

- ◆ **Issue and defect management.** Database that allows you to manage issues and defects, such as to log, control, and resolve an issue or defect. You can also find the status of the issue or the defect from this database.

- ◆ **Financial database.** The financial information related to the project, such as budget, work hours, and cost overruns.

- ◆ **Configuration management database.** This contains the change history: different versions and baselines for the company standards and policies and for the archived project documents.

Study Checkpoint 1.4

What is the core difference between enterprise environmental factors and organizational process assets?

In a nutshell, enterprise environmental factors and organizational process assets contribute to the project environment in addition to the organizational culture and organizational structure.

 NOTE

Enterprise environmental factors and organizational process assets are common input to many project management processes. Sometimes they can also appear as output from a process, such as archived documents and lessons learned.

Once you enter the field of project management, you will immediately run into two neighbors of a project: program and portfolio.

Triangular Relationship: Project, Program, and Portfolio

As a project manager, you should know the basic concepts of program and portfolio and how they are related to each other and to projects. A program may be a part of a higher-level program; it certainly contains some interrelated projects, and it may contain some non-project work. Program management focuses on optimally managing the interdependencies among the projects in the program. To that end, the program manager's responsibilities include the following:

◆ Prioritize to resolve resource conflict and constraints that affect multiple projects within the program.

◆ Keep your priorities aligned with the strategic goals and objectives of the organization.

◆ Resolve issues and manage change within the governance structure of the organization.

Just like a project is managed by a project manager, a program is managed by a program manager, who oversees the projects and provides high-level guidance to the project managers. In other words, a program manager oversees projects and coordinates efforts between projects but does not manage the projects: the project managers manage the projects. A portfolio contains both programs and projects and is managed by a portfolio manager. The portfolio is drawn directly from the strategic business plan of the organization.

The strategy of an organization is an action plan to achieve its business goals and objectives. It's also called a *strategic plan* or a *strategic business plan*. The strategy determines the portfolio of projects and programs that the organization will execute. A portfolio is a set of projects, programs, or both that is managed in a coordinated fashion to obtain control and benefits not available from managing them individually.

Portfolio management is the centralized management of one or more portfolios, and it includes identifying, prioritizing, authorizing, managing, and controlling projects, programs, and other related work in order to obtain specific strategic business objectives. Just as a program is managed by a program manager, a portfolio is managed by a portfolio manager.

To understand the relationship of a portfolio to projects and programs, note the following:

◆ If an organization does not have any programs but has only individual projects, all these projects can be grouped into one or more portfolios.

◆ If an organization has programs and no individual project external to all programs, all these programs can be grouped into one or more portfolios.

◆ If an organization has some programs and some individual projects, all these programs and projects can be grouped into one or more portfolios.

Portfolio management focuses on making sure that programs and projects are prioritized for resources to serve the organization's strategy. Therefore, investment decisions are usually made at the portfolio level. Program management focuses on achieving the benefits that would be aligned with the portfolio and hence with the strategic objectives of the organization. So, a portfolio is part of the interface between the programs and strategic business objectives of the organization for which the programs are run.

> **NOTE**
>
> Information typically flows from a program to its projects during early stages (or phases), such as initiating and planning, and from projects to program during later stages, such as executing, controlling, and closing.

The triangular relationship among portfolios, programs, and projects is shown in Figure 1.6, in which an arrow represents containment. As the figure illustrates, all portfolios are composed of programs, projects, or both. A program consists of only projects and not portfolios. The figure also illustrates that both a program and a portfolio can have projects. That means a project may have a membership in a portfolio directly or through a program.

As compared to projects and programs, a portfolio is closer to an organization's business objectives, and therefore this is where most of the investment decisions are made. If you want to learn about an organization's business intent and direction (or strategy), look at its portfolio.

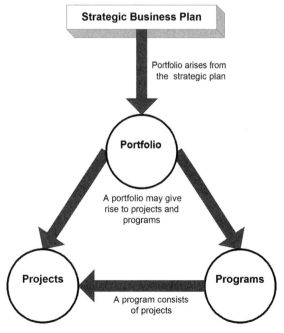

FIGURE 1.6 *The triangular relationship between projects, programs, and portfolios.*

It's also important to note that an operation is not part of a project. However, a program can include a non-project work. Similarly, a portfolio can also include work that is not included in any of its constituent projects and programs.

Table 1.6 presents a comparison between some characteristics of a project, a program, and a portfolio.

Study Checkpoint 1.5

Match each item in the first column of the following table with one or more suitable items in the second column.

Entity	May Contain
A. Operation	1. Non-project work
B. Project	2. Projects
C. Program	3. Programs
D. Portfolio	4. Portfolios
	5. Activities to create a well-defined, unique product

You have learned how the five process groups (the different stages in the project lifecycle) and the nine project management knowledge areas constitute the project management framework. The actual implementation of project management is greatly influenced by the facts on the ground—the organizational structure, for example. Throughout the book, you will be exploring the details of project management, and, therefore, getting introduced to some advanced concepts up front will make that journey more pleasant and smoother.

Some Advanced Concepts

Throughout this book, you will be encountering concepts such as probability, baseline, project team, and project management team. Those concepts are introduced in the following sections.

Probability-Related Concepts

The theory of probability has its early seventeenth-century roots in the investigations of games of chance, such as roulette and cards. Since then, a multitude of mathematicians and scientists have contributed to the development of the theory of probability. Today, the concepts of probability appear in almost every discipline, ranging from physics to project management. Risk (an important aspect of a project) and probability have the same origin: uncertainty. In project management, there is always an important question: What is the probability of this risk to occur? In the modern age, probability has already entered into the folk psyche through phrases such as, "What are the odds that this will happen?"

Table 1.6 Comparison between a Project, a Program, and Portfolio

Characteristic	Project	Program	Portfolio
Definition	A limited set of efforts (work) to create a unique product, service, or results.	A group of related projects and possibly some related work that does not belong to any project.	A collection of projects, programs, and other related work.
Change	Project manager expects change and implements processes to manage and control it.	Program manager must expect changes from both inside and outside the program and thrive on them if they help maximize the strategic benefits and objectives of the program.	Portfolio manager continually monitors changes in the broader context of the strategic plan of the organization.
Management	Project manager manages or coordinates the project team to lead the project to its success.	Program manager manages the program staff and the project managers and provide overall leadership, including vision.	Portfolio manager may coordinate or manage the portfolio management staff.
Monitoring	Project manager monitors and controls the project activities (tasks) undertaken to produce the planned products, results, or services of the project.	Program manager monitors the progress of program components, including projects and program-related non-project work, to lead the program to success, which means overall goals and benefits will be achieved within the planned budget and schedule.	Portfolio manager manages the aggregated portfolio performance and value indicators.
Planning	Project manager develops, monitors, and controls project plans from high-level information throughout the project lifecycle by using progressive elaboration.	Program manager develops the program plan and performs high-level planning to provide guidance at component-level planning, such as project planning.	Portfolio manager performs planning at the portfolio level, which includes developing and executing necessary processes, including communication.
Scope	At a given time, a project has a scope limited to meeting its objectives, including delivering the planned product. The scope is developed and monitored and controlled throughout the lifecycle of the program by using progressive elaboration.	A program has a wider scope dedicated to meeting the benefits in context of the strategic goals of the organization.	A portfolio has a business scope that changes with the change in the strategic plan and goals of the organization.
Success	Success relates to the project and is measured generally by the criteria of completing the project within the planned budget, cost, and scope. The degree of customer satisfaction is another parameter to measure success.	Success relates to the overall program and is measured in terms of benefit delivery expected from the program.	Success relates to the overall portfolio performance, which is an aggregated performance of all of its components: programs and projects.

Probability. Probability is defined as a chance that something will happen. For example, when you play the lottery and you wonder what the odds are that you will win, you are thinking of probability. The simplest example of probability is tossing a coin. The question is, when you toss a coin, what is the probability that the coin will land heads up? When you toss a coin, there are only two possibilities: It will land either heads up or tails up. Each possibility is equally likely if you are not cheating. Therefore, the probability that the coin will land heads up is 1 out of 2, or 50 percent, or 0.5. In general, if there are n possible outcomes of an event, and each outcome is equally likely, then the probability of a specific outcome is $1/n$.

Another useful concept in probability is the combined probability of several events. For example, if you toss two coins, the probability that the first coin will land heads up and the second coin will land tails up is 0.5×0.5=0.25. In general, to calculate the combined probability, you multiply the individual probabilities. If the probability that an event X will happen is a, the probability that event Y will happen is b, and the probability that event Z will happen is c, then the probability that all the three events (X, Y, and Z) will happen is a×b×c. To summarize, the probability that a number of independent events will occur is calculated by multiplying the probabilities of occurrence of all the individual events.

Random variable. A random variable can acquire any value within a given range or out of a set of values. For example, you can use a random variable to represent the results of rolling a fair die, which has six sides numbered by dots from 1 to 6. The possible outcome of rolling a die could be any number from the set of outcomes: {1, 2, 3, 4, 5, 6}.

Expected value. This is the expected value of an outcome. As an example, assume you get into a bet that you will win $10 if a coin toss results in heads, and you will lose $5 if it results in tails. Given that the probability for heads or tails is 0.5 for each, the expected value for the money that you will win is $10×0.5=$5, and the expected value for the money that you will lose is $5×0.5=$2.5.

Variance. The variance of a random variable is the deviation from the expected value. It is computed as the average squared deviation of each number from its mean. For example, assume that the values of a random variable are 2, 4, 5, 7, and 2 in five measurements. The mean value for these measurements is:

(2+4+5+7+2)/5=4

The variance of the spread of these values is:

$$V=\sigma^2=[(2-4)^2+(4-4)^2+(7-4)^2+(2-4)^2]/5=3.4$$

Standard deviation. This is the square root of the variance—that is, σ. So, in our example, the standard deviation is the square root of 3.4—that is, 1.84.

Algebraic equations. Project/program management and some questions in the CAPM, PMP, and PgMP exams will assume that you can do simple mathematical calculations. You should also have a very simple understanding of algebraic equations. You should be able to make simple manipulations, such as the following:

CPI=EV/AC implies EV=CPI×AC

CV=EV−AC implies EV=AC+CV

STUDY CHECKPOINT 1.6

You are about to throw a quarter and a dime several times. What is the probability that the following will happen?

- A. The quarter will land heads up on the first try.
- B. The dime will land tails up on the first try.
- C. The quarter will land heads up and the dime will land tails up on the first try.
- D. Both the quarter and the dime will land heads up on the first try.
- E. The quarter will land heads up on the first try and also heads up on the second try.

Global Project Variables

There are some significant factors in projects and project management that vary their values throughout the project lifecycle. You must keep your eyes on these variables from the very beginning of the project:

- ◆ **Cost and number of team members (staff).** Low in the beginning, maximum when the project is being executed, with a rapid drop when the project draws to a close.

- ◆ **Ability to influence the characteristics of the project product without significantly changing the cost.** Highest in the beginning and gradually decreases as the project progresses.

- ◆ **Risk and stakeholder influences.** Highest in the beginning and decreases as the project progresses. This is true about uncertainty, too, as risks arise from uncertainty.

Study Checkpoint 1.7

In the following table, match each item in the first column with the corresponding item in the second column.

Project Variable	Value
A. Level of staff	1. Highest in the beginning and end of the project and lowest when the project is being executed.
B. Risk	2. Highest in the beginning and decreases as the project progresses.
C. Ability to influence the characteristics of the project product without significantly impacting the project cost	3. Low in the beginning and maximum when the project is being executed.
D. Cost	4. Uniform throughout the project

Baseline

The project baseline is defined as the approved plan for the cost, schedule, and scope of the project. The project performance is measured against this baseline. The project baseline is also referred to in terms of its components—cost baseline, schedule baseline, and scope baseline. How do you know how the project is performing? You compare the performance against the baseline. Approved changes in cost, schedule, and scope will also change the baseline.

Project Management Office

The project management office (PMO) refers to an entity in an organization that is responsible for providing centralized coordinated management and support for projects in the organization. The projects supported by the PMO may or may not be related to one another. Some functions of the PMO depend upon the organization. In general, a PMO is an interface between the business objectives of the organization and the projects. For example, depending on the organization, it may act as a stakeholder in projects and a key decision maker in the beginning of any project in order to ensure that the projects consistently support the business objectives of the organization. To that end, it may be involved in selecting, prioritizing, allocating, and managing the project resources.

A primary function of the PMO is to support project managers in multiple ways, including the following:

- ◆ **Coaching.** Provide coaching, training, mentoring, and oversight.
- ◆ **Uniformity and consistency in standards:**
  - ◆ Identify and develop management methodology, best practices, and standards for the projects.
  - ◆ Develop and manage procedures, policies, templates, and other documentation shared by the projects.
  - ◆ Audit projects to ensure the compliance of standards, policies, procedures, and templates.
- ◆ **Resource management.** Manage shared resources across all the projects administered by the PMO.
- ◆ **Communication.** Coordinate communication across projects.

To understand the relationship between the roles of a project manager and the PMO, remember the following three things:

- ◆ **Scope.** A project manager focuses on the objectives of the project, whereas the PMO manages the scope at the program level and handles scope changes at the program level that may be seen as potential opportunities to meet the strategic business objectives of the organization.
- ◆ **Resources.** The project manager controls and manages the project resources to best meet the project objectives, whereas the PMO works to optimize the use of project resources across all the projects.

◆ **Project aspects.** The project manager handles aspects (or constraints) such as cost, quality, risk, and schedule specific to the individual project, whereas the PMO manages the interdependencies among the projects and the organization-level standards, such as project management methodologies, policies, and procedures.

In this chapter, you have been introduced to many concepts in order to build a high-level big picture of project management.

Big Picture of Project Management

In this chapter, you have learned what project management is and how project management is performed by applying knowledge and skills to project activities in order to meet the project objectives. Applying knowledge boils down to performing processes.

Figure 1.7 shows the big picture of project management in terms of project, processes, project lifecycle in terms of project stages, and project aspects managed by different knowledge areas. There are nine important aspects of projects, and each of these nine aspects is managed by using the corresponding knowledge area. For example, cost is managed by using the cost management knowledge area, and communication is managed by using the communication

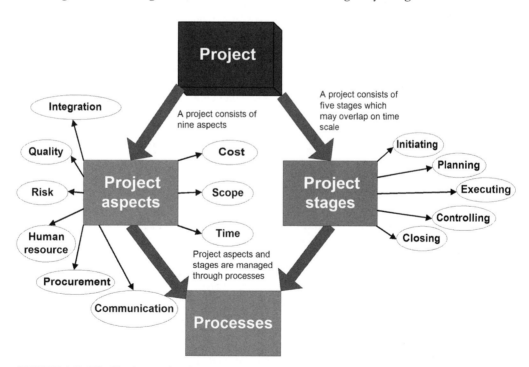

FIGURE 1.7 *The big picture of project management: The aspects of a project that need to be managed at different stages of the project lifecycle by using processes.*

management knowledge area. So, project management is performed by applying processes from certain knowledge areas at certain stages of the project.

The three most important takeaways from this chapter are as follows:

◆ The project lifecycle consists of five stages, technically called process groups: initiating, planning, executing, monitoring/controlling, and closing. These process groups can be mapped to commonly known project stages: starting, organizing and preparing, carrying out the work, and closing.

◆ The project processes that are performed to manage projects constitute nine project management knowledge areas: communication management, cost management, human resource management, integration management, procurement management, quality management, risk management, scope management, and time management.

◆ A project is performed in a project environment that is shaped by many elements, such as organizational culture, organizational structure, enterprise environmental factors, organizational process assets, and the maturity of the organization.

Summary

The activities inside an organization are generally organized into groups, which fall into two categories—operations and projects. Operations usually consist of ongoing routine work, whereas a project has a goal to generate a unique product, service, or result in a finite time— that is, it has a planned beginning and a planned end. Organizations launch projects for different reasons, such as to meet a business or legal requirement or to take on an opportunity offered by the market. The underlying motivation behind taking on these opportunities, however, is the business strategy of the organization. A project, like anything else in an organization, needs to be managed. Project management is the application of knowledge and skills to project activities in order to meet the project objectives. It involves performing a set of processes that constitute nine knowledge areas of project management: communication management, cost management, human resource management, integration management, procurement management, quality management, risk management, scope management, and time management. Each process is part of a knowledge area and has a membership in one of five process groups: initiating, planning, executing, monitoring/controlling, and closing. The process groups represent different stages of a project lifecycle.

Each project has a set of individuals or organizations that it influences positively or negatively, and these individuals and organizations are accordingly called *positive* and *negative stakeholders*. Some of these stakeholders may influence the project. Therefore, you must identify all the project stakeholders, positive and negative. The different project stakeholders might have different and conflicting expectations, which you need to analyze and manage. Besides, each project runs in an environment that influences it. This project environment consists of elements such as organizational culture, organizational structure, enterprise environmental factors, and organizational process assets. The structure of the performing organization could be functional, projectized, or matrix. On one end of the spectrum, a project manager is usually part-time and has little or no authority in a functional organization. On the other end, the project manager is full-time and has high to full authority in a projectized organization. In the middle of the spectrum are matrix organizations, in which a project manager has low to high authority. Some organizations have a composite structure, which is a hybrid of these three basic structures.

A project can be standalone or part of a program, which is a collection of interrelated projects and possibly non-project work. A project can also be part of a portfolio, which is a collection of programs, projects, and other related work.

As you learned in this chapter, the first stage of the project lifecycle is initiating. You will start your journey of project management by exploring the initiating stage in the next chapter.

Exam's Eye View

Comprehend

◆ The way PMI views it, the discipline of project management is composed of nine knowledge areas: scope management, cost management, human resource management, quality management, risk management, time management, procurement management, communication management, and integration management.

◆ Depending upon the stage of the project lifecycle in which they are executed, the processes are grouped into five process groups: initiating, planning, executing, monitoring and controlling, and closing.

◆ A process belongs exactly to one knowledge area and one process group, the same input may appear in more than one process, and you do not have to perform all the processes in each project.

◆ A project is run in an environment constituted by organizational structure, organizational culture, enterprise environmental factors, and organizational process assets.

◆ The project manager's authority is none to little in a functional organization, limited to high in a matrix organization, and high to full in a projectized organization.

Look Out

◆ For a work effort to be qualified as a project, it must be temporary (that is, have a start and a finish), and the outcome must be a unique product, result, or service. Routine, ongoing work is an operation, not a project.

◆ Any individual or organization that is positively or negatively affected by a project is a project stakeholder. Stakeholders can exist outside of the performing organization.

◆ You must identify both positive and negative stakeholders of your project, and you must not ignore the negative stakeholders.

◆ In a weak matrix, the role of a project manager is more of a coordinator or an expediter; in a strong matrix, the project manager may have considerable authority and his or her role may be very close to a true project manager.

◆ Regardless of the structure of the performing organization, project managers are responsible for the project results.

◆ A project may vary in size, it may be few days long or it may be few months long, and it may involve one person or quite a few individuals.

◆ A project may or may not be part of a program, but a program always consists of projects.

◆ A program may contain related work that is not part of any constituent project.

Memorize

◆ Nine knowledge areas and five process groups listed under **Comprehend**.

◆ There are four kinds of organizational structures: Functional, matrix, projectized, and composite.

◆ Knowledge, performance, and personal abilities are the three kinds of characteristics necessary for a project manager to effectively manage projects.

◆ In functional organizations, project management might be conducted under other names, such as project coordinator or team leader.

◆ Process groups are not a project phases.

Key Terms and Definitions

◆ **enterprise environmental factors.** Factors internal or external to the performing organization that can influence the project's success, such as the organization's culture, infrastructure, existing skill set, market conditions, and project management software. These are input to both the project charter and the preliminary project scope statement.

◆ **knowledge area.** A knowledge area in project management is defined by its knowledge requirements related to managing a specific aspect of a project, such as cost, by using a set of processes. PMI recognizes a total of nine knowledge areas, such as cost management and human resource management.

◆ **organization.** A group of individuals organized to work for some purpose or mission.

◆ **organizational process assets.** The processes and process-related assets of the organizations participating in the project that can be used to perform the project successfully, such as templates, guidelines, knowledge base, and policies and procedures.

◆ **performing organization.** The organization that is performing the project.

- **portfolio.** A set of projects, programs, and related work that is managed in a coordinated fashion to obtain business objectives in the strategic plan of the organization.

- **portfolio management.** The centralized management of one or more portfolios, which includes identifying, authorizing, prioritizing, managing, and controlling projects, programs, and other related work in order to obtain specific business objectives in the strategic plan of the organization.

- **process.** A set of interrelated activities performed to obtain a specified set of products, results, or services.

- **program.** A set of related projects managed in a coordinated fashion to improve overall efficiency and effectiveness that may not be obtained by managing the projects individually.

- **program management.** The centralized coordinated management of a specific program to achieve its strategic goals, objectives, and benefits.

- **program management office (PMO).** An entity in an organization that is responsible for providing centralized coordinated support to the program managers managing programs and unrelated projects.

- **progressive elaboration.** A technique used to continuously improving a plan by working out more details and better accuracy as more detailed and specific information becomes available as the project progresses.

- **project.** A work effort made over a finite period of time, with a start and a finish, to create a unique product, service, or result. A process consists of three elements: input, tools and techniques, and output.

- **project management.** Application of knowledge, skills, and tools and techniques to project activities in order to meet project objectives. You do this by performing some processes at various stages of the project.

- **project management office (PMO).** An entity in an organization that is responsible for providing centralized coordinated management for projects in the organization.

- **project stakeholder.** An individual or an organization that is positively or negatively affected by the project.

Review Questions

1. Which of the following are the essential characteristics that make a group of activities a project?

   A. It takes multiple individuals to perform these activities and it creates a new product.

   B. The work is managed by a project manager.

   C. The group has a plan and a budget.

   D. The group has a start date and a finish date, and its outcome will be a new product.

2. Which of the following is a project?
   A. Running a donut shop
   B. Building another library in your area
   C. Keeping a network up and running in a university department
   D. Running a warehouse

3. Which of the following are the process groups?
   A. Starting, planning, executing, monitoring and controlling, and closing
   B. Initiating, organizing and preparing, executing, monitoring and controlling, and closing
   C. Initiating, planning, implementing, monitoring and controlling, and closing
   D. Initiating, planning, executing, monitoring and controlling, and closing

4. Which of the following is not a project management knowledge area?
   A. Project procurement management
   B. Project risk management
   C. Project quality management
   D. Project team management

5. Which of the following is the best definition of progressive elaboration?
   A. Taking the project from concept to project management plan
   B. Taking the project from conception to completion
   C. Taking the project from initiating to closing
   D. Decomposing the project objectives into smaller, more manageable work pieces

6. In which of the following organizational structures does the project manager have the greatest authority?
   A. Functional
   B. Projectized
   C. Matrix
   D. Leveled

7. In which of the following organizational structures does the project manager have the least authority?
   A. Functional
   B. Projectized
   C. Matrix
   D. Leveled

8. Your project depends on two business partners: On The Fly, Inc. (OTF) and The Sure Thing, Inc. (ST) delivering their products to you on time. The chances are three out of four that OTF will make the delivery on time and two out of three that ST will *not* make the delivery on time. The probability that OTF and ST will both deliver on time is equal to:

   A. 0.25

   B. 0.5

   C. 5/7

   D. 4/7

9. All of the following are true about a project except:

   A. Cost is low and stakeholder influence is highest in the beginning.

   B. Staffing levels and the ability to influence the product characteristics are both low at the end of the project.

   C. When the project is executing, both cost and stakeholders' influence are at their highest.

   D. Uncertainty is at its highest in the beginning of the project.

10. Both projects and operations share all the following characteristics except:

    A. Performed by individuals

    B. Planned, executed, monitored and controlled, and closed

    C. Limited by constraints

    D. Performed to achieve the strategic objectives of the organization

11. You are being interviewed by a functional manager who says, "We have this huge undertaking of launching an online education website that contains different components, such as designing the website; developing the content; developing the administrative system, including registration and payment; marketing the courses on the website; integrating different components of the website; and finally going live. Each component is functionally complex and large enough that it will be better served under a different management." The manager is most likely describing a:

    A. Project

    B. Program

    C. Operation

    D. Portfolio

12. Effective project management requires that a project manger must have the following characteristics:

    A. Project management knowledge, ability to apply the knowledge effectively to the project at hand, and computer expertise

    B. Project management knowledge, leadership skills, and expertise in the application area of the project

    C. Project management knowledge; ability to apply the knowledge to the project at hand; and personal style and behavior, including personal effectiveness and leadership

    D. Project management knowledge, ability to apply the knowledge effectively to the project at hand, and project management experience

13. The role of a project manager is more of a coordinator or an expediter in organizations with the following structures:

    A. Strong matrix and weak matrix

    B. Projectized

    C. Functional and weak matrix

    D. Hierarchical

14. The project manager is responsible for achieving project objectives in an organization with the following structure:

    A. Projectized only

    B. Strong matrix and projectized only

    C. Matrix and projectized only

    D. All structures

15. You have just joined an organization as a project manager and are studying the enterprise environmental factors of the organization to find out how you can leverage them for the success of your upcoming projects. Enterprise environmental factors may have what kind of influence on the projects?

    A. Positive only

    B. Negative only

    C. Positive or negative

    D. None

Chapter 2

Initiating the Project

PMP Exam Objectives

Objective	What It Really Means
1.1 Conduct Project Selection Methods	Understand the origin of projects. You must know the project selection methods, such as benefit measurement methods and expert judgment.
1.2 Define Scope	Know how to define the initial project scope based on the business need with the purpose of meeting customer expectations. Understand the big picture of how projects are initiated to meet business needs in line with the organization's business strategy.
1.3 Document High-Level Risks, Assumptions, and Constraints	Understand the basic concepts of assumptions, constraints, and risks and how risk is connected to assumptions and constraints. Understand how documenting these starts at the initiating stage of the project.
1.4 Identify and Perform Stakeholder Analysis	Understand how to identify both negative and positive stakeholders. You must know the key stakeholders in any project, such as the project manager, sponsor, and project team members. Know how to perform the Identify Stakeholders process.
1.5 Develop a Project Charter	Understand the Develop Project Charter process. You must know that the project charter authorizes the project and names and authorizes the project manager.
1.6 Obtain Project Charter Approval	Understand that the project charter approval process depends upon the project and the performing organization. You must know that the project charter approval officially starts a project.

Introduction

As you learned in the previous chapter, you manage projects through processes. You also learned that a process is composed of input, tools and techniques, and output. You use the tools and techniques on the input of a process to generate its output. You manage the initiation of a project through a process group called the *initiating process group*, which consists of two processes: Develop Project Charter and Identify Stakeholders. Before you can initiate a project, it must originate from somewhere.

So the central question in this chapter is, how is a project initiated? In search of the answer, you will explore three avenues with me: the origin and selection of projects, developing the project charter, and identifying stakeholders.

Initiating a Project: Big Picture

Initiating a project means defining the project, getting approval to start it, and identifying and analyzing project stakeholders. During this stage the initial scope of the project is defined; accordingly, initial resources are determined and allocated, a project manager with an appropriate authority level is assigned, and project stakeholders are identified. Defining the project includes the following:

- Developing project objectives and describing how they are related to the organization's business objectives and strategy.
- Specifying the project deliverables, such as products, services, or results, that will meet the objectives. In some cases, a deliverable and an objective may be the same.
- Based on the objectives and deliverables, defining the initial scope of the project by explaining what will be done and drawing boundaries around what will be done; this means stating where necessary what will not be included.
- Based on the initial scope, estimating the project duration and the resources needed. More accurate estimates will be made during planning.
- Defining the success criteria, which may be improved during planning. The project definition is incomplete without defining its success.
- Assigning the initial project resources. For example, some initial resources are needed just to define and plan the project before even beginning to execute it.
- Assigning a project manager if one is not already assigned.
- Authorizing the project. While different organizations may have a different process to approve the processes, the standard way to do it is to approve the document that holds the definition of the project, such as the project charter.

CAUTION

The processes in the initiating process group, just like any other process group, can also be used to initiate a phase of a project that has multiple phases.

Based on the project definition, you will identify the project stakeholders.

Figure 2.1 presents the big picture of initiating a project by illustrating the relationships among major elements of this stage. The business need to be met by the project emerges from the organization's business strategy, and based on the business need, somebody writes the statement of work and makes the business case. The business case and statement of work are the starting points to develop the initial project scope and thereby determine the initial resources. All this information becomes input to developing the project charter, which, in turn, is an input to the process of identifying stakeholders.

FIGURE 2.1 *Illustration of the relationship among the major building blocks of the big picture of initiating a project.*

TIP

It's a good policy to involve customers and other important stakeholders in the initiating stage of the project. It gives them the feeling of shared ownership that will greatly contribute to the success of the project by positively influencing factors such as deliverable acceptance and stakeholder satisfaction.

NOTE

If your project is divided into different phases, you will be going through the initiation stage at the beginning of each phase to check whether the decisions and plans made during the initiation of the project are still relevant to this phase. It helps to ensure that the project is still focused on the business need for which it was started.

Included in Figure 2.1 are two processes performed during the initiating stage: Develop Project Charter and Identify Stakeholders. We will explore all these processes in detail further on in this chapter. However, before you can begin the project initiation, someone must request the project. So let's back up a little and ask a fundamental question: Where do projects originally come from?

Origins of Projects

Projects often originate from sources external to the project, such as a sponsor, project management office, or portfolio steering committee—internally or externally, by an enterprise or a government agency. A project may originate as a result of one or more of the following categories of reasons:

◆ **Business/legal requirements.** This category includes projects based on a business need or a legal requirement. For example, perhaps a web design company authorizes a project to automate certain aspects of maintaining websites to increase its efficiency and revenue. As another example, consider a building owner authorizing a project to make the building accessible to physically disabled persons in order to meet the legal requirements for using the building for a specific business.

◆ **Opportunities.** The projects that fall into this category might include the following:

　◆ Those based on the market demand. For example, a car manufacturer begins a project to make electric cars based on high oil prices that the customer cannot afford.

　◆ Those based on a customer request. For example, one of the customers of your company requests a product that could be a source of revenue for the company.

- ◆ Strategic opportunity/business need. A project that helps implement the business strategy of the organization. However, all other opportunities taken by the organization must also be aligned with the business strategy.

- ◆ Those based on a technological advance. For example, several electronics companies authorized projects to manufacture MP3 players following the invention and popularity of MP3 technology.

- ◆ **Problems.** Projects are also authorized to offer solutions to certain problems in a company or a country or to address social needs in a society. For example, the government might start a project to help victims of a natural disaster, such as a hurricane. A company might authorize a project to analyze the problem of low employee productivity and to design a solution for this problem.

- ◆ **Ecological impact.** For example, a company undertakes a project to lessen the negative impact that its operations or products may have on the environment.

- ◆ **Social needs.** Governmental or nongovernmental organizations initiate projects to satisfy some social needs, such as a project to provide access to the Internet in an underprivileged community or a project to set up latrines and a sewer system in a remote community. These kinds of projects based on social needs are often run by nonprofit organizations. Even if not for profit, the projects in such organizations are also linked to the business needs of the organization because in order to perform the projects, the organization must survive, and in order to survive, the organization must work according to its strategic business plan.

The sources of project requests can vary widely in different organizations. Depending upon your organization, the origins of projects might be inside the organization, outside the organization, or both. Regardless of these sources, an organization performs a project to meet some business objectives in the organization's strategic plan. So the strategic plan of an organization is still the grand origin of all projects.

So, a project can originate from multiple possible sources. Not all requested projects are authorized by the organization, however. How does an organization decide which projects to select?

Understanding Project Selection

The underlying motivation behind project selection is the business strategy of the organization. That said, a project can be selected by using one or more project selection methods that fall into three categories: benefit measurement methods, constrained optimization methods, and expert judgment.

Benefit Measurement Methods

These methods use comparative approaches to compare the benefits obtained from the candidate projects so that the project with the maximum benefit will be selected. These methods fall into three categories: scoring models, benefit contributions, and economic models.

Scoring Models

A scoring model evaluates projects by using a set of criteria with a weight (score) assigned to each criterion. You can assign different weights to different criteria to represent the varied degree of importance given to various criteria. All projects are evaluated (scored) against this set of criteria, and the project with the maximum score is selected. The set of criteria can include both objective and subjective criteria, such as financial data, organizational expertise, market value, innovation, and fit with the corporate culture. The advantage of a scoring model is that you have the freedom to assign different weights to different criteria in order to select projects consistent with the goals, mission, and vision of your corporation. This freedom, however, is also a disadvantage because your selection is only as good as the criteria with larger weights. Furthermore, developing a good scoring model is a difficult task that requires unbiased cross-departmental feedback from different levels of the organization.

Benefit Contributions

These methods are based on comparing the benefit contributions from different projects. These contributions can be estimated by performing a cost-benefit analysis, which typically calculates the projected cost, revenue, and savings of a project. This method favors the projects that create profit in the shortest time and ignores the long-term benefits of projects that might not be tangible at the current time, such as innovation and strategic values.

Economic Models

An economic model is used to estimate the economic efficiency of a project, and it involves a set of calculations to provide overall financial data about the project. The common terms involved in economic models are explained in the following list.

- ◆ **Benefit Cost Ratio (BCR).** This is the value obtained by dividing the benefit by the cost. The greater the value, the more attractive the project is. For example, if the projected cost of producing a product is $20,000, and you expect to sell it for $60,000, then the BCR is equal to $60,000/$20,000, which is equal to 3. For the benefit to exceed cost, the BCR must be greater than 1.

- ◆ **Cash flow.** Whereas cash refers to money, cash flow refers to both the money coming in and the money going out of an organization. Positive cash flow means more money is coming in than going out. Cash inflow is benefit (income), and cash outflow is cost (expenses).

- ◆ **Internal Return Rate (IRR).** This is just another way of interpreting the benefit from the project. It looks at the cost of the project as the capital investment and translates the profit into the interest rate over the life of that investment. Calculations for IRR are outside the scope of this book. Just understand that the greater the value for IRR, the more beneficial the project is.

- ◆ **Present Value (PV) and Net Present Value (NPV).** To understand these two concepts, understand that one dollar today can buy you more than what one dollar next year can buy. (Think about inflation and return.) The issue arises because it takes time to complete a project, and even when a project is completed, its benefits are reaped over a period of time, not immediately. In other words, the project is costing you today but will benefit you tomorrow. So, to make an accurate calculation for the profit, the cost and benefits must be converted to the same point in time. The NPV of a project is the present value of the future cash inflows (benefits) minus the present value of the current and future cash outflows (cost). For a project to be worthwhile economically, the NPV must be positive. As an example, assume you invest $300,000 today to build a house, which will be completed and sold after three years for $500,000. Also assume that real estate that is worth $400,000 today will be worth $500,000 after three years. So the present value of the cash inflow on your house is $400,000, and hence the NPV is the present value of the cash inflow minus the present value of the cash outflow, which equals $400,000–$300,000, which equals $100,000.

◆ **Opportunity cost.** This refers to selecting a project over another due to the scarcity of resources. In other words, by spending this dollar on this project, you are passing on the opportunity to spend this dollar on another project. How big an opportunity are you missing? The smaller the opportunity cost, the better it is.

◆ **Discounted Cash Flow (DCF).** The discounted cash flow refers to the amount that someone is willing to pay today in anticipation of receiving the cash flow in the future. DCF is calculated by taking the amount that you anticipate to receive in the future and discounting (converting) it back to today on the time scale. This conversion factors in the interest rate and opportunity cost between now (when you are spending cash) and the time when you will receive the cash back.

◆ **Return on Investment (ROI).** The ROI is the percentage profit from the project. For example, if you spend $400,000 on the project, and the benefit for the first year is $500,000, then ROI equals ($500,000–$400,000)/$400,000, which equals 25%.

The details and calculations for these quantities are outside the scope of this book. Just understand the basic concepts and whether a larger or a smaller value for a given quantity favors the project selection.

Study Checkpoint 2.1

You have been offered a project B that will earn you a profit of $100,000 in three months. You already have an offer of a project A that will earn you a profit of $70,000 in three months. You can only do one project during these three months, and the project requesters are unable to move the project durations.

A. What is the opportunity cost of project A?
B. What is the opportunity cost of project B?
C. Just based on the opportunity cost, which project will you select?
D. Describe what can change your decision based just on the opportunity cost.

As the name suggests, all the benefit measurement methods are based on calculating some kind of benefit from the given project. However, the benefit will never be realized if the project fails. This concern has given rise to methods based on calculating the success of the projects; these methods are called *constrained optimization methods*.

Constrained Optimization Methods

Constrained optimization methods are concerned with predicting the success of the project. These methods are based on complex mathematical models that use formulae and algorithms to predict the success of a project. These models use the following kinds of algorithms:

◆ Linear

◆ Nonlinear

◆ Dynamic

◆ Integer

◆ Multiple objective programming

 TIP

For the exam, you need to know two things about constrained optimization methods: the names of the types of algorithms and the fact that these methods are only used for complex projects and therefore are not typically used for most projects.

The details of these models are outside the scope of this book.

Either in conjunction with other methods or in absence of them, organizations often rely on expert judgment in making selection decisions.

Expert Judgment

Expert judgment is one of the techniques used in project management to accomplish various tasks, including project selection. It refers to making a decision by relying on expert advice from one or more of the following sources:

◆ Senior management

◆ An appropriate unit within the organization

◆ The project stakeholders, including customers and sponsors

◆ Consultants

◆ Professional and technical associations

- ◆ Industry groups
- ◆ Subject matter experts from within or outside of the performing organization
- ◆ Project management office (PMO)

The use of expert judgment is not limited to the project selection; it can be used in many processes, such as developing a project charter. Expert judgment can be obtained by using a suitable method, such as individual consultation, interview, survey, and panel group discussion.

CAUTION

Keep in mind that expert judgment can be very subjective at times and might include political influence. An excellent salesperson or an executive with great influence can exploit this method successfully.

An organization might use multiple selection methods to make a decision. During the project selection process, you might start interacting with a very important group of people called project stakeholders. For effective identification of stakeholders, you need the project charter.

Developing a Project Charter

The project charter is a document that states the initial requirements to satisfy the stakeholders' needs and expectations, and it also formally authorizes the project. The single most important task for the develop project charter process, the standard process used to develop the project charter, is to authorize the project. To accomplish that, it is necessary to document the business needs and the new product or service that the project will launch to satisfy those needs. This way, the project charter links the proposed project to the ongoing work in the organization and clears the way to authorize the project.

NOTE

The project charter is the document that formally authorizes a project, which includes naming the project manager and determining the authority level of the project manager. Obviously, we are referring to the approved project charter.

The output of the Develop Project Charter process is, of course, the project charter, and this output is generated by applying the tools and techniques to the input of this process, as shown in Figure 2.2.

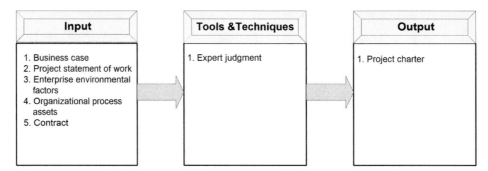

FIGURE 2.2 *The Develop Project Charter process: input, tools and techniques, and output.*

The input to developing the project charter comes from the origin of the project and from within the organization that will perform the project. The possible input items for the process of developing a project charter are the following:

Business case. The origins of the business case are pretty much the same as the origins of a project discussed earlier in this chapter. The business case is built on the business need addressed by the project that justifies the project. This will determine whether the project is worth the effort and the investment. The business case may contain the cost benefit analysis described further on in this chapter. The business case is written by either the person or the group within the performing organization that is proposing the project or by an external organization or the customer who is requesting the project or the product that will be produced by the project.

If the organization that is requesting the project is a separate legal entity than the organization that is performing the project, both may have their own business cases. In this case, the business case that goes into the project is the business case of the performing organization. The business case of the requesting organization will make its way to the project through the contract or the statement of work.

TIP

Periodic reviews of the business case in the early stages of a project help to confirm that the project is still required. If the project has multiple phases, the business case may be reviewed at the beginning of each phase to ensure that the project is still on track to deliver the business benefits.

Project statement of work (SOW). The statement of work is a document that describes the products, services, or results that will be delivered by the project. For an internal project, the SOW is provided by the project initiator or the project sponsor, whereas for an external project, the SOW is received from the customer as part of a bid document, such as a request for proposal, a request for bid, or a request for information. Alternatively, it could come as part of the contract. The SOW includes or refers to the business need that the project will satisfy, the product scope, and the strategic plan of the organization supported by the project.

CAUTION

Do not confuse the *project* scope with the *product* scope: These are related though different concepts. Product scope is defined as features and functions that characterize a product, service, or result to be delivered by the project, whereas the project scope is the scope of the whole project and is defined as the entire work required to create the project deliverables.

Enterprise environmental factors. During the development of the project charter, you must consider the performing organization's environmental factors relevant to this task, which include the following:

- **Government and industry standards**, such as legal requirements, product standards, and quality standards relevant to the project
- **Performing organization's infrastructure**, such as facilities and equipment to do the project
- **Marketplace conditions** relevant to the project

Note that the environmental factors can be internal to the performing organization, such as the organization's culture, or external to the organization, such as market conditions.

Organizational process assets. As you learned in Chapter 1, the organizational process assets are typically grouped into two categories: processes and procedures for conducting work and a corporate knowledge base for storing and retrieving information to help the processes. For example, the performing organization might have its own guidelines, policies, and procedures, whose effect on the project must be considered while developing the project charter and other project documents that will follow. Another example of an organization's process assets are the knowledge and learning base acquired from the previous projects. Here are some specific examples from the organizational process assets that can be useful in developing the project charter:

- Templates to support some project management tasks, such as project charter templates
- Standard policies and procedures of the organization relevant to developing the project charter
- Procedures for issuing work authorizations
- The knowledge base of the organization that contains historical information from previous projects, such as lessons learned

Contract. A project for a customer who is external to the performing organization is usually done based on a contract.

To summarize, the input items to developing the project charter may include the business case, the statement of work, enterprise environmental factors, organizational process assets, and possibly a contract. You take the available input and apply the relevant tools and techniques to develop the project charter. The most important tool used in developing the project charter is the expert judgment described earlier in this chapter.

The output of the Develop Project Charter process is a formal document called the *project charter*. It is a high-level document that summarizes the business needs, the understanding of customer requirements and needs, and how the new product or service will satisfy these requirements. To be specific, the project charter should include the following information.

◆ **The project justification**, which includes the purpose of the project and the business case for the project, which in turn may include return on investment.

◆ **A high-level project description** that includes the business needs that the project addresses and the high-level product requirements.

◆ **High-level project requirements** based on the needs of the customer, the sponsor, and other stakeholders.

◆ **Project objectives and success criteria**, which are derived from the purpose section. These explain what exactly is going to be accomplished to meet the purpose—that is, what the outcome of the project will be. Each objective should be measurable and have a success criterion assigned to it. The project objectives must be measurable.

◆ **High-level risks**, which will be identified during the project planning. However, some high-level risks may be apparent during the time of developing the project charter.

◆ **Milestone schedule**—some kind of high-level schedule included in the charter.

◆ **A budget summary.** A high-level summary of the project cost estimate with some kind of timeline.

◆ **Project approval and acceptance requirements**, which include the name and responsibility of the person or committee that will approve and accept the project when it's finished:

   ◆ What constitutes the project success?

   ◆ Who decides whether the project is successful?

   ◆ Who signs off on the project completion?

◆ **An assigned project manager**, a specified authority level for that project manager, and defined stakeholder influences.

◆ **Project sponsor**—the name and authority level of the project sponsor authorizing the project charter.

Depending on the project and the organization, the charter may include other elements as well, such as a list of participating functional departments of the organization and their roles in the project, and organizational, environmental, and external assumptions and constraints.

An *assumption* is a factor that you consider to be true without any proof or verification. For example, an obvious assumption that you might make during planning for an in-house project could be the availability of the required skill set to perform the project.

It's important to document assumptions clearly and validate them at various stages of the project because assumptions carry a certain degree of uncertainty with them, and uncertainty means risk. Assumptions can appear in both the input and the output of various processes.

A *constraint* is a restriction (or a limitation) that can affect the performance of the project. It can appear in both the input and the output of various processes. For example, there could be a schedule constraint that the project must be completed by a predetermined date. Similarly, a cost constraint would limit the budget available for the project.

The project charter provides the project manager with the authority to use organizational resources to run the project. Remember that formally speaking, project charters are prepared external to project management by an individual or a committee in the organization. In other words, project management starts where the project charter ends. However, practically, the would-be project manager might actually be involved in writing the project charter or a part of it. The project approval and funding will still be external to the project management boundaries.

 NOTE

Some organizations might perform a feasibility study or its equivalent to justify the project before developing the project charter and initiating the project. The feasibility study may itself become a project.

Once you have the project charter, you know the high-level product (or service) requirements that the project will satisfy. However, a high-level requirement written in a certain way might mean different things to different stakeholders. So, after you get the project charter, your first task is to develop a common understanding of the project among the project stakeholders. You accomplish this by drawing boundaries around the project—that is, what is included and what is not—thereby spelling out what exactly the deliverables are. By doing this, you are determining the scope of the project.

 NOTE

If a project includes multiple phases, the initiation process may be performed at the beginning of each phase to validate the assumptions made during the previous phases.

Once the project charter is developed, you are well equipped to identify the project stakeholders.

Identifying the Project Stakeholders

As mentioned in Chapter 1, project stakeholders are individuals and organizations whose interests are affected (positively or negatively) by the project's execution and completion. In other words, a project stakeholder has something to gain from the project or something to lose to the project. Accordingly, the stakeholders fall into two categories: positive stakeholders, who will normally benefit from the success of the project, and negative stakeholders, who see some kind of disadvantage coming from the project. The implications, obviously, are that the positive stakeholders would like to see the project succeed, and the negative stakeholders' interests will be better served if the project is delayed or cancelled altogether. For example, your city mayor might be a positive stakeholder in a project to open a Walmart store in your neighborhood because it brings business to the city, whereas some local business leaders might look at it as a threat to the local businesses and thereby may act as negative stakeholders.

Negative stakeholders are often overlooked by the project manager and the project team, which increases the project risk. Ignoring positive or negative project stakeholders will have a damaging impact on the project. Therefore, it's important that you, as a project manager, start identifying the project stakeholders early on in the project. The different project stakeholders might have different and conflicting expectations that you need to analyze and manage.

Identifying all the project stakeholders might be a difficult task, but the obvious ones include the project manager, program manager, portfolio manager, customers and users, project sponsor, project management office, project team, operations management, sellers and business partners, and functional managers. In addition to these key stakeholders, discussed in Chapter 1, there can be a number of other less obvious stakeholders inside and outside of your organization. Depending upon the project, these might include investors, sellers, contractors, family members of the project team members, government agencies, media outlets, lobbying organizations, individual citizens, and society at large.

It is critical for the success of the project that you identify positive and negative stakeholders early on in the project, understand and analyze their varying and conflicting expectations, and manage those expectations throughout the project.

Figure 2.3 illustrates the Identify Stakeholders process. Identifying stakeholders includes the following:

◆ Identify individuals and organizations that will influence the project and will be impacted by the project.

◆ Document relevant information about the individuals and organizations and about their interests and involvement in the project.

◆ Document how these individuals and organizations can influence the project and how they can be impacted by the project.

◆ Determine their levels of importance.

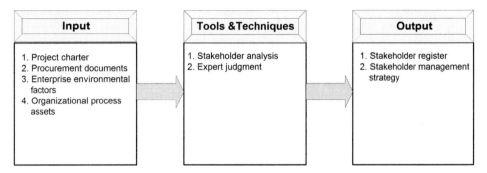

FIGURE 2.3 *The Identify Stakeholders process: input, tools and techniques, and output.*

As stated earlier, stakeholder identification is necessary in order to manage stakeholder expectations and to manage their influence on the project. They can influence various aspects of the project, such as definition, changes, execution, deliverables, and ultimately the success. They may come from inside the organization with different levels of authority or from outside the organization.

Identifying stakeholders is an iterative process—that is, you might have to perform the identification over and over again because some old stakeholders may become irrelevant, and some new stakeholders may appear during the life of the project. Because identifying and analyzing the stakeholders and managing their expectations and influence is so critical to the success of the project, you should start this task early on in the project.

Input to Identifying Stakeholders

The following items are the input to the process of developing stakeholders:

Project charter. The project charter greatly helps to identify stakeholders by revealing the internal and external individuals and groups who either are directly involved in the project or will potentially be impacted by it. Project sponsors, customers, and departments of the performing organization participating in the project are some examples of stakeholders identified by the project charter.

Procurement documents. If the project originated from procurement activity, then the procurement documents, such as the contract, will be useful to identify the stakeholders. Even if this project is going to use procurement in order to produce part of its product, the procurement documents will help to identify some stakeholders, such as sellers and suppliers.

Enterprise environmental factors. Examples of the enterprise environmental factors that help identify stakeholders include governmental and industry standards, organizational cultures, and organizational structure. It's important to understand the organization's culture and structure in order to identify some stakeholders and their possible impact on the project, because different people will have different levels of authority and influence under different cultures and structures, as discussed in Chapter 1.

Organizational process assets. The stakeholder register templates and the stakeholder registers from previous projects can be useful to create the stakeholder registers for the project at hand. Another example of the organizational process assets helpful in identifying stakeholders are the lessons learned from previous projects. For instance, you learned from a previous project how you ignored a negative stakeholder that caused great damage to the project.

You identify stakeholders by applying the tools and techniques discussed in the next section to this input.

Tools and Techniques for Identifying Stakeholders

The tools and techniques used to identify stakeholders include expert judgment and stakeholder analysis. Expert judgment was discussed in a previous section, and stakeholder analysis is discussed in an upcoming section in this chapter.

Output of Identifying Stakeholders

The output items of the Identify Stakeholders process are the stakeholder register and the stakeholder management strategy. The stakeholder management strategy is discussed in an upcoming section in this chapter.

You store information about the stakeholders that you identified in a document called the *stakeholder register*. This information includes the following items:

◆ **Identification.** For example, name, location, organizational position, project role (if any), and contact information.

◆ **Assessment.** Requirements and expectations coming from this stakeholder, the part or the phase of the project that is of most interest to this stakeholder, and assessment of potential influence on the project.

◆ **Classification.** There will be a whole array of different kinds of project stakeholders with varied influence. So it's helpful to classify them by using suitable criteria, such as whether they are internal or external to the performing organization, proponents or opponents of the project, and so on.

So, the minimum information in the stakeholder register is based on your work: identify, assess, and classify. This work is part of what is called *stakeholder analysis*, a technique used for identifying the stakeholders.

Stakeholder Analysis

Stakeholder analysis is an activity to gather and analyze information about the stakeholders. Following are the three major steps in this process:

1. **Identify.** Identify in all potential stakeholders the important characteristics of each identified stakeholder, such as the following:

   A. **Name, department, and role.** For example, Dr. John Serri, Vice President, Research and Development.

   B. **Interest in the project.** Why should the stakeholder be interested in the project—seeking to benefit or threatened?

   C. **Knowledge level.** What is the knowledge level of the stakeholder, especially about the project and in the application area of the project?

   D. **Expectations.** What are the expectations of the stakeholder from the project?

   E. **Kind and level of influence.** In which way and how much can the stakeholder influence the project?

2. **Assess.** Make an assessment of how a stakeholder is going to react to various situations in the project. This will help you prepare to influence them in order to get their support to enhance the chances for project success.

3. **Classify.** When there are so many stakeholders, it's important for effective stakeholder management to classify and prioritize the stakeholders. This will help in efficient use of management efforts, including communication and expectations management. For example, an obvious classification is positive and negative stakeholders. For more sophisticated classifications, there are several criteria and models, including the following:

   A. **Power/interest grid.** In this model you place the stakeholders on a two-dimensional plot: authority level versus interest level. For example, if a powerful stakeholder has a lot of interest in the project, he is of great priority. If, on the other hand, a stakeholder lacks interest in the project—even if he has a lot of authority—then he potentially will not influence the project that much.

   B. **Power/involvement grid.** Also called *power/influence grid*, this model plots the stakeholders in a two-dimensional space: authority level versus involvement in the project.

   C. **Involvement/impact grid.** Also called *influence/impact grid*, this model plots the stakeholders in a two-dimensional space: involvement in the project versus ability to impact the project. For example, a project stakeholder may be highly involved in the project but have no ability to impact the project, such as influence the changes in the project. In that case, this stakeholder is of lower priority compared to the stakeholder who has high involvement and high impact.

   D. **Salience model.** This model classifies stakeholders based on multiple characteristics, such as the ability to impose their will (power); the urgency of their needs, expectations, or requirements; and the legitimacy of their involvement.

Based on the stakeholder analysis, you develop the strategy for managing the stakeholders.

Stakeholder Management Strategy

The stakeholder management strategy is the approach developed to deal with the stakeholders in the best interests of the project. The strategy should include the following elements:

◆ Key stakeholders

◆ For each stakeholder, level of influence on the project and level of impact on the stakeholder from the project

◆ How to manage individual stakeholders

◆ How to manage groups of stakeholders

For example, you can maintain the strategy in a matrix like the one shown in Table 2.1.

Table 2.1 Example Template for the Stakeholder Management Strategy Matrix

Stakeholder	Interest in the Project	Assessment of Impact of the Project on the Stakeholder	Level of Influence of the Stakeholder on the Project	Positive Stakeholder or Negative Stakeholder?	Strategy for Maximizing Support or Minimizing Negative Impact

TIP

The stakeholder management strategy should include both the positive and the negative stakeholders. You should develop and implement the stakeholder management strategy with one goal in mind: to optimize the project success by maximizing the support from the positive stakeholders and minimizing (or mitigating) the damaging impact on the project from the negative stakeholders.

As mentioned in the previous section, during the analysis you can draw a variable against another variable and see where the stakeholders fit in that plot. If the variables are chosen carefully, the plot will suggest how much attention should be given to various stakeholders in the plot. As an example, Figure 2.4 presents such a plot, in which the X axis represents the level of interest from very low to very high, and the Y axis represents the authority level (capability of influencing the project) from very low to very high. Stakeholders 1, 2, and 3 have a low interest in the project and low power, and therefore they do not deserve much of your time

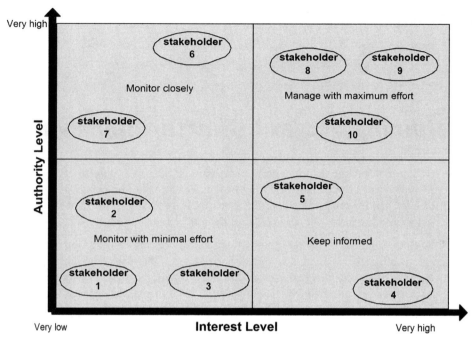

FIGURE 2.4 *An example of determining the strategy by plotting stakeholders against different variables.*

and effort. However, they must be monitored because the interest and the power may change over time. On the other extreme, Stakeholders 8, 9, and 10 have a high interest in the project and a very high capability to influence the project due to high power. Now, these stakeholders should obviously be managed with maximum effort.

 CAUTION

Communication of information about the stakeholders is an important part of the stakeholder management strategy. For example, some of the information about certain stakeholders may be too sensitive to be included in a publicly shared document. As a project manager, you must exercise your discreet judgment on which information about which stakeholder can be shared with whom and to what detail.

So, the project charter and the stakeholder register are the two important documents of the project initiating stage. However, the project does not initiate until the project charter is approved.

A. What is the first process you perform in managing a project?
B. What do you need before you can begin initiating your project?

Obtaining Project Charter Approval

The single most important outcome of the project initiation process group is the project charter approval. In other words, a project is initiated through an approval of the project charter by an appropriate person in the performing organization. Who this person is depends on the organization and the project. This person, for example, could be the CEO of the company, the project sponsor, or a representative of the project selection committee.

With the approval of the project charter, the project is officially authorized, the project manager is officially assigned, and the authority level of the project manager is determined. In practice, it does happen that the (future) project manager participates in developing the project charter, but project approval and resource assignments, such as funding, generally happen outside the boundaries of project management.

Study Checkpoint 2.3

In the following table, match each item in the first column to one or more items in the second column to describe its role during project initiating:

Item	Role
A. Statement of work	1. Input to developing project charter
B. Project charter	2. Output of developing project charter
C. Procurement documents	3. Input to identifying stakeholders
D. Project management strategy	4. Output of identifying stakeholders

 CAUTION

It's important to realize that approval and funding of a project occurs outside the boundaries of the project. However, the project management team may help and be involved in writing the project charter.

In a nutshell, issuing an approved project charter moves the project from the initiating stage into the planning stage.

The three most important takeaways from this chapter are as follows:

◆ A project can originate inside the performing organization or outside of it, in order to meet business requirements, take on an opportunity, or offer a solution to a problem. But the grand origin of a project is always the strategic plan of the organization.

◆ The project charter officially authorizes the project, names the project manager, and determines the authority level of the project manager.

◆ The process of identifying the stakeholders generates the stakeholder register and the stakeholder management strategy.

Summary

Organizations start projects for different reasons, such as to meet a business or legal requirement, to take on a business opportunity, or to develop a solution for a problem. However, the underlying motivation is always to meet some business objectives in the strategic plan of the organization. Three categories of methods are available to select from the proposed projects. The first method is the benefit measurement method, which evaluates the benefits from the project. Constrained optimization methods focus on the probability of completing the project successfully, and expert judgment relies on expert advice. As a project manager, you need to identify each stakeholder: an individual or an organization that is going to gain or lose from the successful completion of the project.

The initiating project stage (also called starting) is constituted by two processes: Develop Project Charter and Identify Stakeholders. The two documents generated by the initiating stage are the project charter, which names and authorizes the project manager, and the stakeholder register, which identifies the project stakeholders and relevant information about them. Based on this information, you develop the stakeholder management strategy. The project charter also includes project justification based on the business needs and a high-level description of the product or service that the project will offer to meet those business needs.

Issuing an approved project charter moves the project from the initiation stage into the planning stage, which is composed of a number of processes collectively called the *planning process group*. These processes are explored in the next Part of the book.

Exam's Eye View

Comprehend

◆ The project manager and project sponsor are also project stakeholders.

◆ A contract can be an input item for developing the project charter but not for developing the preliminary project scope statement.

◆ The project charter, which is an output of the Develop Project Charter process, is an input to the Identify Stakeholder process.

◆ The Develop Charter Process needs to be performed before the Identify Stakeholders process because the project charter is an input to identifying project stakeholders.

Look Out

◆ A contract can be an input item to both the Develop Project Charter process and the Identify Stakeholders process. For identifying stakeholders, a contract could be a part of the procurement documents.

◆ A project stakeholder is an individual or organization that has anything to gain or lose from the successful completion of the project. It could be anyone from the CEO of the performing organization to an ordinary citizen.

Memorize

◆ Project stakeholders are individuals and organizations whose interests are affected (positively or negatively) by the project execution and completion.

◆ The project charter is the document that formally authorizes a project, which includes naming a project manager.

◆ Constrained optimization methods used for project selection use these kinds of algorithms: linear, nonlinear, dynamic, integer, and multiple objective programming.

◆ The major output items of project initiating are the project charter, stakeholder register, and stakeholder management strategy.

◆ The project statement of work is an input to the Develop Project Charter process, and not to the Identify Stakeholders process.

Key Terms and Definitions

- **assumption.** A factor that you consider to be true without any proof or verification. Assumptions can appear in both the input and the output of various processes.

- **constraint.** A restriction (or a limitation) that can affect the performance of the project. Assumptions can appear in both the input and the output of various processes.

- **initiating process group.** A process group that contains two processes: develop project charter and develop preliminary project scope statement.

- **project charter.** A document that states the initial requirements to satisfy the stakeholders' needs and expectations and also formally authorizes the project.

- **Project Management Information System (PMIS).** An information system that consists of tools used to store, integrate, and retrieve the outputs of the project management processes. This can be used to support all stages of the project from initiating to closing.

- **project scope.** The work that must be performed to deliver a product, service, or results with the specified features. The project scope draws the boundaries around the project: what is included and what is not.

- **stakeholder management strategy.** The approach developed to deal with the stakeholders in the best interests of the project.

- **stakeholder register.** A document that identifies the project stakeholders and the relevant information about them.

- **statement of work (SOW).** A document that describes the products or services to be delivered by the project. It is an input to developing the project charter and the preliminary project scope statement.

Review Questions

1. Which of the following issues the project charter document?
   - **A.** The performing organization's higher management
   - **B.** Any stakeholder
   - **C.** The customer
   - **D.** The project manager

2. What document is the result of the project initiation process group?
   - **A.** Statement of work
   - **B.** Project charter
   - **C.** Scope plan document
   - **D.** Preliminary scope statement

3. The project charter is important for which of the following reasons?
   A. It authorizes the sponsor.
   B. It names the project manager and authorizes the project manager to use the organization's resources for the project.
   C. It identifies all the stakeholders.
   D. It produces the stakeholder management strategy.

4. Which of the following is not included in the project charter?
   A. The purpose of the project
   B. High-level product requirements
   C. Budget summary
   D. Project schedule

5. Which of the following is not an input to identifying stakeholders?
   A. Project charter
   B. Contract
   C. Approved project schedule
   D. Stakeholder register template

6. Which of the following lists the documents in the order their first drafts are written?
   A. Statement of work, project charter, stakeholder register
   B. Project charter, statement of work, stakeholder register
   C. Stakeholder register, project charter, statement of work
   D. Statement of work, stakeholder register, project charter

7. You have been named the project manager for a project in your company codenamed Thank You Mr. Glad. The project must complete before Thanksgiving Day this year. This represents which of the following project characteristics?
   A. Assumption
   B. Constraint
   C. Schedule
   D. Crashing

8. Which of the following is true about assumptions in the project initiation?

   A. Because assumptions are a part of the project charter that you did not write, you don't need to validate them. Just assume the assumptions are true, and if the project fails, it's not your fault.

   B. Because assumptions represent risk, you must validate them at various stages of the project.

   C. An assumption is a condition that has been verified to be true, so you don't need to validate it.

   D. You must not start a project until all the assumptions have been proven to be true.

9. Which of the following is not an example of a project selection method?

   A. Enterprise environmental factors

   B. Scoring models

   C. Benefit cost ratio

   D. Constrained optimization methods

10. Your company runs a website that makes digital music downloads available to end users. You have been assigned a project that involves adding parental guidance warnings attached to various downloads. This project originated due to which of the following?

    A. Business requirements that may include legal requirements

    B. Opportunity

    C. Problems

    D. Internal business needs

11. You are preparing to develop the project charter for a project codenamed Plum Dog Millionaire. As part of this effort, you are studying the project statement of work. You must be able to find the following three elements that the SOW includes or refers to:

    A. Project scope, business need, and strategic plan

    B. Contract, business need, and human resources

    C. Project manager, project sponsor, and work required

    D. Product scope, business need, and strategic plan

12. The initiating stage of a project produces the following documents:

    A. Project charter and preliminary project scope statement

    B. Project charter and stakeholder register

    C. Stakeholder management plan and detailed project scope statement

    D. Strategic plan and project charter

13. The three important output items of initiating a project are the project charter, stakeholder register, and:

   A. Stakeholder management strategy

   B. Organizational process assets

   C. Preliminary scope statement

PART II

Planning the Project

Congratulations, you have already defined your project as described in Part I. You can't wait to begin executing. But hold on! I have a couple of questions for you. First, when you are executing your project, how will you know that you are on the right track? Second, during the execution, how will you know that the project is performing in such a way that it will end in success? To address these two and other related questions, you will need to do some planning before you begin the execution. Also, to lead the project to success, you want to monitor and control it throughout its lifetime. Planning gives you the tools and the framework to do exactly that—for example, a performance baseline against which you will be measuring the progress of the project, an important part of monitoring and controlling, is developed during planning. This baseline is comprised of the scope baseline, schedule baseline, and cost baseline, which are developed during scope, schedule, and cost planning. You will also need to plan for the resources needed to complete the project. Furthermore, any management task has a potential of increasing or decreasing a potential risk. Therefore, all project management is inherently connected to risk management. You need to plan for managing risks, and also quality.

Initiation determines what will be done, whereas planning embraces that what, refines it, and determines how it will be done.

Chapter 3

Planning the Project Scope

PMP Exam Objectives

Objective	*What It Really Means*
1.2 Define Scope	You must know how to define the project scope based on the business need with the purpose of meeting customer expectations. Understand how to develop the project scope statement by performing the Define Scope process.
2.1 Define and Record Requirements, Constraints, and Assumptions	Understand the elements of the project scope statement, such as assumptions and constraints, product description, and initial risk identification. Understand the Collect Requirements process and how the collected requirements are used to determine the project scope.
2.3 Create the WBS	Understand the process of creating the work breakdown structure, called Create WBS. You must know how to use the WBS in various planning tasks, such as estimating costs, planning human resources, developing the schedule, planning procurements, and planning for quality. In this chapter, we cover the Create WBS process.

(continues)

PMP Exam Objectives (continued)

Objective	*What It Really Means*
2.4 Develop Change Management Plan	You must understand that you develop the change management plan as part of developing the project management plan. You should understand that the project management plan contains all the subsidiary plans.
2.6 Obtain Plan Approval	You must know that the final project management plan must be approved before you start executing it. Understand the Develop Project Management Plan process.

Introduction

After the project has been initiated, as discussed in the previous chapter, you need to develop a project management plan, which becomes the primary source of information for how the project at hand will be executed, monitored and controlled, and closed. One component of the project management plan is scope planning, which you will explore in this chapter. The primary purpose of project scope management is to ensure that the required work (and *only* the required work) is performed to complete the project successfully. If changes in the work requirements are made, they must be controlled—that is, the scope must be controlled.

Before you start defining the scope, you need to know what the project and product requirements are. In other words, you need to collect requirements based on the needs and expectations of the stakeholders. Once you have defined the scope, it needs to be broken down into concrete, manageable tasks that can be assigned and performed. This is accomplished through what is called the *work breakdown structure* (WBS).

In a nutshell, the central issue in this chapter is planning for the project scope. To be able to wrap your mind around this issue, you will explore three avenues: collecting requirements, defining the project scope, and creating the WBS.

Planning the Project: Big Picture

Once the project has been initiated, it's time to do some planning. This includes determining the project scope, during which time you'll refine the project objectives and determine some how-to's: how the scope will be executed, how the execution will be monitored and controlled, and how the project will be brought to a proper closure. Project planning is embodied in the project management plan that is developed through progressive elaboration, a concept explained in Chapter 1. The project management plan is a document that defines, prepares, coordinates, and integrates all subsidiary plans, such as scope and risk management plans, into one plan. The goal here is to develop a source of information that will work as a guideline for how the project will be executed, monitored and controlled, and closed.

In this section you will get a bird's-eye view of how different elements of project planning integrate into developing the project management plan.

Elements of Project Planning

Project planning means the following three things:

♦ Refining the project objectives defined during project initiation and collecting requirements based on the stakeholder needs and expectations.

♦ Determining the scope of the project.

♦ Determining the course of action required to attain these objectives, which involves breaking down the scope and objectives into concrete, manageable tasks.

It is important to plan the project because not all projects need all the planning processes, nor do they all need them to the same degree. Therefore, the content of the project management plan, the ultimate document developed from project planning, will depend upon a specific project. As the project goes through different stages, the project management plan may be updated and revised through the change control process. Following is an incomplete list of issues that project planning addresses:

♦ Which project management processes will be used for the project, what the level of implementation for each of the processes will be, and what the inputs and tools and techniques for the processes are

♦ The project baseline against which the performance of the project will be measured and against which the project will be monitored and controlled

♦ How the changes to the approved plan will be monitored and controlled

♦ What the needs and techniques for communication among the stakeholders are

♦ How the project lifecycle looks, including the project phases if the project is a multi-phase one

 NOTE

The project baseline is defined as the approved plan for the scope, schedule, and cost of the project. The project performance is measured against this baseline, and therefore this baseline is also called the *performance baseline*. The project baseline is also referred to in terms of its components: cost baseline, schedule baseline, and scope baseline. How do you know how the project is performing? You compare the performance to the baseline. Approved changes in scope, schedule, or cost will obviously change the baseline.

Figure 3.1 presents the big picture of project planning and its relationship with executing. This figure and other figures like this only present a high-level view. The details may be more complex. For example, the project management plan is initially an input to executing but can be influenced and changed as a result of execution. Depending upon the complexity of the

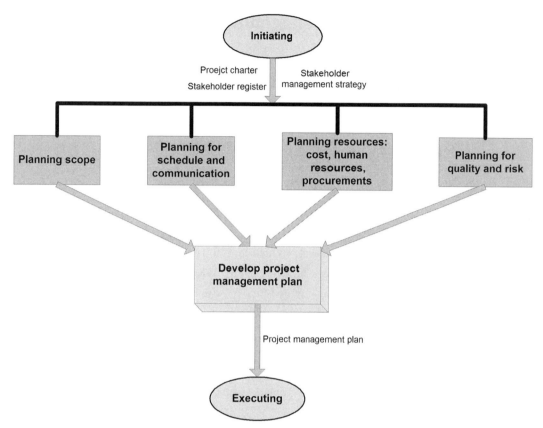

FIGURE 3.1 *A high-level view of interactions and data flow between different components of project planning.*

project, the project management plan can be either a summary or a collection of subsidiary plans and components, which might include the following:

◆ Standard plans from different aspects of project planning, such as the cost management plan, communication management plan, scope management plan, and risk management plan.

◆ Other components, such as the milestones list, the resource calendar, and baselines for scope, schedule, cost, and quality. A baseline is a reference plan against which all the performance deviations are measured. This reference plan can be the original or the updated plan.

In a nutshell, project planning involves determining exactly what will be done and how it will be done. Executing a project means implementing the project management plan for that project. Therefore, the project management plan contains the project scope that defines what needs to be done to meet the project objectives. But how is the project management plan actually developed?

Developing the Project Management Plan

Once the project has been initiated, it is time to do some planning. Project planning starts with the process of developing a project management plan, which defines, prepares, coordinates, and integrates all subsidiary plans, such as scope and risk management plans, into one plan called the *project management plan*. The goal here is to develop a source of information that will work as a guideline for how the project will be planned, executed, controlled, and closed.

One reason why it is important to develop a project management plan is that not all projects need all the planning processes, and to the same degree. Therefore, the content of the project management plan will depend upon a specific project. As the project goes through different stages, the project management plan may be updated and revised through the change control process. Following is an incomplete list of issues that a project management plan addresses.

◆ Which project management processes will be used for this process, what the level of implementation for each of these processes will be, and what the inputs and tools and techniques for these processes are

◆ How the changes will be monitored and controlled

◆ What the needs and techniques for communication among the stakeholders are

◆ How the project lifecycle looks, including the project phases if the project is a multi-phase project

◆ The lifecycle selected for the project at hand

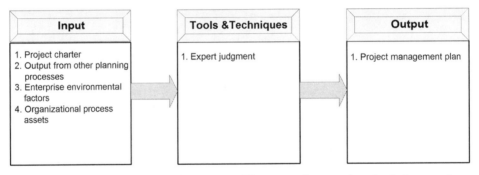

Input	Tools &Techniques	Output
1. Project charter 2. Output from other planning processes 3. Enterprise environmental factors 4. Organizational process assets	1. Expert judgment	1. Project management plan

FIGURE 3.2 *The Develop Project Management Plan process: input, tools and techniques, and output.*

Depending upon the complexity of the project, the project management plan can be either a summary or a collection of subsidiary plans and components, which might include the following:

◆ Standard plans from the project planning process group, such as the cost management plan, communication management plan, process scope management plan, and risk management plan.

◆ Some necessary plans, which may not be generated by standard processes, such as a change management plan that describes how changes will be monitored and controlled.

◆ Other components, such as the milestones list, resource calendar, and baselines for schedule, cost, and quality. A baseline is a reference plan against which all the performance deviations are measured. This reference plan can be the original or the updated plan.

The process of developing the project management plan falls in the knowledge area of integration management because it coordinates the various processes and activities. Therefore, project management processes, in addition to the preliminary project scope statement, are the obvious inputs to this process. The other inputs are enterprise environmental factors and organizational process assets. To develop the project management plan, you apply the following tools and techniques to this input: expert judgment, project management information systems, and project management methodology.

One of the crucial parts of managing any project is scope management, which is discussed next.

Managing Scope

The *scope* of a project consists of the project scope and the product scope. The project scope is defined as the work that must be performed to deliver the required products, services, or results with the specified functions and features. The product scope is the set of functions and features that characterize a product, service, or result to be delivered by the project. It is about both what is included in the project and what is not. In other words, scoping a project means drawing boundaries around it. The importance of managing the project scope cannot be overemphasized because it has a profound impact on the overall success of the project.

 CAUTION

Project scope is not the same thing as the product scope. Project scope is the work required to deliver the product scope.

STUDY CHECKPOINT 3.1

Among the following attributes, identify which are part of the product scope and which are part of the project scope.

   A. Develop software modules to support a website.
   B. The user can only access this website after logging in.
   C. The drug should not have more than two side effects.
   D. The drug must be developed within one year.
   E. The drug must be tested in-house before it goes to the Food and Drug Administration.

Developing the Project Scope Management Plan

Before starting to perform the five scope management processes, you develop the scope management plan. This work is recommended to be part of the effort of developing the project management plan. This plan will work as a guide for handling the following:

- **How can you define the scope?** To answer this question, the scope management plan includes the following:
  - A process to prepare a detailed project scope statement based on the preliminary project scope statement.
  - A process that will enable the creation of the work breakdown structure (WBS) from the detailed project scope statement and will establish how the WBS will be maintained and approved.
- **How can you verify the scope?** The scope management plan answers this question by including a process that describes how the formal verification and acceptance of the completed project deliverables will be obtained.
- **How can you control the scope?** The scope management plan answers this question by including a process that specifies how the requests for changes to the detailed project scope statement (which we also refer to as the *scope statement*) will be processed.

Whether the project scope management plan is informal and high-level (without too much detail) or formal and detailed depends upon the size, complexity, and needs of the project.

The project scope management plan becomes part of the project management plan.

 CAUTION

If you are familiar with the PMBOK Guide, Third Edition, note that there was a process called *scope planning* to develop the scope management plan. There is no such formal process in the PMBOK Guide, Fourth Edition. You develop the scope management plan as part of the effort of developing the project management plan.

Project Scope Management: Big Picture

The major goal of scope management is to ensure that the required work and only the required work is included and performed in the project. As shown in Figure 3.3, this goal is accomplished by the following functions of project management:

- **Collect requirements.** Define the project and product requirements and develop a plan to manage those requirements. This will help clarify what needs to be done.
- **Define scope.** Develop a detailed description of the project and the product that will determine what needs to be done.

◆ **Create work breakdown structure (WBS).** Break down the scope into concrete, manageable components. In other words, decompose the project deliverables into manageable tasks that can be assigned to team members.

◆ **Verify scope.** Formalize the acceptance of the completed project deliverables—that is, determine how to verify that the project scope has been executed as planned.

◆ **Control scope.** Determine how to monitor the status of the project and product scope and monitor and control changes to the scope.

 NOTE

Figure 3.3 presents the big picture of project scope management by showing the high-level view of the interaction of various scope management processes. Note that only the flow of key data items (inputs and outputs) are shown, which is true for all such diagrams throughout the book.

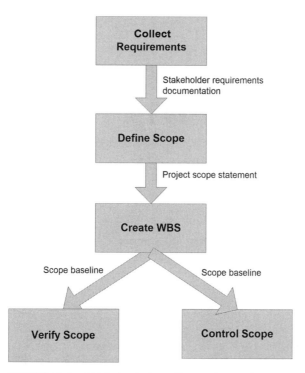

FIGURE 3.3 *A high-level view of interactions and data flow between different components of scope management.*

These functions are executed by performing the corresponding processes listed in Table 3.1. The Verify Scope and Control Scope processes will be discussed further on in this book, whereas other processes of scope management are discussed in this chapter.

Table 3.1 Processes of Scope Management Mapped to the Process Groups

Scope Management Process	Process Group	Major Output
Collect Requirements	Planning	Requirement management plan and other requirement documents
Define Scope	Planning	Project scope statement
Create WBS	Planning	WBS and scope baseline
Verify Scope	Monitoring and controlling	Acceptance of deliverables and change requests
Control Scope	Monitoring and controlling	Work performance measurements

So, the project scope planning specifies how to define, verify, and control the project. Before you can actually define the scope, though, you need to have a very crucial item in place: stakeholder requirements.

Collecting Requirements for the Project

The project success is defined as the delivery of the planned outcome with full scope, on time, and within the budget. To realize this success, it's very important that there is an agreement on what exactly is being delivered with what requirements. A requirement is a condition, characteristics, or a capability that a specific outcome of the project must have. For example, an online banking website is an outcome of the project, and the condition that it must record the number of users who have visited the site each day is a requirement. Requirements may come from different sources, such as from standards, specifications, and contracts. Stakeholder expectations and needs often materialize into requirements as well.

 NOTE

Generally speaking, project requirements should include the product requirements. However, many organizations distinguish between project requirements and product requirements, in which case project requirements include strictly project-related requirements, such as schedule and delivery requirements, business-related requirements, and other project management requirements, whereas product requirements include the product-related requirements, such as requirements related to performance, security, and defects.

You need to do some requirements planning, which includes:

◆ Defining and documenting the project requirements

◆ Defining and documenting the product requirements

◆ Developing a plan to manage the requirements—the requirements management plan

You do all this in order to determine and fulfill stakeholder expectations and needs.

TIP

How effective you are in capturing requirements will determine how effective you will be in getting agreement on these requirements from the stakeholders and in managing the stakeholder expectations and needs. Also, these requirements go right into the foundations of the WBS, along with the deliverables. Therefore, collecting requirements effectively is critical for the success of the project.

You collect requirements by using the Collect Requirements process illustrated in Figure 3.4 in terms of input, tools and techniques, and output. During project initiation, you created the project charter and the stakeholder register, both discussed in Chapter 2. These two documents are the input to the Collect Requirements process. Recall that the project charter contains the high-level product description and requirements. You get information about the stakeholders from the stakeholder register to identify those stakeholders who can provide information about requirements.

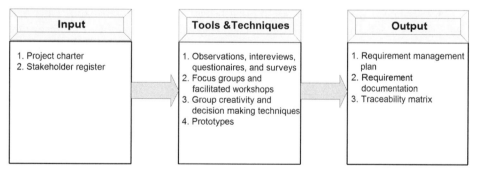

FIGURE 3.4 *The Collect Requirements process: input, tools and techniques, and output.*

With these input items at your disposal, you use some tools and techniques to collect the requirements.

Tools and Techniques for Collecting Requirements

You collect the needed information about the requirements by using various techniques, such as observations, interviews, questionnaires and surveys, focus groups, facilitated workshops, group creativity and decision-making techniques, and prototypes. These tools and techniques are discussed in the following paragraphs.

Observations. Observation is the technique in which the requirements about a product or process are gathered by directly observing the user using the product or performing the process. In other words, the process or product is observed in action in the real world with people on the job. For that reason, this techniques is also called *job shadowing*. Depending on the situation, the observer can simply observe the user doing the job, or he or she can participate in it.

Interviews, questionnaires, and surveys. An interview is typically performed by asking predetermined and on-the-spot questions and recording the responses. Depending on the situation, interviews may take several forms, such as one on one, multiple interviewees, or multiple interviewers. For example, by interviewing subject matter experts and individuals who ran similar projects before, you may identify and define some features and functions of the project deliverables.

When you want to cover a large number of respondents quickly, questionnaires and surveys will be more appropriate. These are based on written sets of questions.

Focus groups and facilitated workshops. A focus group is a set of prequalified stakeholders and subject matter experts that are brought together with the purpose of learning about their opinions, expectations, and attitudes about a product, service, or result that will be the output of the project. Generally speaking, a moderator facilitates the interactive discussion to make this experience more conversational than one-on-one interviews.

A facilitated workshop is a session that brings together the cross-functional stakeholders to focus on defining product requirements. It generally proves to be an effective technique for quickly defining cross-functional requirements and reconciling differences among the stakeholders regarding the requirements. These workshops also help in developing trust and improving communication among the stakeholders and therefore fostering relationships that will help the project to succeed.

Group creativity techniques. These are group activities organized to identify project (including product) requirements. Here are some examples of such activities:

- ◆ **Affinity diagram.** In this technique, a large number of ideas are classified into different groups by using some criteria. This facilitates an effective and efficient review and analysis.
- ◆ **Brainstorming.** This is a creative technique generally used in a group environment to gather ideas as candidates for a solution to a problem or an issue without any immediate evaluation of these ideas. The evaluation and analysis of these ideas

happens later. Obviously, this technique can also be used to collect requirements. Here are examples of two specific kinds of brainstorming:

◆ **Idea/mind mapping.** This is an individual brainstorming technique in which a multitude of ideas are mapped around a central or key concept in order to expose commonalities and differences among ideas and generate new consolidated ideas. Mapping also helps in classifying ideas into groups by discovering relationships among them. In addition to project management, this technique is also used in other areas, such as personal, family, and education. It helps in summarizing, clarifying, and revising ideas.

◆ **Nominal group technique.** This is the brainstorming technique with voting. The voting process is used to rank the ideas generated by brainstorming for further brainstorming or for prioritization.

◆ **Delphi technique.** This refers to an information-gathering technique used for experts to reach a consensus while sharing their ideas and preferences anonymously.

Group decision-making techniques. Group decision making is, in general, a process used to collectively assess and evaluate multiple alternatives in terms of expected outcomes. The decisions usually result in taking specific actions. This general technique can also be used to identify/generate, classify, and prioritize project requirements, including the product requirements. To reach a group decision, multiple methods are available, including the following:

◆ **Dictatorship.** One person has the authority to make the decision. While this expedites the decision making, it may not be the most effective decision-making method.

◆ **Unanimity.** This is opposite of dictatorship: A decision is accepted only if everyone agrees.

◆ **Majority.** A decision must be supported by more than 50 percent of the members of the group.

◆ **Plurality.** The alternative supported by largest number of members wins even if this number does not make a majority. This situation arises when there are more than two alternatives. Plurality with two alternatives is simply a majority method.

Prototypes. A prototype is a working model of a product put together without developing the actual product. Organizations usually make prototypes for developing proof of concept. Prototypes can also be used to collect requirements by experimenting with the prototype and by letting stakeholders experiment with it and offer feedback. A prototype is more tangible than the abstract idea of a product. Prototypes can be improved and modified based on feedback from the stakeholders. In this way, prototypes support the progressive elaboration process of developing requirements.

You use one or more of these techniques to generate the output of the Collect Requirements process.

Output of Collecting Requirements

During this process of collecting the requirements, you will produce two documents: the stakeholder requirements document and the requirements management plan.

Requirements documentation. Also called the *stakeholder requirements document*, this document consists of a list of requirements and any necessary detail for each item in the list. The details of the requirements and the format of the document depend on the project and the rules within the performing organization. Following are some essential elements of the requirements document:

- ◆ **Sources of requirements.** This describes the overall project outcome to which the requirements apply and the purpose of the project, such as the opportunity being seized or the business problem being solved.

- ◆ **Types of requirements.** For effective management, you can organize the requirements into different categories using some criteria. For example, all requirements can be broadly organized into two categories: functional requirements, referring to the functionality of the project outcome, and nonfunctional requirements, such as compliance, compatibility, and support. Furthermore, these broad categories can be subdivided into more specific types, such as the following:

  - ◆ Quality requirements, such as not more than three bugs per software module.
  - ◆ Support and training requirements, such as that the product will be released with a manual.
  - ◆ Requirements that are based on assumptions and requirements that lead to constraints—for example, phase one of the project must be completed before a specific date.

- ◆ **Impacts of the requirements.** This element describes the impact of requirements on the project and on entities external to the project, such as different groups in the organization.

 CAUTION

The requirements must be well defined and not vague. As a test, always ask this question: How will I be able to measure or test it? Also, make sure that a requirement is consistent within itself and with other requirements.

The requirements that you collected will need to be managed.

Requirements management plan. This plan documents how the requirements will be managed throughout the project life, which includes how they will be documented and analyzed.

The requirements management plan includes the following elements:

◆ **Prioritization.** The process and criteria to prioritize the requirements.

◆ **Configuration management.** How the changes to the requirements will be processed: initiated, analyzed, tracked, and reported.

◆ **Reporting.** How, by whom, and to whom the activities related to the requirements will be reported.

◆ **Traceability.** What the traceability structure of the requirements will be—for example, which attributes of a requirement will be captured on the traceability matrix.

Requirements are usually tracked by using a tool called a *requirements traceability matrix.*

Requirements traceability matrix. As the name suggests, the requirements traceability matrix is a table that traces each requirement back to its origin, such as product or business objective, and tracks its progress throughout the project life. Linking a requirement to the business objective underlines its value. Tracking the requirement throughout the lifecycle of the project ensures that it will be delivered before the project is completed. So, this table becomes a very useful tool to remind the team how important these requirements are, when they are going to be implemented, and how they are progressing in implementing them. The requirements traceability matrix includes the following links:

◆ Requirements linked to the origin of the project, such as the opportunity or business need

◆ Requirements linked to the project objectives and deliverables

◆ Requirements linked to the project scope and the product scope

◆ Requirements linked to the product design, development, and testing

◆ High-level requirements linked to their details

◆ The attributes linked to a requirement

The key information about a requirement can be stored in the form of its attributes. Here are some examples of attributes of a requirement: a unique identifier, description, owner, source, priority, status, and completion date.

With the definition of the project determined during project initiation and the requirements collected during planning, and with the project scope management plan in your hands, you are all set to begin defining the project scope.

Defining the Project Scope

The project charter developed during initiation and the stakeholder requirements document, also called the *requirement documentation*, contain enough information about the project and the product to start defining the project scope. Now that the project is in the planning stage, you have more information than you had in the initiation stage. Therefore, you are in a better position to analyze the needs and expectations related to the project and convert them into requirements. Furthermore, the assumptions and constraints can be revisited and analyzed at greater length, and additional assumptions and constraints can be identified. This will help to define the project scope with more clarity and specificity.

 NOTE

When we say *scope* or *project scope*, it generally includes both the scope of the project and the scope of the product that it will deliver, unless stated otherwise.

The scope is defined by using the Define Scope process illustrated in Figure 3.5.

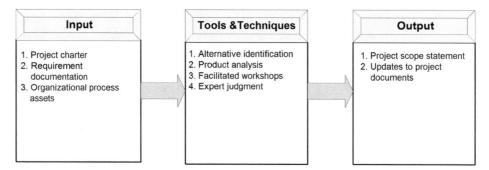

Input	Tools &Techniques	Output

1. Project charter
2. Requirement
  documentation
3. Organizational process
  assets
	1. Alternative identification
	2. Product analysis
	3. Facilitated workshops
	4. Expert judgment
		1. Project scope statement
		2. Updates to project
		  documents

FIGURE 3.5 *Define Scope: input, tools and techniques, and output.*

Input to Scope Definition

The project charter developed during project initiation presents the high-level project and product description. It also contains other information relevant to defining the scope, such as the project approval requirements. Project and product requirements listed in the requirement documentation described earlier in this chapter also contain critical information for defining the scope.

Here are some examples of the organizational process assets that can be helpful in defining the scope:

◆ Template for the project scope statement
◆ Scope-related project files from previous projects
◆ Lessons learned from previous projects or from previous phases of this project
◆ Policies and procedures relevant to defining the project scope

TIP

It's critical to the success of the project that you determine the scope correctly: only the required features and functions for the product and only the required work to produce those features and functions; nothing less, nothing more.

Once you have input for the scope definition, you apply the tools and techniques discussed next to define (or redefine) the project scope.

Tools and Techniques for Scope Definition

This section discusses tools and techniques used in the scope definition process.

♦ **Identification of alternatives.** This is a technique used to apply nonstandard approaches to perform project work—in this case, to define the project scope. A host of general management techniques can be used in this category; the most common ones are brainstorming and lateral thinking. Brainstorming, discussed earlier in this chapter, is a creative technique generally used in a group environment to gather ideas as candidates for a solution to a problem or an issue. The evaluation and analysis of these ideas happens later. Lateral thinking is synonymous with thinking outside the box. The idea is to think beyond the realm of your experience to search for new solutions and methods, not just better uses of the current ones.

♦ **Product analysis.** To hammer out the details of the project scope, you might need to perform product analysis, which might include techniques such as product breakdown, requirement analysis, system analysis, system engineering, value analysis, and value engineering. The goal is to translate the project objectives into tangible deliverables and requirements. Each application area has different product analysis methods to accomplish this.

♦ **Facilitated workshops.** The facilitated workshops described earlier in this chapter can also be used in defining the scope.

♦ **Expert judgment.** You can use help from relevant experts in the organization to develop parts of the detailed project scope.

You apply one of these tools or techniques to the input to hammer out the output of the scope definition process.

Output of Scope Definition

Depending on the input, the scope definition process can generate two kinds of output: the project scope statement that contains the original scope definition and updates to some project documents. Recall that the project scope statement is a component of the baseline used to manage the change requests to the project.

Changes and Updates

In the process of defining the project scope, you may end up modifying the existing requirements or adding new requirements. You may also learn more about the stakeholders. Accordingly, the documents that may be updated as a result of defining the scope include:

- Requirements documentation
- Requirements traceability matrix
- Stakeholder register

Project Scope Statement

The key output item of the Define Project process is the project scope statement, which is
sometimes also called the *detailed project scope statement* or just the *scope statement*. The scope
statement basically states what needs to be accomplished by the project: product and work to
generate the product. It provides a documented basis for the following:

- Developing a common understanding among the stakeholders about the project
  scope
- Making project decisions throughout the lifecycle of the project
- Measuring performance deviations from the scope

The specific elements of the project scope statement are discussed in the following list.

- **Project assumptions and constraints.** Assumptions and constraints are initially
  included in the project charter. However, at this stage, you have more information
  about the project, and therefore you can revisit the initial assumptions and constraints, and you might be able to identify more assumptions and constraints. You
  should document the specific assumptions related to the project scope and also analyze their impact in case they turn out to be false. Due to the uncertainty built into
  them, the assumptions are potential sources of risk.

  The constraints related to the project scope must also be documented in the scope
  statement. Because the constraints limit the team's options, the constraints' impact
  on the project must be evaluated. The constraints can come from various sources,
  such as a predetermined deadline (also called a *hard deadline*) for the completion of
  the project or a milestone, limits on the funds available for the project, and contractual provisions. However, the following are common constraints to consider across
  all projects:
  - Quality
  - Resources
  - Scope
  - Time (or schedule)

We will be exploring these items throughout the book.

◆ **Project deliverables.** A deliverable is a unique and verifiable product, a capability to provide a service, or a result that must be produced to complete a project, a process, or a phase of the project. The deliverables can also include project management reports and documents. The scope statement provides the list of deliverables and their descriptions.

◆ **Project exclusions.** This involves drawing boundaries around the project by specifying what is included and what is not, especially focusing on the gray areas where the stakeholders can make their own assumptions, different from each other. It generally identifies what is excluded from the project, which helps to manage stakeholder expectations.

◆ **Product description.** The scope statement must describe the product scope and the product acceptance criteria:

  ◆ **Product scope description.** Product scope is defined as features and functions that characterize a product, service, or result to be delivered by the project. The requirements documentation produced during the Collect Requirements process will help define the product scope.

  ◆ **Product acceptance criteria.** This defines the process and criteria for accepting the completed products that the project will deliver.

TIP

You must be able to make a distinction between objectives, deliverables, and requirements. For example, in a project to launch a website, the website is a deliverable. That the website must print a warning message at the login time is a requirement, and that the website should increase the company revenue by 3 percent is an objective.

The project scope statement serves the following purposes:

◆ It serves as a component to the baseline that will be used to evaluate whether the request for a change or additional work falls within or beyond the scope of the project.

◆ By providing a common understanding of the project scope, the scope statement helps bring the stakeholders onto the same page in their expectations.

◆ Because the scope statement describes the deliverables and the work required to create those deliverables, it is used to create a WBS, which helps in scheduling the project.

◆ It serves as a guide for the project team to do more detailed planning, if necessary, and to perform work during project execution.

STUDY CHECKPOINT 3.2

In the following table, match each item in the first column with an appropriate item in the second column.

A. The software product must run on both the Microsoft 3) Windows and Apple Macintosh platforms.	1. Project deliverable
B. An online education website. 1	2. Project constraint
C. The drug must be developed within six months. 2	3. Product requirement
D. The software module must not have more than 10 bugs. 5	4. Project management requirement
E. The project manager must have a PMP certification. 4	5. Product acceptance criteria

In a nutshell, the project scope statement specifies the scope of the project in terms of the products, services, or results with specified features to be delivered by the project. From the perspective of actually performing the work, the scope statement is still a high-level document. To be able to schedule the project, identify and assign resources, and manage the project successfully, these deliverables need to be broken down into manageable tasks. This is accomplished by creating an entity called the *work breakdown structure* (WBS).

Creating a Work Breakdown Structure (WBS)

What is the secret behind accomplishing seemingly impossible tasks in any area? The answer is to break down the required work into smaller, manageable pieces. This is also a very important process in project management. To be able to actually execute the project, the project scope is broken down into manageable tasks by creating a work breakdown structure (WBS). In other words, a WBS is a deliverable-oriented hierarchy of the work that must be performed to accomplish the objectives of and create the deliverables for the project.

Figure 3.6 shows the input, tools and techniques, and output of creating the WBS. The project scope statement contains the list of deliverables and the product description. The requirements documentation describes the product and project requirements. Information in these two items provides the basis for creating the WBS. You should always consider organizational process assets while going through this and several other processes. In this case, the organizational policies and procedure related to creating the WBS, as well as relevant project files and lessons learned from previous projects, are some examples of organizational process assets that can be helpful.

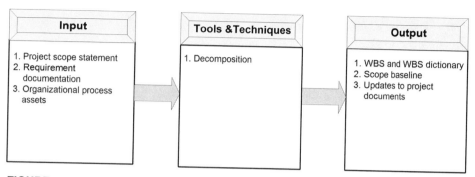

FIGURE 3.6 *The Create WBS process: input, tools and techniques, and output.*

Furthermore, even though each project is unique, there are similarities among sets of projects in an organization. These similarities can be used to prepare templates that will be used as a starting point for the WBS, to avoid the duplication of work. With or without templates, you will need to go through breaking down the deliverables, a very important step in creating the WBS.

Decomposition

Decomposition is a technique for subdividing the project deliverables into smaller, manageable tasks called *work packages*. The WBS is a hierarchical structure with work packages at the lowest level of each branch. Based on their complexity, different deliverables can have different levels of decomposition, as shown in the examples presented in Figure 3.7. In a WBS such as the one presented in Figure 3.7, the lines are called *branches*, and the boxes are called *nodes*.

You decompose the project work by executing the following steps:

1. Identify the deliverables and the work involved by analyzing the project scope statement and the requirements documentation.

2. Understand the relationships among the deliverables.

3. Structure and organize the first level (just below the root of the hierarchical tree) of the WBS hierarchy. Based on the project at hand, you can use one of the following approaches:

    ◆ Use the deliverables as the components in the first level.

    ◆ Use the phases of the project as the components in the first level.

    ◆ Use the subprojects as components in the first level. A subproject is a part of the project that is independent enough of the rest of the project that it can be performed by another project team. This approach is useful when you want to outsource (or procure) parts of the project.

    ◆ Use different approaches within each branch of the WBS—for example, a subproject and deliverables in the first level.

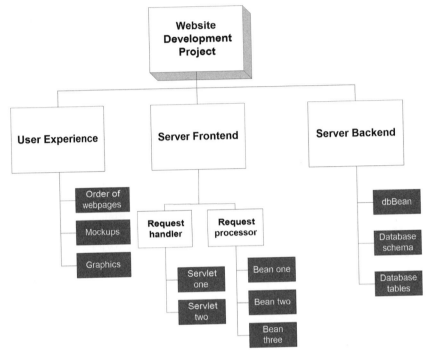

FIGURE 3.7 *An example of a WBS. The work packages are represented by the dark boxes at the end of each branch. Servlet and Bean refer to the programs that will need to be written.*

4. Decompose the upper level into more detailed components for the lower level.

5. Keep decomposing to lower levels until necessary and sufficient decomposition has been achieved.

6. Assign identification codes to the WBS components.

As the work is decomposed to lower levels of detail, work components become more concrete and manageable. However, you should avoid excessive decomposition, because it will lead to a large number of work packages, and it will not be possible to manage all of them effectively. In other words, excessive decomposition leads to inefficient use of management and other resources. Necessary and sufficient decomposition is the key.

 TIP

During decomposition, the components are defined in terms of how the project work will actually be executed and controlled. You must verify the correctness of the decomposition at each level by requiring that the lower-level components are necessary and sufficient to the completion of the corresponding higher-level deliverables.

One final point. While using the technique of decomposition, remember a useful concept or trick: *rolling wave planning*. It's a fancy term that refers to handling a deliverable or subproject that currently cannot be decomposed fully because you don't know the details about it yet—for example, it is to be executed far into the future. You leave the decomposition of such a deliverable at a level allowed by the available information and wait for further decomposition until more information becomes available. Yes, it is an example of progressive elaboration.

The WBS document is the key item of the Create WBS process, but there are some other output items as well.

Output of Creating WBS

The output of the Create WBS process consists of the items discussed in the following list.

◆ **Work breakdown structure.** As explained earlier, the WBS is a deliverable-oriented hierarchical structure that decomposes the deliverables into the work that will be executed by the project team to create the planned deliverables and to accomplish the planned project objectives. The project manager creates this document with the help of the project team. Following are some important characteristics of the WBS:

   ◆ **Control account.** Remember that each node represents a deliverable or a component of it at certain level, and each deliverable will have scope, schedule, and cost attached to it. Some suitable nodes in the WBS are selected as management control points. At each of these control points, scope, schedule, and cost are integrated for the purposes of monitoring and controlling the performance. For example, the integrated scope, schedule, and actual cost at these points can be compared to the earned value to measure the project performance. (You will learn about earned value in an upcoming chapter.) Such management points are called *control accounts*. Each control account may have one or more work packages under it. Obviously, each work package must belong to only one account; otherwise, some factors, such as cost, will be double counted or counted multiple times. A WBS component that is below the control account, that has a well-defined work content but does not yet have a detailed schedule, is called a *planning package*.

   ◆ **Code of account.** Each component in the WBS hierarchy, including work packages, is assigned a unique identifier called a *code of account* identifier. These identifiers can then be used in estimating costs, scheduling, and assigning resources.

   ◆ **Scope.** The WBS embraces the full scope of the project. If a task is not included in the WBS, it will not be done as a part of the project.

   ◆ **Step toward team building.** Because the project manager creates the WBS with the help of the project team, it is also the beginning of the team-building process on the part of the project manager.

- ◆ **Step toward scheduling.** The WBS decomposes the project work into manageable pieces (work packages) that can be assigned to individuals. This helps define the responsibilities for the team members and is the starting point for building the schedule.
- ◆ **Reference for communication.** Throughout the project, the WBS works as a reference for communication regarding what is included in the project and what is not.
- ◆ **WBS dictionary.** This is a supporting document for the main WBS document to provide details about the components of the WBS. The details about a component might include elements such as a code of account identifier, description of work involved, quality requirements, acceptance criteria, a list of milestones schedule, cost estimates, required resources, contract information (if any), and the organization or group responsible for this component.
- ◆ **Updates.** During the create WBS process, the project team might realize that something out of the existing scope must be included in order to accomplish something in the scope. This will give rise to a change request, which might also come from other stakeholders during or after the first creation of the WBS. After the change request has been approved, not only the WBS will be changed—the scope statement must also be updated accordingly. The impact of the approved change request on the project scope management plan must be evaluated, and the plan must be updated accordingly.
- ◆ **Scope baseline.** This is not a different item in and of itself. The scope statement, the WBS document, and the WBS dictionary combined constitute the scope baseline against which all the change requests will be evaluated.

 NOTE

Do not confuse the WBS with other information breakdown structures, such as the organizational breakdown structure (OBS), which provides a hierarchy of the performing organization and can be used to identify organizational units for assigning the WBS work packages. Remember, the end goal of the WBS is to specify the project scope in terms of work packages; this is what distinguishes the WBS from other information breakdown structures.

You might wonder who creates the WBS. Well, it is your responsibility, and you, the project manager, create it with the help of the team. Which team? The work packages do not exist before the WBS is complete; therefore, no assignments have been made yet. Catch 22? Yes, you are right—depending upon the project, the final formal project team might not even exist yet. However, practically speaking, there will already be some people working with you on the project by now. Some of them are the potential team members. In addition to them, you can use the help of relevant experts in the organization and some stakeholders. Also, by now you have a very good idea of who will probably be working to generate the outcome of the project. It's a good idea to involve those individuals in creating the WBS. This will give them a sense of participation and ownership. After all, the WBS will be the reference for the work throughout the project.

CAUTION

The PMP exam expects you to know the ropes of the formal standard terminology. For example, if I say *project plan*, you should be able to figure out that I'm referring to the project management plan. Another example: If I say *defining scope*, you should be able to translate it to the Define Scope process, the same way you will translate the planning stage to the planning process group.

STUDY CHECKPOINT 3.3

A. What is the difference between management control points and control accounts?

B. What is the difference between control accounts and a code of account?

Before and After the WBS

From the initiating process group until now, I have discussed quite a few documents created in various processes. Some of these documents become input into another process that creates some other document. It is important to understand the order in which these documents are created and which document is an input to creating which other document. This is shown in Figure 3.8.

The WBS is at the heart of project management. It affects directly or indirectly almost all the processes that are performed after its creation. Figure 3.9 shows some of the processes that are directly based on the WBS as a component of scope baseline.

The three most important takeaways from this chapter are as follows:

◆ You need to collect requirements by using the Collect Requirements process before you can define the project scope.

◆ The requirements documentation generated by the Collect Requirements process and the project charter generated during the project initiation are used to define the scope, which is documented in the project scope statement.

◆ The requirements documentation and the project scope statement are input items to create the work breakdown structure (WBS), which is a breakdown of project deliverables into manageable pieces called *work packages*. The WBS is supported by another document called the *WBS dictionary*, which offers details for the WBS components.

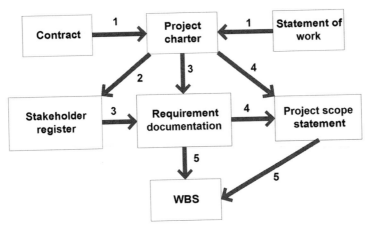

FIGURE 3.8 *A number of documents are created during the initiation and scope planning processes. An arrow shows the documents that are inputs to creating other documents, and the numbers indicate the order in which these documents are created.*

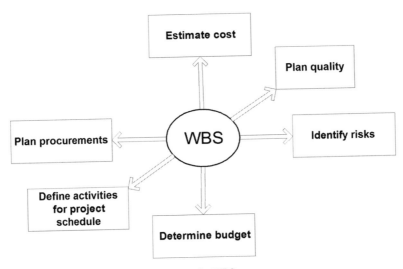

FIGURE 3.9 *Some processes based on the WBS.*

Summary

After a project has been initiated, the project management plan is developed to specify how the project at hand will be executed, monitored and controlled, and closed. The project management plan can contain subsidiary plans, such as a quality management plan, a risk management plan, a project scope management plan, and a scope baseline. The scope baseline consists of the project scope statement, work breakdown structure (WBS), and WBS dictionary. Collecting requirements is part of the scope planning, which creates requirements documentation. The project charter and requirements documentation are used to define the scope, which creates the project scope statement.

The project scope statement is a document that defines the scope of a project, including the product scope, by stating what needs to be accomplished by the project. It includes project deliverables, product description, product acceptance criteria, assumptions and constraints, and project exclusions. The project scope statement and requirements documentation are input items to creating the work breakdown structure (WBS), which is a breakdown of project deliverables into manageable pieces called *work packages*, which in turn are used to develop the project schedule. The WBS is supported by another document called the *WBS dictionary*, which offers details for the WBS components.

The scope statement, the WBS document, and the WBS dictionary combined constitute the scope baseline against which all change requests are evaluated. The WBS is the heart of project management, as it is used in managing many aspects of the project, including developing the schedule. The schedule and communication planning are the topics of the next chapter.

Exam's Eye View

Comprehend

- The project charter and stakeholder register are input items to collecting requirements.

- The project charter and the requirements documentation are input items to the Define Scope process that is used to develop the project scope statement.

- The project scope statement and requirements documentation are input items to creating the WBS.

- The scope statement, the WBS document, and the WBS dictionary combined constitute the scope baseline against which all change requests are evaluated.

Look Out

◆ Do not confuse project scope with product scope. The product scope consists of the features and functions that characterize a product, service, or result to be delivered by the project, whereas the project scope is composed of the work that must be performed (and only that work) to deliver products, services, or results with specified features.

◆ There is no formal standard process to develop the project scope management plan; it's created as a part of the effort to develop the project management plan.

Memorize

◆ The project scope statement includes these elements: project assumptions and constraints, project deliverables, project exclusions, product scope description, and product acceptance criteria.

◆ Quality, resources, scope, predefined budgets, and imposed dates or deadlines are some common constraints you should consider across all projects.

◆ The scope baseline consists of the WBS, WBS dictionary, and project scope statement.

◆ All subsidiary plans are integrated into one plan called the *project management plan*.

Key Terms and Definitions

◆ **alternatives identification.** A technique used to apply nonstandard approaches, such as brainstorming and lateral thinking, to perform project work.

◆ **baseline.** A reference plan for components, such as schedule, scope, and cost, against which performance deviations are measured. The reference plan can be the original or the modified plan.

◆ **brainstorming.** A creative technique generally used in a group environment to gather ideas as candidates for a solution to a problem or an issue without any immediate evaluation of these ideas. The evaluation and analysis of these ideas happens later.

◆ **code of accounts.** A numbering system used to uniquely identify each component of a WBS.

◆ **configuration management.** Refers to controlling the characteristics of a product, a service, or a result of a project. It includes documenting the features of a product or a service, controlling and documenting changes to the features, and providing support for auditing the products for conformance to requirements.

◆ **control account.** A node in the WBS that acts as a management control point where scope, schedule, and actual cost are integrated and compared to the earned value to measure the project performance.

◆ **decomposition.** A planning technique to subdivide the project scope, including deliverables, into smaller, manageable tasks called *work packages.*

◆ **deliverable.** A unique and verifiable product, a capability to provide a service, or a result that must be produced to complete a project or a process or phase of the project.

◆ **lateral thinking.** Thinking outside the box, beyond the realm of your experience, to search for new solutions and methods, rather than only better uses of the current solutions and methods.

◆ **planning package.** A WBS component that is below the control account that has a well-defined work content but does not yet have a detailed schedule.

◆ **product scope.** Features and functions that characterize a product, service, or result to be delivered by the project.

◆ **project management plan.** An approved document that describes how the project will be executed, monitored and controlled, and closed.

◆ **project scope.** The work that must be performed (and only that work) to deliver products, services, or results with specified features that were promised by the project. The project scope draws the boundaries around the project—what is included and what is not.

◆ **project scope statement.** A document that defines the scope of a project by stating what needs to be accomplished by the project.

◆ **requirement.** A condition, characteristic, or capability that a specific outcome of the project must have.

◆ **rolling wave planning.** A case of progressive elaboration in which the deliverables about which full information is available are decomposed to the lowest level, whereas the deliverables for which full information is not available are left at higher levels until the information becomes available.

◆ **scope baseline.** The reference scope against which all the scope deviations are measured. It consists of the scope statement, the WBS document, and the WBS dictionary.

◆ **scope definition.** The process used to develop the detailed project scope statement.

◆ **scope planning.** The process of developing the project scope management plan.

◆ **subprojects.** Parts of the main projects that are independent enough that each can be performed by separate project teams.

◆ **work breakdown structure (WBS).** A deliverable-oriented hierarchical structure that displays the decomposition of deliverables into work, which must be performed to accomplish the project objectives and create the project deliverables.

◆ **work package.** A deliverable or a task at the lowest level of each branch of the WBS.

Review Questions

1. Which of the following is a false statement about the WBS?

    A. Each item in the WBS (not just the work packages) is assigned a unique identi-fier called a *code of account identifier*.

    B. You should keep decomposing WBS components to lower levels until necessary and sufficient decomposition has been achieved.

    C. Each work component appears in the WBS once and only once.

     **D.** The work packages should appear from left to right in the order in which the work will be performed.

2. Which of the following is done first?

    A. Creating the scope statement

    B. Creating the WBS

    C. Creating the requirements documentation

    D. Creating the project charter ✓

3. The WBS is the output of which of the following processes?

    A. The Create WBS process

    B. The Define Scope process

    C. The Develop WBS process

    D. The Project Initiating process

4. The project scope statement is the output of which of the following processes?

    A. The Create WBS process

    B. The Define Scope process ✓

    C. The Create Project Scope process

    D. The Project Initiating process

5. Which of the following is a false statement about the project scope management plan?

    A. It describes how to verify the scope.

    B. It describes how to control the scope.

    C. It serves as the baseline for the project scope.

    D. It describes how to create the WBS.

6. What are the components in the lowest level of the WBS hierarchy collectively called?
   A. Work packages ✓
   B. Milestones
   C. Phases
   D. Features

7. Which of the following is not a constraint common to the projects?
   A. Resources
   B. Imposed date
   C. Schedule milestone
   D. Skill set ✓

8. Which of the following constitutes the project scope baseline?
   A. The WBS document and the scope statement
   B. The scope statement
   C. The WBS document
   D. The WBS, the WBS dictionary, and the scope statement ✓

9. Who creates the WBS?
   A. The project manager alone
   B. The upper management in the performing organization
   C. The customer
   D. The project manager with help from the project team ✓

10. Which of the following is not included in the project scope statement?
    A. Project assumptions and constraints
    B. The WBS ✓
    C. Product description
    D. Project deliverables

11. You are in the process of developing the scope management plan for your project. You will develop this plan:
    A. By performing the Scope Planning process
    B. By performing the Define Scope process
    C. As a part of the effort to develop the project management plan ✓
    D. During the initiation stage of the project

12. You are in the planning stage of a project. Walking down the hallway, your supervisor mumbles, "Don't forget job shadowing." Job shadowing is a technique used in:
    A. Defining the project scope
    B. Collecting product requirements ✓
    C. Creating the WBS
    D. Developing the stakeholder management strategy

13. You are planning the scope for your project. You have just created the requirements documentation after meeting with the stakeholders and studying the project charter. This requirements documentation can be used in developing:
    A. The stakeholder register and project scope statement
    B. The project charter and the WBS
    C. The stakeholder register and the project charter
    D. The project scope statement and the WBS ✓

14. Which of the following is the correct order of running processes?
    A. Develop project charter, Collect Requirements, and Create WBS
    B. Collect Requirements, Develop Project Charter, and Define WBS
    C. Identify Stakeholders, Define Scope, and Collect Requirements
    D. Collect Requirements, Create WBS, Define Scope

15. You have selected a node in the hierarchy of the WBS that you will use to compare schedule, cost, and scope with the earned value in order to measure the project performance. This node or component in the WBS is called:
    A. Code of accounts
    B. Control account
    C. Management account
    D. Performance node

Chapter 4

Planning for Project Schedule and Communication

PMP Exam Objectives

Objective	*What It Really Means*
2.2 Identify Project Team	Identify the key project team members in order to develop the communication plan. You must also define roles and responsibilities of the team members, discussed in Chapter 5. You should understand the Plan Communication process discussed in this chapter.
2.3 Create the WBS	Understand the process of creating the WBS covered in Chapter 3. You must know how to define activities, sequence activities, estimate activity durations, estimate activity resources, and subsequently develop the project schedule, starting with the WBS. These topics are covered in this chapter. You must know that the WBS is part of the scope baseline.
2.6 Obtain Plan Approval	You must know that the final project management plan must be approved before you start executing it. You must also know that you might end up developing multiple versions of the project schedule, but it is the approved version that will be considered as a schedule baseline against which the project progress will be measured.

Introduction

At its core, a project consists of two main components: the project work that needs to be performed and the schedule to perform that work. The overall project work is broken down into smaller, manageable components. These components in the WBS are called *work packages*. However, a work package might not be suitable to assign to an individual to perform. So, work packages can be rearranged, such as decomposed into smaller components called *activities*. A project schedule contains not only the activities to be performed, but also the order (sequence) in which the activities will be performed and a start and a finish date. The sequencing of activities is constrained by the dependencies among the activities.

A realistic project schedule can be created from the bottom up by identifying the activities, estimating the resources for the activities, and determining the time that each activity will take with the given resources available. The resources required to complete the activities include human resources. Before, during, and after schedule development, you will need to communicate effectively.

To enable you to wrap your mind around this issue, I will explore the following three avenues: generating the data about project activities, such as determining activities and their characteristics, including resource requirements and activity durations; building a project schedule from the data on the activities; and planning communication.

The Long and Winding Road to the Project Schedule

Planning the project schedule is all about time management. To complete a project, you need to perform some activities to produce the project deliverables. To make that happen, you need to assign resources to the activities and schedule them. But before all this can happen, you need to identify the activities. Although all this sounds like common sense, it makes sense to define the following terms so we are all on the same page.

- ◆ **Activity.** A component of project work.
- ◆ **Activity duration.** The time measured in calendar units between the start and finish of a schedule activity.
- ◆ **Schedule activity.** A scheduled task (component of work) performed during the lifecycle of a project.

◆ **Logical relationship.** A dependency between two project schedule activities or between a schedule activity and a schedule milestone.

◆ **Schedule milestone.** A milestone is a significant point (or event) in the life of a project, and a schedule milestone is a milestone on the project schedule. A milestone refers to the completion of an activity, marking possibly the completion of a set of activities, and therefore has zero duration. The completion of a major deliverable is an example of a milestone.

Project time management includes the processes required to complete the project in a timely manner. Figure 4.1 presents the flow diagram for the time management processes that lead to schedule development.

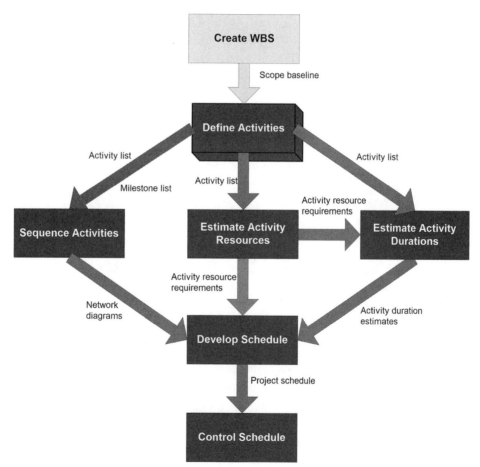

FIGURE 4.1 *The time management processes that lead to schedule development.*

The usages of these processes are listed here:

◆ **Define Activities.** Identifies the specific schedule activities that must be performed to produce the project deliverables.

◆ **Sequence Activities.** Identifies the dependencies among the schedule activities and orders the activities accordingly.

◆ **Estimate Activity Resources.** Estimates the types and amounts of resources that will be required to perform each schedule activity. Examples of resources are materials, equipment, supplies, and people.

◆ **Estimate Activity Duration.** Estimates the time in work periods individually for each schedule activity required for the activity's completion. A work period is a measurement of time when the work is in progress; it is measured in hours, days, or months, depending upon the size of the activity. This estimate is performed for given resources.

◆ **Develop Schedule.** Develops the project schedule by analyzing schedule activity sequences, schedule activity durations, resource requirements, and schedule constraints.

◆ **Control Schedule.** Monitors the status of the project progress and controls the changes to the schedule baseline.

 NOTE

The underlying philosophy of project management for schedule development is to first develop the schedule based on the work required to complete the project tasks and then see how you can make it conform to other constraints, calendar requirements, and strategic goals of the organization. You, the project manager, build the schedule through cold, hard mathematical analysis, and you don't just accept whatever schedule goals come down the pipeline from elsewhere, such as from the customer or the project sponsor.

All these processes, except the Control Schedule process, belong to planning and therefore are discussed in this chapter, whereas the Control Schedule process is explored in an upcoming chapter.

In a nutshell, the path to schedule development includes defining activities, arranging the activities in the correct order, and estimating the resources required to complete the activities. In other words, the work necessary for completing the project is expressed in terms of activities, and the resources are required to complete those activities. So, the first step toward schedule planning after creating the WBS is defining activities.

Defining Activities

Activities that need to be performed to produce the project deliverables are identified using the activity definition process shown in Figure 4.2. The starting point for defining the activities is the lowest level of the WBS that contains work packages. Each work package can be broken down into one or more activities. So, the key input items to the activity definition process are the WBS and the WBS dictionary.

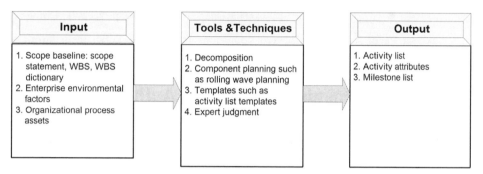

FIGURE 4.2 *The Define Activities process: input, tools and techniques, and output.*

Input to Defining Activities

Identifying project activities starts with the work packages in the WBS, which in turn are derived from the project scope statement. These two obvious input items, along with others, are discussed here.

Project scope baseline. Elements of the scope baseline, such as deliverables, assumptions, and constraints, will be useful in defining activities. All the following three components of the project scope statement are needed to define activities:

◆ **WBS and WBS dictionary.** The work packages in the WBS are decomposed into project activities. To define activities in detail so that you can assign appropriate resources to them, you need the details about work packages, which are provided in the WBS dictionary.

◆ **Project scope statement.** The WBS is built from the project scope statement. While dealing with the WBS, you might need to go back to the project scope statement. The following elements of the project scope statement are especially important to consider while identifying activities:

  ◆ Assumptions related to the activities or schedule planning, such as work hours per week

  ◆ Constraints that will limit the schedule options, such as predetermined deadlines on project milestones

  ◆ Project deliverables, to ensure that everything is covered in WBS work packages

- ◆ **Enterprise environmental factors.** The enterprise environmental factors relevant to identifying schedule activities include project management information systems and project scheduling software tools.
- ◆ **Organizational process assets.** Following are examples of organizational process assets that can be useful in the process of identifying activities:
  - ◆ Organizational policies related to activity planning
  - ◆ Organizational procedures and guidelines used in defining activities
  - ◆ Knowledge base of lessons learned from previous projects regarding activity lists

So, the major input to the activity definition process is the WBS, whose work packages are decomposed into activities using some tools and techniques discussed in the following section.

Tools and Techniques for Defining Activities

The major task in the Define Activities process is to decompose the work packages in the WBS into activities. This decomposition, along with other tools and techniques, is discussed here.

Decomposition. Recall that you used the decomposition technique to create the WBS by subdividing the project deliverables into smaller manageable tasks called *work packages*. Decomposition is also used in the activity definition process for subdividing the work packages into smaller, more manageable components called *schedule activities*.

 TIP

You create the WBS and decompose the work packages to project activities with the help of the project team. Even though the schedule is not yet developed and the resources are not fully assigned, the project team in some initial form will be there. When decomposing a work package into activities, involve the individuals who either are familiar with the work packages or will be responsible for them.

Component planning. If there are areas of the project scope for which sufficient information is not available yet, there will definitely be corresponding components in the WBS that are not decomposed to the level of work packages. You can only develop a high-level schedule for these planning components. You accommodate this kind of high-level scheduling by using a technique called *rolling wave planning* to plan the project work at various levels of detail depending upon the availability of information. Work to be performed in the near future is planned to the low level of the WBS, whereas work to be performed far into the future can be planned at the relatively high level of the WBS. So, a WBS component at the bottom level of a branch of WBS hierarchy for which some planning can be performed is called a *planning component*.

NOTE

Rolling wave planning is an example of progressive elaboration, which was discussed in Chapter 1.

Templates. As a timesaver and a guide, you can use a standard activity list or an activity list from a previous project similar to the project at hand as a template. The template can also contain information about the activities in it, such as required hours of effort.

Expert judgment. Activities make the core of a project. So, it's very important to identify and define them correctly to make the project schedule efficient and effective. Therefore, expert judgment is a very important tool that can be used in this process. For example, during the process of decomposing the work packages into schedule activities, you can use the help of team members and other experts who are experienced in developing WBS and project schedules.

Using these techniques, you convert the work packages in the WBS into schedule activities, which, along with some other items, make the output of the activity definition process.

Output of Defining Activities

The key output item of the activity definition process is a comprehensive list of all the schedule activities that need to be performed to produce the project deliverables. This and other output items are discussed in the following list.

Activity list. This is a list of all the activities that are necessary and sufficient to produce the project deliverables. In other words, these activities are derived from the WBS and hence are within the scope of the project. Also, the scope of each schedule activity should be described to sufficient detail in concrete terms, so that the team member responsible for it will understand what work needs to be performed. Examples of schedule activities include a book chapter with a summary of content, a computer program that will accomplish a well-defined task, and an application to be installed on a computer.

Activity attributes. These attributes are in addition to the scope description of the activity in the activity list. The list of attributes of an activity can include the following:

- ◆ Activity identifier and code
- ◆ Activity description
- ◆ Assumptions and constraints related to this activity, such as imposed date
- ◆ Predecessor and successor activities
- ◆ Resource requirements
- ◆ Team member responsible for performing the work and information about the work—for example, where it will be performed

Some attributes evolve over time. The attributes are used to arrange the activities in the correct order (sequencing) and to schedule them.

Milestone list. A schedule milestone is a significant event in the project schedule, such as the completion of a major deliverable. A milestone can be mandatory, such as one required by a contract, or optional, such as one determined by the team to run the project more smoothly. The milestone list includes all the milestones and specifies whether a milestone is mandatory or optional. Milestones are used in building the schedule.

CAUTION

The Define Activities process generates the final output as activities and not deliverables. Therefore, ideally speaking, the WBS and the WBS dictionary should be generated before defining activities. However, practically speaking, the activity list, the WBS, and the WBS dictionary can be developed concurrently.

To summarize, the output items of the activity definition process are a schedule activity list, a list of attributes for each activity, and a list of milestones. Before you can schedule them, the identified activities need to be arranged in the correct order, which is called *sequencing*.

Sequencing Activities

The activity sequencing process is used to arrange the schedule activities in the appropriate order, which takes into account the dependencies among the activities. For example, if Activity B depends upon the product of Activity A, then Activity A must be performed before Activity B. So the activity sequencing has a two-pronged goal—to identify the dependencies among the schedule activities and to order the activities accordingly. Figure 4.3 shows the activity sequencing process.

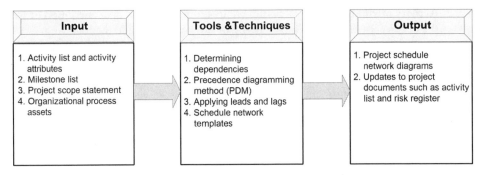

FIGURE 4.3 *The Sequence Activities process: input, tools and techniques, and output.*

Comparing Figure 4.3 with Figure 4.2 reveals that all the output items of the activity definition process are the input into the activity sequencing process. The project scope statement is an additional input item, and it can be used as a source to check the accuracy of the activity list and to ensure that the activity list covers the scope of the project and the products.

You use the appropriate tools and techniques to determine the dependencies among the schedule activities and sequence them accordingly.

Tools and Techniques for Sequencing Activities

Dependency determination is the prerequisite to determine sequencing. Therefore, most of the tools and techniques used for sequencing are focused on determining and displaying the dependencies.

Determining dependencies. To properly sequence the schedule activities, you need to determine the dependencies among them. As illustrated in Figure 4.4, a dependency relationship between two activities is defined by two terms: predecessor and successor. In other words, when two activities are in a dependency relationship with each other, one of them is a predecessor of the other, and the other one is the successor. In Figure 4.4, Activity A is a predecessor of Activity B, and Activity B is successor of Activity A. That means A must start before B.

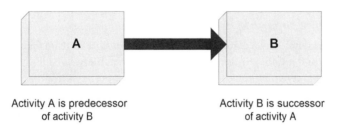

Activity A is predecessor
of activity B

Activity B is successor
of activity A

FIGURE 4.4 *Predecessor/successor relationship between two activities.*

By definition, the successor activity must start after the predecessor activity has already started. But exactly when can the successor activity start after the predecessor activity has already been started? Well, both the predecessor and the successor have a start and a finish, and there are at maximum four possible combinations between the start and finish points of the predecessor and the successor activities. Accordingly, there are four kinds of dependencies, also called *precedence relationships* or *logical relationships*, listed here:

◆ **Finish to start.** The initiation of the successor activity depends upon the completion of the predecessor activity—that is, the successor activity cannot be started until the predecessor activity has already been completed.

◆ **Finish to finish.** The completion of the successor activity depends upon the completion of the predecessor activity—that is, the successor activity cannot be completed until the predecessor activity has already been completed.

◆ **Start to start.** The initiation of the successor activity depends upon the initiation of the predecessor activity—that is, the successor activity cannot be initiated until the predecessor activity has already been initiated.

◆ **Start to finish.** The completion of the successor activity depends upon the initiation of the predecessor activity—that is, the successor activity cannot be completed until the predecessor activity has already been initiated.

These types of dependencies describe the logical relationships between activities. Where do these relationships come from? To answer this question, the dependencies can be grouped into three categories:

◆ **Mandatory dependencies.** These are the dependencies inherent to the schedule activities. For example, a software program must be developed before it can be tested. Mandatory dependencies are also referred to as *hard logic*.

◆ **Discretionary dependencies.** These are the dependencies at the discretion of the project team. For example, perhaps it was possible to perform Activities A and B simultaneously or to perform A after B was finished, but the team decided, for whatever reason, to perform B after A was finished. Some of the guidelines for establishing discretionary dependencies can come from the knowledge of best practices within the given application area and from the previous experience of performing a similar project. Discretionary dependencies are also referred to as *soft logic*, *preferential logic*, or *preferred logic*.

◆ **External dependencies.** An external dependency involves a relationship between a project activity and a non-project activity—that is, an activity outside the project. For example, in a movie production project, think of a project activity that involves shooting scenes with lots of tourists skiing. This scene is planned to be shot at a skiing resort during the skiing season. This is an example of an external dependency.

The dependency between two schedule activities is an example of the logical relationships defined earlier in this chapter. Logical relationships can be displayed in schematic diagrams, called *project schedule network diagrams*, or just *network diagrams* for brevity. A common method to develop network diagrams is called the *precedence diagramming method (PDM)*.

Precedence diagramming method (PDM). The precedence diagramming method is the method to construct a project schedule network diagram in which a box (for example, a rectangle) is used to represent an activity and an arrow is used to represent dependency between two activities. The boxes representing activities are called *nodes*. Figure 4.5 presents an example of a network diagram constructed by using PDM, in which Activity A is a predecessor of Activity B, Activity C is a predecessor of Activities D and G, and so on.

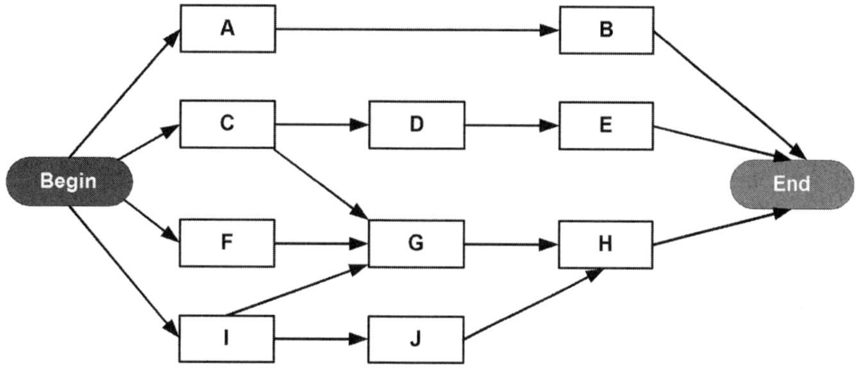

FIGURE 4.5 *An example of a project schedule network diagram constructed by using the precedence diagramming method (PDM).*

In this diagram, only C and I have more than one successor. In general, PDM supports all four kinds of precedence relationships discussed earlier, but the most commonly used dependency relationship in PDM is finish to start. The start-to-finish relationship is rarely used.

Applying leads and lags. In the real world, some activities may need or lend themselves to what are called *leads and lags* to accurately or effectively define the logical relationships. For example, the finish-to-start dependency means that the successor activity starts where the predecessor activity finishes. Applying a lead means you allow the successor activity to start before the predecessor activity finishes, and applying a lag means you start the successor activity a few days after the predecessor activity finishes. Sometimes you might need to make such adjustments in the schedule for effectiveness and efficiency.

Schedule network templates. You can use standardized network diagram templates to expedite the process of activity sequencing. You can also use network diagrams from previous projects and modify them for the project at hand.

STUDY CHECKPOINT 4.1

A. What is the most common logical relationship used in schedule network diagrams?
B. What is the least common logical relationship used in schedule network diagrams?

You use these methods to construct project schedule network diagrams, which are the major output of the activity sequencing process.

Output of Sequencing Activities

The goal of the activity sequencing process is to determine the dependencies among the schedule activities and sequence the activities accordingly. The sequencing is presented in network diagrams. Following are the output items from the activity sequencing process:

◆ **Project schedule network diagrams.** These diagrams, discussed in the previous section, can be created manually or by using an appropriate project management software application. Depending upon a project's size, you might have multiple network diagrams for it.

◆ **Updates to project documents.** During the process of sequencing activities, you may identify new necessary activities, split an activity into two, modify activity attributes, add new attributes, or identify a risk related to an activity. Accordingly, you may need to modify some project documents, such as the activity list, activity attributes, and the risk register.

You can make the activity list, and you can sequence the activities. These are important steps that must be executed. However, to perform the activities, you need resources.

Estimating Activity Resource Requirements

The resource requirements for an activity are estimated by using the Estimate Activity Resources process. The main purpose of this process is to accomplish the following goals:

◆ Estimate the types of resources needed for a given activity

◆ Estimate the quantities of each type of resource needed for the activity

Figure 4.6 shows the Estimate Activity Resources process with its input, tools and techniques, and output.

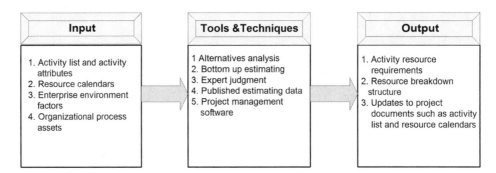

FIGURE 4.6 *The Estimate Activity Resources process: input, tools and techniques, and output.*

The activity list and attributes determined by the Define Activities process are the major input items to activity resource estimating.

Input to Activity Resource Estimating

The activity list and attributes are the obvious and major input to the activity resource estimating process. These and other input items are discussed in the following list.

◆ **Activity list and activity attributes.** The activity list originally developed during the activity definition process identifies the schedule activities that need the resources. The activity attributes provide the details for the activities, which will be helpful in estimating the resources.

◆ **Resource calendars.** Resource estimating will require information on the available quantity of resources of different types, such as human, equipment, and material. This information is usually available in the resource calendars, which may also have detailed information about human resources, such as skill level, experience, and the geographical location from where the resource will come. Typically, the resource calendar contains the following useful information about the resources:

   ◆ Days and times of day when a resource is available

   ◆ The passive time for the resource—for example, holidays for human resources

   ◆ The quantity of each type of available resource

   ◆ The capability of each resource

◆ **Enterprise environmental factors.** Information about the infrastructure of the performing organization, such as existing facilities, will be used in identifying the resources and their availability.

◆ **Organizational process assets.** The organizational process assets useful for activity resource estimating include organizational policies for staffing and purchase of supplies, historical information on what types of resources were used for similar activities in a previous project, and the like.

Once you understand the activities, you can use some tools and techniques to determine the resources required to perform those activities.

Tools and Techniques for Activity Resource Estimating

Following are the tools and techniques used to determine the resources required to perform schedule activities.

◆ **Alternative analysis.** Alternative analysis is all about exploring alternative solutions to a problem. In the case of estimating resource requirements, you will need to consider alternatives available for resources needed for some schedule activities. For example, you might need to decide whether you want to buy or develop a tool needed to perform an activity, what types of machines (for example, Windows or Linux) to use, which computers to use to do the development, or what level of skills is needed.

◆ **Bottom-up estimating.** You might discover that it is rather complex to estimate resources for a given schedule activity. If the problem is inherent to the activity, it might be helpful in certain cases to decompose the activity into smaller components for the purpose of resource estimating and, then estimate the resource for each component, and then aggregate the resources to get an estimate for the whole activity. In aggregation, you must consider the possible relationships (overlaps and such) among different components of the activity so you don't double-count the resources.

◆ **Expert judgment.** Expert judgment can be used to assess the input and determine the output of the resource estimating process.

◆ **Published estimating data.** Information published by various vendors, such as costs for resources, can be useful in estimating the resources.

◆ **Project management software.** Depending upon the sophistication of the resource requirements and the capabilities of the available features, project management software might be useful in estimating and managing the resources. It can also be used to create resource breakdown structures.

You can use a combination of these tools and techniques to generate the output of the resource estimating process.

Output of Activity Resource Estimating

The resource requirements are the major output of the resource estimating process. These and other output items are discussed in the following list.

Activity resource requirements. The main purpose of the activity resource estimating process is to determine the resource requirements for each activity, and therefore this is the major output item from this process. You identify the types of resources required to perform each activity and estimate the required quantity of each identified resource. If a work package in the WBS has multiple activities, the resource estimates for those activities can be aggregated to estimate the resource requirements for the work package. The requirement documents may also include information such as the basis for each estimate, the assumptions made for the estimate, and the availability of the resources.

Resource breakdown structure. The resource breakdown structure (RBS) is a hierarchical structure of resource categories and types required to complete the schedule activities of a project. The RBS can be used to identify and analyze the project human resource assignments.

Updates to project documents. The identified types of required resources for an activity and the estimated quantity for each identified resource become activity attributes and must be added to the attribute list for the activity. Activity resource estimating might generate modifications to the activity list—for example, to add or delete an activity. It may also cause you to change the resource calendar.

Once the activities have been identified and resources required to perform each activity have been estimated, you have enough information to begin estimating the time needed to complete each activity, which is called the *activity duration*.

Estimating Activity Duration

Activity duration is the time between the start and finish of a schedule activity. Activity duration is estimated in work periods by using the Estimate Activity Durations process. A work period is a measurement of time when the work is in progress; it is measured in hours, days, or months, depending upon the size of the activity. This estimate can be converted to calendar units of time by factoring in the resource's passive time, such as holidays. For an example, suppose you have estimated that it will take one programmer four days (with eight work hours in a day) to write a program. You also know that the work will start on a Friday and there will be no work on Saturday and Sunday. Therefore, the activity duration estimate is four days (or 32 hours) measured in work periods and six days measured in calendar units.

Figure 4.7 shows the input, tools and techniques, and output for activity duration estimating.

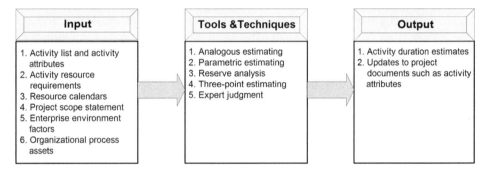

FIGURE 4.7 *The Estimate Activity Durations process: input, tools and techniques, and output.*

Input to Activity Duration Estimating

To estimate the activity duration, you will need information about the activity, the resource requirements for the activity, and the resources available for the activity. This underlines the major input items to the activity duration estimating process. These and other input items are discussed here.

Activity list and activity attributes. Because you want to estimate the duration of the activities, the activity list along with the activity attributes, originally developed in the Define Activities process, are the obvious input items to the activity duration estimating process.

Activity resource requirements. The work periods required to complete an activity depend on the resources assigned to the activity. For example, suppose it will take four work days to complete an activity that involves having two programmers write two programs. If only one programmer is available, it will take roughly eight work days to finish this activity. However, while assigning additional resources to an activity, always consider the following:

◆ Sometimes assigning additional resources might reduce the overall efficiency and productivity. For example, think of two engineers with different skill levels assigned to work on the interrelated components of an activity.

◆ Most of the activities have a threshold beyond which assigning additional resources does not help. For example, installing an operating system on a machine will take the same amount of time regardless of how many system administrators have been assigned to this activity.

Resource calendar. The resource calendar, finalized (or modified) during activity resource estimating, contains the type, quantity, availability, and capability of each resource, including the skills of a human resource, which must be considered during activity duration estimating. For example, an experienced programmer can finish the same program in less time than a beginner can. Capability and quantity of available resources, both human and material, can affect the activity duration estimate. For example, if an activity will take four work days for an engineer to finish, and the engineer can work only four hours a day on this activity, it will take eight calendar days to finish.

Project scope statement. Some assumptions and constraints in the project scope statement can affect activity duration estimates and therefore must be considered. For example, there might be an assumption that part of the work related to an activity has already been performed in a previous project and can be used in this project. If the assumption is true, the activity duration will be less than otherwise. An example of a constraint might be that a specific work package must be finished before a predetermined deadline. This will put a maximum limit on the duration for the activities corresponding to this work package.

Enterprise environmental factors. Examples of enterprise environmental factors are some databases that contain reference data relevant to the activity duration—for instance, how long it takes for a specific government agency to respond to a request. Published commercial information and metrics to measure productivity can also be helpful in duration estimates.

Organizational process assets. Organizational process assets that will be useful in estimating activity duration include information from previous projects and a calendar of working days and non-working days.

In a nutshell, the activity list and activity resource requirements are the major inputs to the activity duration process. The activity duration estimate is a nontrivial task, and there are various tools and techniques available to perform this task effectively and reliably.

Tools and Techniques for Activity Duration Estimating

The project schedule depends upon the activity duration estimates. The duration estimates of activities on the critical path will determine the finish date of a project for a given start date. However, there might be many uncertainties involved in the estimate. For example, two programmers, due to the differences in their experience, will take different amounts of time to write the same program. The good news is that there are a number of tools and techniques that you can use in activity duration estimating.

Analogous estimating. Analogous estimating techniques estimate the duration of an activity based on the duration of a similar activity in a previous project. The accuracy of the estimate depends upon how similar the activities are and whether the team member who will perform the activity has the same level of expertise and experience as the team member from the previous project. This technique is useful when there is not enough detail information about the project or a project activity available—for example, in the early stages of a project.

Parametric estimating. This is a quantitative technique used to calculate the activity duration when the productivity rate of the resource performing the activity is available. You use a formula such as the following one to calculate the duration:

Activity duration = Units of work in the activity / Productivity rate of the resources

For example, if you know that a team assigned to the activity of burying 40 miles of cable can bury two miles of cable in one day, the duration calculation can be performed as follows:

Activity duration = 40 miles / (2 miles/day) = 20 days

Three-point estimating. This method addresses the issue of uncertainty in estimating the activity duration. The uncertainty in the duration estimate can be calculated by making a three-point estimate in which each point corresponds to one of the following estimate types:

◆ **Most likely scenario.** The activity duration is calculated in most practical terms by factoring in resources likely to be assigned, realistic expectations of the resources, dependencies, and interruptions.

◆ **Optimistic scenario.** This is the best-case version of the situation described in the most likely scenario.

◆ **Pessimistic scenario**. This is the worst-case version of the situation described in the most likely scenario.

The spread of these three estimates determines the uncertainty. The resultant duration is calculated by taking the average of the three estimates. For example, if the duration for an activity is estimated to be 20 days for the most likely scenario, 18 days for the optimistic scenario, and 22 days for the pessimistic scenario, then the average duration is 20 days, and the uncertainty is ± 2 days, which can be expressed as:

Duration = 20 ± 2 days

It's equivalent to saying that the activity duration is 20 days, give or take two days.

However, the most likely scenario may be given more weight than the other two scenarios. Therefore, the expected duration can be calculated by using the following formula:

$t_e = (nt_m + t_o + t_p)/(n+2)$

where t_e is the expected duration, t_m is the duration in the most likely scenario, t_o is the duration in the optimistic scenario, t_p is the duration in the pessimistic scenario, and n is the weight given to the most likely scenario.

STUDY CHECKPOINT 4.2

In the program evaluation and review technique (PERT), the most likely scenario is given a weight of 4 as compared to the weight of 1 for each of the pessimistic and optimistic scenarios. The pessimistic estimate for an activity is 25 days, the optimistic estimate is 5 days, and the most likely estimate is 10 days. Calculate the expected estimate by using the PERT technique.

Reserve analysis. Reserve analysis is used to incorporate a time cushion into your schedule; this cushion is called a *contingency reserve*, a *time reserve*, or a *time buffer*. The whole idea is to accommodate the possibility of schedule risks. One method of calculating the contingency reserve is to take a percentage of the original activity duration estimate as the contingency reserve. It can also be estimated by using quantitative analysis methods. Later, when more information about the project becomes available, the contingency reserve can be reduced or eliminated.

Expert judgment. Expert judgment can be used to estimate the whole duration of an activity when not enough information is available. It can also be used to estimate some parameters to be used in other methods—for example, what percentage of the original activity duration estimate should be used as a contingency reserve—and in comparing an activity to a similar activity in a previous project during analogous estimating.

Note that, in general, a combination of techniques is used to estimate the duration of an activity. For example, you can use the analogous technique and expert judgment to estimate the productivity rate of resources and then use that productivity rate in parametric analysis to calculate the activity duration.

Output of Activity Duration Estimating

Guess what the output of the activity duration estimating process is. Yes, you are right: It is the activity duration estimates! Regardless of which technique you use, these estimates are quantitative assessments of the required time units to finish activities, such as five days or 10 weeks. As shown earlier, you can also assign an uncertainty to the estimate, such as 20±2 days to say that the activity will take at least 18 days and at most 22 days.

The duration of an activity is an attribute of the activity. Therefore, you update the activity attributes, originally developed in the Define Activities process, to include the activity durations.

In a nutshell, there are two output items of the activity duration estimating process:

♦ Activity duration estimates
♦ Updates to activity attributes and assumptions about skill level and availability of resources

By using various processes discussed in this chapter, you have identified schedule activities, arranged them in proper sequence, determined resource requirements for them, and estimated their durations. All these tasks and accomplishments are a means to an end called *project schedule development*.

Developing the Project Schedule

The project work is composed of individual activities. So, the processes previously discussed in this chapter deal with the activities: defining activities, estimating activity durations, and estimating resource requirements of the activities. By using these processes, you work out a few schedule-related pieces at the activity level, which come together as the project schedule when you crank them through the schedule development process, formally called Develop Schedule. Until you have a realistic project schedule, you do not have a project. A project schedule has schedule activities sandwiched between the project start date and the project finish date. Figure 4.8 shows the Develop Schedule process used to develop the project schedule.

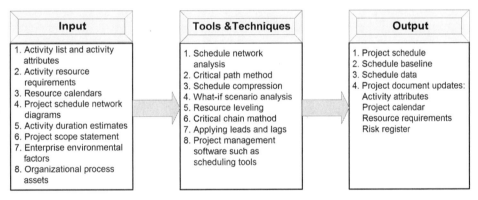

FIGURE 4.8 *The Develop Schedule process: input, tools and techniques, and output.*

All the processes discussed in this chapter so far had a common goal: schedule development. Therefore, the major output items of all the processes discussed in this chapter are the input to the schedule development process.

Input to Schedule Development

The following output items from the schedule-related processes discussed in this chapter directly support the schedule development process:

- ◆ Activity list and activity attributes
- ◆ Project schedule network diagrams showing the dependencies among activities
- ◆ Activity resource requirements and resource calendars
- ◆ Activity duration estimates

The project scope statement and two other input items that can be useful in ways are described in the following list.

Project scope statement. The assumptions and constraints in the project scope statement can affect the project schedule and therefore must be considered in developing the schedule. The following two types of time-related constraints should get special attention.

♦ **Hard deadlines for start and finish dates.** Some activities or work packages might have constraints on their start or finish dates. For example, there might be a situation in which an activity cannot be started before a certain date, or must be finished before a certain date, or both. Where do these date constraints come from? They can come from various sources, such as a date in the contract, a date determined by the market window, a date determined by delivery of material from an external vendor, and the like.

♦ **Time constraints on deliverables.** These constraints can come from the customer, the sponsor, or any other stakeholder in terms of deadlines for certain major deliverables or milestones. Other projects inside or outside your organization might be depending on these constraints. So, once scheduled, these deadlines are constraints and can only be changed through the approval process.

Enterprise environmental factors and process assets. Scheduling tools are an example of enterprise environmental factors and scheduling methodology and project calendars are examples of organizational process assets that can be useful in developing the schedule.

To summarize, the output of various time management processes is used as input to the schedule development process, which uses a variety of tools and techniques to iron out the project schedule.

Tools and Techniques for Schedule Development

Once you have the network diagrams for the activities, as well as the activity duration estimates, you are well equipped to start scheduling the project. The remaining main concerns include the following:

♦ The actual start date

♦ Uncertainty of the availability of resources

♦ Identification of and preparation for activities on the critical path

♦ Risks involved or what-if scenarios

♦ The hard start/finish dates for activities or for the project that came down the pipeline from very important stakeholders

Various tools and techniques discussed in the following sections can be used to address these concerns while you are hammering out the project schedule.

Schedule Network Analysis

Schedule network analysis is a technique used to generate a project schedule by identifying the early and late start and finish dates for the project. The analysis accomplishes this task by using various analytical techniques, such as critical path method, critical chain method, what-if analysis, and resource leveling. These techniques are discussed in the following list.

Critical path method. This is the schedule network analysis technique used to identify the schedule flexibility and the critical path of the project schedule network diagram. The critical path is the longest path (sequence of activities) in a project schedule network diagram. Because it is the longest path, it determines the duration of the project and hence the finish date of the project given the start date. An example will explain this. Consider the network diagram presented in Figure 4.9. The boxes in the figure represent activities, such as Activity A followed by Activity B, and the number on top of a box represents the duration of the activity in time units, such as days.

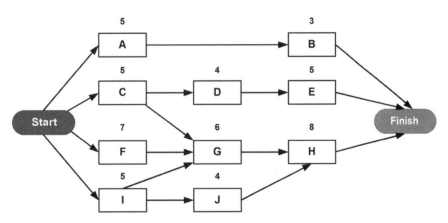

FIGURE 4.9 *An example of a project schedule network diagram. The duration of an activity is represented by the number shown on top of the box that represents the activity.*

Table 4.1 shows the calculations for the duration of each path of the network diagram by adding the durations of the individual activities on the path. You can see from Table 4.1 that Start-F-G-H-Finish is the critical path because it is the longest path in the diagram, at 21 days. This means if the project start date is January 2, the project finish date will be January 23 (2+21), given that the duration is shown in calendar time units.

The second important feature of the critical path method is to identify the flexibility in the project schedule by calculating the early and late start and finish dates of each activity on each path. The schedule flexibility of an activity is measured by the positive difference between the late start date and the early start date for the activity and is called *float time* or *total float*.

Table 4.1 Path Durations Calculated from the Network Diagram Shown in Figure 4.9

Path	Durations of Activities	Path Duration
Start-A-B-Finish	5+3	8
Start-C-D-E-Finish	5+4+5	14
Start-C-G-H-Finish	5+6+8	19
Start-F-G-H-Finish	7+6+8	21
Start-I-G-H-Finish	5+6+8	19
Start-I-J-H-Finish	5+4+8	17

Table 4.2 shows calculations for the early and late start and finish dates and the float time for each activity in the network diagram being analyzed. The early start and finish dates of activities on a path are calculated by using the forward-pass method, which means you start your calculations from the start point (leftmost) and make your way forward.

Table 4.2 Early and Late Start and Finish Dates for Activities in the Network Diagram Shown in Figure 4.9

Activity	Early Start	Early Finish	Late Start	Late Finish	Float Time
A	0	5	13	18	13
B	5	8	18	21	13
C	0	5	2 (not 7)	7	2
D	5	9	12	16	7
E	9	14	16	21	7
F	0	7	0	7	0
G	7	13	7	13	0
H	13	21	13	21	0
I	0	5	2 (not 4)	9	2
J	5	9	9	13	4

As an example, consider the path Start-A-B-Finish in the network diagram shown in Figure 4.9. Because A is the first activity on the path, its early start is Day 0. Because B depends on the completion of A, and A takes 5 days to finish, the early start date for B is the early start date of A plus the duration of A—that is, 0+5=5. The late start and finish dates are calculated using the backward-pass method, which means you start your calculations from the finish point. The project finish date determined by the critical path is Day 21, given that the project start date is Day 0. Because Activity B has a duration of 3 days, it must be started no later than Day 18 (21–3=18). Therefore, Day 18 is the late start date of Activity B. Activity A has a duration of 5 days, so given that B must start on Day 18, A must not start later than Day 13 (18–5=13). Therefore the late start date for A is Day 13. The float times are calculated as follows:

Float time for A = late start – early start = 13–0 = 13

Float time for B = late start – early start = 18–5 = 13

Note that each of the activities on the critical path (F, G, and H) has a float time of zero. This obviously is a source of schedule risk.

 NOTE

Each activity on a critical path has zero float time and therefore poses a schedule risk. So, you must monitor the activities on all critical paths very closely during the execution of the project.

Critical chain method. This is an alternative schedule network analysis technique that takes into account the uncertainties of the activity durations due the uncertainty of the availability of resources. It uses schedule network diagrams to identify the critical paths and the schedule flexibility, just like the critical path method. The only difference is that in this technique, you work from more than one network diagram. For example, the durations in the first network are based on the planned scenario regarding the availability of resources. You can draw another network diagram based on the pessimistic scenario regarding the availability of resources. The durations of some activities in the second diagram will be longer than the first diagram, and the second diagram might even have a different or an additional critical path. The extra durations in the second diagram are called *duration buffers*. So, the focus of the critical chain method is on managing the duration buffers and the uncertainties in the availability of resources applied to the planned schedule activities.

Resource leveling. Resource leveling is not an independent schedule network analysis method. It is applied to the schedule that has already been analyzed using other methods, such as the critical path method or the critical chain method. The resource leveling technique is applied to address the resource needs of activities that must be performed to meet specific delivery dates. Resource leveling involves taking a part of the resources from one activity and assigning it to another. This will change the activity durations and can also result in a change of critical paths.

What-if scenario analysis. The purpose of what-if scenario analysis is to calculate the effects of a specific scenario on the schedule—for example, how the schedule will be affected if a vendor does not make the delivery of a major component on the promised date. Because a what-if scenario by definition represents uncertainty, this analysis often leads to risk planning, which might include changing the schedule or changing the network diagram to get a few activities out of harm's way if possible.

As you have seen, the critical path method is used to develop a schedule for given resources, whereas the critical chain method factors in the uncertainty of the availability of the resources. The resource leveling technique is used to move the resources around to meet the resource needs of the activities that must be accomplished on a specific date. In other words, in an ideal world in which the required (or planned) resources are guaranteed, you do not need the critical chain method and resource leveling; just the critical path method will do.

Let's assume you have used the critical path method to determine the schedule for a project. You have also applied other techniques, such as the critical chain method and resource leveling. The final realistic schedule that you have come up with has an unacceptable project duration (the length of the critical path). What do you do? This is where the schedule compression technique comes to your rescue.

Schedule Compression

Schedule compression is an attempt to shorten the project schedule without changing the project scope. It may be necessary in order to deal with schedule-related constraints and objectives. It is true that you, the project manager, build the schedule through cold, hard mathematical analysis, and you don't just accept whatever schedule goals come down the pipeline from elsewhere, such as from the customer or the project sponsor. However, once you have the schedule built through analysis, you can attempt to accommodate some critical stakeholder expectations or hard deadlines, such as a predetermined project finish date. I have already discussed one such method, called resource leveling, to accommodate hard deadlines for activities. In this section, I will discuss two more methods for schedule compression: crashing and fast tracking.

Crashing. This is a project schedule compression technique in which cost and schedule trade-offs are analyzed to decrease the project duration with minimal additional cost. A number of alternatives are analyzed, including the assignment of additional resources. Approving overtime is another example of crashing.

Fast tracking. This is a project schedule compression technique used to decrease the project duration by performing project phases or some schedule activities within a phase in parallel that would normally be performed in sequence. For example, testing of a product can start when some of its components are finished, rather than waiting for the whole product to be completed.

TIP

Crashing usually involves assigning more resources and hence increasing the cost. However, guard yourself against the misconception that additional resources will linearly improve the performance. For example, if one programmer can develop a program in eight days, it does not necessarily mean that two programmers will develop the same program in four days, because there will be overheads, such as the initial less-productive stage of the newly assigned resource, the time taken to reallocate the work, the interaction among the resources, and so on.

Other Tools and Techniques

In addition to the main techniques to develop the project schedule, which I already discussed, there are some other tools and techniques for developing the project schedule that I will discuss in this list.

Applying leads and lags. Just like in the activity sequencing process, leads and lags can be applied during the development of project schedule. If you applied some leads and lags during the activity sequencing process, it is time to consider whether you need to adjust those. This adjustment might be necessary to create a realistic schedule.

Project management software. After you have the data for the schedule development created by the processes discussed in this chapter, it is a common practice to use project management software to build the actual schedule. Because they are automated, the scheduling tools expedite the scheduling process and reduce the probability of errors in the schedule.

In a nutshell, the main techniques to develop a project schedule include network diagram analysis (critical path method and critical chain method), schedule compression (fast tracking and crashing), and resource leveling. You use these techniques to generate the output of the schedule development process.

Output of the Schedule Development Process

The planned project schedule is an obvious output of the schedule development process. This and other output items are discussed in this list.

Project schedule. The project schedule includes a planned start date and a planned finish date for each schedule activity. The schedule will be considered preliminary until the resources have been assigned to perform the activities according to the schedule. Although a schedule for a simple project might be presented in a tabular form, typically a project schedule is presented in one of the following graphical formats:

◆ **Project schedule network diagram.** These diagrams present the schedule activities on a timescale with a start and a finish date for each activity and hence show the dependencies of activities on each other. Because they show the dependencies—that is, the logic—they are also called *logic charts*.

◆ **Bar chart.** In these charts the activities are represented by bars, with each bar showing the start date, the finish date, and the duration of the activity. They are easy to read and are often used in presentations.

◆ **Milestone chart.** These are typically the bar charts representing only the milestones, not all the schedule activities.

Schedule data. This is the supporting data for the project schedule and consists of the following:

◆ The essential data consists of schedule activities, schedule milestones, activity attributes, and documentation of all identified assumptions and constraints.

◆ Resource requirements by time periods.

◆ Alternative schedules—for example, schedules based on best-case and worst-case scenarios.

◆ Schedule contingency reserves.

 TIP

The schedule data may be enriched by items such as delivery schedules, order schedules, and resource histograms depending on the nature of the project.

This data is used to create the version of the schedule that is approved by the project management team and becomes the schedule baseline.

Schedule baseline. This is a specific version of the project schedule that is accepted and approved by the project management team as a baseline against which the progress of the project will be measured. This version of the schedule is developed from the schedule network analysis described earlier.

Updates to project documents. During the process of developing the schedule, updates to the following documents may happen:

◆ **Resource requirements.** The schedule development process might change the initial estimate for the types and quantities of required resources.

♦ **Activity attributes.** Resource requirements or any other activity attributes that have changed must be updated.

♦ **Project calendar.** Any update to the project calendar must be documented. For example, each project may use different calendar units in the project schedule.

 NOTE

Project schedule development is an iterative process. For example, it might be necessary to review and revise the duration and resource estimates for some activities to create a project schedule that will be approved. The approved project schedule will act as a baseline against which project progress will be tracked.

As mentioned earlier, the approved project schedule is used as a baseline to track the project progress. To some extent, the schedule development (or modification) continues throughout the project execution due to the approved changes and the risk occurrences.

STUDY CHECKPOINT 4.3

Lora Nirvana is the project manager for the Sequence the DNA of a Buffalo (SDB) project. Match each item in the first column of the following table to the correct item in the second column.

Output of the Develop Schedule Process   Description

A. Schedule data

1. A bar chart that includes all the activities of the project and also includes milestones. Lora points to this bar chart for the project sponsor to show where they are in the execution of the project.

B. Project document updates

2. A bar chart hanging on the calendar that has never changed once it was approved. Lora compares the current bar chart with this bar chart to show the progress.

C. Schedule

3. On a bar chart, Lora points to the dates when she will have the DNA sample isolated and purified, when she will get the DNA sample run through the genetic analyzer, when she will receive the results from the analyzer, and when the results will be published on the Internet.

D. Schedule baseline

4. After realizing that their chosen vendor has a track record of sending the DNA analysis kits late, Lora writes something into the risk register.

While developing the project schedule, you will be doing lots of communication. Managing project communication is indeed very critical to the project success.

Managing Project Communication: Big Picture

There is a common thread that runs through almost all activities and processes in project management, and that is communication. The project and its activities will fail without effective communication. Communication is an exchange of information among persons and groups by using an effectively common system of signs, symbols, and behavior. I used the term "effectively common" to take into account the fact that even if two communicating entities are using two different systems, the "translators" between the communicating entities produce the results as if the two entities were using a common system. For example, I might be using a Windows computer and you might be using a Macintosh, but we can exchange e-mails without having to deal with the differences between the two machines.

TIP

Communication is a common thread that runs through almost all activities and processes in project management.

The importance of communication in project management cannot be overemphasized. Even a well-scheduled and well-funded project can fail in the hands of a hardworking team of experts due to the lack of proper communication. As a project manager, you may be dealing with a wide functional variety of individuals, ranging from executives, marketing personnel, to sales folks, to technologists. You should be able to wear different communication hats depending upon who you are communicating with. For example, you will not be talking in terms of technical jargon with executives or marketing folks, and you will not speak marketing lingo to software developers. You will be speaking to different stakeholders in their language, while filling the language gap between different functional groups and eliminating misunderstandings due to miscommunication. The key point is that you put on the appropriate communication hat depending on which individual you are communicating with. Be able to switch communication hats quickly and avoid technical jargon and acronyms that are not understood by the person or the group you are communicating with. The goal is the clarity of the language to convey the message accurately.

In a project, you will be communicating with project stakeholders. The different components of project communication management are illustrated in Figure 4.10.

In this chapter we discuss communication in general and how to plan for it. Other components of communication management will be discussed in forthcoming chapters.

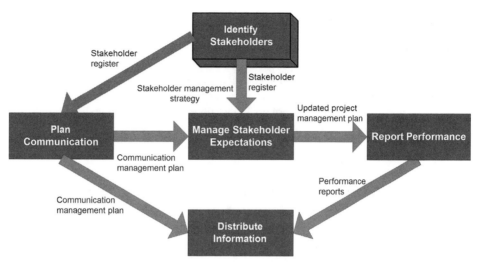

FIGURE 4.10 *Big picture of project communication management.*

TIP

The major goal of communication management is to deliver the right information to the right stakeholders at the right time by using the right communication means to produce the desired impact.

Planning Project Communication

In a project environment, communication means communicating with the project stakeholders. Plan Communication is the process of determining the information needs of the project stakeholders and accordingly designing the communication approach.

To be specific, communication planning determines the following:

◆ The communication and information needs of the program stakeholders

◆ The four Ws: what information is needed, when it is needed, who needs it, and who will deliver it

◆ How the information will be delivered—for example, by e-mail, phone call, or presentation

In Chapter 2, you learned how to identify stakeholders. During the process of identifying stakeholders, you create the stakeholder register and develop the stakeholder management strategy. Both of these items are used in planning the project communication.

CAUTION

Planning communication is the process of determining the information needs of the project stakeholders and accordingly the communication approach. Misplanning will produce undesired results, such as incorrect individuals getting sensitive information, necessary information not getting to the right stakeholders in time, wrong communication methods being used, and so on.

As mentioned earlier, the stakeholder register and stakeholder management strategy developed during the Identify Stakeholders process will be the major input into the Plan Communication process illustrated in Figure 4.11. Also, because communication is the common thread running through the whole project and because it must be adapted to the whole project environment, all the enterprise environmental factors and all the organizational process assets should be considered as input. Historical information and lessons learned are particularly important because they can be used for wisely planning the communication based on past experience.

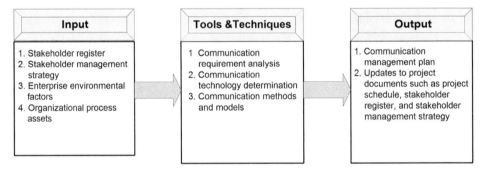

FIGURE 4.11 *The Plan Communication process: input, tools and techniques, and output.*

With these documents and past experience at hand, it's important to use some tools and techniques to finalize the communication plan.

Tools and Techniques for Communication Planning

Recall that communication is transferring information from one point to another. It expends resources. To optimize the use of resources and the benefits of communication, you need to analyze the communication requirements and determine the communication technology to be used. These and other relevant tools and techniques are discussed in the following sections.

Communication Requirements Analysis

Communication requirements, needed for the communication planning process, must be analyzed. This analysis will generate the communication needs of the project stakeholders. For example, a communication requirement may specify the type of information and the format in which this information should be delivered. The analysis of this requirement will estimate the value of this communication requirement—for example, fulfillment of this requirement will significantly contribute to the success of the project, or the lack of it will result in the failure of the project or one of its components. So, one of the purposes of communication requirements analysis is to optimize the use of resources in communication.

TIP

Communication requirements need to be analyzed to generate the communication needs of the project stakeholders. This is important for optimal use of the communication resources and for project success.

Following are some examples of what types of information you will need to analyze the communication requirements for your project:

◆ **Relationships.** Organizational and stakeholder responsibility relationships. Organizational charts can be helpful to figure out some of this information.

◆ **Groups.** Different groups, disciplines, departments, and specialties involved in this project—for example, marketing, sales, and engineering as departments and software engineering and testing as groups in the engineering department.

◆ **Logistics.** How many individuals and groups will be involved in the project and where they are located. Obviously, this information is necessary to plan communication.

◆ **Information needs.** Communication is performed to deliver or exchange some kind of information. So to plan communication effectively, it's important to know the following information needs:

◆ Information needs of the stakeholders

◆ Internal information needs—for example, communication across the performing organization and communication within the project team

◆ External information needs—for example, communicating with contractors, media, and the public

You can appreciate the complexity of communication by realizing that there are $n(n-1)/2$ possible communication channels among n stakeholders, as discussed earlier in this chapter. For example, if there are 20 stakeholders, the possible number of communication channels is $20 \times 19/2 = 190$.

Based on communication needs, you can determine which communication technology will be appropriate to meet these needs.

Communication Technology Determination

Depending on the communication needs and the nature of the information, a communication technology may vary from a conversation in a hallway to a sophisticated information system. The following factors can contribute to determining the communication technology to be used for your project:

- ◆ **Availability.** If you are considering a number of options, obviously the technology that's already in place is more likely to be chosen.

- ◆ **Project environment.** The project environment can also affect the choice of communication technology. For example, the communication technology requirements for a project team that meets face to face will be different from that of a virtual team.

- ◆ **Project length.** The length of the project affects communication technology requirements in the following ways:
  - ◆ Is it worth it to spend time on a technology for the given length of the project?
  - ◆ Will the technology under consideration change during the course of the project? If yes, that will mean extra cost for the new technology and for training the team members to use it.

- ◆ **Urgency of the information need.** How frequently the information needs to be updated will also play a role in determining the communication technology. For example, information that does not need to change frequently can be delivered in written reports, whereas information that can change very frequently can be delivered through web pages.

- ◆ **Staffing preparation level.** Another factor that can be considered in making the communication technology decision is the users' (project team and other stakeholders) level of preparation for using a given technology. Are the users already fluent in this technology or will they need to be trained? Training and learning for the project staff could be the valid issues on the table.

 NOTE

The factors that can contribute to determining the communication technology to be used include availability, project environment, project length, urgency of the information need, and preparation level.

Communication Models and Methods

If you have some experience in IT or in the field of communication, be aware that when PMI refers to communication models and methods, it has very specific things in mind. Although it's a very broad topic, we will confine our discussion to what PMI means by communication models and methods, for the purpose of the exam.

Communication models. PMI's basic communication model is illustrated in Figure 4.12, and its different components are explained in the following list:

◆ **Sender.** The individual that initiates the communication by sending the original message.

◆ **Receiver.** The individual that receives the original message sent by the sender.

◆ **Encode.** To convert thoughts into a format that can be sent as a message to the receiver.

◆ **Message.** Encoded piece of information that travels from one individual to another.

◆ **Feedback message.** The response sent by the receiver to the sender. It may be a simple acknowledgment or it may be a full message that may require a response.

◆ **Decode.** To convert the encoded message back into thoughts and ideas upon which one could act.

◆ **Medium.** The means of communication used to send and receive the message. E-mail, telephone, and face-to-face conversation are some examples of media.

◆ **Noise.** While the message travels through the medium, it can be interrupted and modified by some interfering entity called *noise*. Anything that interferes with the transmission and understanding of the message is called noise. Some examples are distance, lack of background information or context in which the message is composed, and unfamiliar technology being used. For example, e-mailing and texting have their own lingo, acronyms, and symbols that can become noise for people who are new to these technologies.

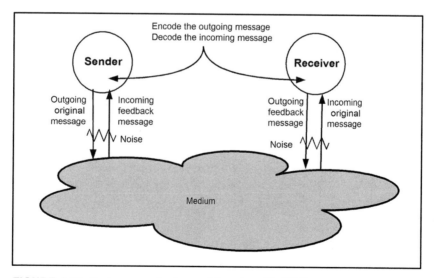

FIGURE 4.12 *Basic communication model as viewed by PMI.*

For the communication to work, both the senders and the receivers have some responsibilities. The responsibilities of the sender include ensuring that the message being sent conveys the complete information clearly and ensuring that the information is received correctly and understood properly by the receiver. The responsibilities of the receiver include ensuring that the information is received correctly and understood properly in its entirety and that it is acknowledged.

STUDY CHECKPOINT 4.4

Lora Nirvana is the project manager for the Sequence the DNA of a Buffalo (SDB) project. Match each item in the first column of the following table to the correct item in the second column.

Term	*Action*
A. Message	1. While developing the schedule, Lora realized that there was a risk involved in the project. So, she put her thoughts into a note that she wrote on her computer.
B. Medium	2. She sent the note to the project sponsor.
C. Encode	3. She used e-mail to send the message.
D. Noise	4. The sponsor received the message.
E. Receiver	5. The sponsor could not understand some of the acronyms and terms in the e-mail message, such as variable number of tandem repeats (VNTR) and central dogma of molecular biology.
F. Feedback	6 The sponsor responded to Lora expressing his concern that he could not exactly understand her concerns.

Communication methods. In its most basic form, communication is an exchange of information between two entities. Even communication among several entities is better handled by looking at it as a set of exchanges between two entities. For example, A communicating with B, C, and D is a set of exchanges between A and B, A and C, and A and D. In other words, exchange between two entities is the basic building block of communication. So we can always break down a communication as an exchange between a sender and a receiver.

From the perspective of how the sender and the receiver are involved with each other through the communication system, communication can be classified into the following two categories:

1. **Interactive communication**. In this type of communication, the receiver receives the message and sends a response to it. This way, the communicating entities keep switching the roles of sender and receiver. There are two kinds of interactive communication:

   ◆ **Asynchronous communication.** A communication in which the two communicating entities do not have to be present on both ends of the communication line at the same time. E-mail is an example of asynchronous communication because when the sender of the e-mail pushes the send button, the intended recipient of the e-mail message does not have to be logged on to the e-mail server. The recipient can log on later, retrieve the message, and read it.

♦ **Synchronous communication.** A communication in which the two communicating entities have to be present on both ends of the communication line at the same time. It's a live, real-time communication—if you are not present when the sender is sending the message, you miss the message. Speaking with someone face to face and conversing with someone on the phone are two examples of synchronous communication.

2. **One-way communication.** There are two kinds of one-way communication:

♦ **Pull communication.** In this kind of communication, the receiver pulls the information from a pool of information. Downloading from websites is an example of this communication.

♦ **Push communication.** In this kind of communication, the sender broadcasts the information to a set of entities without waiting for the request of information and without the need to confirm that the information reached its destination. Marketing e-mails and letters are examples of push communication.

The pull and push methods can also be used in conjunction with each other. For example, the sender can also push the information to a pool, and the receivers can pull it from there at their own convenience.

Communication types discussed here are called *communication methods* in the PMI Standard. Depending on the purpose, the project manager can decide which of these communication methods to use. Quite often a hybrid approach is used in the real world—that is, a mix of more than one method.

You use these tools and techniques to generate the output of the communication planning process.

Output of Communication Planning

The major output of communication planning is the communication management plan. This and other output items are discussed in this section.

Communication Management Plan

This is the document that describes the communication expectations, needs, and plans for the project. It specifies what information will be communicated, when and how it will be communicated, and who will communicate it and to whom. It includes the following:

♦ Communication requirements of the project stakeholders

♦ Information to be communicated: content, format, and level of detail

♦ Who will communicate the information, who will receive it, and why

♦ The person responsible for authorizing the release of confidential information

◆ Methods of communication that will be used, such as e-mail, presentation, and press release

◆ The frequency of communication, such as daily or weekly

◆ The method and procedure for escalating the issues that cannot be resolved at a lower staff level, such as project level

◆ A glossary of common communication terminology

◆ Methods and procedures for updating and refining the communication management plan if needed as the program progresses

◆ Communication constraints

The communication management plan may also include the technology requirements plan. Executing a project in this information age, more likely than not, you will need multiple technologies for communication, such as e-mail, web calendars, and video conferencing. Therefore, it is important that you plan for the communication technology requirements. This planning has two components: the tools that are needed and the usage of those tools. To determine which tools are needed, ask questions such as the following:

◆ How frequently do you need to update the information?

◆ Will the team hold face-to-face or virtual meetings?

For the information that does not change often, the written reports will be sufficient, whereas the information that needs to be updated frequently and on a moment's notice needs web communication tools. To plan effective usage of the tools, ask the following questions:

◆ Are the tools (communication systems) already in place and ready to be used?

◆ Will the available communication tools change before the program ends?

◆ Are the team members familiar with the tools or do they need training to use them?

 TIP

The communication management plan describes the communication expectations, needs, and plans for the project.

Updates to Project Documents

During communication planning, you might realize that you need to make some changes in the project schedule, stakeholder register, and stakeholder management strategy. Accordingly, you will need to change these documents.

TIP

While planning for communication (or doing anything, for that matter), pay attention to details, ask questions, and probe the situation to come to a better understanding. A well understood problem is already half solved. Be an active and effective listener.

The three most important takeaways from this chapter are as follows:

◆ Various time management processes are used to produce schedule data—a list of schedule activities and attributes for each activity, such as required resources and the duration of the activity.

◆ The schedule data is used to develop the project schedule, which is an iterative process due to the uncertainties in the schedule data and due to the changes during the project execution. Nevertheless, the approved version of the planned schedule is used as a baseline to track the project progress.

◆ Communication is a common thread that runs through the project lifecycle. It's important to develop a communication plan in order to ensure that the communication mantra is implemented: Deliver right information to the right people at the right time by using the right communication methods to produce the desired impact.

Summary

Project schedule development is a journey that begins with decomposing the work packages in the WBS to project activities and ends with an approved schedule for performing those activities. Schedule planning addresses some basic questions: What are the activities that need to be performed to complete the project, who is going to perform these activities, and when?

The Define Activities process is used to decompose the work packages in the WBS into schedule activities. The resulting activity list is used by the activity sequencing process to generate network diagrams, which display the dependencies among the activities. The commonly used method to construct network diagrams is the precedence diagramming method (PDM). The activity list and attributes are also used to determine the resource requirements for the project. Given the available resource, you can estimate the activity duration—that is, the time it will take to perform the activity.

By using various time-management processes discussed in this chapter, you identify schedule activities, arrange them in proper sequence, determine resource requirements for them, and estimate their durations. All these tasks and accomplishments are a means to an end called the *Develop Schedule* process. You typically use the critical path method to develop the project schedule from a network diagram. After you have a schedule, you can use schedule compression methods, such as fast tracking and crashing, to accommodate hard deadlines. Schedule development is an iterative process that can continue well into the project execution due to approved changes and risk occurrences. However, the approved planned project schedule is used as a baseline to track the project progress.

Communication, the lifeline of the project, is a common thread that runs through the whole lifecycle of the project. Therefore it's crucial to plan for communication management as early as possible. The output of the Plan Communication process is the communication management plan that describes the communication needs and expectations of the project and how to meet them.

So, now that you have a project schedule and you have planned communication, are you ready to execute the project? Well, not really. You need resources, such as human resources that will do the project work and funding to get the human resources. You need to plan for these resources. This is the topic of the next chapter.

Exam's Eye View

Comprehend
◆ The major task of the Define Activities process is to generate the activity list (output) by decomposing (or arranging) the work packages of the WBS (input) into activities.
◆ The major task of the Sequence Activities process is to determine the dependencies among the activities in the activity list (input) and display those dependencies in the network diagrams (output).
◆ After the activity resource requirements have been determined, the duration for an activity can be estimated for a given resource.
◆ Network diagrams with activity durations assigned to each activity can be used to develop the schedule. The approved project schedule acts as a baseline against which the project progress is tracked.
◆ The Plan Communication process is used to develop the communication management plan.

Look Out

◆ Activity duration is estimated for a given resource committed to the activity. Changing the quantity of the resource will change the duration estimate.

◆ Activity duration measured in work periods does not include holidays, whereas duration measured in calendar units does. For example, the activity duration from Friday to the following Tuesday is three days when measured in work units and five days when measured in calendar units, given that no work is done on Saturday and Sunday.

◆ Each activity on a critical path has zero float time and thus poses a schedule risk. Therefore, you must monitor the activities on all critical paths very closely during the execution of the project.

Memorize

◆ The communication management plan, generated as an output of the Plan Communication process, becomes a component of the project management plan.

◆ The approved project schedule, called the *schedule baseline*, becomes part of the project management plan.

◆ In PDM, finish to start is the most commonly used dependency relationship, whereas start to finish is the least used.

◆ Fast tracking compresses the schedule by performing activities simultaneously that would otherwise be performed in sequence, whereas crashing compresses the schedule by assigning more resources.

Key Terms and Definitions

◆ **activity.** A component of project work.

◆ **activity definition.** The process of identifying the specific schedule activities that need to be performed to produce the project deliverables.

◆ **activity duration.** The time measured in calendar units between the start and finish of a schedule activity.

◆ **activity duration estimating.** The process of estimating the time in work periods individually for each schedule activity required for its completion. A work period is a measurement of time when the work is in progress; it is measured in hours, days, or months depending upon the size of the activity.

◆ **activity resource estimating.** The process of estimating the types and amounts of resources that will be required to perform each schedule activity.

◆ **activity sequencing.** The process of identifying and documenting the dependencies among schedule activities.

◆ **analogous estimating.** A technique used to estimate the duration of an activity based on the duration of a similar activity in a previous project.

◆ **communication management plan.** A document that describes the communications needs and expectations of the project and how these needs and expectations will be met.

◆ **crashing.** A project schedule compression technique used to decrease the project duration with minimal additional cost. A number of alternatives are analyzed, including the assignment of additional resources.

◆ **critical path.** The longest path (sequence of activities) in a project schedule network diagram. Because it is the longest path, it determines the duration of the project.

◆ **critical path method (CPM).** A schedule network analysis technique used to identify the schedule flexibility and the critical path of the project schedule network diagram.

◆ **decode.** To convert the received message from the media back into useful ideas and thoughts.

◆ **encode.** To convert thoughts and idea into a message that could be transmitted through the media.

◆ **fast tracking.** A project schedule compression technique used to decrease the project duration by performing project phases or some schedule activities within a phase simultaneously, when they would normally be performed in sequence.

◆ **float time.** The positive difference between the late start date and the early start date of a schedule activity.

◆ **lag.** A technique to modify a dependency relationship by delaying the successor activity. For example, a lag of five days in a finish-to-start relationship means the successor activity cannot start until five days after the predecessor activity has ended.

◆ **lead.** A technique to modify a dependency relationship by accelerating the successor activity. For example, a lead of five days in a finish-to-start relationship means the successor activity can start up until five days before the finish date of the predecessor activity.

◆ **logical relationship.** A dependency between two project schedule activities or between a schedule activity and a schedule milestone.

◆ **milestone.** A significant point (or event) in the life of a project.

◆ **parametric estimating.** A quantitative technique used to calculate the activity duration when the productivity rate of the resource performing the activity is available.

◆ **planning component.** A WBS component at the bottom level of a branch of the WBS hierarchy for which some planning can be performed.

◆ **precedence diagramming method (PDM).** A technique used to construct a project schedule network diagram in which a node (a box) represents an activity and an arrow represents the dependency relationship.

◆ **project calendar.** A calendar of working days or shifts used to establish when a schedule activity can be performed. A calendar typically specifies holidays and weekends when a schedule activity cannot be performed.

◆ **project schedule.** A schedule that consists of planned dates for performing schedule activities and meeting schedule milestones.

◆ **project schedule network diagram.** A schematic display of logical relationships among the project schedule activities. The time flow in these diagrams is from left to right.

◆ **resource breakdown structure (RBS).** A hierarchical structure of resource types required to complete the schedule activities of a project.

◆ **role.** A defined function that contains a set of responsibilities to be performed by a team member, such as a programmer or a tester.

◆ **rolling wave planning.** A technique used to plan the project work at various levels of detail, depending upon the availability of information. Work to be performed in the near future is planned at a low level of the WBS, whereas work to be performed far into the future is planned at a relatively high level of the WBS.

◆ **schedule activity.** A scheduled task (component of work) performed during the lifecycle of a project.

◆ **schedule baseline.** A specific version of the project schedule that is approved by the project management team as a baseline against which the progress of the project will be measured. This version of the schedule is developed from the schedule network analysis of the schedule model data.

◆ **schedule development.** The process of creating the project schedule by analyzing schedule activity sequences, schedule activity durations, resource requirements, and schedule constraints.

◆ **schedule milestone.** A significant event in the project schedule, such as the completion of a major deliverable.

◆ **schedule network analysis.** A technique used to generate a project schedule by identifying the early and late start and finish dates for the project.

Review Questions

1. Which of the following is the most commonly used network diagramming method?
   A. Critical path method (CPM)
   B. Critical chain method (CCM)
   C. Precedence diagramming method (PDM)
   D. Arrow diagramming method (ADM)

2. What is the crashing technique used for?
   A. Network diagramming
   B. Duration compression
   C. Cost reduction
   D. Activity sequencing

3. Which of the following is a true statement about the critical path?
   A. Each activity on the critical path has zero float time.
   B. It controls the project finish date.
   C. It controls the project start date.
   D. It is the shortest sequence in the network diagram.

4. In your research project on tourism, you must collect data before the tourist season ends because the project involves interviewing tourists. The data-collection activity has which of the following kinds of dependency?
   A. Mandatory
   B. External
   C. Internal
   D. Discretionary

5. You know from a network diagram that Activity B cannot start until Activity A is finished. Which of the following are true?
   A. Activities A and B have a start-to-finish dependency.
   B. Activities A and B have a finish-to-start dependency.
   C. Activity B has a mandatory dependency on Activity A.
   D. Activities A and B are on a critical path.

6. Why should you monitor the activities on the critical path more closely?

   A. Because each activity on the critical path has a zero float time and thereby poses a schedule risk.

   B. Because the activities on the critical path need to be performed before the activities on other paths.

   C. Because the activities on the critical path are critical to the organization's strategy.

   D. Because the activities on noncritical paths depend upon the activities on the critical path.

7. You estimate the duration of an activity as five days because an expert told you that it took five days to complete a similar activity in a previous project. Which of the following methods have you used for your activity duration estimate?

   A. Parametric estimating

   B. Expert judgment

   C. Analogous estimating

   D. Delphi technique

8. You have developed the schedule for your project, and you've called the kickoff meeting. A team member who is responsible for an activity comes to you and tells you that the activity cannot be performed within the allocated time because some pieces were left out during activity definition. The revised estimate will add two more days to the activity duration, but the activity is not on the critical path. Which of the following actions will you take?

   A. Go to the team member's functional manager and find out whether the team member's estimate is correct.

   B. Accept the new estimate but do not change the schedule.

   C. Accept the new estimate and update the schedule accordingly.

   D. Put the new estimate through the integrated change control process.

9. The amount of time by which an activity can be delayed without changing the project finish date is called:

   A. Float time

   B. Lag time

   C. Grace time

   D. Activity gradient

10. You are the project manager of a project that is running behind schedule. The project sponsor is very unhappy at the new finish date that you proposed, but he has accepted it. However, you also requested extra funds to support the extended time of work, and the sponsor has refused to supply more funds and is threatening to cancel the project if you cannot finish the project within the planned budget. What are your options?

   A. Crashing

   B. Fast tracking

   C. Asking the executive management for a new sponsor

   D. Speaking with the customer directly without involving the sponsor to see whether the customer can increase the budget

11. Consider the following network diagram. Which of the following is the critical path?

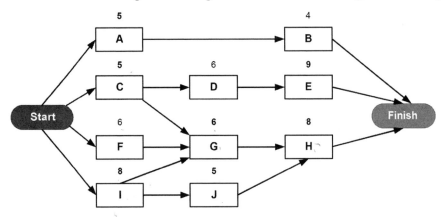

   A. Start-C-D-E-Finish 20

   B. Start-I-G-E-Finish ✗

   C. Start-I-G-H-Finish ✓ 22

   D. Start-I-J-H-Finish 21

   E. Start-I-G-H-E-Finish ✗

12. What is the float for Activity G in the network diagram in Question 11?

   A. 3

   B. 2

   C. 1

   D. 0

13. What is the length of the critical path in the network diagram shown in Question 11?

   A. 20

   B. 21

   C. 22

   D. 31

   E. 9

14. You use a three-point estimate for activity duration estimating. An activity has a duration of 9 days for an optimistic scenario, 18 days for a pessimistic scenario, and 12 days for the most likely scenario. Which of the following will you take as the duration estimate for this activity if you use the PERT analysis?

   A. 13 days

   B. 12.5 days

   C. 12 days

   D. 18 days

15. Which of the following is not an input item to the Define Activities process?

   A. The WBS

   B. The activity duration

   C. The project scope statement

   D. The WBS dictionary

16. You are trying to understand the message sent to you by one of your team member who lives on the other side of the globe. The team member has used lots of local phrases and acronyms that you are trying to understand. According to the basic communication model, what are you dealing with here?

   A. Noise and decoding

   B. Encoding and feedback

   C. Message and feedback

   D. Broken English

17. Which of the following is not an output of communication planning?

   A. Methods of communication

   B. Communication constraints

   C. Frequency of reporting the project status

   D. Stakeholder management strategy

Chapter 5

Planning for Project Resources

PMP Exam Objectives

Objective	What It Really Means
3.4 Manage Resource Allocation	Understand how to estimate and assign resources to the project tasks included in the project management plan. You must know the processes related to resource planning, such as Develop Human Resource Plan, Estimate Costs, and Determine Budget.
2.3 Create the WBS	Understand the process of creating the work breakdown structure, called Create WBS. You must know how to use the WBS in various planning tasks, such as estimating costs, planning human resources, developing the schedule, planning procurements, and planning for quality. In this chapter, we cover the planning processes related to resources and procurement needed to complete the project.

Introduction

Once you have developed the project schedule, as discussed in the previous chapter, you need resources to execute the schedule. For example, you need the team members—the human resources—to perform the project activities, such as a computer programmer to design and develop a program. Furthermore, you also need financial resources to support these human resources and to make purchases and acquisitions required for the project. These financial resources are managed in the form of cost in project management. Some of the expected outcome items of the project will be developed by the project team, and others will be purchased or acquired in a process called *procurement*, which may also include items that are needed to complete the project and are not necessarily the end product of the project.

So, the core question in this chapter is: How do you plan for the project resources? This issue breaks down into three avenues that we will explore: human resource planning, cost planning, and procurement planning.

Planning for Resources: Big Picture

As you learned in the previous chapter, resource requirements are estimated by using the Estimate Activity Resources process, and the schedule is developed by using the Develop Schedule process. As illustrated in Figure 5.1, the activity resource requirements estimated this way are used to develop the human resource plan for the project. The human resource plan and the project schedule, in turn, are used to make cost estimates for activities, which are aggregated to determine the project budget.

The approved budget with a timeline assigned to it is called the *cost baseline*, against which the project performance is measured. This baseline is also used to plan for procurements—that is, purchases and acquisitions that are needed to complete the project but cannot be produced by the project team.

While developing the project schedule, the availability of resources required to perform the schedule activities is an obvious assumption. An important category of resources is human resources—for example, a computer programmer who will write a computer program. You need to plan for these resources.

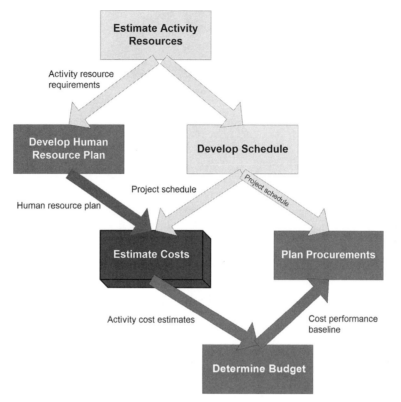

FIGURE 5.1 *Relationships among major processes of resource planning.*

Developing the Human Resource Plan

In order to avoid confusion, you must understand the logical relationships among the project, activity resource requirements, roles, and responsibilities, as illustrated in Figure 5.2. Roles are determined from the resource requirements, and responsibilities are assigned to the roles to perform the project activities. In a nutshell, project work is generally performed in the form of roles and responsibilities. Project roles, responsibilities of the roles, and reporting relationships among the roles need to be determined in order to perform a project. The usefulness of the concept of a role is that you can talk about it during planning, even before hiring a person who will play this role. So, a role is a defined function to be performed by a team member, such as a programmer or a tester. The other issue that needs to be addressed before the project can be performed is how and when the project team members (who will perform the project work) will be acquired. The human resource planning process addresses these issues.

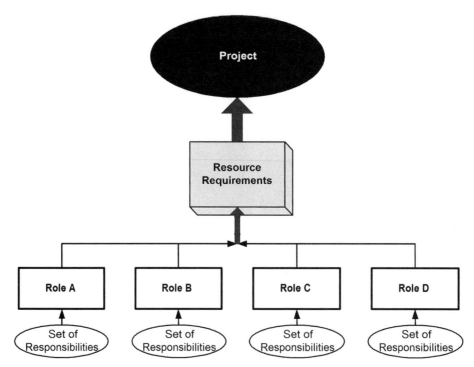

FIGURE 5.2 *Relationships among the project, project activity requirements, roles, and responsibilities.*

Therefore, two main goals of the human resource planning process are the following:

◆ Identify and document project roles, responsibilities for each role, and reporting relationships among the roles.

◆ Develop the staff management plan.

All this planning will go into a document called the *human resource plan*, which is developed by the Develop Human Resource Plan process illustrated in Figure 5.3.

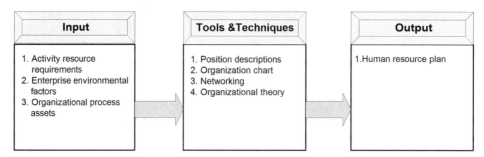

FIGURE 5.3 *The Develop Human Resource Plan process: input, tools and techniques, and output.*

Input to Human Resource Planning

Before you can assign the resources to a project, you need to know the resource requirements of the project, which are the main items that you need to plan resources. The other two items are the familiar ones: enterprise environmental factors and organizational process assets.

Enterprise environmental factors. The enterprise environmental factors that can influence human resource planning include human resources that already exist in the organization and are available for the project, organizational culture, organizational structure, human resource and personnel administration policies of the organization, and marketplace conditions. For example, how do the different departments and the people within the performing organization interact with each other? This will have a profound effect on defining the roles and responsibilities. Overall, while planning human resources, you must consider the following enterprise environmental factors:

◆ **Interpersonal.** The interpersonal environmental factor should be explored while considering the candidates within the performing organization for the project team members. You should seek answers to interpersonal questions, such as the following:

   ◆ What are the job descriptions of the candidates? This will tell you what kind of project activities they might be able to perform.

   ◆ What are the skills and experiences of the candidates beyond their current job descriptions?

   ◆ What types of formal and informal reporting relationships exist among the candidates? This will help determine who can fit in where.

   ◆ What cultural or language differences will possibly affect the working relationships among the candidates? This should be used to optimize the project work results by honoring cultural diversity.

◆ **Logistical.** The logistical factor deals with the issue of how the project team is spread out geographically. For example, a relevant question to ask is, are the team members spread out in different buildings, time zones, or countries? Virtual communication, discussed in the next chapter, will be an important consideration here.

◆ **Organizational.** The organizational factor relevant to human resource planning can be identified by answering the following questions:

   ◆ Which departments of the performing organization will participate in the project?

   ◆ What are the current relationships between these departments? In other words, how do these departments interact?

◆ **Political.** Playing politics could be a dirty word for a social reformer, but you need to deal with it tactically by recognizing it as a project reality. To explore the effect of the political factor on human resource planning, you should ask questions such as the following:

   ◆ What are the individual goals and agendas of the project stakeholders?

   ◆ Which individuals or groups are influential in areas important to the project?

   ◆ What are the formal or informal alliances that exist between individuals or departments relevant to the project?

◆ **Technical.** Almost all the projects these days include the use of some kind of technology. To explore the effects of technical factors on human resource planning, you should explore answers to questions such as:

  ◆ What are the technical specialties, such as software, programming languages, and technical equipment, needed to perform the project?

  ◆ Which of these specialties need to be coordinated?

  ◆ Are there any technical challenges this project might face?

Organizational process assets. The organizational process assets that can be useful in human resource planning include checklists, templates, organizational standards and procedures, standardized role descriptions, and historical information from previous projects. Some examples of checklists are common project roles in your organization, typical competencies, training programs to consider, team ground rules, and safety considerations. Examples of templates include project organizational charts and standard conflict management approach. Conflict management is discussed in an upcoming chapter.

Activity resource requirements. In the previous chapter, we explored the process of determining the resource requirements for the schedule activities. These requirements include human resource requirements, which are needed to develop the human resource plan. The human resource requirements begin as preliminary requirements and are progressively elaborated during planning.

The human resource requirements, a subset of activity resource requirements, are the raw material to determine the roles that will perform the activities. Various tools and techniques are available to convert requirements into roles.

Tools and Techniques for Human Resource Planning

At the heart of resource planning lays the art of converting activities and activity resource requirements into roles and responsibilities. For example, consider an activity in a project—writing a software program. The program will be written by a programmer, which is a human resource. However, before you even know the name of the programmer, you can work with this programmer as a role whose main responsibility is to write the program, and you can assign a real individual to fill this role later. This approach allows for planning before hiring. The tools and techniques used to determine the roles for a project are discussed in the following list.

Organizational charts and position descriptions. These charts identify and document the roles of the project team members, the responsibilities assigned to the roles, and the reporting relationships among the roles. Most of the chart formats fall into three categories—hierarchical, matrix, and text-oriented.

◆ **Hierarchical.** Hierarchical charts are the traditional way to represent the reporting relationships in an organization in a top-down format. Such a chart is also called an *organizational breakdown structure* (OBS), and it is arranged according to the organization's existing departments, units, or teams. The OBS will help you to identify team members for the project.

◆ **Matrix.** A matrix is used to specify the relationships between schedule activities, roles to perform those activities, and team members assigned to the roles. Such a matrix is generally called a *responsibility assignment matrix* (RAM). Different matrixes can show these relationships at different levels. For example, you can use the RAM to document resource requirements for each activity, as shown in Table 5.1. For example, the second row of Table 5.1 shows that it will take six developers, six workstations on which the developers will work, and one server to perform Activity B. You can also use the RAM to document the specific responsibilities assigned to specific team members for the schedule activities, as shown in Table 5.2.

Table 5.1   A Responsibility Assignment Matrix (RAM) Depicting the Resources Required to Perform Schedule Activities

Activity	Designer	Developer	Tester	Marketer	Workstation	Server
A	1					
B		6			6	1
C			3		3	2
D				2		
E	1	1	1		1	

◆ **Text-oriented charts.** These charts are useful when the team member responsibilities need to be described in greater detail. A text-oriented chart may include information about role responsibilities, authority, competencies, and required qualifications. In the real world, these charts are known by different names, such as *job descriptions* and *job responsibilities*.

 CAUTION

Information about some responsibilities of the human resources will be scattered across the project management plan. For example, the risk register lists the risk owners, and the communication management plan lists individuals responsible for some types of communications, such as status reports.

Depending upon the project needs, you can use both RAM and text-oriented charts to document roles and responsibilities of those roles. Also, remember that the RAM can be used for various purposes. For example, the RAM in Table 5.1 documents the resource requirements for the schedule activities, while the RAM in Table 5.2 depicts the roles of team members for schedule activities. In Table 5.2, letters are used as symbols to represent roles: R for responsible, A for accountable, C for consult, and I for inform.

Table 5.2 A Responsibility Assignment Matrix (RAM) Depicting the Roles Assigned to Team Members for Various Activities

Activity	Susan	Cathleen	Pappu	Maya	Kiruba
Design	R	A	I	I	C
Develop	I	I	R	I	C
Test	C	R	A	I	C
Deploy	I	I	A	I	R

The RAM in Table 5.2 is also called the *RACI chart* because it assigns four roles to team members for various activities: responsible (R), accountable (A), consult (C), and inform (I). For example, Susan has the responsibility of designing the product, Cathleen will be held accountable for the design, Kiruba will play the role of a consultant for designing the product, while Pappu and Maya will play the role of keeping everybody informed of the status and progress.

TIP

Each activity or task should have an owner who is responsible for its successful completion. For complex tasks and activities, there may be more roles assigned, but there must be only one principle owner. Joint ownership usually gives rise to confusion, finger pointing, conflict, more overhead, and dilution of commitment.

Networking. Burn it in your head: Networking is one of the golden secrets you have for succeeding as a project manager, especially in an organization in which functional managers hold all the powers (hiring, firing, bonuses) and the project managers are running around with nothing in their hands other than the project schedules and status reports. To network effectively, you should understand the influence of political and interpersonal factors in your organization that might impact various staffing management options. Some of the essential networking happens at the beginning of each project, and you must make full use of it. However, networking is a regular practice, and you should be using all the human resource network activities, such as proactive correspondence, informal conversations, luncheon meetings, and trade conferences.

Organizational theories. Various organizational theories provide information and insight on how people behave in a team or an organization, what motivates team members, and the like. If you have knowledge of these theories, it will help you plan human resources quickly and use them more effectively. By understanding organizational theories, you can also comprehend why different organizational structures support different kinds of relationships among the organization's members and different kinds of responses to the same situation.

To summarize, organizational charts, networking, and organizational theories are the main tools and techniques used to determine roles and develop the human resource plan.

Output of Human Resource Planning: The Human Resource Plan

The results of your efforts of human resource planning are documented in what is called the *human resource plan*. It's a document that describes roles and responsibilities, reporting relationships among the roles, and staffing management. Following are the main elements of this document.

Roles and responsibilities. This section contains roles and the responsibilities assigned to each role. The schedule project activities will be completed by individuals working in certain roles and performing responsibilities that come with the roles. So, roles and responsibilities are an important output of human resource planning. While determining roles and responsibilities, you must be clear about the following concepts:

- ◆ **Role.** In real life, most activities are performed by people playing certain roles, such as a parent, a teacher, or a student. Similarly, in project management, a role is essentially a set of responsibilities, such as the responsibilities of a developer, a tester, or a manager. A role is assigned to a team member who will perform the responsibilities included in the role to complete one or more project activities.

- ◆ **Responsibility.** A responsibility is a piece of work (task) that must be performed as part of completing a project activity. Responsibilities can be grouped together as a role.

- ◆ **Competency.** Competency is the ability of a team member to play a certain role— that is, to perform the responsibilities assigned to the role. While assigning a role to a team member, you should know whether the team member possesses the skills required to perform the responsibilities of the role. You might need to respond to a mismatch with training, hiring, schedule changes, or scope changes.

- ◆ **Authority.** Authority is a right assigned to a role that enables the person playing the role to apply project resources, make certain decisions, or sign approvals. Poorly defined or undefined authorities can cause confusion and conflicts.

 TIP

Roles must be clarified by specifying the responsibilities and the authorities assigned to each role. A good match between the levels of responsibility and authority for each team member generally produces the best results. This gives the team members a sense of ownership. If you own it, you will less likely break it.

Project organizational charts. A project organizational chart displays the project team members and the reporting relationships among them. The level of formality and detail of these charts depends upon the size and needs of the project at hand.

Staffing management plan. After you have determined the roles to perform the activities, you need to identify individuals to fill those roles. The staff management plan describes when and how human resource requirements for a project will be met. When preparing the staff management plan for your project, you must consider the following items:

◆ **Staff acquisition.** This will document how the staff for the project will be acquired. To be specific, while planning staff acquisition, you might need to struggle with some of the following questions:

  ◆ What are the levels of expertise needed for the project, and what are the assigned costs?

  ◆ Will the human resources come from within the organization, outside the organization, or both?

  ◆ Will the team members be required to work in a central location, or can they work from distant locations?

  ◆ Will you need the assistance of the human resources department of your organization to acquire the staff?

◆ **Timetable and release criteria.** You need to have a timetable for the human resource requirements, describing when and for how long a staff member is needed. The project schedule will help you determine that. The time commitment of human resources can be displayed in charts, such as resource histograms. A resource histogram is a bar chart that illustrates the number of hours of a human resource entity needed each week or month during the project lifecycle. The human resource entity may refer to an individual, a department, or the whole project team. You should also determine the release criteria and the time to release each team member from the project. Planning of release criteria is very important for a smooth transition of team members from one project to another and for the optimal use of the resources.

◆ **Training needs.** If some team members lack the adequate level of skills needed for the project, a training plan can be developed as part of the project.

◆ **Compliance and safety.** The staff management plan can also include strategies for complying with relevant government regulations, union contracts, and human resource policies. Your organization might have some policies and procedures that protect the team members from safety hazards. These policies and procedures must be included in the staff management plan.

◆ **Recognition and rewards.** Recognition and rewards are good tools to promote and reinforce desired behavior. However, to use these tools effectively, you must have clear criteria for rewards based on activities and performance of team members. The potential candidate for a reward must have an appropriate level of control over the activity for which the reward will be offered. For example, if a team member is to be rewarded for completing the project within the budget, the team member must have an adequate level of control over the decision-making that affected the spending.

In a nutshell, human resource planning accomplishes two things: It determines roles to perform the schedule activities, and it develops a staff management plan to fill those roles with team members. All this information is stored in the document called the *human resource plan*.

Human resources will cost you, and this leads us to cost management, which starts with making cost estimates, discussed next.

Estimating Costs and Determining Budget

First of all, we need to distinguish between cost and budget. Cost is the value of the inputs that have been (or will be) used up to perform a task or to produce an item: product, service, or result. This value is usually measured in units of money. For example, you paid two programmers $500 each for developing a software program, and you paid $100 to a tester to test the program. So, the cost for the task of developing and testing the software program is $1,100. You can add the costs of components of a system, and the sum will represent the cost of the system, but it's still a cost and not a budget. Budget is an aggregated cost with a timeline. You aggregate the costs of all the resources needed to perform the project and put a timeline on it: the availability of funds over time. That is called a *budget*.

As illustrated in Figure 5.4, cost management consists of estimating project costs, determining budget from the cost estimates, and controlling the cost while the project is being executed. In this chapter, we explore estimating costs and determining budget. Cost control is discussed in forthcoming chapters.

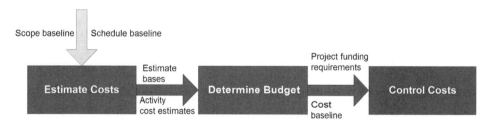

FIGURE 5.4 *Big picture of cost management.*

Cost management starts with making cost estimates.

Estimating Project Costs

Estimating project cost means developing an estimate for the monetary resources needed to complete the project work—that is, activities. These estimates are based on the information available at a given time. The estimates in the beginning are less accurate—for example, their accuracy may be only as good as ±50 percent. For example, if you say the cost will be $50,000, it could be anywhere between $25,000 and $75,000. As the project moves along and more information becomes available, the cost estimates can be improved to get better estimates.

The standard process used to estimate costs is called the *Estimate Costs* process and is illustrated in Figure 5.5. Estimating project cost means estimating the costs required to complete the project scope by executing schedule activities. Therefore, you need the scope baseline and the schedule baseline for estimating costs. Recall that the scope baseline is constituted by the scope statement, the WBS, and the WBS dictionary, and the schedule baseline is the approved project schedule. These and other items that you may need to determine costs are discussed in the following list:

◆ **Human resource plan.** The information in the human resource plan useful for estimating costs includes the list of roles and responsibilities, personnel rates, and recognitions and rewards.

◆ **Project schedule.** An approved project schedule will give you the information about the resources needed to complete the project work. This information is crucial to make cost estimates. As you learned in the previous chapter, activity resources are estimated by performing the Estimate Activity Resources process. Therefore, the Estimate Costs process should be closely coordinated with the Estimate Activity Resources process, which in turn depends on the Estimate Activity Durations process because an activity duration is determined for the given resources.

◆ **Scope baseline.** All three components of the scope baseline—scope statement, WBS, and WBS dictionary—are useful in estimating the project cost. The scope statement will provide the cost-relevant information, such as project and product acceptance criteria, assumptions and constraints, product description, key deliverables, and project boundaries around the scope. An example of a cost-related assumption is whether you are only counting the direct cost of the project or you are also counting the indirect cost. The indirect costs are those costs that cannot be directly traced to a specific project and therefore are usually shared by multiple projects and determined by some approved accounting procedure. An example would be

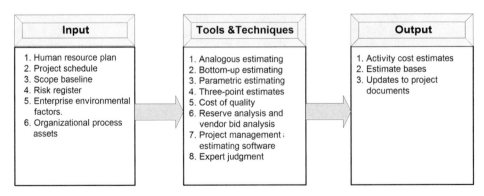

FIGURE 5.5 *The Estimate Costs process: input, tools and techniques, and output.*

the utility bill of the building or a computer network shared by many projects in the company. The WBS will be useful by providing the relationships among the different components of the projects that must be understood to make the cost estimates. The WBS dictionary will provide the description of the work.

◆ **Risk register.** Both kinds of risks—threats and opportunities—have an impact on the cost in the form of risk mitigation costs and revenues or savings from the opportunities.

◆ **Enterprise environmental factors.** Enterprise environmental factors relevant to estimating costs include market conditions and published commercial information that will provide the cost of resources, including human resources, materials, and equipment. This will also provide the information related to the availability of products and services and their cost and rates. Supply and demand conditions can also influence the project cost.

◆ **Organizational process assets.** This includes the organization's policies regarding cost estimates, cost estimating templates, and information from previous projects, including lessons learned.

Some tools and techniques that can be used in cost estimating and budgeting are discussed in the following paragraphs.

Analogous estimation. Analogous cost estimation is a technique that uses cost-related variables, such as rate, cost of a component, cost of an activity from similar tasks and activities in previous projects, or cost of a similar project from the past, to measure the same variable in the current project. This technique is useful when very limited component information is available, especially in the beginning of a project, and is usually used for estimating the gross values and not the detailed component-based values. It's generally less costly and less time consuming than other techniques, but it also is less accurate. Its accuracy and reliability improve if the person making the estimate is an expert and the components or activities being compared are actually similar.

Parametric estimation. This is a technique that uses some parameters and statistical relationships among them to make the estimate. For example, if the unit cost is known, say from historical data, the cost of the whole package containing a number of units can be calculated. This technique can generate quite accurate results depending on the accuracy of the quantity of resources and other data that goes into the estimation.

Bottom-up estimation. This technique involves estimating the cost of the parts of a component and then aggregating the cost of those parts to calculate the cost of the whole component. This technique can generate accurate results when you can generally make a better estimate of a part than the whole, which is usually the case when enough information is available.

STUDY CHECKPOINT 5.1

An activity cost estimate goes like this: It will take a programmer 20 hours to write this program. The average rate to hire a programmer is $50 per hour. Therefore, the cost of writing this program, assuming that everything else needed to write the program (such as a computer) is in place, is 20×$50=$1,000. What kind of estimation technique is at work here?

Contingency reserve analysis. The following two problems are associated with the estimates:

◆ Estimates are approximations, and approximations imply uncertainty, which means risk.

◆ Some stakeholders will always push the envelope on the project scope, and each organization has some tolerance for overrunning the objectives. This will mean more cost.

You will need some funds to deal with both of these situations. What comes to your rescue here is called *contingency reserve*. The contingency reserve, in general, is an amount of resource (funds or time) allocated in addition to the calculated estimates to reduce the risk arising from various sources—for example, from the overruns of project objectives to a level acceptable to the performing organization. In other words, the contingency reserves are the funds reserved to deal with events that are anticipated but not certain. Contingency reserves can be used at the discretion of the project manager. The overall cost estimate should include the contingency reserves.

 CAUTION

Contingency reserves may artificially raise the overall cost estimates. So if they are included in the cost estimates, they should be put into a separate category. These contingency reserves are usually not part of the budget included in the cost baseline used to evaluate the project performance.

Vendor bid analysis. Bids from qualified vendors on parts of the project or even the whole project can help in estimating the project cost.

Cost of quality. Cost of quality, discussed in the next chapter, should also be considered when making cost estimates.

Three-point estimates. Three-point estimates, discussed in the previous chapter for duration estimates, can also be applied in the same way to cost estimates.

TIP

Note that the accuracy of cost estimates depends on many other estimates, such as activity duration estimates and resource requirement estimates, which go into developing the schedule baseline used for making cost estimates. It is important to keep this dependency in mind just in case you need to change any of these estimates.

STUDY CHECKPOINT 5.2

The pessimistic cost estimate for an activity is $6,000, the optimistic estimate is $3,000, and the most likely estimate is $5,000. Calculate the expected estimate by using the PERT technique.

The output of the Estimate Costs process consists of the items discussed in the following paragraphs.

Activity cost estimates. These are the quantitative estimates of various costs required to complete the project work. Depending on the project and the stage of the project, cost estimates may be documented in summary form or in detail. These estimates include costs for all resources needed to complete the project work, including equipment, facilities, information technology, labor directly applied to the project work, material, and services. Indirect costs and special categories, such as allowances and contingency reserves, must also be included.

Estimate bases. It's important to document what the bases of the cost estimates were. These may highly depend on the application area of the project. At a higher level, the following elements must be included in the documentation:

◆ Assumptions made in making the estimates—for example, the labor rate and where this data came from.

◆ Constraints that affected the estimates—for example, a milestone must be met by a certain date.

◆ The methods used to develop the estimate—for example, a three-point estimate.

◆ The uncertainty, such as ±10%, and the confidence level must be assigned to an estimate.

In a nutshell, the outcome of estimating costs will include a cost estimate for each project activity and the basis for that estimate, which can be used to determine the project budget.

Determining Project Budget

Determining the project budget is the process of aggregating the cost estimates for all project activities and assigning a timeline to them. Cost aggregation is the technique used to calculate the cost of a whole by summing up the costs of the parts of which the whole is made. You can use the bottom-up estimation technique to aggregate the costs of all the components and activities to calculate the total cost of the project. The timeline assigned to this cost will be important to reconcile the expenditure with the funding limits. The reconciliation may require rescheduling some activities.

The budget is determined by using the Determine Budget process illustrated in Figure 5.6. Most of the items in the input to this process are already described in this chapter. Organizational process assets may include organizational policies and tools for determining the budget. The reserve analysis at budget level includes management reserve in addition to contingency reserve, and you must understand the difference between the two. Contingency reserves are the funds that can be used to deal with the unplanned events that can potentially transpire in case one or more identified risks occur, whereas management reserves are the funds that can be used in case of yet unplanned but future changes in some aspects of the project, such as the project scope.

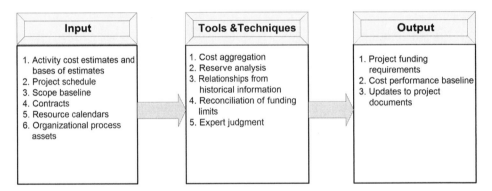

FIGURE 5.6 *The Determine Budget process: input, tools and techniques, and output.*

The approved budget that includes the aggregated cost with timeline is called the *cost baseline*. The cost performance of the project is monitored, measured, and controlled against this baseline. This is why it's also called the *cost performance baseline*. Funding requirements for the project are derived from the cost baseline and the reserve analysis.

Do not leave out the cost of the internal employees of the organization who will work on the project. They are not free, for two reasons: The organization pays for them, and they do not have infinite numbers of hours to put into the project. Their cost to the project will be determined just like any other project role based on the hours of work they will put into the project.

In the process of determining the budget, you may need to update the project schedule, cost estimates, and the risk register.

Your organization may not have the resources to complete all parts of the project. For those parts of the project, you will need to use what is called *procurement*.

CAUTION

The standard practice is not to include the reserves in the cost baseline, but they may be included in the overall budget of the project. That means the reserves will not be used in the calculations of earned value measurements discussed in an upcoming chapter.

Procuring the Project Resources

Procurement refers to obtaining—purchasing or renting—products, services, or results from outside the project team to complete the project. Accordingly, procurement management is an execution of a set of processes used to obtain (procure) the products, services, or results from outside the project team to complete the project. There are two main roles involved in procurement management:

◆ **Buyer.** The party purchasing (procuring) the product or service.

◆ **Seller.** The party delivering the product or service to the buyer.

As illustrated in Figure 5.7, procurement management includes the following components:

◆ **Plan procurements.** This is the process of making and documenting purchasing decisions, identifying potential sellers, and determining the approach toward these issues.

◆ **Conduct procurements.** This is the process of soliciting seller responses, selecting sellers, and awarding contracts.

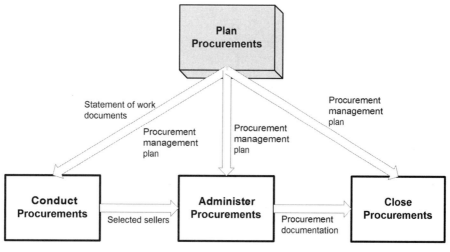

FIGURE 5.7 *Big picture of procurement management.*

◆ **Administer procurements.** This is the process of monitoring the contract execution, making approved changes and corrections, and managing relationships among the parties involved in the procurement.

◆ **Close procurements.** This is the process of completing each project procurement and giving it a proper closure as planned.

In this chapter, we will explore the plan procurements part of procurement management. Other components will be discussed in forthcoming chapters.

STUDY CHECKPOINT 5.3

Rajinder Preeti is in the process of estimating costs and preparing the budget for her project. In the following table, match each of her activities in the first column with the corresponding technique in the second column.

Activity	Technique
A. Rajinder discovers that there are lots of unknowns about an activity that could cost a lot more than has been estimated because it could take longer. So she puts some money aside to deal with this situation.	1. Parametric estimation
B. There is a complicated activity for which there is much disagreement among the team about its cost estimate. So, Rajinder makes an estimate by taking the average of the most optimistic estimate, the most pessimistic estimate, and the most realistic estimate.	2. Reserve analysis
C. Rajinder shows the estimate in Point B to her supervisor. The supervisor expresses her doubts about the final figure. Rajinder then splits the complex activity into smaller pieces, estimates the costs of each piece, and adds up the cost to reach the final figure.	3. Cost aggregation
D. For another activity, Rajinder just multiplies the number of work hours with the hourly rate for each team member involved in the activity and adds those numbers to reach the final cost estimate for the activity.	4. Reconciliation of funding limits
E. Rajinder adds up cost estimates for all the activities of the project in order to determine the budget.	5. Bottom-up estimating
F. Rajinder discovers that the overall budget is not consistent with the availability of funding. So, she has a careful look at the schedule to solve this problem.	6. Three-point estimate

Planning for Procurement

Planning procurements includes making and documenting purchasing decisions, identifying potential sellers, and developing a procurement approach. Although the procurement planning should be done early in the project, like any other planning, it might be necessary at any stage of the project as the need arises due to approved changes or other circumstances.

Procurement is planned by performing the Plan Procurements process illustrated in Figure 5.8. During procurement planning, you will be looking at lots of information, such as the scope baseline, stakeholder requirements, partner agreements, risk registers, activity resource requirements, and cost baseline. All this information will help you identify what needs to be done to complete the project, what the risks involved are, and what needs to be procured. Enterprise environmental factors, such as market conditions, availability of the product in the market, past performance of potential suppliers, and unique local conditions, must be considered as input to this process. The organizational process assets that can influence procurement planning include procurement policies and procedures of the performing organization, a supplier system of already established sellers that the organization currently deals with, and an information system that can be used to develop the procurement management plan. You will also need to know how to make make-or-buy decisions and what the different contract types are.

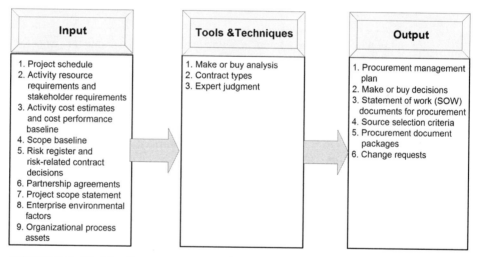

FIGURE 5.8 *The Plan Procurements process: input, tools and techniques, and output.*

Make-or-Buy Decisions

Obviously, procurement refers to buying something as compared to making it in-house. The decision to buy or make can be based on one or more of the reasons listed in Table 5.3. Buy can mean to purchase or to rent. The decision to purchase or to rent should be based on the effective cost in the long term. For example, if it is a piece of hardware that will be used only in this project, you do not anticipate its use in any future project, and renting is significantly cheaper than buying, you should probably rent it. You might decide to buy it if this hardware is of common use in the kind of work your organization does and therefore it will be used in other projects as well.

Table 5.3 Some Reasons to Make or Buy

Factor	Reasons to Make In-House	Reasons to Buy
Cost	Less cost	Less cost
Skills availability	Use in-house skills	In-house skills don't exist or are not available
Skills acquisition	Learn new skills that will be used even after this project	These skills are not important to the organization
Risks	Deal with the risk in-house	Transfer the risk
Work	Core project work	Not core project work
Human resource availability	Staff available	Vendor available

 NOTE

An output of the procurement planning process is the statement of work (SOW), which is a document summarizing the work to be performed. The SOW can be written by the buyer or the seller to specify what products will be delivered or what services will be performed. It is also called the *contract statement of work.*

Before you can buy, you need to get information from the sellers. In other words, you need to request seller responses. Make-or-buy analysis is a technique used in the plan purchases and acquisitions process. Also in this process, you need to use a technique to determine the type of contract you will use for the procurement.

Determining Contract Types

A contract is a mutually binding agreement between a buyer and a seller that obligates the seller to provide the specified product, service, or result and obligates the buyer to make the payment for it. Contracts generally fall into the three categories discussed in this list.

Fixed-price (lump-sum) contracts. A fixed-price contract, also called a *lump-sum contract* or a *firm fixed-price contract*, is an agreement that specifies the fixed total price for the product, service, or result to be procured. An example of a fixed-price contract is a purchase order for the specified item to be delivered by a specified date for a specified price. This category of contracts is generally used for products and services that are well-defined and have good historical information. A fixed-price contract for a poorly defined product or a service with very little historical record is a source of high risk for both the seller and the buyer.

Cost-reimbursable contracts. A contract in this category includes two kinds of costs:

♦ **Actual cost.** This is the payment (reimbursement) to the seller for the actual cost of the item, which includes the direct cost and the indirect cost (overhead). An actual cost, such as the salary of the project staff working on the item, is incurred directly from the work on the item, whereas an indirect cost, such as the cost of utilities and equipment for the office of the staff member, is the cost of doing business. Indirect cost is generally calculated as a percentage of the actual cost. The actual cost is also called the *project cost*. The project here refers to the project of the seller to produce the items for the buyer.

♦ **Fee.** This typically represents the seller's profit.

As discussed in the following list, there are three types of cost-reimbursable contracts:

♦ **Cost plus fee (CPF) or cost plus percentage of cost (CPPC).** The payment to the seller includes the actual cost and the fee, which is a percentage of the actual cost. Note that the fee is not fixed; it varies with the actual cost.

♦ **Cost plus fixed fee (CPFF).** The payment to the seller includes the actual cost and a fixed fee, which can be calculated as a percentage of the estimated project cost. Note that the fee is fixed and does not vary with the actual project cost.

♦ **Cost plus incentive fee (CPIF).** The payment to the seller includes the actual cost and a predetermined incentive bonus based on achieving certain objectives.

 NOTE

Both fixed-price contracts and cost-reimbursable contracts can optionally include incentives—for example, a bonus from the buyer to the seller if the seller meets certain target schedule dates or exceeds some other predetermined expectations.

Because cost overrun can occur in any type of cost-reimbursable contract, and the cost overrun will be paid by the buyer, this category of contract poses risk to the buyer.

Time and material (T&M) contracts. This type of contract is based on the rates of time and materials used to produce the procured product. This is a hybrid that contains some aspects from both the fixed-price category and the cost-reimbursable category. The contracts in this category resemble the contracts in the cost-reimbursable category because the total cost and the exact quantity of the items is not fixed at the time of the agreement. The contracts resemble fixed-price contracts because the unit rates can be fixed in the contract. These types of contracts are useful when you do not know the quantity of the procured items. For example, you do not know how much time a contract programmer will take to develop a software program, so you determine the hourly rate in the contract, but not the total cost for writing the program. In this category of contracts, the risk is high for the buyer because the buyer agreed to pay for all the time the seller takes to produce the deliverables.

Table 5.4 lists different types of contracts and the corresponding risk bearers.

Table 5.4 Risk Bearers in Different Categories of Contracts

Contract Type	Risk Bearer	Explanation
Fixed price (FP)	Buyer and seller	The cost overrun is borne by the seller, whereas the price fixed higher than the actual cost hurts the buyer.
Time and Material (T&M)	Buyer	The increased cost due to the increased quantity of resources, such as work hours by a contractor, is borne by the buyer.
Cost plus fixed fee (CPFF)	Buyer	Cost overrun is paid by the buyer.
Cost plus percentage of cost (CPPC)	Buyer	Cost overrun is paid by the buyer. Because the fee increases with the increase in cost, this type poses maximum risk to the buyer.
Cost plus incentive fee (CPIF)	Buyer	Cost overrun is paid by the buyer.

STUDY CHECKPOINT 5.4

Rajinder, the project manager, is now working on procurement planning for a portion of the project. She is looking at all the following options for procuring different pieces. Match each consideration in the first column of the following table to the corresponding contract type in the second column.

Consideration

A. Rajinder will pay $3,000 for the use of facility and $5,000 per month for the employees working for the procured piece for the duration of work. However, there is a cap of $50,000 for the maximum cost.

B. Rajinder will pay for the cost of the labor and a lump sum of $5,000.

C. Rajinder will provide $50,000 to maintain the website for the project for two years.

D. Rajinder will provide $10,000 for developing a software program and an extra $1,000 if fewer than 10 bugs are discovered in the program in the first year of its use.

E. Rajinder will pay the labor cost each month plus 5% of this cost as coffee and snacks at work and for recognition and rewards for the labor.

Contract type

1. Fixed price (FP)

2. Time and Material (T&M)

3. Cost plus fixed fee (CPFF)

4. Cost plus percentage of cost (CPPC)

5. Cost plus incentive fee (CPIF)

The major output of procurement planning is the procurement management plan.

Procurement Management Plan

This document describes how the procurement will be managed throughout the project. The plan includes the following:

- How the make-or-buy decisions will be made and handled
- Contracts
    - What types of contracts will be used for this project
    - The form and format for the statement of work related to a procurement or a contract
    - Metrics to be used to evaluate potential sellers and to manage contracts
    - Requirements for performance bonds or insurance contracts that might be put in place to mitigate some project risks
- Management and coordination
    - How to manage multiple sellers.
    - How to coordinate procurement with other aspects of the project, such as the project schedule, scope, budget, and status progress reporting.
    - Evaluation criteria for selecting sellers and measuring their performance. It is also called *source selection criteria* and is described in Chapter 7 when we discuss conducting procurements.
- A list of assumptions and constraints that could affect the procurement
- Any needed standardized procurement documents

In a nutshell, the major tasks of procurement planning are making make-or-buy decisions, preparing the procurement management plan, preparing the statement of work, determining a suitable type of contract, and preparing or acquiring the procurement documents. Once you have these elements in place, you are ready to implement the procurement plan, which will be discussed further on in the book.

Exam's Eye View

Comprehend
◆ Human resource planning is used to determine the roles that will perform the schedule activities and to develop the staff management plan to fill the roles with team members.
◆ The human resource plan and the project schedule are used to make cost estimates for activities, which are aggregated to determine the project budget.

♦ The accuracy of cost estimates depends on the accuracy of other estimates, such as activity duration estimates and activity resource requirements estimates.

♦ The major tasks of procurement planning are making make-or-buy decisions, preparing the procurement management plan, preparing the statement of work, determining a suitable type of contract, and preparing or acquiring the procurement documents.

♦ Of all the contract types discussed in this chapter, only the firm fixed-price contract can present risk to the seller.

♦ The contract type that presents the most risk to the buyer is the cost plus percentage of cost because the fee (which is a percentage cost) also increases if cost overrun occurs.

Look Out

♦ Information about the responsibilities of the human resources will be scattered across different parts of the project management plan.

♦ The approved budget that includes the aggregated cost with timeline is called the *cost baseline*. The cost performance of the project is monitored, measured, and controlled against this baseline.

♦ The standard practice is not to include the reserves in the cost baseline, but they may be included in the overall budget of the project. That means the reserves will not be used in the calculations of earned value measurements.

♦ A fixed-price contract is the riskiest contract for the seller.

♦ The contract type that presents the most risk to the buyer is the cost plus percentage of cost contract because the fee (which is a percentage cost) also increases if cost overrun occurs.

Memorize

♦ The responsibility assignment matrix (RAM) is a matrix used to specify the relationships between schedule activities, roles to perform those activities, and team members assigned to the roles.

♦ The project budget is the time-phased project cost obtained by aggregating the individual activity costs.

♦ Contingency reserves are used for two purposes: to deal with uncertainties in the duration used in the schedule and the cost used in the budget and to deal with overruns of the project objectives to meet the stakeholder expectations.

♦ Analogous estimation is less time consuming but also less accurate than parametric estimation and bottom-up estimation.

Key Terms and Definitions

◆ **budget.** Aggregation of cost estimates with a timeline assigned to it.

◆ **contingency reserve.** Funds or time reserved in addition to the calculated estimates to deal with the uncertainties in the duration used in the schedule and the cost used in the budget and to deal with overruns of the project objectives to meet the stakeholder expectations.

◆ **contract.** A mutually binding agreement between a buyer and a seller that obligates the seller to provide the specified product, service, or result and obligates the buyer to make the payment for it.

◆ **cost baseline.** Approved budget used as a baseline to determine the project progress.

◆ **CPFF.** Cost plus fixed fee; a contract type.

◆ **CPIF.** Cost plus incentive fee; a contract type.

◆ **CPPC.** Cost plus percentage of cost; a contract type.

◆ **FP.** Fixed price; a contract type.

◆ **human resource plan.** A document that describes roles and responsibilities, reporting relationships among the roles, and staffing management.

◆ **procurement management plan.** A document that describes how procurements will be managed.

◆ **procurements.** Purchases and acquisitions that are needed to complete the project but that cannot be produced by the in-house project team.

◆ **RAM.** Responsibility assignment matrix; a matrix used to specify the relationships between schedule activities, roles to perform those activities, and team members assigned to the roles.

◆ **role.** A defined function to be performed by a team member, such as a programmer or a tester.

◆ **staff management plan.** A document that describes when and how human resource requirements for a project will be met.

◆ **T&M.** Time and material; a contract type.

Review Questions

1. Management has asked you to produce a chart that depicts the resource needs for all the activities in the project. Which of the following charts is management referring to?
   - **A.** The project organizational chart
   - **B.** The WBS
   - **C.** The roles and responsibilities chart
   - **D.** The responsibility assignment matrix

2. Which of the following is not an output of the Develop Human Resource Plan process?
   - **A.** Project organizational chart
   - **B.** Roles and responsibilities
   - **C.** Project schedule
   - **D.** Staff management plan

3. Which of the following is a true statement about the staff management plan?
   - **A.** It is created by the human resources department.
   - **B.** It is a tool for team development.
   - **C.** It is created by the project management team as an output of the human resource planning efforts.
   - **D.** It is provided by the project sponsor.

4. You are in the process of developing the cost baseline for your project. What is the name of this process?
   - **A.** Determine Budget
   - **B.** Develop Cost Baseline
   - **C.** Estimate Costs
   - **D.** Develop Budget

5. Your project is in the planning stage. You first want to make the cost estimates for the planned project activities, and then you want to aggregate those costs. Which process will you perform first?
   - **A.** Determine Budget
   - **B.** Develop Human Resource Plan
   - **C.** Estimate Costs
   - **D.** Develop Budget

6. Which of the following processes will you perform first?

   A. Plan Procurements

   B. Determine Budget

   C. Estimate Costs

   D. Develop Schedule

7. Your supervisor has asked you to put some contingency reserve into your project plans. Which of the following is not true about contingency reserve?

   A. These are the funds and not the time.

   B. These are not included in the cost baseline.

   C. These are included in the budget.

   D. These are not used in earned value measurements.

8. You are a project manager at a company that is a seller for another company. You are coordinating the efforts to bid on a contract with another company to sell the product of your company. Which of the following contract types carries the most risk for your company?

   A. CPIF

   B. T&M

   C. CPPC

   D. FP

9. Ron Collins is the project manager for a biotechnology company. He is outsourcing a part of the project to a foreign company. The foreign company will charge Ron $10 per hour for each employee that will be involved in the outsourced part of the project. Ron will also be charged an extra amount of $100 per month for other charges, such as using the facilities for the duration of the project. What type of contract is it?

   A. T&M

   B. FP

   C. CPPC

   D. CPIF

10. Which of the following is not true about planning procurements?

   A. Scope baseline is an input to planning procurements.

   B. Contract types are an input to planning procurements.

   C. Make-or-buy decisions are an output of planning procurements.

   D. Make-or-buy analysis is a technique used in planning procurements.

11. In procurement, which of the following contract types presents the highest risk for the buyer?

    A. Firm fixed-price

    B. Cost plus fixed fee

    C. Cost plus percentage of cost

    D. Cost plus incentive fee

12. You are managing a software project. The project is already in the execution stage when you discover that a whole software module is missing from the work breakdown structure. Your company does not have the programmers to write the module in a timely fashion, so you decide to procure this piece of work. The module will have a number of small programs working together, and it will take almost the same effort to write any of these programs. The software experts have given you an estimate of how much that effort will be. However, it is not clear at this stage how many programs will be needed. Which type of contract will you choose in this situation?

    A. Time and material

    B. Cost plus fixed fee

    C. Cost plus percentage of cost

    D. Firm fixed-price

Chapter 6

Planning Quality and Risk Management

PMP Exam Objectives

Objective	What It Really Means
1.3 Document Project Risks, Assumptions, and Constraints	You must know the relationship of assumptions and constraints to risks. You must know that risks are the product of uncertainties. You also must know that there can be both positive and negative risks and that negative risks pose threats, whereas positive risks offer opportunities.
2.3 Create the WBS	Understand the process of creating the work breakdown structure, called Create WBS. You must know how to use the WBS in various planning tasks, such as estimating costs, planning human resources, developing the schedule, planning procurements, and planning for quality. In this chapter, we cover the process for planning quality, formally called Plan Quality.
2.5 Identify Risks and Define Risk Strategies	You must know how to develop the risk management plan by using risk management processes. That means you also must understand all the risk management planning processes: Plan Risk Management, Identify Risks, Perform Qualitative Risk Analysis, Perform Quantitative Risk Analysis, and Plan Risk Responses.

Introduction

Quality and risk are two important interrelated aspects of any project that need to be managed. While quality refers to the degree to which a set of characteristics of project deliverables and objectives fulfill the project requirements, risk refers to an uncertain event or condition that, if it occurs, has a positive or negative effect on meeting the project objectives. After you have planned the project scope to the WBS level, as discussed in the previous chapter, you are ready to plan the quality and risk management. After the project starts executing, you will not have enough time to plan a response to a risk if it occurs, so you need to plan risk responses before the project starts executing. To do that, you need to identify the risks and analyze them.

The core question in this chapter is: How do you plan for quality and risk management? In search of an answer, we will explore three avenues: planning quality, identifying and analyzing risks, and planning risk responses.

Managing Quality: Big Picture

Quality refers to the degree to which a set of characteristics of project deliverables and objectives fulfills the project requirements. In other words, it is the sum of project and product characteristics that help fulfill the requirements. The broader goal of quality management is to ensure that a given project will satisfy the needs for which it was undertaken. Quality management has two components: project quality management and product quality management. Whereas product quality management techniques depend upon the specific product that the project is going to produce, project quality management applies to all projects independent of the nature of the products.

While dealing with quality, you should be able to distinguish between the terms in the following pairs:

◆ **Grade and quality.** Grade is a category assigned to products with the same overall functional use but that differ in their technical characteristics and features, whereas quality is the degree to which the inherent characteristics of a product meet the requirements. Number of defects is an example of poor quality, whereas a limited number of features is an example of low grade.

◆ **Precision and accuracy.** Precision is a spread of different measurements of the same quantity, constant, or variable, such as gravity or cost. The smaller the spread of measured values, the better the precision. Accuracy is a measurement of how close the measured values are to the true value of the quantity. The closer the measured value is to the actual (or true) value, the better the accuracy of measurements.

◆ **Prevention and inspection.** Prevention is a direction to perform an activity that will keep an error from entering the product and the process. Inspection is a technique to examine whether an activity, component, product, result, or service complies with planned requirements. So, the goal of inspection is to ensure that errors do not reach the customer.

 NOTE

PMI's approach to quality management is intended to be compatible with that of International Organization for Standardization (ISO) and is compatible with proprietary approaches to quality, such as those proposed by Crosby, Deming, Juan, and others. It is also compatible with proprietary approaches to quality management, such as continuous improvement, cost of quality (COQ), design reviews, failure mode and effect analysis (FMEA), Six Sigma, Total Quality Management (TQM), and the voice of the customer.

Project management and quality management have come a long way as separate disciplines of knowledge and practice. It should not come as a surprise that quality management is one of nine knowledge areas in standard project management. In a complementary way, both modern quality management and project management recognize the importance of the following critical issues:

Continuous improvement. Continuous improvement means continuing to improve the quality through a process of planning for quality, implementing quality, auditing quality, and re-planning based on lessons learned or auditing. So really, quality improvement is an endless cycle, called a *plan-do-check-act cycle* as defined by Shewhart and modified by Deming. Performing organizations can also use techniques such as Six Sigma and TQM to improve the quality.

Customer satisfaction. Customer satisfaction can be a very vague notion that can mean different things to different parties. However, in project management and quality management, customer satisfaction means planned customer requirements are met. To achieve customer satisfaction in the real world, you need to understand, define, and evaluate the customer expectations and also manage those expectations, in addition to meeting the planned requirements. Otherwise, you might meet the planned requirements, and the customer may still be dissatisfied.

Management responsibility. This refers to the responsibility of management to provide resources needed for the project team to succeed. Although all team members should be responsible for the success of their parts of the project, they cannot succeed without management responsibility.

Prevention over inspection. One of the fundamental tenets of modern quality management is plan, design, and build in quality as opposed to inspect in. The cost of preventing mistakes is much less than finding them through inspections and then fixing them. Therefore, cost of quality (COQ) is less in prevention than through inspection. The COQ is defined as the total cost of quality-related efforts throughout the product lifecycle.

STUDY CHECKPOINT 6.1

You are trying out a Monte Carlo simulation program that estimates the value of a parameter by using some random variables. You know through the data that the exact value should be 50. You ran the program three times, and it gave you three values: 60, 61, and 62. Based on these values, answer the following questions:

A. How precise is the program in making the estimates?
B. How accurate are the estimates?
C. Are the values generated by the program more accurate or more precise?

The performing organization might have its own quality policy and procedures in addition to the three quality management processes shown in Figure 6.1 and explained in the following list.

◆ **Plan Quality.** This process is used to identify which quality requirements and standards are relevant to the project at hand and to determine how to meet these requirements and standards, as well as how compliance to the quality requirements will be demonstrated.

◆ **Perform Quality Assurance.** This process is used to audit the fulfillment of quality requirements to ensure that the project employs all the planned quality requirements and standards.

◆ **Perform Quality Control.** This process monitors project results to ensure that they meet the agreed-upon quality standards and identifies ways to eliminate the factors that keep the project results from meeting standards—that is, to make recommendations for changes or actions.

The processes for quality assurance are used as part of executing the project, and quality control is used as part of monitoring and controlling the project. These processes are therefore discussed in forthcoming chapters. Quality planning is performed during the project planning stage and is discussed next.

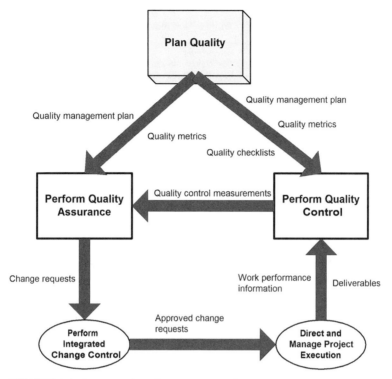

FIGURE 6.1 *Processes of quality management in a big picture.*

Planning Quality

According to PMBOK, quality is defined as the degree to which a set of characteristics of project deliverables and objectives fulfill the project requirements. Therefore, any characteristic that influences the satisfaction of the stakeholders is included in determining the quality. The project quality management processes include performing quality planning, quality assurance, and quality control. Quality planning is the quality process that is performed during the planning phase to accomplish the following goals.

- ◆ Identify which quality standards are relevant to the project at hand
- ◆ Determine how to satisfy these standards

Figure 6.2 depicts the quality planning process.

The project scope statement is the key input to the quality planning process, in addition to other input items discussed next.

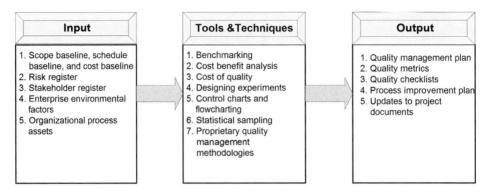

FIGURE 6.2 *The Plan Quality process: input, tools and techniques, and output.*

Input to Quality Planning

This section details items that can be used as input to the quality planning process, as shown in the following paragraphs:

Project performance baseline. The project performance baseline constituted by the scope baseline, schedule baseline, and cost baseline contains the list of all the deliverables and objectives to which the quality needs to be applied. For example, the following components of the project scope statement are especially relevant to quality planning:

◆ Project deliverables.

◆ Project objectives.

◆ Project requirements.

◆ A product scope description that may contain the details of technical issues and other quality-related concerns.

◆ Product acceptance criteria. The definition of acceptance criteria has an impact on the quality cost.

You find out the accepted schedule performance from the schedule baseline and the accepted cost performance from the cost baseline.

Stakeholder register and risk register. The stakeholder register may help in identifying the stakeholders that will have interests in quality. The risk register will help identify positive risks (opportunities) and negative risks (threats) that may have impact on quality.

Enterprise environmental factors. Guidelines, regulations from a government agency, rules, and standards relevant to the project at hand are examples of enterprise environmental factors that must be considered during quality planning. For example, procedures relevant to the application area of this project should be followed. Working or operating conditions and environment can also affect the project quality.

Organizational process assets. The following organizational process assets can affect the project from the perspective of quality planning:

- Information from previous projects and lessons learned
- Quality-related historical database
- An organizational quality policy, which is composed of overall intentions and high-level direction of an organization with respect to quality, established by the management at executive level

If the performing organization lacks a quality policy, the project team will need to develop a quality policy for the project. Once a quality policy is in place, it is your responsibility to ensure that the project stakeholders are aware of it and are on the same page.

With the input items in place, you use some tools and techniques to perform quality planning, as discussed in the following section.

Tools and Techniques Used for Quality Planning

The tools and techniques used for quality planning include benchmarking, cost/benefit analysis, experiment design, and brainstorming.

Benchmarking. Benchmarking is comparing practices, products, or services of a project with those of some reference projects for the purposes of learning, improving, and creating the basis for measuring performance. These reference projects might be previous projects performed inside or outside of the performing organization. Improvement and performance are of course quality-related factors. For example, you might have a similar project performed in the past that accepted no more than two defects in each feature. You might use that as a quality criterion—a benchmark—for your project.

Cost of quality and cost/benefit analysis. As mentioned earlier, the cost of quality is the total quality-related cost during the lifecycle of the product. That includes the costs incurred in implementing conformance to the requirements, reworking due to the defects resulting from failure to meet the requirements, and updating the product or service to meet the requirements. The cost of performance consists of prevention costs and appraisal costs. Prevention costs include the costs of appropriate equipment, documenting and performing processes, time and effort to perform the project work the right way, and needed training of the team members. The appraisal costs include the costs of inspecting, testing, and loss due to destructive testing. Cost of nonconformance includes rework and waste if the product is rejected internally because it did not meet the quality standards. If the problems with the product were found by the customer, however, the results could be more much more costly, including liabilities and loss of business.

During quality planning, you must consider the tradeoff between the cost and the benefit of quality and strike the appropriate balance for a given project. Implementing quality has its costs, including quality management and fulfilling quality requirements. The benefits of meeting quality requirements include less rework, resulting in overall higher productivity; lower costs of maintaining the product or service; and higher customer satisfaction.

Experiment design. Also called *design of experiments (DOE)*, this is a statistical method that can be used to identify the factors that might influence a set of specific variables for a product or a process under development or in production. You look for optimal conditions by changing the values of a number of variables simultaneously rather than changing one variable at a time. By using the results from this technique, you can optimize the products and processes. For example, you can use DOE to strike the right balance between cost of quality and its benefits. During planning, DOE can also be used to determine the types of tests and their impact on cost of quality.

Other quality planning tools. Other tools that you can use in quality planning, depending upon the project, include brainstorming, flowcharting, control charts, and statistical sampling. Statistical sampling involves randomly selecting a part of the population for study. Control charts, flowcharting, and statistical sampling are discussed further on in this book, when we discuss quality control. Some other tools of quality planning are included in the following list:

- **Affinity diagrams.** A business tool used to organize a large set of data and ideas into logical groups based on the relationships among these ideas.
- **Force field analysis.** A technique to understand the forces (factors) influencing a situation. It can be used to separate the forces that drive movement toward a goal from those that either block that movement or drive it away from the goal.
- **Matrix diagrams.** This method is used to explore the relationships between different entities, such as objectives and causes, by displaying these entities in a matrix, with cells of the matrix representing the relationships.
- **Nominal group techniques.** These are the decision-making methods that are used among groups of different sizes with two goals in mind: Make the decision quickly and take everyone's opinion into account. One example involves decision making by a group of one size, then a review of all those ideas from brainstorming by a group of another size, and then making the final decision by a group of yet another size.
- **Prioritization matrices.** This is the method of prioritizing entities, such as problems, ideas, and issues, by using some ranking criteria.

 NOTE

Part of the cost of quality is failure cost, which is the cost of rework due to failure to meet the requirements during product development. Failure cost, also called *cost of poor quality*, is grouped into two categories: external failure cost, which is the cost of fixing problems found by the customer, and internal failure cost, which is the cost of fixing problems found within the project.

You can use one or more of these techniques to generate the output of quality planning.

Output of Quality Planning

A major output of the quality planning process is the quality management plan. This section discusses the quality management plan and other output items.

Quality management plan. The quality management plan describes how the quality policy for this project will be implemented by the project management team. It includes approaches to quality assurance, quality control, and continuous process improvement. The quality management plan also contains the quality baseline that sets the criteria that specify the quality objectives for the project and thereby makes the basis for measuring and reporting quality performance. For example, a project that is finished on time, with everything delivered in scope, and that stayed within its cost is a project with high quality performance.

This plan becomes a component of the overall project management plan.

TIP

Whether the quality management plan is informal and high level or formal and detailed depends upon the size, complexity, and needs of the project.

Quality metrics. This is an operational criterion that defines in specific terms what something (such as a characteristic or a feature) is and how the quality control process measures it. For example, it is not specific enough to say the defects in the product will be minimized. Rather, specifying something such as that no feature will have more than two defects is a measurable criterion and hence a metric. Some examples of quality metrics are cost performance, schedule performance, defect frequency, failure rate, and test coverage. The metrics that you set during quality planning will be used in quality assurance and quality control.

Quality checklist. A checklist is a structured tool used to verify that a predetermined set of required steps has been performed. The checklists can come in imperative form ("to do" lists) or in interrogative form ("have you done this" lists). Checklists are prepared (or identified if they already exist in the organization) in quality planning and used in quality control.

Process improvement plan. This plan describes how to improve some of the processes that will be used in the project. For example, one purpose of improvement is to prevent activities in the processes that are not needed for this project. This is accomplished by describing the purpose, start, and end of a given process, the input to the process, and the output of the process. This is equivalent to drawing boundaries around the process. The process improvement plan may also include some metrics used to measure the efficiency of the process.

Updates to project documents. During quality planning, you may end up making changes that will require modifying corresponding documents, such as the stakeholder register and responsibility assignment matrix (RAM).

Note that quality planning might influence other planning processes. For example, implementing the identified quality standards will impact the cost and the schedule. Furthermore, the implementation of a quality characteristic might require a risk analysis of the problem that the quality characteristic addresses.

Managing Risks: The Big Picture

To most of us, risk means danger—if it happens, it will result in negative, undesired consequences. However, according to PMI, risk is an uncertain event or condition that, if it occurs, has a positive or negative effect on meeting the project objectives related to components such as schedule (time), cost, scope, or quality. For example, one of the obvious schedule objectives for a project is to complete the project by the scheduled deadline. If a risk related to the schedule occurs, it can delay the completion of the project, or it can make it possible to finish the project earlier. So, the two characteristics of a risk in project management are the following:

◆ It stems from elements of uncertainty.

◆ It might have negative or positive effects on meeting the project objectives.

Risk management includes planning risk management, identifying and analyzing the risks, preparing the response plan, monitoring the risk, and implementing the risk response if the risk occurs. Figure 6.3 shows the corresponding processes used to accomplish these tasks, which are also explained in the following list:

◆ **Plan Risk Management.** A process to determine the *how* of risk management: how to conduct risk management for the project at hand.

◆ **Identify Risks.** A process to identify and document the risks that might occur for a given project.

◆ **Perform Qualitative Risk Analysis.** A process used to estimate the overall probability for risks to occur and their impact and to prioritize them accordingly for further analysis.

◆ **Perform Quantitative Risk Analysis.** A process used to analyze numerically the effect of identified risks on meeting the project objectives.

◆ **Plan Risk Responses.** A process used to prepare a risk response plan in order to increase the positive impact and decrease the negative impact of risks on the project.

◆ **Monitor and Control Risks.** A process used for tracking identified risks, identifying new risks, executing risk response plans, and evaluating the effectiveness of executing responses throughout the lifecycle of the project.

The risk monitoring and control process is part of the control process group; therefore, we will discuss this process in Chapter 11, "Monitoring and Controlling Quality and Risk." The other five processes are discussed in the following sections, starting with risk management planning.

FIGURE 6.3 *Processes used in risk management.*

 TIP

The data flow between the different processes shown in Figure 6.3 is true in general. However, note that depending upon the project and the experience of the risk management team, shortcuts can be taken. For example, you can go directly from risk identification to quantitative risk analysis, or even to risk response planning.

Planning Risk Management

Risk management planning is the process used to decide how the risk management activities for the project at hand will be performed. The major goals for planning risk management are threefold: Ensure that the type, level, and visibility of risk management are proportionate to the actual risk involved in the project and the importance of the project to the organization; secure sufficient resources, including time for risk management activities; and set up an agreed-upon basis for evaluating risks. To be specific, you use the risk management planning process to determine the following:

- How to approach the risk management activities for this project
- How to plan the risk management activities
- How to execute the risk management activities

Figure 6.4 illustrates the Plan Risk Management process used for planning risk management.

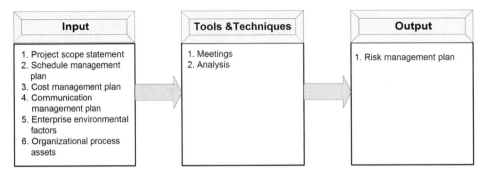

FIGURE 6.4 *The Plan Risk Management process: input, tools and techniques, and output.*

The first document to look for risks is the project scope statement, and it is therefore an input to risk management planning.

Developing the Risk Management Plan

You perform risk management planning to develop a document called the *risk management plan*. As an input to this development process, you need to look at the project scope statement, which contains elements such as the following, which are relevant to risk management planning:

◆ **Assumptions and constraints.** Assumptions should be evaluated for their uncertainty and thereby the possible risks. Constraints represent fixed parameters, such as available funds and deadlines that can also pose risks to the project.

◆ **Project objectives and requirements.** You must address the risks that might prevent the team from meeting the project objectives and requirements.

◆ **Product description.** There might be risks involved in performing the work for meeting the product description.

◆ **Initial risk identification.** The project scope statement might contain some of the risks you initially identified. Now you have more information to build on that work.

The cost management plan may have information on risks related to budget, contingency, and management reserves. The schedule management plan may have information on how the schedule contingencies will be used and reported. The communication management plan should have information on who should receive reports about the different risks.

The enterprise environmental factors relevant to risk planning include the organizational attitude toward risks and the risk tolerance level of the organization. This information can be found from the policy statements of the organization and from actual experience with previous projects. The organizational process assets relevant to risk planning include organizational approaches toward risk management, definitions of concepts and terms used within the organization, standard risk templates you can use, a roles and responsibilities list, and authority levels for decision making.

You develop the risk management plan by holding planning meetings, which might include the following attendees:

- ◆ Project manager
- ◆ Selected members from the project team
- ◆ Selected stakeholders
- ◆ Any member from the performing organization who has responsibility for risk planning and executing

In these meetings, the input items are used to develop the risk management plan, the only output of the risk management planning process.

Risk Management Plan

The only output of the Plan Risk Management process is the risk management plan, which includes the following elements.

Methodology. This specifies the system of approaches, tools, and data sources that will be used to perform risk management on the project at hand. These tools and approaches might vary over projects, so you have to make the best selection for the given project.

Identifying and assigning resources. This identifies and assigns resources for risk management, such as human resources, cost, and time.

- ◆ **Roles and responsibilities.** This specifies the roles and responsibilities for each role involved in risk management. These roles are assigned to members of the risk management team. The risk management team might include members from outside the project team.
- ◆ **Budgeting.** The cost for risk management activities needs to be estimated and included in the budget and the project cost baseline.
- ◆ **Timing and scheduling.** The plan specifies how often risk management processes will be performed and which risk management activities will be included in the project schedule, which is planned and developed by using processes discussed in Chapter 4, "Planning for Project Schedule and Communication."

TIP

It's a good idea for the risk management team to include members from outside the project team to ensure unbiased risk evaluations.

Risk categories. This element specifies how the risks will be categorized. The risk categories typically correspond to the sources of risks. Depending upon the size and complexity of the project, you might need to develop a risk breakdown structure (RBS), which is a hierarchical structure that breaks the identified risk categories into subcategories. In developing this structure, you will end up identifying various areas and causes of potential risks. The performing organization might already have prepared a categorization of typical risks. However, you need to examine this categorization for each project and tailor it according to the needs of the project at hand. The risk categorization helps you identify risks to the extent that you will be identifying various areas and causes of potential risks for your project.

TIP

Some project management literature and some PMP exam questions might use the terms *risk sources* and *risk categories* synonymously.

Risk probability and impact. Defining different levels of risk probabilities and impacts is necessary to ensure the quality and credibility of the qualitative risk analysis that we will discuss later in this chapter. The basic issues are defining the scale of likelihood that the risk will happen and defining the scale of the strength of its impact if the risk occurs. These definitions, even if they already exist in the organization, must be examined and tailored to the needs of the specific project.

You can define the risk probability scale from very unlikely to almost certainly, called the *relative scale*. As an alternative, you can define a numerical scale in which the probability is represented by numbers, in which a value close to 0.0 means very unlikely and a value close to 1.0 means almost certainly. The impact scale represents the size of the risk impact on the given project objective should the risk occur. Just like the probability scale, you can define the impact scale relatively or numerically. The relative scale can range from very low impact to very high impact, with points in the middle such as low, moderate, and high. As an alternative, you can define the impact numerically; it might be linear, such as the first point at 0.1, the second point at 0.2, and the tenth point at 1.0, or it might be nonlinear, such as the first point at 0.001, the second point at 0.01, and the third point at 0.1. Figure 6.5 shows an example of linear and nonlinear impact scales, in which the impact scale for Objective 1 is nonlinear and the impact scale for Objective 2 is linear. You can think of the X axis as a variable on which the risk impact depends.

Risks are prioritized according to the size of their impact on the project objectives, which can be recorded in what is called an *impact matrix* or *lookup table*. Even if your organization already has a typical impact matrix, you should examine it and tailor it to the needs of the specific project at hand. I will discuss the probability and impact matrix in more detail later in this chapter.

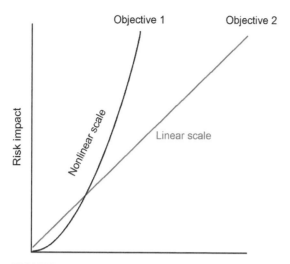

FIGURE 6.5 *An example of a linear and a nonlinear impact scale. The impact scale for Objective 1 is nonlinear, whereas the scale for Objective 2 is linear.*

As an example, Table 6.1 shows the risk impact definitions for four project objectives: cost, quality, scope, and time. Note that this example only shows the negative impact. The first row of the table presents the impact scale, and each cell in the following rows from Column 2 to Column 6 specifies the impact on a specific objective corresponding to a point on the overall impact scale. For example, the cell corresponding to the second row and fifth column reads that high impact (0.65) means a 50 to 80% increase in cost.

Table 6.1 Risk Impact Definitions for Four Project Objectives

	Risk Impact				
Project Objectives	**Very Low (0.05)**	**Low (0.10)**	**Moderate (0.35)**	**High (0.65)**	**Very High (0.90)**
Cost	Less than 1% cost increase	1–20% cost increase	20–50% cost increase	50-80% cost increase	80-100% cost increase
Time	Insignificant time increase	1–10% time increase	10–30% time increase	30–60% time increase	60–100% time increase
Scope	Scope decrease unnoticeable	Scope of only a few minor areas affected	Sponsor approval necessary for scope reduction	Scope reduction unacceptable to the sponsor	Project and item are effectively useless
Quality	Unnoticeable quality reduction	Only a few applications will be affected	Quality requires sponsor approval	Quality reduction unacceptable	Project and item are effectively useless

Risk reporting and tracking. This element describes the format of risk reports, such as the risk register, a document that contains the results of risk analysis and risk response planning. Furthermore, it describes how different aspects of risk activities will be recorded so that the risks can be monitored for the current project. Also, should the performing organization decide to audit the risk management process, one should be able to track these activities. Another reason for recording these activities could be to save the information for the benefit of future projects in the form of lessons learned.

During the process of planning risk management for a specific project, you revisit the tolerance levels of the stakeholders for certain risks, and these levels may be revised. Risk management planning is the process that generates the risk management plan document, which contains the information that will be used in risk identification, risk analysis, and risk response planning.

You cannot manage a risk if it's not identified.

Identifying Risks

Risks are identified by using the risk identification process. An unidentified risk is a danger lurking out of your sight and waiting to attack the project. The significance of the risk identification process cannot be overemphasized. You use the risk identification process to accomplish the following tasks:

◆ Identify which risks might affect the project at hand
◆ Document the characteristics of the identified risks in a document called the *risk register*

Figure 6.6 shows the input, tools and techniques, and the output for the risk identification process.

Note that the risk identification process has the risk management plan as an input item, in addition to all the input items that the quality planning and risk management planning processes have.

Input to Risk Identification

The risk management plan and the project scope baseline are obvious inputs to identifying risks. As in many other processes, the enterprise environmental factors and organizational process assets relevant to the project at hand must also be considered. These and other input items are discussed in the following paragraphs.

Project scope baseline. Assumptions in the project scope statement, an element of the scope baseline, are potential sources of uncertainty, hence the risk. Constraints pose a risk by presenting predetermined factors, such as hard deadlines and fixed costs, thereby posing questions such as, "What is the probability that we can meet this constraint with the available resources?"

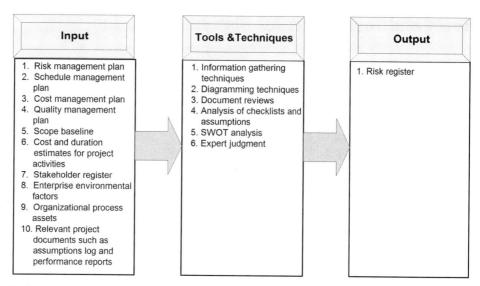

FIGURE 6.6 *The Identify Risks process: input, tools and techniques, and output.*

The WBS, another component of the scope baseline, can be used to recognize risks at different levels of the WBS hierarchy.

Management plans. In the process of identifying risks, you need to look at the cost management plan, schedule management plan, risk management plan, and quality management plan. The approach that any of these plans takes may pose some risks of its own or may enhance some other risks. The key items from the risk management plan useful for risk identification are risk categories, roles and responsibilities, and the budget and timing available for the risk management activities.

Cost and duration estimates. Estimates such as activity cost estimates and activity duration estimates by definition have a degree of uncertainty built into them. They should be looked at to identify the potential risks hiding behind this uncertainty.

Stakeholder register. If you look at the stakeholder register, you might find some stakeholders who can give useful input to identifying risks.

Enterprise environmental factors. The environmental factors internal or external to the performing organization that can influence the project must be considered in the risk identification process. This might include academic and industry studies, published information, benchmarking, and commercial databases.

Organizational process assets. This might include information from previous projects (the knowledge base), including lessons learned, process controls, and risk-related templates.

With this handful of input for your use, you are ready to use a number of tools and techniques available for risk identification.

Tools and Techniques for Risk Identification

Risk identification is crucial to risk management: If you fail to identify a risk, you will not be able to manage it. There are a multitude of tools and techniques available to aid you in identifying risks.

Assumptions analysis. Assumptions in the project scope statement represent uncertainty. You analyze these assumptions to identify the risks. Assumptions analysis is the technique used to examine the validity of the assumptions and thereby to identify the risks resulting from the inaccuracies, inconsistencies, or incompleteness of each assumption. For example, suppose there is only one person in the organization who has a rare skill needed for the project. An obvious assumption would be that the person will not quit the organization before completing the assignment. The inaccuracy of this assumption amounts to the risk.

Checklist analysis. The carefully prepared checklists in any process are great no-brainer time-savers. Projects in the same organization will more often than not have similarities. As a result, you can develop a risk identification checklist based on the information gathered from a similar set of projects previously performed. Also, if you developed the risk breakdown structure (RBS) in risk planning, the lowest level of the RBS can be used as a checklist.

 NOTE

Risk identification checklists are rarely exhaustive. Always explore what is left out of the checklist you are using. Also, improve the checklist when you close the project to enhance its value for future projects.

Diagramming techniques. These techniques use diagrams to identify risks by exposing and exploring the risks' causes. Here are a few examples:

◆ **Cause-and-effect diagram.** A cause-and-effect diagram illustrates how various factors (causes) can be linked to potential problems (effects).

◆ **Flowchart diagram.** A flowchart depicts how the elements of a system are related to each other and shows the logical flow of a process. By examining the flowchart of a process, the risk management team can identify points of potential problems in the flowchart diagram.

◆ **Influence diagram.** An influence diagram is a graphical representation of situations that shows relationships among various variables and outcomes, such as causal influences and time-ordering of events. By examining these diagrams, the risk management team can recognize potential problem areas and thereby identify risks.

Documentation reviews. A structured review of the relevant parts of input documents, such as the project scope statement and the project management plan, will certainly help in identifying risks. Furthermore, the knowledge base related to risk management from previous projects can also be reviewed.

Information-gathering techniques. To identify risks, you need to gather risk-related information. Following are some of the information-gathering techniques used in risk identification:

- **Brainstorming.** The goal here is to get a comprehensive list of potential risks so that no risk goes unidentified. The project team, along with relevant experts from different disciplines, can participate in the brainstorming session. Brainstorming is better performed under the guidance of a facilitator. You can use the categories of risks or the RBS as a framework to keep the session focused on the issue.

- **Delphi technique.** The goal here is for experts to reach a consensus without biases toward each other. I'm sure you will have no problem recalling a time when a decision was made because somebody (usually higher in the management hierarchy) said so. Contrary to this, the Delphi technique is used to ensure that it is the quality of the information and the argument that are important, not who is saying them. A facilitator circulates a questionnaire among the experts to solicit ideas about the risks of the given project. The experts respond anonymously. The responses are compiled and circulated among the participating experts for further evaluation without attaching a name to a response. It might take a few iterations before a general consensus is reached.

- **Interviewing.** This is one of the common methods used for information gathering for risk identification. You interview the appropriate stakeholders and subject-matter experts to gather information that will help identify risks for the project at hand.

- **Root cause identification.** A powerful way to identify risk is to look for anything in the project that might generate a risk. In other words, if you can spot a potential cause for risks, it's simple to identify the risks resulting from that cause. Furthermore, if you know the cause of a risk, it helps to plan an effective response. You can also look for risks at the opposite side of causes—that is, impacts.

- **SWOT analysis.** While root cause identification techniques look into the causes of risks to identify risks, a SWOT analysis looks at the potential impacts of risks to identify risks. If you examine the strengths, weaknesses, opportunities, and threats (SWOT) of a given project, you will be exposing the risks involved. Remember that a strength is an opportunity, a weakness is a threat, and opportunities and threats are posed by risks. This helps broaden the spectrum of risks considered. For example, a strength of your project might be that most of its parts are well understood from previously executed similar projects. Therefore, the risks involved in those parts will be easy to identify. A weakness of your project might be that one of the parts involves new technology that is not well-tested. So, this is a source of unknown risks. An opportunity might be that your organization will be the first one to take this product to market. An example of a threat might be that the government is considering a bill that, if it becomes a law, will have profound implications for your project.

Of course, you can always use the judgment of experts on the topic. You will generally be using more than one of these tools and techniques to identify risks. During risk identification, you might discover the causes of the risks, and you might even think of some potential risk responses. All this is part of the output of the risk identification process.

The Risk Register: The Output of Risk Identification

The risk register is a document that contains the output of the risk identification process. You will see later in this chapter that the risk register, which is initiated in the risk identification process, will also contain information from other risk management processes. To begin, you store the following information from the risk identification process in the risk register:

- **List of identified risks.** These are the risks that you identified in the risk identification process. These risks should be described in reasonable detail, which may include the following:
  - **The risks.** The definition and nature of each risk and the causes that will give rise to the risk.
  - **List of the root causes of the risks.** This is a list of events or conditions that might give rise to the identified risks.
  - **Updates to risk categories.** Risks categories were originally identified in the risk management planning process. However, in the process of identifying risks, you might discover new categories or modify existing categories. The updated risk categories must be included in the risk register.
- **List of potential responses.** Risk response planning is a separate process that is performed after risk analysis. However, during risk identification, you might identify potential risk responses that you must document in the risk register. These responses can be further examined and planned in the risk response planning process.

The results of the risk identification process usually lead to qualitative risk analysis. However, depending upon the project and the experience of the risk management team, risk identification might lead directly to quantitative risk analysis and even to risk response planning.

Analyzing Risks

Once the risks have been identified, you need to answer two main questions for each identified risk: What are the odds that the risk will occur, and, if it does, what will its impact be on the project objectives? You get the answers by performing risk analysis, which comes in two forms: qualitative and quantitative.

- **Qualitative risk analysis.** This is used to prioritize risks by estimating the probability of their occurrence and their impact on the project.
- **Quantitative risk analysis.** This is used to perform numerical analysis to estimate the effect of each identified risk on the overall project objectives and deliverables.

Usually, you prioritize risks by performing qualitative analysis on them before you perform quantitative analysis.

Performing Qualitative Analysis

Because qualitative analysis is an estimate, it is less precise than quantitative analysis, which is based on numbers and hence is more precise. However, qualitative analysis is quick and cheaper. It gives you some feel about the risks, and then you can determine which risks needs to be analyzed further by using quantitative analysis.

Figure 6.7 shows the input, tools and techniques, and output for the qualitative analysis, which are discussed in the following section.

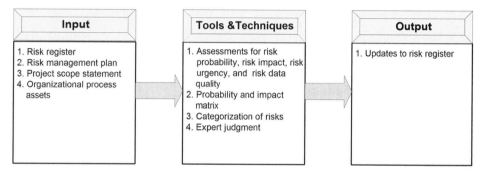

Input	Tools &Techniques	Output
1. Risk register 2. Risk management plan 3. Project scope statement 4. Organizational process assets	1. Assessments for risk probability, risk impact, risk urgency, and risk data quality 2. Probability and impact matrix 3. Categorization of risks 4. Expert judgment	1. Updates to risk register

FIGURE 6.7 *The Perform Qualitative Risk Analysis process: input, tools and techniques, and output.*

Input to Qualitative Risk Analysis

In addition to the risk register, qualitative risk analysis can also use the risk management plan, the project scope statement, and the organizational process assets as input items.

Project scope statement. When you are performing qualitative risk analysis, you want to know what kinds of risks you are dealing with. For example, are you already familiar with these risks? If your project is similar to previous projects, it might have well-understood risks. If it is a new and complex project, it might involve risks that are not well understood in your organization. So, how do you know what kind of project you are dealing with? Simple—you take a look at the project scope statement and search for uncertainties.

Risk management plan. To generate the output of qualitative risk analysis, you will need the following elements of the risk management plan:

- Roles and responsibilities for performing risk management
- Budgeting
- Definitions of probabilities and impacts
- The probability and impact matrices
- Risk categories
- Risk timing and scheduling
- Stakeholders' risk tolerances

If any of these input items was not developed during risk management planning, it can be developed during qualitative analysis.

Risk register. The risk register contains the list of identified risks that will be the key input to the qualitative risk analysis. Updated risk categories and causes of risks can also be useful elements of the risk register, which can be used in the qualitative risk analysis.

Organizational process assets. While analyzing risks, you will make use of the risk-related components of the knowledge base from previous projects, such as data about risks and lessons learned. You can also look into risk databases that may be available from industry organizations and proprietary sources.

Tools and Techniques for Qualitative Risk Analysis

Prioritizing risks based on their probability of occurrence and their impact if they do occur is the central goal of qualitative risk analysis. Accordingly, most of the tools and techniques used involve estimating probability and impact.

Risk probability and impact assessment. Risk probability refers to the likelihood that a risk will occur, and impact refers to the effect the risk will have on a project objective if it occurs. The probability for each risk and the impact of each risk on project objectives, such as cost, quality, scope, and time, must be assessed. Note that probability and impact are assessed for each identified risk.

Methods used in making the probability and impact assessment include holding meetings, interviewing, considering expert judgment, and using an information base from previous projects. A risk with a high probability might have a very low impact, and a risk with a low probability might have a very high impact. To prioritize the risks, you need to look at both probability and impact.

Assessment of the risk data quality. Qualitative risk analysis is performed to analyze the risk data to prioritize risks. However, before you do it, you must examine the risk data for its quality, which is crucial because the credibility of the results of qualitative risk analysis depend upon the quality of the risk data. If the quality of the risk data is found to be unacceptable, you might decide to gather better-quality data. The technique to assess the risk data quality involves examining the accuracy, reliability, and integrity of the data and also examining how good that data is relevant to the specific risk and project for which it is being used.

Risk urgency assessment. This is a risk prioritization technique based on time urgency. For example, a risk that is going to occur now is more urgent to address than a risk that might occur a month from now.

Probability and impact matrix. Risks need to be prioritized for quantitative analysis, response planning, or both. The prioritization can be performed by using a probability and impact matrix—a lookup table that can be used to rate a risk based on where it falls both on the probability scale and on the impact scale. Table 6.2 presents an example of a probability and impact matrix by showing both the probability scale and the impact scale. Here is an example of how to read this matrix: Risk R_{35} has a probability of 0.70 (that is, seven out of 10 chances) for occurrence and an impact of 0.45 on the project objective for which this matrix is prepared. How to calculate the numerical scales for the probability and impact matrix and what they mean depends upon the project and the organization. However, remember the relative meaning: Higher value of a risk on the probability scale means greater likelihood of risk occurrence, and higher value on the impact scale means greater effect on the project objectives. The higher the value for a risk, the higher its priority is. For example, Risk R_{38} has higher priority than Risk R_{27}.

Table 6.2 A Risk Probability and Impact Matrix for an Objective*

Probability	Impact								
0.00	0.05	0.15	0.25	0.35	0.45	0.55	0.65	0.75	0.90
0.10	R_{11}	R_{12}	R_{13}	R_{14}	R_{15}	R_{16}	R_{17}	R_{18}	R_{19}
0.30	R_{21}	R_{22}	R_{23}	R_{24}	R_{25}	R_{26}	R_{27}	R_{28}	R_{29}
0.50	R_{31}	R_{32}	R_{33}	R_{34}	R_{35}	R_{36}	R_{37}	R_{38}	R_{39}
0.70	R_{41}	R_{42}	R_{43}	R_{44}	R_{45}	R_{46}	R_{47}	R_{48}	R_{49}
0.90	R_{51}	R_{52}	R_{53}	R_{54}	R_{55}	R_{56}	R_{57}	R_{58}	R_{59}

R_{ij}, where i and j are integers, represents risks in the two-dimensional (probability and impact) space.

Each risk is rated (prioritized) according to the probability and the impact value assigned to it separately for each objective. Generally, you can divide the matrix in Table 6.2 into three areas—high-priority risks represented by higher numbers, such as R_{59}, medium-priority risks represented by moderate numbers, such as R_{23}, and low-priority risks represented by lower numbers, such as R_{12}. However, each organization has to design its own risk score and risk threshold to guide the risk response plan.

Note that impact can be a threat (a negative effect) or an opportunity (a positive effect). You will have separate matrices for threats and opportunities. Threats in the high-priority area might require priority actions and aggressive responses. Also, you will want to capitalize on those opportunities in the high-priority area, which you can do with relatively little effort. Risks posing threats in the low-priority area might not need any response, but they must be kept on the watch list.

Risk categorization. You defined the risk categories during the risk management planning and risk identification processes. Now you can assign the identified risks to those categories. You can also revisit the categorization scheme, such as RBS, that you developed for your project, because now you have more information about risks for the project. Categorizing risks by their causes often helps you develop effective risk responses.

Expert judgment. You may need expert judgment to assess the probability and impact of each risk. To find an expert, look for people who've had experience with similar projects in the not too distant past. While weighing the expert judgment, look for possible biases. Often experts are biased toward their area.

You need to update the risk register with the output of the qualitative risk analysis.

Output of the Qualitative Risk Analysis: Updated Risk Register

The risk register was initiated during the Identify Risks process and is updated with the results from the qualitative risk analysis. The updates include the following:

- ◆ **Risks categorizations.** This means arranging risks in different categories. This helps you identify the common root causes of the risks and the areas of the project that might require special attention. Furthermore, categorizing risks can bring order to a chaotic situation and makes the management of these risks easier and more effective.

- ◆ **Prioritized list of risks.** The risk register has lists of risks prioritized according to the probability and impact matrix discussed earlier in this chapter. A separate list can be created for each project objective, such as cost, quality, scope, and time. These lists help you prioritize efforts for preparing and executing risk responses. The risks may be ranked as high, medium, or low.

- ◆ **Lists of risks.** Using some criteria, you can make different lists of risks for effective management. Following are some examples:

  - ◆ **List of risks with time urgency.** This list includes urgent risks that require attention now or will in the near future.

  - ◆ **Watch list of low-priority risks.** This list contains risks that are deemed unimportant by the qualitative risk analysis but that need to be monitored continually.

  - ◆ **List of risks for additional analysis and response.** This list includes risks that need further analysis, such as quantitative analysis or a response action.

- ◆ **Trends in the analysis results.** By examining the results from the qualitative risk analysis, you might recognize a trend for specific risks. That trend might suggest further analysis or a specific risk response.

The main output of qualitative risk analysis is the prioritization of risks based on a probability and impact matrix for each objective. So each objective can have its own prioritized list of risks.

Qualitative risk analysis is a relatively quick and cost-effective way to prioritize risks for risk planning. It also lays the groundwork for the quantitative risk analysis if one is required for some risks.

Performing Quantitative Analysis

Quantitative risk analysis is generally performed on risks that have been prioritized by using the qualitative risk analysis. However, depending upon the experience of the team and their familiarity with the risk, it is possible to skip the qualitative risk analysis and, after the risk identification, move directly to the quantitative risk analysis. The quantitative risk analysis has three major goals:

◆ Assess the probabilities of achieving specific project objectives

◆ Quantify the effect of the risks on the overall project objectives

◆ Prioritize risks by their contributions to the overall project risk

Figure 6.8 illustrates the Perform Quantitative Risk Analysis process in terms of input, tools and techniques, and output.

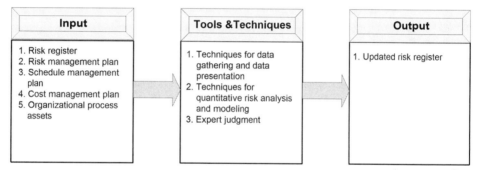

FIGURE 6.8   *The Perform Quantitative Risk Analysis process: input, tools and techniques, and output.*

Input to Quantitative Analysis

All the items that are input for the qualitative risk analysis are also input for the quantitative risk analysis. Because the quantitative risk analysis generally requires more information, it also includes project management plans in its list of input items, which are discussed in the following list.

◆ **Risk register.** The key input items from the risk register are the following:

    ◆ List of identified risks

    ◆ Priority list of risks if the qualitative risk analysis was performed

    ◆ Risks with categories assigned to them

◆ **Management plan.** To perform quantitative risk analysis, you must look at the risk management plan, cost management plan, and schedule management plan. To generate the output of the quantitative risk analysis, you need the following elements of the risk management plan:

   ◆ Budgeting
   ◆ Definitions of probabilities and impacts
   ◆ Probability and impact matrix
   ◆ Risk categories
   ◆ Risk timing and scheduling

To analyze the effect of risks on the project objectives, you need to know the project schedule and the project cost. These can be found in the cost management plan and schedule management plan. Also, the approaches taken by these plans can affect quantitative risk analysis.

◆ **Organization process assets.** The following organizational process assets might be useful in the quantitative analysis:

   ◆ Information on previously performed similar projects
   ◆ Studies performed by risk specialists on similar projects
   ◆ Proprietary risk databases or risk databases available from the industry

Obviously, the quantitative risk analysis will use techniques that are of a more numerical nature.

Tools and Techniques for Quantitative Analysis

The quantitative risk analysis can be looked upon as a two-step process—gathering and representing the data, and analyzing and modeling the data. Accordingly, all the techniques fall into two categories: data gathering and representation techniques, such as interviewing, probability distributions, and expert judgment; and analysis and modeling techniques, such as sensitivity analysis, EMV analysis, decision tree analysis, and modeling and simulation.

Interviewing. This technique is used to collect the data for assessing the probabilities of achieving specific project objectives. You are looking for results such as: We have a 70% probability of finishing the project within the schedule desired by the customer. Or perhaps: We have a 60% probability of finishing the project within the budget of $100,000. The goal is to determine the scale of probabilities for a given objective; for example, there is a 20% probability that the project will cost $50,000, a 60% probability that it will cost $100,000, and a 20% probability that it will cost $150,000.

The data is collected by interviewing relevant stakeholders and subject-matter experts. Most commonly, you will be exploring the optimistic (best case), pessimistic (worst case), and most likely scenarios for a given objective. For example, for the project cost, the optimistic estimate might be $10 million, the pessimistic estimate might be $50 million, and the most likely estimate might be $25 million.

Probability distributions. After you have collected the data on meeting the project objectives, you can present it in a probability distribution for each objective under study. Note that a distribution represents uncertainty, and uncertainty represents risk. For example, if you know for sure the project will cost $25 million, there will be no distribution because it is only one data point. Distribution comes into the picture when you have several possible values with a probability assigned to each value. There are distributions of different shapes in which the data can be presented. Figure 6.9 shows some of them, such as for the cost objective. The X axis represents the cost, and the Y axis represents the corresponding probability that the project will be completed within that cost.

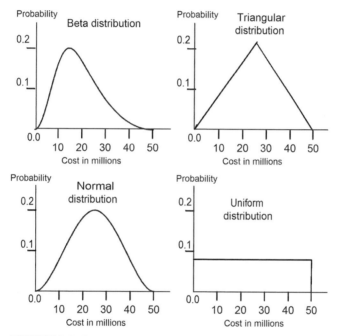

FIGURE 6.9 *Examples of probability distributions commonly used in quantitative risk analysis.*

The beta distribution and the triangular distribution are the most frequently used distributions. The other commonly used distributions that could be suitable under given circumstances are normal distribution and uniform distribution. The uniform distribution is used when all the values of an objective have the same chance of being true.

Sensitivity analysis. This is a technique used to determine which risk has the greatest impact on the project. You study the impact of one uncertain element on a project objective by keeping all other uncertain elements fixed at their baseline values. You can repeat this analysis for several objectives, one at a time. You can also repeat this study for several uncertain elements (creating risks), one element at a time. This way, you can see the impact of each element (or risk) on the overall project separate from other elements (or risks).

Expected monetary value analysis. The expected monetary value (EMV) analysis is used to calculate the expected value of an outcome when different possible scenarios exist for different values of the outcome with some probabilities assigned to them. The goal here is to calculate the expected final result of a probabilistic situation. EMV is calculated by multiplying the value of each possible outcome by the probability of its occurrence and adding the results. For example, if there is 60% probability that an opportunity will earn you $1,000 and a 40% probability that it will only earn you $500, the EMV is calculated as follows:

$$EMV=0.60\times1000+0.40\times500=600+200=800$$

So the EMV in this case is $800. When you are using opportunities and threats in the same calculation, you should express EMV for an opportunity as a positive value and EMV for a threat as a negative value. For example, if there is a 60% chance that you will benefit from a risk by $1,000 and a 40% probability that you will lose $500 as a result of this risk, the EMV is calculated as follows:

$$EMV=0.60\times1000-0.40\times500=600-200=400$$

Therefore, the EMV in this case is $400.

The concept of EMV can be presented in a decision-making technique, such as a decision tree analysis.

Decision tree analysis. This technique uses the decision tree diagram to choose from different available options; each option is represented by a branch of the tree. This technique is used when there are multiple possible outcomes with different threats or opportunities with certain probabilities assigned to them. EMV analysis is done along each branch, which helps to make a decision about which option to choose.

Figure 6.10 presents a very simple decision tree diagram that depicts two options: updating an existing product or building a new product from scratch. The initial cost for the update option is $50,000, whereas the initial cost for the build-from-scratch option is $70,000. However, the probability for failure is 40% for the update option, compared to 10% for the build-from-scratch option, and the impact from failure in both cases is a loss of $200,000. As Study Checkpoint 6.2 shows, even though the initial cost for the update option is less than the initial cost for the build-from-scratch option, the decision will be made in favor of the build-from-scratch option because when you combine the initial cost with the EMV resulting from the probability of failure, the build-from-scratch option turns out to be a better deal.

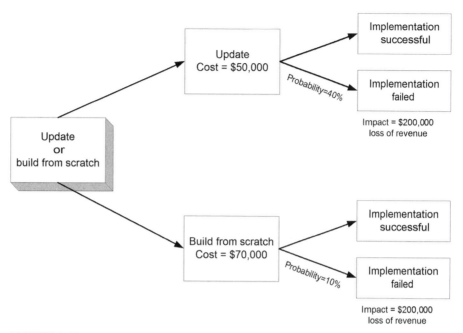

FIGURE 6.10 *Example of a decision tree diagram.*

STUDY CHECKPOINT 6.2

Perform the EMV analysis of the decision tree presented in Figure 6.10 to make a decision on which option to take.

Option	Initial Cost	Risk Cost	Probability	EMV for Risk Cost	Total Cost
Update	$50,000	$200,000	40%	0.40×$200,000=$80,000	$50,000+$80,000=$130,000
Build from scratch	$70,000	$200,000	10%	0.10×$200,000=$20,000	$70,000+$20,000=$90,000

Modeling and simulation. A *model* is a set of rules to describe how something works; it takes input and makes predictions as output. The rules might include formulas and functions based on facts, assumptions, or both. A *simulation* is any analytical method used to imitate a real-life system. Simulations in risk analysis are created using the Monte Carlo technique, which is named after the city of Monte Carlo—known for its casinos that present games of chance based on random behavior. Monte Carlo simulation models take random input iteratively to generate output for certain quantities as predictions. This technique is used in several disciplines, such as physics and biology, in addition to project management. In risk analysis, the input is taken randomly from a probability distribution, and the output for impact on the project objectives is predicted. The name "Monte Carlo" refers to the random behavior of the input. (In that spirit, it could easily be called Las Vegas.)

Expert judgment. In quantitative risk analysis, expert judgment can be used to validate the collected risk data and the analysis used for the project at hand.

The risk register is updated with the results of the quantitative risk analysis.

Output of the Quantitative Risk Analysis: Updated Risk Register

The risk register that was used as an input item to the quantitative risk analysis is updated with the results of this analysis. The updates include the following:

◆ **Probabilistic analysis of the project.** This includes the estimates of the project schedule and cost with a confidence level attached to each estimate. Confidence level is expressed in percentage form, such as 95%, and it represents how certain you are about the estimate. You can compare these estimates to the stakeholders' risk tolerances to see whether the project is within the acceptable limits.

◆ **Probability of achieving the project objectives.** Factoring in project risks, you can estimate the probability of meeting project objectives, such as cost and schedule, set forth by the current project plan. For example, the likelihood of completing the project within the current budget plan of $2 million is 70%.

◆ **Prioritized list of risks.** Risks are prioritized according to the threats they pose or the opportunities they offer. Risks with greater threats (or opportunities) are higher on the list. The goal is to prioritize the response plan efforts to eliminate (or minimize) the impact of the threats and capitalize on the opportunities. The priorities are determined based on the total effect of each risk to the overall project objectives.

◆ **Trends in the results.** By repeating the analysis several times and examining the results, you might recognize a trend for specific risks. That trend might suggest further analysis or a specific risk response. In finding the trend, you can also take a look at the historical information on project cost, quality, schedule, and performance.

The emphasis in quantitative analysis is on two tasks: Assess the probability of meeting each project objective and prioritize the risks based on the total effect of each risk on the overall project objectives. Subsequently, the resultant prioritized list of risks can be used to prepare the risk response plan.

Planning Risk Response

Depending on the project, the nature of risks, and the experience of the team, risk response planning can start after risk identification, qualitative risk analysis, or quantitative risk analysis. But if qualitative risk analysis and quantitative risk analysis are performed on the risk, then the response planning must come after these analyses. Recall that risks can include threats (negative risks) and opportunities (positive risks). Accordingly, the central task in risk response planning is to develop actions and options to meet the following two goals:

- Minimize threats to meeting project objectives
- Maximize opportunities

TIP

Remember the five-pronged golden rule for risk response planning, AARCO: A risk response must be *appropriate* to the significance of the risk, *agreed* upon, *realistic* within the context of the project, *cost* effective, and *owned* by a team member.

As shown in Figure 6.11, the risk management plan and risk register are the input items to risk response planning.

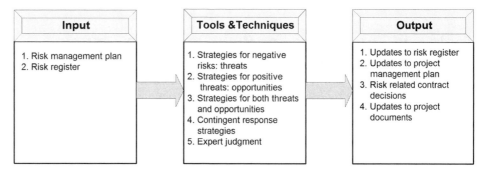

Input	Tools &Techniques	Output
1. Risk management plan 2. Risk register	1. Strategies for negative risks: threats 2. Strategies for positive threats: opportunities 3. Strategies for both threats and opportunities 4. Contingent response strategies 5. Expert judgment	1. Updates to risk register 2. Updates to project management plan 3. Risk related contract decisions 4. Updates to project documents

FIGURE 6.11 *The risk response planning process: input, tools and techniques, and output.*

Input to Risk Response Planning

The only two input items for risk response planning are the risk register and the risk management plan.

Risk register. The risk register contains the results from risk identification, qualitative risk analysis, and quantitative risk analysis. The following elements of the risk register are especially useful for risk response planning:

◆ List of identified risks

◆ Root causes of risks

◆ Prioritized list of risks

◆ List of risks that need immediate attention

◆ Trends in analysis results

Risk management plan. The elements of the risk management plan that can be useful for risk response planning include the following:

◆ Organizations' and stakeholders' thresholds for low, moderate, and high risks to sort out those risks for which response is needed.

◆ Roles and responsibilities that specify the positions and functions for each position involved in risk management. These roles are assigned to members of the risk management team, which might include members from inside or outside the project team.

◆ Timing and a schedule that specifies how often the risk management processes will be performed and which risk management activities will be included in the project schedule.

Because there is a wide spectrum of risks that can occur, there are a multitude of tools and techniques available to plan responses for these risks.

Tools and Techniques for Risk Response Planning

Risk, as you have already learned, can come in two categories: negative risks, which pose threats to meeting the project objectives, and positive risks, which offer opportunities. The goal here is to minimize the threats and maximize the opportunities. In project management, there are three kinds of possible responses to risks—take an action, take no action, or take a conditional action. When you want to take an action, different response strategies for negative and positive risks need to be planned. Accordingly, there are three kinds of strategies available to handle three kinds of scenarios:

◆ Strategies to respond to negative risks (threats) when action is required

◆ Strategies to respond to positive risks (opportunities) when action is required

◆ Strategies that can be used to respond to both negative and positive risks when no action or a conditional action is taken

Response Strategies for Threats

There are only three commonsense ways to take an action against a potential problem: Get out of harm's way, pass it to someone else, or confront it to minimize the damage. In project management, these three strategies are called *avoid*, *transfer*, and *mitigate*—the ATM approach.

Avoid. You avoid risk by changing your project management plan in such a way that the risk is eliminated. Depending upon the situation, this can be accomplished in various ways, including the following:

- ◆ Obtaining information and clarifying requirements for risks based on misunderstanding or miscommunication. This answers two questions: Do we really have this risk, and, if yes, how can we avoid it?
- ◆ Acquiring expertise for risks that exist due to a lack of expertise.
- ◆ Isolating the project objectives from the risk whenever possible.
- ◆ Relaxing the objective that is under threat, such as extending the project schedule.

Transfer. Risk transfer means you shift the responsibility for responding to the risk (the ownership of the risk), the negative impact of the risk, or both to another party. Note that transferring the risk transfers the responsibility for risk management and does not necessarily eliminate the risk. Risk transfer almost always involves making payment of a risk premium to the party to which the risk has been transferred. Some examples include buying an insurance policy and contracting out the tasks involving risk.

Mitigate. Mitigation in general means taking action to reduce or prevent the impact of a disaster that is expected to occur. Risk mitigation means reducing the probability of risk occurrence, reducing the impact of the risk if it does occur, or both. A good mitigation strategy is to take action early on to first reduce the probability of the risk happening, and then to plan for reducing its impact if it does occur, rather than letting it occur and then trying to reduce the impact or repair the damage. Following are some examples of mitigation:

- ◆ Adopting less complex processes
- ◆ Conducting more tests on the product or service of the project
- ◆ Choosing a more stable supplier for the project supplies
- ◆ Designing redundancy into a system so that if one part fails, the redundant part takes over and the system keeps working

Each of these three strategies has a counter-strategy to deal with the opportunities.

Response Strategies for Opportunities

Just like in the case of threats, you have three strategies to deal with opportunities. Not surprisingly, each response strategy to deal with an opportunity is a counterpart of a response strategy to deal with a threat—a one-to-one correspondence:

- ◆ Share corresponds to transfer
- ◆ Exploit corresponds to avoid
- ◆ Enhance corresponds to mitigate

You use the SEE (share, exploit, enhance) approach to deal with opportunities presented by the positive risks.

Share. Sharing a positive risk that presents an opportunity means transferring ownership of the risk to another party that is better equipped to capitalize on the opportunity. Some examples of sharing are:

- Forming risk-sharing partnerships
- Starting a joint venture with the purpose of capitalizing on an opportunity
- Forming teams or special-purpose companies to exploit opportunities presented by positive risks

Exploit. Exploiting an opportunity means ensuring that the opportunity is realized—that is, the positive risk that presents the opportunity does occur. This is accomplished by eliminating or minimizing the uncertainty associated with the risk occurrence. An example of exploiting is assigning more talented resources to the project to reduce the completion time and therefore to be the first to market. Another example could be to provide better quality than planned to beat a competitor. Whereas exploiting refers to ensuring that the positive risk occurs, enhancing refers to increasing the impact of the risk once it occurs.

Enhance. This strategy means increasing the size of the opportunity by increasing the probability, impact, or both. You can increase the probability by maximizing the key drivers of the positive risks or by strengthening the causes of the risks. Similarly, you can increase the impact by increasing the project's susceptibility to the positive risk.

You have just learned the different strategies that you need to plan for negative and positive risks if you intend to take action. If, on the other hand, you intend to take no action or a conditional action, then the response planning strategies for both negative and positive risks are the same.

Response Strategies for Both Threats and Opportunities

There are two response strategies that you need to plan for the risks for which you need to take either a conditional action or no action.

Acceptance. Acceptance of a risk means letting it be. Generally, it is not possible to take action against all risks. Depending upon their probabilities and impacts, some risks will simply be accepted. There are two kinds of acceptance:

- Passive acceptance that requires no action
- Active acceptance that requires a conditional action, called a *contingent response*

Contingency. Generally speaking, contingency means a future event or condition that is possible but cannot be predicted with certainty. So, your action will be contingent upon the condition; that is, it will be executed only if the condition happens. In risk management, a contingent response is a response that is executed only if certain predefined conditions (or events) happen. These events trigger the contingency response. Some examples of such triggers are missing a milestone or escalating the priority of a feature by the customer. The events that can trigger contingency response must be clearly defined and tracked.

CAUTION

While designing a response to a risk, also design a backup plan to fall back on in case the response does not work. Also, think through and plan for responding to the risks that the response to the original (primary) risk may cause. These risks are called *secondary risks*.

You use these strategies to generate the output of the risk response planning process.

STUDY CHECKPOINT 6.3

You are the project manager of a movie-shooting project. The first column in the following table lists some actions you are taking to deal with risks. Match each item in the first column with one item in the second column of this table.

Action	*Risk Response Type*
A. One of the scenes is to be shot in a country that has enormous bureaucracy and red tape. They might create roadblocks and make it difficult for you. There isn't much you can plan about it.	1. Avoid
B. The jungle where you are going to shoot a few scenes is a wetland and very hot and humid, and the probability of damage happening to the equipment is very high. So, you have decided to buy insurance to protect you against this possible damage.	2. Accept
C. You have learned that during certain parts of the year, the locals come to the jungle in big numbers for hunting. So, you have decided not to do the shoot during that part of the year.	3. Exploit
D. Although the movie does not depend on it, it will add a lot of marketing value to the movie if your cameras could capture an endangered species of bird that lives in the jungle. You are choosing the specific time of the year for shooting and taking some other actions to increase the probability that the birds will show up.	4. Share
E. The movie has something to do with Thanksgiving Day. You have put some extra resources to ensure that the movie is completed in a timely manner for release on Thanksgiving Day.	5. Mitigate
F. You have learned that there could be mosquitoes in the area that you are going to shoot. So you have planned to take plenty of mosquito repellent and other products to prevent mosquito bites.	6. Enhance
G. You know that another movie team is going to shoot some scenes in the same jungle during a different time of the year. You have signed a contract with them to share or trade shots of the endangered bird species.	7. Transfer

Output of Risk Response Planning

The output of risk response planning might include risk register updates, risk-related contractual agreements, and project management plan updates.

Risk register updates. The appropriate risk responses planned and agreed upon by the risk management team are included in the risk register. The responses to high and moderate risks are entered in detail, while the low-priority risks can be put on a watch list for monitoring. After the risk register is updated, it includes the following main elements:

- A list of identified risks, descriptions of the risks, root causes of the risks, WBS elements affected by the risks, and impacts of the risks on the project objectives.
- Roles and responsibilities in managing the risks—that is, risk owners and the responsibilities assigned to them.
- Results from qualitative and quantitative risk analyses, including a prioritized list of risks, a probabilistic analysis of the project objectives, and a list of risks with time urgency.
- Planned and agreed-upon risk response strategies and specific actions to implement each strategy.
- Symptoms and warning signs of risk occurrences, contingency plans, and triggers for contingency risks.
- Budget and schedule requirements to implement the planned responses, including the contingency reserve, which is the amount of funds, time, or both needed in addition to the estimates in order to meet the organization's and stakeholders' risk tolerances and thresholds.
- Fallback plans in case the planned responses prove to be inadequate
- A list of risks to remain, which include the following:
    - Passive, accepted risks
    - Residual risks that will remain after planned responses have been performed
- A list of secondary risks that will arise as a result of implementing the responses. You must plan for these risks like any other risk.

Updates to the project management plan. Risk response planning is a very involved and serious process. It may affect many components of the project management plan. You should go back and modify that component accordingly. For example, a risk response plan may require a change in the schedule, and therefore you will need to update the schedule management plan. Similarly, changes in budget and tolerance level as a result of planning a response should trigger updates to the cost management plan and quality management plan. Other plans that may be affected by risk response planning include the procurement management plan and the human resource management plan. These changes may also include or trigger changes in the cost baseline, the schedule baseline, and the WBS.

NOTE

A residual risk is the remains of a risk on which a response has been performed, whereas a secondary risk is a risk that is expected to arise as a result of implementing a risk response; therefore, a response for a secondary risk must be planned.

Risk-related contract decisions. The decisions for risk-related contractual agreements might result, for example, from the decisions of transferring risks. Mitigating the risks may also have an option to contract it out, and hence a contract will be necessary. A positive risk can also be contracted out to maximize the opportunity it offers and share the resulting benefit with the vendor to which it is contracted out.

Updates to project documents. In addition to the risk register and project management plan, risk response planning may also cause updates to other project documents. For example, new information that becomes available during risk planning may change an assumption. This will require an update of the project scope statement (if it contains that assumption) or the assumption document, such as the assumption log, if you are keeping assumptions separate from the scope statement. You may also need to change some technical documents due to changes in the technical approach as a result of risk response plans.

In a nutshell, risk response planning deals with both kinds of risks—those that pose threats to meeting project objectives and those that present opportunities. Three kinds of responses can be planned—take action, take no action, or take a conditional action.

I have discussed quite a few processes used in quality management and risk management. It is time to put them together to show how they are related to each other in the big picture.

The Big Picture of Quality and Risk Management

In this chapter, I have introduced the processes used in managing the quality and risks of a project. As shown in Figure 6.12, quality management and risk management can begin after project scope planning, schedule planning, and cost planning have been performed.

Note that Figure 6.12 presents a general and high-level view of the relationships between different processes used to manage quality and risk, and not all the interactions and data flow are shown. For example, depending on the nature of the risk and the experience of the risk management team, a risk might move directly from the identification process to quantitative risk analysis or even to the risk response planning process.

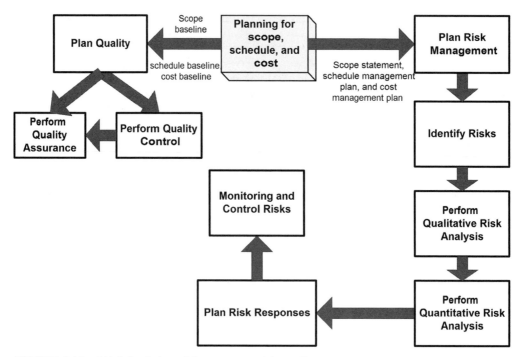

FIGURE 6.12 *A high-level view of the processes used in quality management and risk management.*

You might be overwhelmed by the input items that go into various processes. Table 6.3 presents a unified picture of the main input items for various quality and risk-related processes. Following are the main points emerging from this picture:

◆ The scope statement is an input to quality planning, risk management planning, identifying risks, and performing qualitative risk analysis. You can realize this only if you remember that the scope statement is a component of the scope baseline.

◆ The risk management plan, generated during the Plan Risk Management process, is an input to all other risk planning processes.

◆ The risk register is initiated by the risk identification process and is an input item to, and is updated by, the following risk management processes: Perform Qualitative Risk Analysis, Perform Quantitative Risk Analysis, and Plan Risk Responses. It will also be updated by the Monitor and Control Risks process, which we will explore in an upcoming chapter.

Table 6.3 Some Input Items for Various Processes Used to Manage Quality and Risk*

Input Items	Processes					
	Plan Quality	Plan Risk	Perform Management Identify Risks	Perform Qualitative Risk Analysis	Quantitative Risk Analysis	Plan Risk Responses
Enterprise environmental factors	Yes	Yes	Yes	No	No	No
Organizational process assets	Yes	Yes	Yes	Yes	Yes	No
Project scope statement	Yes	Yes	Yes	Yes	No	No
Schedule management plan	No	Yes	Yes	No	Yes	No
Cost management plan	No	Yes	Yes	No	Yes	No
Risk management plan	No	No	Yes	Yes	Yes	Yes
Risk register	Yes	No	No	Yes	Yes	Yes
Stakeholder register	Yes	No	Yes	No	No	No

*Yes means the item is included in the input list of the corresponding process.

The three most important takeaways from this chapter are as follows:

◆ The goal for quality planning is twofold: Identify which quality standards are relevant to the project at hand and determine how to satisfy these standards.

◆ The risk identification process initiates the risk register by listing the identified risks in it. Qualitative risk analysis prioritizes these risks based on the probability and impact matrix for each objective, whereas the emphasis in quantitative risk analysis is on assessing the probabilities of meeting each project objective and prioritizing the risks based on the total effect of each risk on the overall project objectives.

◆ The goal for risk response planning is to minimize the threats (the negative effects of risks) and maximize the opportunities (the positive effects of risks).

Summary

Quality and risk are two interrelated aspects of any project and need to be managed. While quality refers to the degree to which a set of characteristics of project deliverables and objectives fulfill the requirements, risk refers to an uncertain event or condition that, if it occurs, has a positive or negative effect on meeting the project objectives. Quality management includes quality planning, quality assurance, and quality control. The quality management plan, quality metrics, quality checklist, and process improvement plan are the major output items of the quality planning process called Plan Quality. The only output of risk management planning is the risk management plan, which includes elements such as a list of tools and approaches to be used for risk management, identification and assignment of resources for risk management, risk categories, risk probabilities and impacts, and the format of risk reporting and tracking. This information is used in the remaining processes of risk management—Identify Risks, Perform Qualitative Risk Analysis, Perform Quantitative Risk Analysis, and Plan Risk Responses.

The risk management plan is an input item to the risk identification process. Its only output is the risk register, which includes a list of identified risks, a list of the root causes of the risks, and an initial list of potential responses. The risk register, initially prepared during the risk identification process, is updated during the following processes: Perform Qualitative Risk Analysis, Perform Quantitative Risk Analysis, Plan Risk Responses, and Monitor and Control Risks. The main output of qualitative risk analysis is the prioritization of risks based on a probability and impact matrix for each objective. Each objective might have its own prioritized list of risks. However, the emphasis in quantitative analysis is on two things—assessing the probability of meeting each project objective and prioritizing the risks based on the total effect of each risk on the overall project objectives. Subsequently, the resultant prioritized list of risks can be used to prepare the risk response plan.

Depending upon the priority of the risk, you can choose one of the three options—taking no action, taking an action if some event happens, or taking an action. When you decide to take an action, there are three ways to plan it: avoid, transfer, or mitigate in case of a negative risk; and share, exploit, or enhance in case of a positive risk.

After you have planned for various management aspects of the project, including scope, schedule, cost, quality, and risk, you need to proceed toward executing the project. This subject is explored in the next part of this book.

Exam's Eye View

Comprehend

◆ Quality management has two components: project quality management and product quality management. While product quality management techniques depend upon the specific product that the project is going to produce, project quality management applies to all projects independent of the nature of the products.

◆ Risk categorization is a part of the risk management plan, and it helps in the risk identification process.

◆ Defining risk probability and risk impact are parts of the risk management plan and are used in qualitative risk analysis and in prioritizing risks.

◆ Risk identification is performed before risk analysis, and qualitative risk analysis, if performed, is performed before quantitative risk analysis because it takes less effort and time and its results can be used for quantitative analysis.

◆ An important update added to the risk register by the qualitative risk analysis is the prioritized list of risks. Each objective can have its own prioritized list of risks.

◆ Two important updates added to the risk register by the quantitative risk analysis are:

    ◆ The probabilistic analysis of the project objectives—that is, the probability of meeting the project objectives

    ◆ The prioritized list of risks based on the total effect of each risk on the overall project objectives

Look Out

◆ A fundamental tenet of quality: Quality is planned, designed, and built in, not inspected in.

◆ Risk stems from elements of uncertainty and can have a negative or a positive effect on meeting the project objectives.

◆ Quality planning and risk management planning processes have identical sets of input items.

◆ A residual risk is the remains of a risk on which a response has been performed, whereas a secondary risk is a risk that is expected to arise as a result of implementing a risk response.

◆ Depending upon the experience of the team and the nature of the risk, a risk can be moved directly after identification to the quantitative risk analysis or even to risk response planning.

Memorize

◆ The quality management plan, quality checklists, the process improvement plan, and quality metrics are the major output items of the quality planning process.

◆ The risk register is initially prepared during the risk identification process and is updated during the following processes: qualitative risk analysis, quantitative risk analysis, risk response planning, and risk monitoring and controlling.

◆ The quality management plan and risk management plan become part of the project management plan.

◆ Planning for scope, schedule, and cost needs to be performed before you can plan for quality and risk management.

◆ The only output of risk management planning is the risk management plan.

Key Terms and Definitions

◆ **assumptions analysis.** A technique used to examine the validity of an assumption and thereby identify the risk resulting from the inaccuracy, inconsistency, or incompleteness of each assumption.

◆ **benchmarking.** Comparing practices, products, or services of a project with those of some reference projects for the purposes of learning, improvement, and creating the basis for measuring performance.

◆ **confidence level.** A statistical term that refers to the certainty attached to an estimate and is often represented in percentage form, such as a 95% confidence level.

◆ **contingency.** A future event or condition that is possible but cannot be predicted with certainty. In this case, an action will be contingent upon the condition—that is, the action will be executed only if the condition happens.

◆ **contingency reserve.** The amount of funds, time, or both needed in addition to the estimates in order to meet the organization's and stakeholders' risk tolerances and thresholds.

◆ **COQ.** Cost of quality; the total cost of quality-related efforts throughout the product lifecycle.

◆ **decision tree analysis.** A technique that uses a decision tree diagram to choose from different options available; each option is represented by a branch of the tree. EMV analysis is done along each branch, which helps to make a decision about which option to choose.

◆ **Delphi technique.** An information-gathering technique used for experts to reach a consensus while sharing their ideas and preferences anonymously.

◆ **Expected Monetary Value (EMV) analysis.** A statistical technique used to calculate the expected outcome when there are multiple possible outcome values with probabilities assigned to them.

◆ **experiment design.** A statistical method that can be used to identify the factors that can influence a set of specific variables of a product or a process under development or in production.

◆ **methodology.** A system of procedures and techniques practiced in a discipline to accomplish a task. For example, risk management methodology is used in the discipline of project management to determine how risk management processes will be performed.

◆ **mitigation.** The process of taking actions to reduce or prevent the impact of a disaster that is expected to occur.

◆ **model.** A set of rules to describe how something works, which takes input and makes predictions as output.

◆ **Monte Carlo simulation.** An analysis technique that randomly generates values for uncertain elements (that is, variables) and takes them as input to a model to generate output. In other words, it simulates a model by feeding randomly selected input values.

◆ **performance measurement baseline.** An approved integrated plan for the project specifying some parameters to be included in the performance measurements, such as scope, schedule, and cost. The performance of the project is measured against this baseline. Some technical and quality parameters can also become part of this baseline.

◆ **qualitative risk analysis.** A process used to prioritize risks by estimating the probability of their occurrence and their impact on the project.

◆ **quality.** The degree to which a set of characteristics of project deliverables and objectives fulfills the project requirements.

◆ **quality baseline.** A criterion that specifies the quality objectives for the project and thereby makes the basis for measuring and reporting the quality performance.

◆ **quality management plan.** A management plan that describes how the project management team will implement the quality policy of the performing organization for the specific project.

◆ **quality metrics.** An operational criterion that defines in specific terms what something (such as a characteristic or a feature) is and how the quality control process measures it.

◆ **quality planning.** The process of identifying the quality standards relevant to the project at hand and determining how to satisfy these standards.

◆ **quality policy.** Overall intentions and high-level direction of an organization with respect to quality, established by management at the executive level.

- **quantitative risk analysis.** A process used to perform numerical analysis to estimate the effect of each identified risk on the overall project objectives and deliverables.

- **residual risk.** A risk that remains after the risk response has been performed.

- **risk.** An uncertain event or condition that, if it occurs, has a positive or negative effect on meeting the project objectives.

- **risk breakdown structure (RBS).** A hierarchical structure that breaks down the identified risk categories into subcategories. In developing this structure, you will end up identifying various areas and causes of potential risks.

- **risk identification.** A process used to identify the risks for a given project and record their characteristics in a document called the *risk register*.

- **risk management plan.** A document that describes how risk management will be structured and performed for the project at hand. It becomes part of the project management plan.

- **risk management planning.** A process used to determine how to approach, plan, and execute risk management activities for a given project. This process produces the risk management plan.

- **risk register.** A document that contains the results of risk analysis and risk response planning.

- **secondary risk.** A risk that arises as a result of implementing a risk response.

- **simulation.** Any analytical method used to imitate a real-life system.

- **strengths, weaknesses, opportunities, and threats (SWOT) analysis.** A technique used to gather information for risk identification by examining a given project from the perspectives of its strengths, weaknesses, opportunities, and threats.

Review Questions

1. Which of the following is a false statement about project risks?
    A. A risk arises out of uncertainty.
    B. A risk can only have a negative effect on a project.
    C. Identified risks are usually listed in a document called the *risk register*.
    D. Risks can be categorized by developing a risk breakdown structure (RBS).

2. The risk register is not an input to which of the following processes?
    A. Identify Risks
    B. Perform Qualitative Risk Analysis
    C. Perform Quantitative Risk Analysis
    D. Plan Risk Responses

3. Which of the following is not an information-gathering technique used in the risk identification process?

    A. Brainstorming

    B. Delphi technique

    C. SWOT analysis

    D. Web browsing

4. Which of the following statements about risk analysis is false?

    A. Quantitative risk analysis can only be performed on risks on which a qualitative risk analysis has already been performed.

    B. Qualitative risk analysis is usually performed before quantitative risk analysis.

    C. An updated risk register is the output of both qualitative risk analysis and quantitative risk analysis.

    D. The risk register is an input to both qualitative risk analysis and quantitative risk analysis.

5. You are managing a project to set up data servers to support a website for an enterprise customer. The location for the servers has been chosen close to the customer due to their requirements. However, this location is prone to natural disasters, such as hurricanes and flooding. You have decided to install some extra servers in another city that will act as backup if a disaster happens. This is an example of which of the following?

    A. Risk avoidance

    B. Risk mitigation

    C. Risk acceptance

    D. Risk transfer

6. The risk management team of a software project has decided that due to the lack of adequate talent in your company, development of a specific part of the system is under high risk, so they have decided to outsource it. This is an example of which of the following?

    A. Risk avoidance

    B. Risk mitigation

    C. Risk acceptance

    D. Risk transfer

7. You are in the process of evaluating the probability and impact of a risk by assigning numbers, such as expected monetary value. This is an example of which of the following?

    A. Monte Carlo simulation

    B. Qualitative risk analysis

    C. Quantitative risk analysis

    D. Risk response planning

8. Consider the following figure. Assume that the risk has a 50% probability of occurrence. If the risk does occur, it could have a positive or a negative impact equivalent to $200,000 or $50,000, respectively, with the probabilities shown in the figure. What is the EMV for the positive impact?

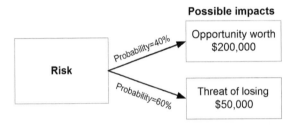

    A. $80,000

    B. $200,000

    C. $50,000

    D. $40,000

9. Consider the following figure. Assume that the risk has a 50% probability of occurrence. If the risk does occur, it could have a positive or a negative impact equivalent to $200,000 or $50,000, respectively, with the probabilities shown in the figure. What is the EMV for the risk?

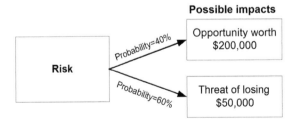

    A. $25,000

    B. $55,000

    C. $110,000

    D. $50,000

10. Which of the following is a correct statement about secondary risks?

    A. These are the residual risks.

    B. These are the risks that have medium or low priority.

    C. These are the risks that will be avoided.

    D. These are the risks that can result from responses to the identified risks.

11. Which of the following is not a valid risk response?

    A. Risk acceptance

    B. Risk sharing

    C. Risk mitigation

    D. Risk rejection

12. Which of the following is a valid statement about SWOT?

    A. It is an analysis technique to identify risks.

    B. It refers to the analysis of scope, work, options, and timing.

    C. It is a technique used to plan a risk response.

    D. It is a technique used to perform quantitative risk analysis.

13. Which of the following is not an output of the qualitative risk analysis?

    A. A prioritized list of risks for a given project objective based on the probability and impact matrix of the objective

    B. A watch list of low-priority risks

    C. A list of risks prioritized based on the total effect of each risk on the overall project objectives

    D. A list of trends in the analysis results

14. Which of the following is not an output of quantitative risk analysis?

    A. Probability of meeting the project objectives, such as cost and schedule

    B. A list of risks prioritized based on the total effect of each risk on the overall project objectives

    C. A list of trends in the analysis results

    D. Decision about a risk-related contractual agreement

15. What is the name of a quality planning technique that involves comparing the results of similar activities?

    A. Brainstorming

    B. Benchmarking

    C. Cost/benefit analysis

    D. Quality metrics

16. The plan-do-check-act cycle of quality management was:
    A. Defined by Shewhart and modified by Deming.
    B. Originally defined by Deming and then modified by Shewhart.
    C. Defined by Crosby and modified by Deming.
    D. Defined by Crosby and modified by Juan.

17. One of the fundamental tenets of modern quality management is:
    A. Inspect the quality and then build it in.
    B. There is no need to design and build in the quality until you do the inspection, if it's needed.
    C. Break all rules: Deliver the product in a timely fashion and then work on the quality.
    D. Plan, design, and build in quality as opposed to inspecting it in.

PART III

III

*Executing
the Project*

After the project is authorized through initiation and planning, it's time to begin the execution. You will be directing and managing the project execution throughout the lifecycle of the project. To perform the project work, you will also need to acquire, develop, and manage the project team. Furthermore, your organization might not have the resources to finish certain parts of the project work. You will need to conduct procurements for those parts of the work. In addition to producing deliverables, project execution will also include assuring quality, distributing information on project progress and issues, and managing stakeholder expectations.

Chapter 7

Managing Project Work

PMP Exam Objectives

Objective	What It Really Means
3.1 Execute Tasks Defined in the Project Plan	You must understand the big picture of project execution discussed in this chapter. You also must understand the Direct and Manage Project Execution process. You should know that the project is executed to implement the project management plan.
3.3 Implement the Procurement of Project Resources	You should know how to implement the procurement management plan. This includes understanding the Conduct Procurements process.
3.5 Implement a Quality Management Plan	You should know how to implement the quality management plan to ensure that the project work is being performed in conformance with the planned quality standards. This requires that you must understand the Perform Quality Assurance process.
3.6 Implement Approved Changes 3.7 Implement Approved Actions and Workarounds	You must understand that implementing approved changes, including approved recommendations for actions and preventions, is part of the project execution and must be managed by using the Direct and Manage Project Execution process. Also understand that these changes and recommendations originate from various sources, including processes in the monitoring and controlling process group.

Introduction

After a project has been planned using the processes in the planning process group, it needs to be executed using the processes in the executing process group. The project team determines which of the processes in the executing process group are relevant to the project at hand. The goal of the execution stage is to complete the project work specified in the project management plan to meet the project requirements. To accomplish that, you will need to acquire, develop, and manage the project team. Your organization might not have the resources to finish certain parts of this work. You will need to use procurement for those parts of the work. You also need to ensure that all the planned quality activities are performed. This is accomplished by using the quality assurance process.

Directing and managing project execution is the process of implementing the project management plan developed during project planning. The end product of this process is the project deliverables. This is a high-level umbrella process under which other execution processes are performed, such as assuring quality and conducting procurements. So the core question in this chapter is how to execute a project as planned. In search of an answer, you will explore three avenues—directing and managing project execution, assuring quality, and conducting procurements.

Executing a Project: Big Picture

The project work defined in the project management plan is executed by using the processes in the executing process group, shown in Figure 7.1. As I said earlier, it is up to the project team to determine which of these processes is relevant for the project at hand. The processes in this group are used to accomplish a three-pronged goal:

◆ Coordinate people and resources used to perform the project activities

◆ Integrate and manage the project activities being performed

◆ Ensure the implementation of the project scope and approved changes

The following list defines the processes shown in Figure 7.1.

◆ **Direct and manage project execution.** Manage various interfaces in the project execution to complete the project work smoothly in order to produce the project outcome, such as deliverables and objectives.

◆ **Acquire project team.** Obtain the project team members needed to perform the project work.

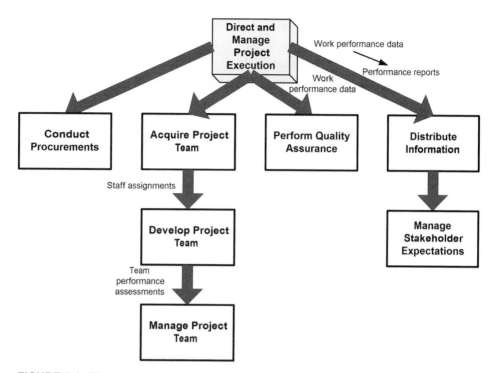

FIGURE 7.1 *The processes used in executing a project. All of these processes (except the Manage Project Team process) belong to the executing process group.*

- ◆ **Develop project team.** Improve the competencies of team members and interaction among team members to enhance project performance.

- ◆ **Manage project team.** Manage the project team, which includes tracking the performance of team members, providing feedback, resolving issues, and managing changes to improve project performance.

- ◆ **Perform quality assurance.** Audit the results from the quality control measurements to ensure that the quality requirements are being met.

- ◆ **Distribute information.** Make the relevant information about the project, such as project progress, available to the stakeholders according to the communication management plan.

- ◆ **Conduct procurements.** Obtain responses from potential sellers in terms of quotes, bids, offers, and proposals for their product or services needed for the project; select sellers; and negotiate written contracts with the selected sellers.

- ◆ **Manage stakeholder expectations.** Stay on the same page with the stakeholders by communicating and working with them on their needs and issues.

> **NOTE**
>
> A project is usually started with a project kickoff meeting that can also be used as the beginning of team development. The kickoff meeting is discussed in Chapter 8, "Developing and Managing the Project Team."

STUDY CHECKPOINT 7.1

List the processes of the executing process group.

In this chapter, we will cover the Direct and Manage Project Execution, Perform Quality Assurance, and Conduct Procurements processes. Once project execution starts, it needs to be managed, which is accomplished by using the Direct and Manage Project Execution process.

Directing and Managing Project Execution

The project work defined in the project management plan is performed using the Direct and Manage Project Execution process. While executing this process, you will be interacting with other processes and departments in your organization. In general, a project team includes people from different departments. Usually the reporting relationships within the same department are very well defined and structured. However, the relationships between different departments (especially between individuals from different departments at the same level of authority) are not well defined. So, managing such project interfaces is a crucial function of a project manager during project execution. Generally speaking, project interfaces are the formal and informal boundaries and relationships among team members, departments, organizations, or functions—for example, how the development department and the QA department interact with each other while working on the same project. Directing and managing project execution is the process used to manage various technical and organizational interfaces in the project to facilitate smooth execution of the project work.

The main purposes of directing and managing project execution are:

◆ Producing the project deliverables by executing the project management plan
◆ Implementing the approved changes, defect repairs, and other actions
◆ Implementing the planned methods, processes, and standards
◆ Producing and distributing status information

The key words during execution are *implement*, *manage*, and *inform* (status). Figure 7.2 illustrates the Direct and Manage Project Execution process with its input, tools and techniques, and output.

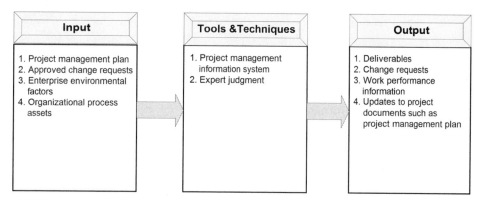

Input	Tools &Techniques	Output
1. Project management plan 2. Approved change requests 3. Enterprise environmental factors 4. Organizational process assets	1. Project management information system 2. Expert judgment	1. Deliverables 2. Change requests 3. Work performance information 4. Updates to project documents such as project management plan

FIGURE 7.2 *The Direct and Manage Project Execution process: input, tools and techniques, and output.*

Input to Directing and Managing Project Execution

The input to directing and managing project execution mainly consists of the items that need to be implemented. The information on the project work that needs to be performed to produce project deliverables is the major input to this process. The specific input items are discussed in the following list.

Project management plan. Directing and managing project execution is all about implementing the project management plan, which contains all the major subsidiary plans, such as the scope baseline, the schedule baseline, the cost baseline, and the quality baseline. It also describes how the work will be executed to meet the project objectives and produce deliverables that satisfy the planned requirements.

Approved change requests. The following approved change-related items are input to the project execution because they must be implemented.

   ◆ **Change requests.** The approved requests for changes to the project schedule, scope, cost, policies, procedures, and project management plan need to be implemented and therefore are the input to the execution process. These change requests are scheduled for execution by the project management team.

   ◆ **Defect repairs.** This is the list of defects found during the quality assurance (QA) process that have been approved for repairs. This may also include the defects that were repaired, but the repair was not good enough to be accepted.

- ◆ **Corrective actions.** The QA process can recommend corrective actions to improve quality, which are directions for executing the project work to bring expected project performance into conformance with the project management plan. The approved corrective actions must be scheduled for implementation.

- ◆ **Preventive actions.** These are directions to perform an activity that will reduce the probability of negative consequences associated with project risks. These preventive actions are recommended by the QA process during process analysis.

Enterprise environmental factors. Items in this category that can be useful or need to be considered in directing and managing project execution include organizational structure and culture; company infrastructure, such as facilities and equipment; personnel administration, such as hiring and firing guidelines; and project management information systems. Stakeholder risk tolerance is also an important input factor to directing and managing project execution.

Organizational process assets. Items in this category that can be useful or need to be considered in directing and managing project execution include standardized work guidelines, workplace security requirements, project files from previous projects, and the issue and defect management database. For example, the defect management database may contain a list of validated defect repairs with information on whether a previously performed defect repair has been accepted or rejected. This will tell you whether you need to implement the defect repair again. Communication requirements and process measurement database are also important input to directing and managing project execution.

STUDY CHECKPOINT 7.2

True or False: Approved change requests are processed through the Perform Integrated Change Control process.

In a nutshell, the project management plan and approved change requests are the major input to directing and managing project execution because executing the project is all about implementing the project management plan along with the approved change requests. You direct and manage the execution by using some tools, which will be discussed in the next section.

Tools and Techniques for Directing and Managing Project Execution

The major tool to direct and manage project execution is the project management information system, which is a collection of tools and techniques—manual and automated—used to gather, integrate, and disseminate the output of project management processes. This may include automated scheduling tools; a configuration management system; an information entry, storage, and distribution system; and interfaces to other online systems. This system is used to facilitate processes from the initiation stage all the way to the closing stage. Microsoft Project, a product that lets you create a project schedule, is an example of such a tool.

Another tool used in directing and managing project execution is expert judgment, which, depending on the issue and the available resources, can be provided by the project manager, other individuals from other departments and groups within the organization, consultants, stakeholders, or professional associations.

The project is executed to produce some results, which will be the output of directing and managing the execution.

Output of Directing and Managing Project Execution

When the project is being executed, at each point in time there are some deliverables with parts thereof completed, and there is a status for the project that can be reported to the stakeholders. These two important output items, along with others, are discussed in the following paragraphs.

Deliverables. A deliverable is a unique and identifiable product, service, or result identified in the project management plan that must be generated to complete the project. The core purpose of executing the project management plan is to produce deliverables.

When you are directing and managing project execution, obviously the items are being implemented. In addition to the work that produces original deliverables, the following items are implemented during project execution:

- Approved change requests
- Approved corrective actions recommended by the QA process
- Approved preventive actions recommended by the QA process
- Approved defect repairs recommended by the QA process

Change requests. During the execution of the project work, requests for changes may arise from sources such as issues and may affect certain aspects of the project, such as the following:

- Project scope
- Project cost
- Project schedule
- Policies or procedures

These change requests might come from inside or outside the performing organization and can be optional or mandated legally or contractually. These change requests must be approved before they can be processed and implemented. These change requests can include the following types:

- **Direct change requests.** These are changes that are not a result of any other action, such as defect repair. Examples are requests for changes to scope, schedule, and cost. Of course, these changes can also result from other change requests, listed below.

♦ **Indirect change requests.** These include:

♦ **Defect repairs.** This is the list of the defects found during the quality assurance (QA) process that have been approved for repairs.

♦ **Corrective actions.** The QA process can recommend corrective actions to improve quality, which are directions for executing the project work to bring expected project performance into conformance with the project management plan. The approved corrective actions must be scheduled for implementation.

♦ **Preventive actions.** These are directions to perform an activity that will reduce the probability of negative consequences associated with project risks. These preventive actions are recommended by the QA process during process analysis.

After some change requests are approved, you may need to change some elements of the project management plan, such as the project baseline, human resource management plan, requirements management plan, or communication management plan.

Work performance information. Monitoring the project status is one of the crucial functions of a project manager during project execution. Work performance information is basically the project status information that is regularly collected and distributed among the stakeholders during project execution. It includes the following items:

♦ The schedule progress information:

♦ Schedule activities that have been finished and those that have started

♦ Estimate to complete the schedule activities that have started and hence are in progress

♦ The portion of each in-progress activity completed in a percentage—for example, Activity A is 30% complete

♦ Deliverables that have been completed and those that have not yet been completed

♦ Incurred costs compared to authorized costs

♦ Resource utilization details

♦ How well the quality standards are being met

♦ Lessons learned and added to the knowledge base

In a nutshell, the main output of directing and managing project execution is the project deliverables specified in the project management plan and the performance data as the work progresses. Between planning the project and producing the deliverables, many things need to happen, and you need to manage them by:

♦ Distributing information

♦ Managing stakeholder expectations

♦ Acquiring, developing, and managing the project team

♦ Performing quality assurance

♦ Conducting procurements

Therefore, the Direct and Manage Project Execution process is a high-level umbrella process, and to execute it you need to perform some other processes too, which are discussed in this and the next chapters. To start with, assuring quality is an integral part of managing project execution.

In addition to performing the project work to produce the project deliverables, a significant task to perform during project execution is quality assurance, an essential component of project work.

Performing Quality Assurance

Quality planning, discussed in Chapter 6, is used to identify which quality standards are relevant to the project at hand and to determine how to meet these standards. Implementing quality management consists of the following two components:

- ◆ **Quality assurance (QA).** Quality assurance is the process of auditing the results from quality control measurements to ensure that the quality requirements are being met. This process is used during the execution of the project, and I discuss it in this section.

- ◆ **Quality control.** This refers to monitoring and controlling the project results to ensure they meet the agreed-upon quality standards. This topic is covered in an upcoming chapter.

Performing organizations typically have a department called quality assurance (QA) that oversees the quality assurance activities and fosters continuous process improvement, which is an iterative method for improving the quality of all processes.

TIP

Continuous process improvement enhances the efficiency and effectiveness of the processes by minimizing waste (unnecessary activities) and duplication of efforts. It includes identifying and reviewing the business processes inside the organization, such as coding of modules within software programs and the process of project approval.

Figure 7.3 depicts the Perform Quality Assurance process.

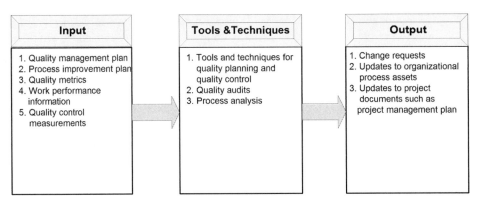

Input	Tools &Techniques	Output
1. Quality management plan 2. Process improvement plan 3. Quality metrics 4. Work performance information 5. Quality control measurements	1. Tools and techniques for quality planning and quality control 2. Quality audits 3. Process analysis	1. Change requests 2. Updates to organizational process assets 3. Updates to project documents such as project management plan

FIGURE 7.3 *The Perform Quality Assurance process: input, tools and techniques, and output.*

Input to Performing Quality Assurance

The input to the quality assurance process comes largely from three sources: quality planning, directing and managing project execution, and quality control. The quality-related output items of these three processes become the input to the quality assurance process. These input items are discussed here.

Output from quality planning. The following output items from the quality planning process become the input to the quality assurance process:

◆ **Quality management plan.** This plan is the output of the quality planning process discussed in Chapter 6, and it describes how QA will be performed for this project.

◆ **Quality metrics.** A quality metric is an operational criterion that defines in specific terms what something (such as a characteristic or a feature) is and how the quality control process measures it. The quality metrics developed during quality planning, such as defect density, failure rates, reliability, and test coverage, must be employed during QA.

◆ **Process improvement plan.** The process improvement plan, discussed in Chapter 6, helps improve the quality of the project and must be implemented during QA.

Output from directing and managing project execution: work performance information. When you are directing and managing project execution, information about work performance and the implementation of a few items will help you determine how the quality is being implemented. Therefore, during QA, you must consider work performance information. Work performance information includes project status information that is regularly collected and distributed among the stakeholders. It includes the following items:

◆ Schedule progress information:

  ◆ Schedule activities that have been finished and those that have started

  ◆ Estimates for the completion of schedule activities that have started and hence are in progress

- Percentages to show the portion of each in-progress activity—for example, Activity A is 30% complete
- Deliverables that have been completed and those that have not yet been completed
- Incurred cost as compared to authorized cost
- Resource utilization details
- How well the quality standards are being met
- Lessons learned added to the knowledge base

When you are directing and managing project execution, obviously the items are being implemented. The following quality-related implemented items must be considered during QA:

- Implemented change requests
- Implemented corrective actions
- Implemented defect repair
- Implemented preventive actions

Output from quality control: quality control measurements. Quality control involves monitoring specific project results to verify whether they meet quality standards. The quality control process sends its results back to QA as feedback.

Approved change requests. Approved change requests, such as modification of work methods, product requirements, quality requirements, scope, and schedule, must be analyzed for their effect on the quality management plan and quality metrics.

TIP

All approved changes should be formally documented. Unapproved and undocumented changes (for example, changes just verbally discussed) must neither be processed nor be implemented.

Some tools and techniques can be used to facilitate the QA process.

Tools and Techniques for Performing Quality Assurance

Quality audits and process analysis, along with the tools and techniques used in quality planning and quality control processes, can be used in the QA process.

Quality audits. A quality audit is a structured and independent review to determine whether project activities comply with the policies, processes, and procedures of the project and the performing organization. It verifies the implementation of approved change requests, corrective actions, defect repairs, and preventive actions. Audits can occur as scheduled or at random and can be conducted by a third party or by properly trained in-house auditors of the performing organization. The main objectives of quality audits are the following:

◆ Identify all good practices

◆ Identify shortcomings and gaps in implementing what was planned

◆ Offer assistance for improvement and share knowledge gathered from the implementation of good practices at similar projects

◆ Record contributions from each audit in the lessons learned database of the project

These audits accomplish the following:

◆ Because one of the objectives of a quality audit is to identify inefficient and ineffective policies, processes, and procedures being used for the project, audits reduce the cost of quality on subsequent projects.

◆ Audits increase customer satisfaction and acceptance of the product or service delivered by the project.

Process analysis. This is a technique used to identify the needed improvements in a process by following the steps outlined in the process improvement plan. It examines the problems, constraints, and unnecessary (non-value-added) activities identified during the implementation of the process. Process analysis typically includes the following steps:

1. Identify a technique to analyze the problem.
2. Identify the underlying causes that led to the problem.
3. Examine the root cause of the problem.
4. Create preventive actions for this and similar problems.

Other tools and techniques. The tools and techniques used in the following processes can also be used in the QA process:

◆ Quality planning, already discussed in Chapter 6

◆ Quality control, discussed in an upcoming chapter

The quality assurance process recommends corrective actions as an output item.

Output of Performing Quality Assurance

The main output of performing quality assurance includes recommended corrective actions and change requests. These and other output items are discussed in the following list.

Change requests. The goal of quality assurance is improving quality, which involves taking actions to increase the effectiveness and efficiency of the policies, procedures, and processes of the performing organization. One way of accomplishing this is to implement the quality-related changes recommended and approved during the process of directing and managing the project execution, including:

◆ Modifications to policies and procedures.

◆ Modifications to project scope, cost, and schedule.

◆ Recommended corrective actions. Implementation of recommended corrective actions will increase the effectiveness and efficiency of the policies, processes, and procedures of the performing organization and will also improve the quality of the product or service delivered by the project. Following are examples of the types of recommended actions:

   ◆ Audits

   ◆ Process analysis that itself might produce a list of preventive actions

   ◆ Defect repair, such as bug fixes in a software program

Updates. As a result of the QA process, you might need to add updates to the following:

◆ **Organizational process assets.** The quality standards, policies, procedures, and processes of the performing organization are the organizational assets that can be updated during the QA process.

◆ **Project management plan.** The quality assurance process can result in updates to the project management plan in the following ways:

   ◆ Changes to the quality management plan, which is a part of the project management plan.

   ◆ Quality audits may cause changes to the schedule management plan and cost management plan.

◆ **Other documents.** Other project documents that may be modified as a result of QA include process documentation, quality audit reports, and training plans.

STUDY CHECKPOINT 7.3

True or False: Quality assurance also uses the tools and techniques of quality planning and quality control.

In some projects you might not find the resources in your organization to complete certain parts of the project. This is where the concept called *procurement* comes into the picture.

Conducting Procurements

As you learned in Chapter 5, procurement refers to obtaining (purchasing or renting) products, services, or results from outside the project team to complete the project. Procurement management is an execution of a set of processes used to obtain (procure) products, services, or results from outside the project team to complete the project. Procurement planning was discussed in Chapter 5, and implementation of this plan, conducting procurement, is discussed in this section. Figure 7.4 illustrates the process used to conduct procurements.

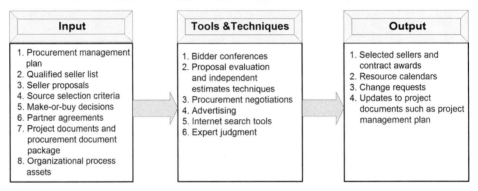

Input	Tools &Techniques	Output
1. Procurement management plan 2. Qualified seller list 3. Seller proposals 4. Source selection criteria 5. Make-or-buy decisions 6. Partner agreements 7. Project documents and procurement document package 8. Organizational process assets	1. Bidder conferences 2. Proposal evaluation and independent estimates techniques 3. Procurement negotiations 4. Advertising 5. Internet search tools 6. Expert judgment	1. Selected sellers and contract awards 2. Resource calendars 3. Change requests 4. Updates to project documents such as project management plan

FIGURE 7.4 *The Conduct Procurements process: input, tools and techniques, and output.*

Input to Conducting Procurements

The input items to conducting procurements include the procurement management plan, procurement documents, and procurement-related organizational process assets. These input items are discussed in the following list.

Procurement management plan. The major input to conducting procurements is the procurement management plan developed during procurement planning. The procurement management plan may have the following items of interest:

◆ Prequalified selected sellers

◆ Procurement metrics to be used to manage contracts and evaluate sellers

◆ Types of contracts to be used and the format for the contract statement of work

◆ Assumptions and constraints that could affect planned purchases and acquisitions

◆ Scheduled dates for contract deliverables

◆ Directions to be provided to the seller on developing and maintaining a contract work breakdown structure

Procurement documents package. This is the set of procurement documents put together during procurement planning. The buyer structures these documents with two goals in mind:

◆ To facilitate an accurate and complete response from each prospective seller

◆ To facilitate easy evaluation of the responses

These documents include the following:

◆ A description of the desired form of the response

◆ A relevant contract statement of work

◆ Any required contractual provisions, such as a copy of a model contract, and non-disclosure provisions

TIP

In government contracting, some or all of the content and structure of a procurement document might already be defined by regulations.

Different terms are used for these documents for different purposes:

◆ A term such as *bid*, *tender*, or *quotation* is used when the seller selection decision will be based on the price, when buying commercial or standard items.

◆ A term such as *proposal* is used when multiple factors are considered, such as cost, technical skills, and technical approach.

◆ Common names for these different kinds of documents include *invitation for bid*, *request for quotation*, *tender notice*, *request for proposal*, and *contractor initial response*.

The procurement documents should be rigorous enough to ensure consistent responses from different sellers that can be fairly compared to one another and flexible enough to allow sellers to offer suggestions on better ways to satisfy the requirements. How are the requests sent to the potential sellers? This is done according to the policies of the buyer's organization—for example, publication of the request in the public media, such as newspapers, magazines, and the Internet.

NOTE

Bids and quotations are typically used to ask for prices, whereas proposals are used to ask for solutions. Invitations for bid, requests for quotation, and requests for proposal travel from buyer to seller, whereas bids, quotations, and proposals travel from seller to buyer.

Source selection criteria. Also called *evaluation criteria*, this is developed by the buyer during procurement planning to rate responses from the sellers. The evaluation criteria could be as simple as the price for off-the-shelf standard items, or it could be a combination of factors for a more complex proposal. Following is a list of some examples of evaluation criteria.

◆ **Cost.** To evaluate the overall cost, you should consider all cost-related factors, such as:
   ◆ Purchase price
   ◆ Delivery cost
   ◆ Operating cost
◆ **Business aspects.** This can include the following factors:
   ◆ **Business size and type.** Does the business size or type meet a condition set forth in the contract, such as being a small business or a disadvantaged small business?
   ◆ **Financial capacity.** Does the seller have the financial capacity to do the job, or is the seller in a position to obtain the necessary financial resources to do the job?
   ◆ **Production capacity and interest.** Does the seller have the capacity and the interest to meet future potential requirements?
   ◆ **References.** Can the seller provide reliable references (such as from previous customers) verifying the seller's work experience and history of compliance with contractual requirements?
◆ **Management approach.** If the procurement itself involves a project, does the seller have the ability to execute management processes and procedures to run a successful project?
◆ **Rights.** The following rights can be considered:
   ◆ **Intellectual property rights.** Will the seller own the intellectual property rights for the work processes or services that will be used to produce the deliverables?
   ◆ **Proprietary rights.** Will the seller have the proprietary rights for the work processes or services that will be used to produce the deliverables?
◆ **Technical aspects.** This includes the technical approach and capability:
   ◆ **Technical approach.** Will the technical methodologies, techniques, solutions, or services proposed by the seller meet the procurement requirements, or will they provide more than the expected results?
   ◆ **Technical capability.** Does the seller have or is the seller capable of acquiring the technical skills and knowledge required to produce the deliverables?

Partner agreements. You might be considering some sellers that already have some contracts or agreements signed with your organization. These agreements, also called *teaming agreements*, must also be honored while conducting procurements.

Organizational process assets. The organizational process assets relevant to requesting seller responses include the following:

◆ A preexisting list of prospective sellers

◆ A list of previously used or qualified sellers

◆ Information about past experiences with previously used sellers

◆ Organizational policies that could affect evaluating the responses and selecting the sellers.

Make-or-buy decisions made during procurement planning should also be considered during this process of conducting procurements. This topic was discussed in Chapter 5.

Tools and Techniques for Conducting Procurements

The first goal for the tools and techniques here is to find sellers and provide them with information about the requests for responses. The list of potential sellers can be developed from various sources, such as the World Wide Web, library directories, relevant local associations, trade catalogs, and the performing organization's internal information base. The main techniques used in soliciting seller responses are advertising and bidder conferences. These and other techniques used in conducting procurements are discussed in the following list.

Bidder conferences. This refers to meetings with prospective sellers prior to preparation of a response to ensure that the sellers have a clear understanding of the procurement, such as the technical and contractual requirements. These meetings can generate amendments to the documents. All potential sellers should be given the same amount of information (or help) during this interaction so that each seller has an equal opportunity to produce the best response. These conferences are also called *contractor conferences*, *vendor conferences*, or *pre-bid conferences*.

 NOTE

In some cases, after a proposal is submitted, the buyer can request that the seller supplement its proposal with an oral presentation to provide some additional information, which can be used to evaluate the seller's proposal.

Proposal evaluation techniques. Different techniques can be used to evaluate responses from sellers. All these techniques can use expert judgment and evaluation criteria. The common factors that can be considered in the evaluation include the following:

◆ **Price.** This can play a primary role in the selection of off-the-shelf standard items. However, you should consider that the lower price does not mean lower cost if the seller does not deliver on time.

◆ **Multiple aspects.** Proposals are usually evaluated for different aspects, such as technical and commercial. Technical refers to the overall approach, whereas commercial refers to the cost.

◆ **Multiple sources.** For products critical to the project, multiple sources (sellers) might be required. This redundancy will help mitigate such risks as failure to meet the delivery schedule or quality requirements.

Some techniques used to make the final selection of sellers are discussed in the following list:

◆ **Independent estimates.** The purpose of independent estimates is to have a check on the proposed pricing by the seller. The procuring organization prepares the independent estimate in house or has it done by a third party. Significant differences between the proposed price and the independent estimate mean that either the market has changed or the seller has failed to offer reasonable pricing due to such reasons as failure to understand the contract statement of work. The independent estimates are also called *should-cost estimates*.

◆ **Seller rating system.** A seller's rating does not depend on a specific response that you are evaluating. Rather, the seller's rating comes from the seller's rating system, which is developed by multiple organizations based on multiple factors related to seller's past performance, such as delivery performance, contractual compliance, and quality rating.

◆ **Weighting system.** The purpose of putting a weighting system in place is to have an objective evaluation as opposed to a subjective evaluation influenced by personal prejudice. The weighting system uses a method to quantify the qualitative data and typically involves the following steps:

1. Assign a numerical weight to each of the evaluation criteria according to its importance, such as w1, w2, and w3 for three criteria, and make these weights the same for each seller.

2. Rate the seller on each criterion, such as r1, r2, and r3. These ratings depend upon the seller.

3. Multiply the weight by the rate for each criterion.

4. Add the results in the previous step to compute an overall score, such as s1 for seller 1: $s1 = r1 \times w1 + r2 \times w2 + r3 \times w3$.

◆ **Expert judgment.** Expert judgment is made by a committee that consists of experts from each of the disciplines covered by the procurement documents and the proposed contract. The committee can include experts from functional disciplines, such as accounting, contracts, engineering, finance, legal, manufacturing, and research and development.

TIP

Sellers in procurement are also sometimes called *sources*.

Screening system. A screening system consists of minimum requirements as a threshold that must be met if the seller is to stay in the list of candidate sellers. It might, for example, consist of one or more evaluation criteria. The screening system can also use the weighting system and independent estimates.

Procurement negotiations. Procurement negotiations, also called the *contract negotiations*, have the following two-pronged goal:

♦ Clarify the structure and requirements of the contract

♦ Reach an agreement

Subjects covered during the negotiations might include the following:

♦ Applicable terms and laws

♦ Authorities, rights, and responsibilities

♦ Business management and technical approaches

♦ Contract financing

♦ Payments and price

♦ Proprietary rights

♦ Schedule

♦ Technical solutions

The conclusion of contract negotiations is a document, the contract, which can be signed by both the buyer and the seller. The final contract signed by both parties can be an offer by the seller or a counteroffer by the buyer. Sometimes for simple procurement items, the contract is nonnegotiable.

TIP

A contract is a mutually binding legal relationship subject to remedy in court. The project manager might not be the lead negotiator on the contract. However, the project manager might be required to be present during negotiations to provide any necessary clarification on the project requirements.

Advertising. The request for seller responses can be advertised in the public media or in relevant professional journals. Whether to use advertising depends on the organization's policy. However, some government jurisdictions require public advertising of pending government contracts.

Internet search and expert judgment are other tools that can also be used during conducting procurements.

Output of Conducting Procurements

The output of conducting procurements includes the list of selected sellers and the contract awards for the selected sellers. These and other output items are discussed in the following paragraphs.

Selected sellers. This is the list of sellers that you have selected as a result of response evaluations.

Procurement awards. These are the contracts awarded to selected sellers. A contract is a legal document that obligates the seller to provide the specified products, services, or results and obligates the buyer to make the payment to the seller. The contract can be a simple purchase order or a complex document, depending on the nature of the procurement. A contract can include, but is not limited to, the following sections:

◆ List of deliverables and statement of work
◆ Schedule
◆ Acceptance criteria
◆ Change-request handling
◆ Inflation adjustments
◆ Insurance
◆ Limitation of liability
◆ Penalties and incentives
◆ Pricing and payment
◆ Product support
◆ Roles and responsibilities
◆ Termination and dispute-handling mechanism
◆ Warranty

Resource calendars. This contains information on the quantity and availability of the contracted (procured) resources—for example, the dates on which a resource will be active or idle.

Changes and updates. Conducting procurements can generate changes and updates such as the following:

◆ **Change requests.** The selection process can generate change requests for the project management plan and its subsidiary plans and components, such as the project schedule and the procurement management plan. These change requests must be processed through the integrated change control system before implementation.

◆ **Updates to the procurement management plan.** If a procurement-related change request is approved, the procurement management plan should be updated to reflect the change. This may include the scope baseline, schedule baseline, cost baseline, and procurement management plan. These changes or updates arise from the fact that procurement and the rest of the project are related to each other. For example, a change in the procurement fulfillment date will affect the schedule that depends on that fulfillment.

STUDY CHECKPOINT 7.4

What is the main goal of the Conduct Procurements process?

The three most important takeaways from this chapter are as follows:

◆ The Direct and Manage Project Execution process is a high-level process to produce project deliverables. To accomplish this, you need to do two things:

1. Acquire the project team, develop it, and manage it to perform the project activities.

2. Procure the items that cannot be produced by the project team.

◆ Use the Perform Quality Assurance process to ensure that the project employs all the planned processes and standards needed to meet all the project quality requirements.

◆ The procurement plan is implemented by using the Conduct Procurements process, which involves requesting seller responses, evaluating seller responses, selecting sellers based on the evaluation, and negotiating and signing contracts with the selected sellers.

Summary

The project management plan is executed using the processes in the executing process group. The high-level umbrella process in this group is the Direct and Manage Project Execution process, whose main goal is to produce the project deliverables. A significant task to perform during project execution is quality assurance, which involves auditing the results from quality control measurements to ensure that quality requirements are being met. Due to a lack of resources in the performing organization, you might need to obtain some products, services, or results from outside the project team to complete the project. This is called *procurement*. The Conduct Procurements process is used to implement the procurement plan, which involves obtaining seller responses, selecting sellers based on the responses, and reaching an agreement with the selected sellers, such as a contract to obtain (procure) the products, services, or results.

To perform the project work, you need to put together a project team and develop and manage the team to obtain optimal results for the success of the project. This is the topic of the next chapter.

Exam's Eye View

Comprehend

◆ Executing the project means implementing the project management plan developed during project planning.

◆ Directing and managing project execution involves managing various technical and organizational interfaces in the project to facilitate smooth execution of the project work.

◆ The execution of a project is managed by performing the process called Direct and Manage Project Execution, a high-level umbrella process for the executing stage, which generates the project deliverables.

◆ Quality assurance, an important task during project execution, is the process of auditing the results from quality control measurements to ensure that the quality requirements are being met.

◆ Conducting procurement is the process of obtaining responses from potential sellers, selecting sellers based on those responses, and awarding contracts to the selected sellers.

Look Out

◆ The two major output items of the Direct and Manage Project Execution process are project deliverables and work performance information or data.

◆ Quality audits are a tool used in quality assurance.

◆ Tools and techniques used in quality planning and quality control are also used in quality assurance.

◆ Invitations for bid, requests for quotation, and requests for proposal travel from buyer to seller, whereas bids, quotations, and proposals travel from seller to buyer.

Memorize

◆ The project management plan is the major input to the Direct and Manage Project Execution process.

◆ The input to the quality assurance (QA) process comes from the output of three processes: quality planning, quality control, and direct and manage project execution.

◆ In procurement, a term such as *bid*, *tender*, or *quotation* is used when the seller selection decision will be based on the price when buying commercial or standard items, whereas a term such as *proposal* is used when multiple factors are considered, such as cost, technical skills, and technical approach.

◆ Bids and quotations are typically used to ask for prices, whereas proposals are used to ask for solutions.

Key Terms and Definitions

◆ **corrective actions.** Directions for executing the project work to bring expected project performance in conformance with the project management plan. This is an output item of the QA process.

◆ **perform quality assurance.** A process used for ensuring that quality requirements are met.

◆ **preventive actions.** Directions to perform an activity that will reduce the probability of negative consequences associated with project risks. These preventive actions are recommended by the QA process during process analysis.

◆ **process analysis.** A technique used to identify the needed improvements in a process by following the steps outlined in the process improvement plan.

◆ **process improvement**. An iterative method for improving the quality of all processes.

◆ **procurement.** Refers to obtaining (purchasing or renting) products, services, or results from outside the project team to complete the project.

◆ **procurement management.** An execution of a set of processes used to obtain products, services, or results from outside the project team to complete the project.

◆ **project interfaces.** The formal and informal boundaries and relationships among team members, departments, organizations, or functions. An example might be how the development department and the QA department interact with each other while working on the same project.

◆ **quality.** The degree to which the set of characteristics inherent to the product or services offered by the project meet the project requirements.

◆ **quality audit.** A structured and independent review to determine whether project activities comply with the policies, processes, and procedures of the project and the performing organization. It verifies the implementation of approved change requests, corrective actions, defect repairs, and preventive actions.

Review Questions

1. Which of the following is not the output of directing and managing project execution?
    A. Deliverables
    B. Implemented defect repairs
    C. Work performance information
    D. Recommended corrective actions

2. Which of the following is not the input to the QA process?
    A. Quality metrics
    B. Quality control measurements
    C. Work performance information
    D. Recommended corrective actions

3. The analysis to make a buy-or-make decision is performed during which of the following stages of procurement?
    A. Conduct procurements
    B. Select sellers
    C. Plan procurements
    D. Estimate costs

4. Your company is outsourcing a part of your project and therefore is preparing the procurement documents. Which of the following is true about the procurement documents?
    A. The documents should have a rigidly fixed format so there are no variations in the responses from different sellers.
    B. The documents should be completely open-ended so each seller has complete freedom to suggest requirements and present their solutions.
    C. The documents should follow the standards required by sellers.
    D. The documents should be flexible enough to allow sellers to be creative in offering solutions for meeting the requirements.

5. Your organization is playing the seller role in doing a part of the project for another company, the buyer. The buyer has incomplete specifications for the work involved and wants you to start the work after signing the agreement. Which of the following contract types will be the most beneficial for your organization?
    A. Fixed-price
    B. Time and material
    C. Cost plus percentage of cost
    D. Cost plus time

6. You are the project manager for the ABC project. You are going to meet with your project team to discuss how to ensure that the project will be completed without any deviations from the project requirements. Which of the following processes are you performing?

    A. Quality control

    B. Quality planning

    C. Quality assurance

    D. Conduct procurements

7. Quality audits are part of which of the following quality management processes?

    A. Quality assurance

    B. Quality control

    C. Quality planning

    D. Quality inspection

8. You are directing and managing the execution of your project. Which of the following is the correct order of executing the processes when you are executing them for the first time during this project?

    A. Quality planning, quality assurance, quality control

    B. Quality planning, quality control, quality assurance

    C. Quality assurance, quality planning, quality control

    D. Quality control, quality assurance, quality planning

9. You are directing and managing the project execution. You see that there are some change requests that some stakeholders are pushing for implementation. However, these change requests have no record of being approved. These change requests:

    A. Should be sent through the approval process and only implemented if approved

    B. Should be sent to the QA department

    C. Must be opposed if they are going to change the scope, schedule, or cost of the project

    D. Should be accepted if they come from an influential stakeholder

10. You are the project manager of the Green Driving project. Your supervisor has asked you to make some self checks and inspections before the stakeholders ask for a formal inspection. It is time to perform which process?

    A. Plan Quality

    B. Perform Quality Control

    C. Inspect Quality

    D. Perform Quality Assurance

Chapter 8

Developing and Managing the Project Team

PMP Exam Objectives

Objective	*What It Really Means*
2.2 Identify Project Team and Define Roles and Responsibilities	You should know how to identify and obtain the right team members who can perform the roles and responsibilities determined during planning. You must understand the Acquire Project Team process.
2.7 Conduct Kickoff Meeting	Understand the importance of a kickoff meeting to start a project. Understand that the main purpose of the kickoff meeting is to bring every team member onto the same page regarding the big picture of the project. You also must understand the project charter, the project plan, and the organizational structure to run a successful kickoff meeting.
3.2 Ensure Common Understanding and Set Expectations	You must understand that during the process of directing and managing project execution, you need to manage the expectations of the stakeholders, and you need to ensure what your expectations of the project team members are. You must understand the Manage Project Team process. Managing stakeholders' expectations is covered in Chapter 9.
3.8 Improve Team Performance	You need to understand how to improve team performance by using tools and techniques such as ground rules, training, and recognition and rewards. You must know the Develop Project Team process.

Introduction

Executing a project requires resources, and executing a project successfully requires the optimal use of resources. Thereby, coordinating and managing resources, including human resources, is an integral part of project execution. During project planning, you define roles and assign responsibilities to those roles. Individuals who play these roles perform the responsibilities of the roles to execute the project work. The process of obtaining the individuals to fill these roles and therefore become the members of the project team is called *acquiring the project team*. A team is a group of individuals who perform individual responsibilities to work interdependently on their independent assignments. From a scientific viewpoint, a team is a dynamic entity, and its dynamics are determined by the interaction among its members. Therefore, for the team to be successful, it has to be effective in both dimensions: Its members must be competent in performing their individual assignments, and the interaction among them must be overall constructive. To ensure that, you need to continually develop and manage the project team. To obtain the right individuals for the project team and to develop and manage the team is an art, whereas the effective team taking the project to success is a science that will unfold itself automatically if you do the art part right.

So the core question in this chapter is how to build and manage a high-performance project team. In search of an answer, we will explore three avenues—acquiring project team members, developing the project team, and managing the project team.

Human Resource Management: Big Picture

As shown in Figure 8.1, human resource management as part of project management means developing the human resource plan, acquiring the project team, developing the project team, and managing the project team.

- ◆ **Acquire Project Team**. This is the process of filling the roles determined during human resource planning with actual staff assignments.
- ◆ **Develop Project Team.** This is the process of developing an optimal team by improving the individual competencies, improving the interaction among the individual team members, and thereby improving the team environment.
- ◆ **Manage Project Team**. This is the process of tracking performance of and providing feedback to the individual team members, managing changes related to the team, and resolving issues.

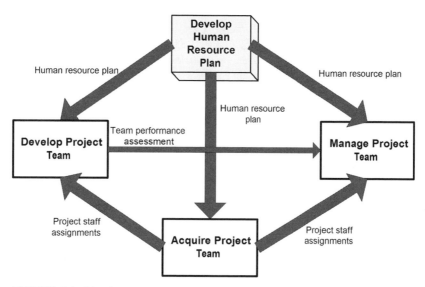

FIGURE 8.1 *Big picture of human resource management.*

The project team has two dimensions: independence and interdependence. Each member has an independent assignment in the sense that the member owns that part of the work, is responsible for completing it, and must have the competency to complete it. However, all these individual assignments may have dependencies among them, requiring the team members to interact effectively.

In a nutshell, you hire the individuals, but you need a team to complete the project successfully. The team needs to be developed from the individuals and managed.

Acquiring a Project Team

The project work will be executed by the project team, and therefore the role of the team in the success of the project is crucial. So, it is critical to acquire the right project team for your project. You accomplish this through the Acquire Project Team process illustrated in Figure 8.2. Roles and responsibilities for the roles required to complete the project are defined during the human resource planning process, discussed in the previous chapter. Before the work can start, the roles need to be assigned to real individuals who will become the members of the project team. These individuals might come from different departments, and the project management team might have no direct control over them. So, these team members need to be acquired through a process like the one shown in Figure 8.2.

The major input to the acquire team process comes from the human resource planning discussed in the previous chapter.

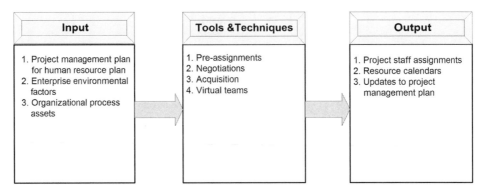

Input	Tools &Techniques	Output
1. Project management plan for human resource plan 2. Enterprise environmental factors 3. Organizational process assets	1. Pre-assignments 2. Negotiations 3. Acquisition 4. Virtual teams	1. Project staff assignments 2. Resource calendars 3. Updates to project management plan

FIGURE 8.2 *The Acquire Project Team process: input, tools and techniques, and output.*

Input to Acquiring the Project Team

The human resource planning process generates the output that contains the staffing management plan, the project organizational chart, and the roles and responsibilities. These items are major inputs to the process of acquiring a project team. These and other input items are discussed in the following paragraphs.

Human resource plan. You need this document because acquiring the project team is one of several processes that implement the human resource plan. It has useful items relevant to acquiring the project team, such as a list of roles and responsibilities required for the project, project organizational charts, and a staffing management plan.

◆ **Roles and responsibilities.** Roles with specific responsibilities are defined in the human resource planning process based on the project work that needs to be performed. These roles will be the guide to finding suitable candidates for the project team, because the team members will play these roles.

◆ **Project organizational chart.** This chart gives you a quick overview of the number of team members needed and their relationships to each other.

◆ **Staffing management plan.** A staffing management plan is an important input item to acquiring the project team because it provides detailed information about the roles that need to be filled, such as the start and end dates for a role. This information is necessary to match the candidates with the roles.

TIP

In the worst-case scenario, you will not be able to negotiate for staff, and you will have no influence on the staff assignments. Unless a team member is not qualified to do the job, you will have to live with the staff assignment decision and make the best of it. If you choose to challenge one of these assignments, make sure you are doing this based on hard facts, such as lack of skills required to perform the assigned activity.

Enterprise environmental factors. The enterprise environmental factors are important in obtaining project team members because the team members can come from various sources inside and outside the performing organization. These factors include organizational structure, administrative policies of your organization regarding outsourcing, availability of team members within the performing organization, and human resource information in the performing organization. For example, the team might include current employees of the performing organization and contractors hired for the project. Depending on your enterprise environment, you, the project manager (or the project management team), may or may not be able to direct or influence the hiring and staff assignments. In either case, you must try to obtain the best team you can. To determine who will be the best team, you need to do your homework, which includes finding out the availability and abilities of the candidate team members. When you do have an influence on making staff assignments, you should consider the following characteristics:

◆ **Availability.** It is important to know whether and when the candidate is available before you attempt to obtain that member.

◆ **Competency.** Does the candidate have the skills needed to complete the schedule activities?

◆ **Experience.** Has the candidate performed similar work well in the past?

◆ **Interests.** What is the candidate's interest level in this project and in the work that will be assigned to him or her?

◆ **Cost.** What is the cost attached to each candidate in terms of pay? This is even more important if the member is a contractor.

Based on this information, build your dream team on paper and attempt to obtain that team. If the team is spread out over different departments and hence the team members are under the control of different functional managers, plan who you will ask for from each functional manager. To make a request, meet with the manager and ask for your most wanted team member first, even though it is very unlikely that you will get everyone you ask for. Before meeting the functional managers, you need to prioritize your staffing needs. The most complex activities and the activities on critical paths should get special attention, and you should make sure these activities have the best members because they have the highest risk potential. Having assigned staff to these activities first, you have more flexibility to agree to a different resource assigned to activities that are less complex and have a non-zero float time. Even though you want to negotiate for the best team, keep a backup plan—that is, if you don't get the best member, try to get the second best member, and so on.

 NOTE

In a traditional organizational structure, you will not have direct control over the project team members, and you will need to acquire them by negotiating with functional managers. But you still need to do the homework that you would do if you were to interview the candidates because you still want to get the best members available for the job.

Organizational process assets. In the process of acquiring the project team, you should consider the following organizational process assets:

♦ Guidelines, policies, or procedures governing staff assignments that your organization may have

♦ Help from the human resources department in recruitment of and orientation for the team members

To put together the best team, you need to understand the tools and techniques available for acquiring the team.

Tools and Techniques for Acquiring the Project Team

You will either negotiate with the functional manager for a team member to fill a role or you will acquire the team member from outside your organization, such as a contractor. Negotiation and acquisition are discussed in the following paragraph, along with other tools and techniques.

Pre-assignment. In some cases, there will be some staff members already assigned to the project. This can happen, for example, due to the following situations:

♦ A staff member was promised as part of a specific proposal to compete with another proposal. Acceptance of this proposal automatically affirms that staff-member assignment.

♦ There is only one person in the organization who has the expertise to perform a specific activity.

♦ A staff assignment was specified in the project charter.

Negotiation. The project manager and the project management team should effectively negotiate and exert influence in a positive way to obtain the best possible team to complete the project work. The failure to acquire an effective team can result in missed deadlines, cost overrun, poor quality, and eventually a failed project. You will most likely need to negotiate with functional managers for the staff assignments for your project. In these negotiations, you have a two-pronged goal—to obtain the best available person for an activity and to obtain the person for the required timeframe. As described in the previous section, you must do your homework in order to get the best results from the negotiations.

 TIP

While negotiating with a functional manager, sometimes it's important to understand the functional manager's perspective in light of the politics of the organization. For example, a functional manager will weigh the benefits (for example, visibility of your project compared to that of competing projects) in determining where to assign the best performers. In this case, it is to your advantage to explain the importance of your project and the activity for which you are asking for the best performer.

You may also be negotiating with project management teams of other projects who might be competing to get team members from the same pool of human resources. Negotiation skills will also be used to communicate with external organizations to hire or contract team members.

Acquisition. If the performing organization does not have the human resources to fill one or more roles needed to finish the project, the required team member can be obtained from outside the organization as a contractor, or the corresponding work can be given to a source outside the performing organization. We will talk more about this area of procurement management later in this chapter.

Virtual teams. Welcome to the information age triggered by the Internet. The process of working for an organization from outside its physical location is called *telecommuting*. The Internet (along with other technological advances, such as teleconferencing, cellular phones, and pagers) makes it possible to telecommute from your home in the same city where the organization is or from a location on the other side of the globe with almost the same ease. Teams composed of telecommuters are called *virtual teams* because the team works together on the same project without holding face-to-face meetings. It is not difficult to find people who have worked on virtual teams and have never seen the other team members face to face. I have worked on several such teams, and I'm sure either you have or you will in the near future. The virtual team format expands the team definition to offer the following benefits:

♦ People working for the same organization but living in different locations can join the same team.

♦ A needed expert can join a team even if the expert does not live in the same location as the rest of the team.

♦ The organization has the option to accommodate employees who can only work from their home offices for a certain period of time.

♦ Due to the availability of asynchronous communication means, such as e-mail and online bulletin boards, it is possible to form a team of members who have different work hours or shifts.

♦ Virtual teams eliminate or reduce the need to travel by using means of communication that are abundantly available, such as e-mail, video conferencing, and the World Wide Web. This enables organizations to perform projects that were previously impossible due to the anticipated travel expenses.

Note that because the virtual team members are not at the same location and do not have regular face-to-face meetings, effective communication is that much more important for the success of the project being performed by the virtual team. Therefore, communication management is crucial to the success of virtual teams.

The team you are going to acquire could be a team at one location or a virtual team, and a team member might be from your organization or from outside your organization. Whatever the case may be, the team itself—that is, the staff assignments—is the major output of the acquire team process—no surprise there.

Output of Acquiring the Project Team

The major outputs of the Acquire Project Team process are the staff assignments to fill the roles defined during human resource planning and the list of time periods for which the staff members will be available. These and other output items are discussed in the following list.

- **Project staff assignments.** This document contains the list of individuals assigned to the project. It can also include memos sent to team members, the project organization chart, and the schedule with the names inserted.

- **Resource calendars.** This document includes the time periods for which each assigned member can work on the project. Possible schedule conflicts, commitments to other projects, and times when a team member is not available can also be recorded.

- **Updates to the project management plan.** As a result of staff assignments, some parts of the project management plan will be modified. For example, the project team is acquired by matching the staffing requirements specified in the staffing management plan to the candidates. Hardly ever is there a perfect match between the two. During the process of acquiring the project team, you might realize that the staffing management plan needs to be updated. Other updates to the staffing management plan might come from the following sources:
  - Promotions
  - Retirements
  - Illnesses
  - Performance issues
  - Changing workloads

After staff assignments have been made, you have the raw material out of which you need to develop the special team for your project.

Developing the Project Team

Your project team can consist of members from different departments and disciplines, regular employees and contractors, and experts from different disciplines. Some of these individuals might not have much appreciation for others' disciplines. You have a challenge to develop this diverse group into a cohesive and efficient team that will perform the project on time, within budget, and with quality. The single goal of team development is to maximize project performance. This is accomplished by introducing three elements:

- Improve the competencies of team members
- Improve the interaction among team members
- Improve the overall team environment

This will help you develop a cohesive and competent team to meet the project objectives effectively.

TIP

Each team member should be the owner of the piece of work assigned to the member, and hence should be fully responsible for it. That said, teamwork and team spirit are critical factors for the project success. It's the responsibility of the project manager to create an environment that supports teamwork and team spirit.

As Figure 8.3 shows, the major output of the Acquire Project Team process is the input to the Develop Project Team process. The team development starts with a list of team members and the staff assignments made during the Acquire Project Team process. The resource availability list provides information about when the team members are available for team development activities. The following items of the staff management plan can be useful for team development:

◆ Training strategies

◆ Plans for developing the project team

◆ Recognition and rewards systems

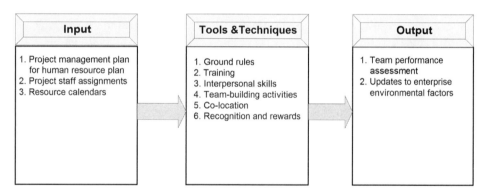

Input	**Tools &Techniques**	**Output**
1. Project management plan for human resource plan 2. Project staff assignments 3. Resource calendars	1. Ground rules 2. Training 3. Interpersonal skills 4. Team-building activities 5. Co-location 6. Recognition and rewards	1. Team performance assessment 2. Updates to enterprise environmental factors

FIGURE 8.3 *The Develop Project Team process: input, tools and techniques, and output.*

As discussed in the following paragraphs, there are some standard tools and techniques that you can use to develop a winning team.

Ground rules. A very important management technique is to establish clear expectations at the very beginning of a project. The expectations can be set up by establishing a set of ground rules. Early commitment to these guidelines will increase cooperation and productivity by decreasing misunderstandings. Once the rules are clearly established, all team members are responsible for enforcing them.

Training. The goal of training is to improve the competencies of the project team members, which in turn helps in meeting the project objectives. Training might be aimed at individual members or at the team as a whole, depending upon the needs. The training might be scheduled in the staff management plan, or it might result from observations, conversations, and project performance appraisals as the project progresses. Following are examples of some training methods:

- Coaching
- Mentoring
- On-the-job training of a team member by another team member
- Online training
- Instructor-led classroom training

Interpersonal and general management skills. General management skills, especially interpersonal skills, are necessary to develop an effective team. You and the project management team can minimize problems and maximize cooperation by understanding the sentiments of team members, anticipating their actions, acknowledging their concerns, and following up on the issues. To accomplish this, the following interpersonal management skills are necessary:

- **Effective communication.** This is needed to facilitate the smooth flow of necessary information among the team members.
- **Ability to influence the organization.** This is needed to get things done.
- **Leadership.** This is needed to develop a vision and strategy and to motivate people to achieve that vision. During a time of possible uncertainty, such as changes in upper management, you should clarify the situation and help the team stay focused on the project.
- **Motivation.** This is needed for energizing team members to achieve high levels of performance and to overcome barriers to change. During times when the team is in a low-morale mode, you should be able to lift the team morale and thereby contribute to team development.
- **Negotiation and conflict management.** This is needed to work with team members to resolve their conflicts and facilitate negotiations when necessary in resolving conflicts or in task assignments. Depending on the nature of the conflict, you can take it as a team development opportunity. Effective resolution of a conflict contributes to team building.
- **Problem solving.** This ability is needed to define, analyze, and solve problems.

Team management is further discussed later in this chapter.

 NOTE

Interpersonal skills are also called *soft skills*, as opposed to *hard skills*, which refer to technical skills and capabilities.

Team-building activities. Team-building activities can range from indirect team-building activities, such as participating in constructing the WBS, to direct team-building activities, such as social gatherings where the team members can get to know each other and start feeling comfortable with each other. While planning such activities, you should keep in mind that team members might have different interests and different levels of tolerance for games and different icebreakers.

The project kickoff meeting is another indirect method to start team development. This can be used as a formal way to introduce team members and other stakeholders and spell out the project goals for everyone at the same time. An ideal kickoff meeting is a combination of serious business and fun. The goal is to align the team with the project goals and to help team members feel comfortable with each other.

In planning the kickoff meeting, you can assume that team members have the following questions in their heads that need to be answered before the end of the meeting:

- ◆ Why am I here?
- ◆ Who are you and what are your expectations of me?
- ◆ What is this team going to do?
- ◆ How is the team going to do its work?
- ◆ How do I fit into all this?

Consider the following steps to make your kickoff meeting successful:

- ◆ **Agenda.** Putting the meeting agenda in the hands of the team members always helps to run the meeting more smoothly and effectively and keep it on the track.

- ◆ **Welcome.** Take immediate charge of the meeting by introducing yourself and welcoming the participants. Quickly walk through the agenda and set the stage for the rest of the meeting.

- ◆ **Project overview.** Define the project, its goals, and its deliverables. Introduce the project team members and briefly describe their roles. The goal is to provide a big picture and to help individual team members figure out how they fit into the big picture.

- ◆ **Expectations.** Many project team members might not already know you and your management style. You should take this opportunity to set expectations about how the team will function. For example, state that you expect all team members to attend weekly status meetings. Remind the team to focus on the project goal, to do their part, and to look out for one another in a team spirit.

- ◆ **Guest speakers.** Depending upon the size and the visibility of the project, you might also invite relevant guest speakers, such as the project sponsor, the customer, or an executive stakeholder. Before the meeting, spend some time communicating with the guest speaker about the message to deliver.

- ◆ **Closure.** Ask for feedback and hold a question-and-answer session before closing the meeting.

Remember that the main purpose of the kickoff meeting is to bring every team member onto the same page regarding the big picture of the project. Don't get bogged down discussing every item in detail.

You should know that team development is not an instant process. Generally speaking, when you form a team, it goes through five stages of development (according to the Tuckman model), as shown in Figure 8.4 and explained in the following list.

◆ **Forming.** This is the orientation stage, with high dependence on the leader (the project manager, in this case) for guidance and direction. Individual roles and responsibilities are unclear, and there is little agreement on the team goals other than those received from the leader. Processes are often ignored, and team members test the tolerance of the system and the leader. It's time to establish ground rules and clear expectations. The leader directs in this stage.

◆ **Storming.** This stage represents the struggle for control and power as team members work to establish themselves relative to other team members. The clarity of team goals increases, but some uncertainties persist. Compromises might be required to make progress. Coaching and training can play effective roles during this stage.

◆ **Norming.** This is the routine stage during which consensus and agreement about team goals generally prevails among team members. Roles and responsibilities are clear and accepted by team members. Major decisions are made by group agreements, and smaller decisions can be delegated to appropriate team members. During this stage, the leader facilitates.

◆ **Performing.** This is the productivity stage in which the team knows what it's doing and why. The team is functioning in a cohesive mode and working toward the common goal in a more autonomous fashion. Disagreements might arise, but they are resolved within the team in a constructive way. During this stage, the leader delegates and oversees.

◆ **Adjourning.** This is the closure stage. When the mission for which the team was formed is accomplished (or cancelled), the team is adjourned to free the team members to move on to other things.

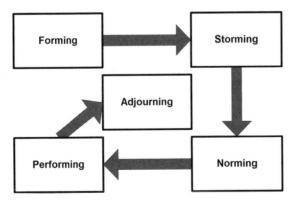

FIGURE 8.4 *The five progressive stages of team development in the Tuckman model.*

Being aware of these stages of team development will help you to better understand the behaviors of team members and thereby develop your team more effectively.

Co-location. This technique keeps all (or most) of the project team members in the same physical location to improve communication and to create a sense of community among team members. In this age of virtual teams, this is not an increasingly popular technique, but when most of the team members are in the same location, this technique is a default choice. It can include a *war room*, which is a meeting room used for regular face-to-face meetings. Also, when the project is being executed by a virtual team, the co-location technique can be used to put together some team members at crucial times of the project.

Recognition and rewards. Generally speaking, people feel motivated if they feel that their contributions and efforts are recognized and valued. Rewards are effective methods to express recognition. The recognition and rewards strategy set up during the human resource planning process can be used to develop the project team. Remember the following rules in setting up a fair reward system:

◆ Only desirable behavior should be rewarded.

◆ Any member should be able to win the reward.

◆ Win-lose rewards, such as team member of the month, can hurt the team cohesiveness.

◆ The cultural diversity of the team should be considered and respected.

The effects of team development efforts are measured by the team performance assessment, the major output of the Develop Project Team process, which includes the following indicators:

◆ Improvement in individual skills that enables a team member to perform project activities more efficiently.

◆ Improvement in team skills that help the team to improve overall performance and work more effectively as a group.

◆ Increased team spirit or cohesiveness: Team members interact in a constructive way and help each other to meet the project objectives.

◆ Reduced staff turnover rate.

While developing your team, you may need to modify some enterprise environmental factors, such as training records and skill assessment.

In addition to team development, the project team needs to be managed throughout the project.

Managing the Project Team

You manage the project team by using the Manage Project Team process, which is aimed at improving the project performance by executing the following tasks:

◆ Resolving issues

◆ Coordinating changes

◆ Tracking the performance of each team member

◆ Providing feedback to the team members

TIP

Managing the project team involves activities from hiring to firing and therefore requires a wide spectrum of management skills, including communication, conflict management, negotiation, and leadership. On one hand you should provide challenging assignments, and on the other hand you should recognize and reward high performance.

Figure 8.5 depicts the Manage Project Team process.

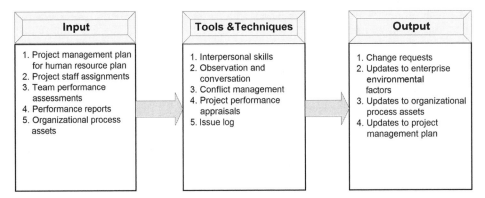

Input	Tools &Techniques	Output
1. Project management plan for human resource plan 2. Project staff assignments 3. Team performance assessments 4. Performance reports 5. Organizational process assets	1. Interpersonal skills 2. Observation and conversation 3. Conflict management 4. Project performance appraisals 5. Issue log	1. Change requests 2. Updates to enterprise environmental factors 3. Updates to organizational process assets 4. Updates to project management plan

FIGURE 8.5 *The Manage Project Team process: input, tools and techniques, and output.*

Input to Managing the Project Team

The main input to managing the project team comes from the output of human resource planning, acquiring the project team, and developing the project team.

Human resource plan. As examples, the following items in the human resource plan, part of project management plan, are the input to the Manage Project Team process:

◆ **Roles and responsibilities.** Used to monitor and evaluate performance.

◆ **Project organizational charts.** Used to find out the reporting relationships among project team members.

◆ **Staffing management plan**. Contains information such as training plans, compliance issues, and certification requirements, along with the time periods when the team members are expected to work.

Project staff assignments. Obviously, you should know who your team members are and what they are supposed to be doing. So, project staff assignments, an output of the Acquire Project Team process, are an obvious input to managing the project team.

Performance information. The following items regarding performance are input to the Manage Project Team process:

◆ **Team performance assessment.** This is the output of the Develop Project Team process discussed earlier in this chapter. Performance assessments provide important information that can be used in managing a team member and in managing the team. These assessments can be the basis to identify issues and address them. Some examples are the need to resolve conflicts, the need for training, and the need to modify communication.

◆ **Performance reports.** Performance reports contain the progress of the project against the baseline data, such as the schedule baseline, the cost baseline, and the quality baseline. They basically reflect how the project resources are being used to achieve the project objectives. The information from the performance reports helps determine future human resource requirements, updates to the staffing management plan, and recognitions and rewards.

Organizational process assets. The project management team can use the following organizational assets in managing the project team:

◆ The organization's policies, procedures, and system for rewarding the team members. Certificates of appreciation, recognition dinners, and bonus structures are some examples.

◆ Other items that should be available to the project management team for use in managing the team, such as bulletin boards, newsletters, and internal websites for information sharing.

To manage the team effectively, you should be aware of the tools and techniques that can be used for that.

Tools and Techniques for Managing the Project Team

The tools and techniques used in managing the team include interpersonal skills, observation and conversation, conflict management, an issue log, and project performance appraisals. Interpersonal skills were discussed earlier in this chapter. Other tools and techniques are discussed in the following paragraphs.

Observation and conversation. Observations and conversations are both means to stay in touch with the work and attitudes of the project team members. The indicators to monitor these include the following:

◆ Progress toward completion of assigned activities and therefore project deliverables
◆ Distinguished accomplishments contributing to the project performance
◆ Interpersonal issues

Conflict management. The purpose of conflict management is to nourish the positive working relationships among the team members that result in increased productivity. Common sources for conflicts include the following:

◆ Scarce resources resulting in unsatisfied needs
◆ Scheduling priorities
◆ Personal work styles
◆ Perceptions, values, feelings, and emotions
◆ Power struggles

You can reduce the number of conflicts by setting ground rules, clearly defining roles and goals, and implementing solid project management practices.

TIP

Differences of opinion should not be considered as sources of conflict. If managed properly, differences can be very healthy and can lead to better solutions and thereby increase productivity.

Initially, project team members who are parties to a conflict should be given the opportunity to resolve it themselves. If the team members fail to resolve the conflict and it becomes a negative factor for the project, you, the project manager, should facilitate the conflict resolution, usually in private and using a direct and collaborative approach. If the conflict continues, you might have no option other than to use formal procedures, such as disciplinary actions.

Different project managers normally use various styles or methods under different situations. The choice of the conflict resolution style or technique may be influenced by the following factors:

◆ Whether the conflict needs to be resolved for the long term or a short-term resolution is fine
◆ The intensity of the conflict and the relative importance of resolution in the context of the project
◆ The urgency of resolving the conflict
◆ The positions taken by the parties involved in the conflict

The first step in conflict management is analyzing the nature and type of conflict, which might involve asking questions. You can meet with (interview) the parties involved in the conflict. The next step is to determine the management strategy. Different management strategies are summarized here:

◆ **Avoidance.** In this strategy, at least one party to the conflict ignores (or withdraws) from the conflict and decides not to deal with the problem. This strategy can be used by the project manager as a cooling-off period, to collect more information, or when the issue is not critical. However, if the issue is critical, this is the worst resolution strategy and can give rise to lose/lose situations if both parties withdraw or yield/lose situations if one party withdraws. This strategy is also called *withdrawal strategy.*

◆ **Competition.** In this approach, one party uses any available means to get its way, often at the expense of the other party. This is a win/lose situation. It can be justified under some situations, such as when the basic rights of a party in conflict are at stake or when you want to set a precedent. However, if used unfairly from a power position (such as if it is a management style), it can be destructive for team development. This strategy can cause the conflict to escalate, and the loser party might attempt to retaliate. When used by a party in power, competition is also called *forcing.*

◆ **Compromising.** In this strategy, both parties gain something and give up something. This is a lose-win/lose-win strategy. You can use this strategy to achieve temporary solutions and to avoid a damaging power struggle when there is time pressure. The downside of this approach is that both parties can look at the solution as a lose/lose situation and can be distracted from the merits of the issues involved. In this way, the short-term solution can hurt the long-term objectives of the project.

◆ **Accommodation.** This strategy is the opposite of the competition strategy. One party attempts to meet the other party's needs at the expense of their own. This might be a justifiable strategy when the concerns of the accommodating party are less significant than the concerns of the other party in the context of the project. Sometimes it's used as a goodwill gesture. However, it is a lose/win approach (the accommodating party loses and the accommodated party wins), and the accommodating party runs the risk of losing credibility and influence in the future. However, when this strategy is applied carefully and both parties become accommodating, they can meet in the areas of agreement, and it can turn into a win/win situation. This is why this technique is also called *smoothing.*

◆ **Collaboration.** This strategy is based on reaching consensus among the parties in the conflict. Both parties work together to explore several solutions and agree on the one that satisfies the needs and concerns of both parties. This is a win/win strategy and is generally considered the best of all the strategies because it helps build commitment and promotes goodwill between the parties involved.

◆ **Confronting.** Some experts consider this approach as a variation of collaboration. You confront the problem causing the conflict head on and then solve that problem through an open dialogue and by examining several alternatives. This approach is also called *problem solving.*

TIP

You should always look for how the different processes overlap and interact with each other. For example, conflict management is a technique for managing the team. However, the purpose of conflict management is to nourish positive working relationships among team members that result in increased productivity, so resolving a conflict can also be looked upon as a team development activity.

Project performance appraisals. Conducting project performance appraisals includes evaluating the performance of project team members and providing them with feedback based on the evaluation. The evaluation is based on information collected from several people interacting with the team member. This method of collecting information is called the *360-degree feedback principle* because the information comes from several sources.

The objectives for conducting performance appraisals include the following:

◆ Providing positive feedback to team members in a possibly hectic environment
◆ Clarifying roles and responsibilities
◆ Discovering new issues and reminding of unresolved issues
◆ Discovering the needs of individual training plans
◆ Setting specific goals for the future

TIP

You might find that the project managers in your organization are not responsible for performance appraisals. The need for formal or informal performance appraisals depends on the organization's policy, the contract requirements, and the size and complexity of the project.

Issue log. Issues generally involve obstacles that can stop the project team from achieving the project objectives. A written log should be maintained that contains the list of team members responsible for resolving the issues by target dates. The purpose of the issue log is to monitor the issues until they are closed.

While you are managing the team using these techniques, you might recommend some actions as an output of the Manage Project Team process.

STUDY CHECKPOINT 8.1

Each comment in the first column of the following table points to a conflict resolution strategy. Match each comment with the corresponding strategy in the second column.

Comment
A. Let's have a face-to-face meeting and hear out both parties.
B. Both of you have to meet halfway; you can't get everything all the time.
C. I'm the one who is running the show here, and I have made the decision.
D. Okay, I see your point now. I was thinking more at a personal level; your view is more compatible with the project's objectives. I guess for that reason I can live with your approach.
E. You guys are not even listening to my argument. I feel I'm wasting my time. So, I'm not going to discuss it with you any longer.
F. Let's sit down, talk it out, and design the best solution for all parties.

Conflict Resolution Technique
1. Avoidance/withdrawal
2. Competition/forcing
3. Compromising/smoothing
4. Accommodation
5. Collaboration
6. Confronting/problem solving

 CAUTION

Not only can you earn quite a few points on the PMP exam, but you can also be a very effective project manager if you realize this: Confront the problem or the issue head on, but do your homework (investigate, research, or analyze) before taking action.

Output of Managing the Project Team

The output from managing the project team includes recommended corrective and preventive actions, change requests, and updates to organizational process assets and the project management plan.

Change requests. The Manage Project Team process might generate recommendations for corrective and preventive actions and other changes as discussed here:

◆ **Recommended corrective actions.** A corrective action is a direction for executing project work to bring future performance in line with what is expected in the project management plan. The corrective actions recommended during project team management might include the following:

   ◆ Staffing changes, such as changing assignments of the team members, replacing team members (for example, ones who leave), and outsourcing some work

- Training for the team or for individual team members
- Recognition and rewards based on the reward system
- Disciplinary actions
- **Recommended preventive actions.** A preventive action is a direction to perform an activity to stop or reduce the probability of an anticipated event occurrence generally associated with a project risk. Preventive action can also be taken to reduce the anticipated impact of an event in case it happens. The preventive actions recommended during project team management might include the following:
  - Cross-training so that, in the absence of a team member, another team member can take over the assignment
  - Role clarifications to ensure that all responsibilities associated with the role are performed
  - Planning for overtime in anticipation of extra work that might be needed to meet project deadlines

Other change requests and updates. The team management activities can generate some change requests for the project management plan. For example, staffing changes can generate requests for extending the schedule, increasing the budget, or reducing the scope. The change requests should be processed through the integrated change control system.

Updates to organizational process assets. Several kinds of organizational process assets can be updated as a result of project team management. Here are some examples:

- **Performance appraisals.** The project staff member that interacts with a project team member in a significant way can offer input to the performance appraisal for that team member.
- **Templates and organization's standard processes.**
- **Lessons-learned database.** The lessons-learned database should be updated with the lessons learned during team management, which can come from different areas that include the following:
  - Issues and solutions in the issue log
  - Special skills and competencies discovered during project work for the team members
  - Successful and unsuccessful ground rules, conflict management techniques, and recognition events

Updates to the project management plan. Approved change requests and corrective actions can result in updates to the staffing management plan, which is a part of the project management plan. New role assignments, training plans, and reward decisions are some examples of updates.

TIP

Managing the project team is a complex task when the team members are accountable to both the project managers and the functional managers—for example, in a matrix organization. Effectively managing this dual relationship is critical to the success of the project and is therefore generally the responsibility of the project manager.

Motivating Your Team

Because you have come so far in studying this book, I must say you are motivated to take the PMP exam, learn about project management, or both. So what is motivation? Motivation is an internal drive to meet a set of objectives. Internal drive is a state of unrest inside of you. This is how it goes. A need is a deficiency, an absence of something, a hole. Out of need arises the desire to fulfill the need. This desire or want represent dissatisfaction, which creates a state of unrest. This unrest is the drive. When drive is directed at a call for action to meet those objectives that will satisfy the need, it becomes motivation. In a nutshell, the need acts as a catalyst, like an enzyme in a biochemical reaction, that sets you on a journey toward meeting a set of objectives that will satisfy the need.

If you want to get optimal results from your computers, you network them appropriately and execute appropriate software programs on appropriate drives in the network. If you want to achieve optimal results from your team, you create the appropriate drive in team members that will execute actions to meet project objectives; in other words, you motivate them.

This is how important motivation is: Motivation to do some task plus the ability to do that task is equal to performance. So, lack of motivation means poor performance. In a project, motivation begins with you, the project manager. You must be motivated for the project and to motivate the project team members. It's always a good idea to have some formal knowledge of something that you are going to go through. So here, in a nutshell, are some theories of motivation.

Maslow's hierarchy of needs theory. According to this theory, people have layers of needs, as illustrated in Figure 8.6, and until the lower-layer needs are satisfied, they will not move to satisfy the upper-layer needs. For example, if you are unemployed and broke, and as a result your very survival is in danger, you don't care about buying health insurance or life insurance or dating to look for a companion.

Herzberg's motivation-hygiene theory. This theory classifies the factors needed to motivate people into two categories: hygiene factors and motivating factors. Hygiene factors are necessary for motivation but not sufficient; they do not bring satisfaction, but they prevent dissatisfaction. Some examples are compensation; company policies; level of supervision or ownership of the assigned work; relationship with superiors, subordinates, and peers; and working conditions. Motivating factors are factors that bring (or increase) job satisfaction. Some examples are challenging work assignment, opportunity for career advancement and accomplishments, opportunity for growth, sense of responsibility, and recognition.

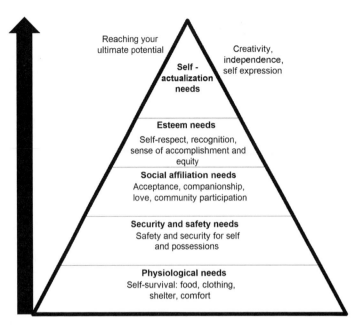

FIGURE 8.6 *Illustration of Maslow's theory of hierarchy of needs. Based on* Motivation and Personality *(Harper and Row, 1970).*

CAUTION

Hygiene factors are related to the work environment, whereas motivating factors (also called *motivators*) are related to the work itself.

McClelland's achievement motivation theory. According to this theory, the following three needs motivate people:

◆ **Achievement.** This is the need to perform well, achieve success, and get recognized for it. The key idea here is the drive to excel.

◆ **Affiliation.** This is the need or desire for good relationships at work. You want to feel connected at work.

◆ **Power.** This is the desire to move things, to influence people or events. The key term here is the *world dominance* or *making a difference*.

McGregor's X-Y theory. According to McGregor, there are the following two types of managers:

◆ **Theory X managers.** These managers believe that most of the people (and hence the workers) are self-centered, are only motivated by their physiological and safety needs, and are indifferent to the needs of the organization they work for. They (the workers) lack ambition and have very little creativity and problem-solving capacity.

As a result, they dislike their work and will try to avoid it. They will also avoid taking responsibility and initiative. There is one word to describe Theory X managers: distrust. They distrust their employees. These managers, therefore, tend to be authoritarian.

◆ **Theory Y managers.** As opposed to Theory X managers, Theory Y managers trust their employees. They believe that most of the people are high performers in a proper work environment. This is because most of the people are creative and committed to meeting the needs of the organization they work for. Theory Y managers also believe that most people like to take responsibility and initiative and are self-disciplined. Finally, they also believe that most people are motivated by all levels of needs in the Maslow's hierarchy of needs. These managers tend to provide more freedom and opportunity for career growth.

Expectancy theory. According to this theory, people are motivated only if they expect a desired outcome or reward. The key idea here is: What is in it for me? The desired outcome here has two components: Objectives will be met with this effort, and the performers will be rewarded.

STUDY CHECKPOINT 8.2

In the following table, match each scenario in the first column with an appropriate theory in the second column.

Scenario	*Motivation Theory*
A. The management is really nice to the employees, and there are lots of perks. But I'm more concerned about my career path once I join this company.	1. Maslow's hierarchy of needs theory
B. Engineering manager Bob has a habit that employees don't like. Every time he passes by a cubicle of an employee, he always peers at the computer screen over the shoulders of the employee to see what the employee is really doing on the computer.	2. Herzberg's motivation-hygiene theory
C. Rachel Janowicz quit her project management job with the Gugu Gaga company immediately after winning the California Super Lotto. She said, "Well, my money problem is solved. Now I will do what I always wanted to do."	3. McClelland's achievement motivation theory
D. I'm not going to attend this seminar. Basically, I'll be listening to their pitches all day long. What are the odds that I'll win the door prize?	4. McGregor's X-Y theory
E. Kushal did not really like the assignment. But he did it anyway because he did not want to let his manager down.	5. Expectancy theory

CAUTION

The expectancy theory applied carelessly can backfire. For example, if the expected reward is unachievable or not worth the effort, people will lose motivation.

The three most important takeaways from this chapter are as follows:

◆ To lay the foundations of your project success, you must negotiate to acquire a team that is capable of performing project work effectively and efficiently.

◆ You obtain individuals, and from those individuals you develop the team, and this development generally goes through these stages: forming, storming, norming, performing, and adjourning.

◆ Conflict resolution is a critical part of managing the team. Successful conflict resolutions are important for the success of the project.

Summary

The project management plan is executed using the processes in the executing process group. The high-level process in this group is the Direct and Manage Project Execution process, whose main goal is to produce the project deliverables. To make that happen, you need to put together a project team that will perform the project work, and you need to develop and manage the team. You put together a project team using the Acquire Project Team process. The main output of this process is the project staff assignments, which become the input to the Develop Project Team process. This process uses training, recognition and rewards, and other team-building techniques to develop a cohesive and efficient team with high performance. You manage the project team using the Manage Project Team process to improve and optimize team performance.

An effective and capable project team is essential for the success of the project. However, even if the project is technically successful, it really is not unless the stakeholders think it is. So, it is critical to manage stakeholder expectations while executing the project. This is the topic of the next chapter.

Exam's Eye View

Comprehend

◆ The goal of the Acquire Project Team process is to fill the roles defined in the staffing management plan with real individuals who will perform those roles to execute the project.

◆ Regardless of how much control you have over staff assignments, always try to obtain the best person for the job by doing your homework, which includes finding out the availability and competencies of the candidate team members.

◆ The staff assignments made through the Acquire Project Team process are the input to the Develop Project Team process, which uses techniques such as training, recognition and rewards, and other team-building activities to develop a high-performance team.

◆ You must manage the team in order to optimize its performance.

Look Out

◆ The project manager and the project management team should effectively negotiate and exert influence in a positive way to obtain the best possible team to complete the project work.

◆ The failure to acquire an effective team can result in missed deadlines, cost overrun, poor quality, and eventually a failed project.

◆ Project staff assignments are an output of the Acquire Project Team process and are an input to the Develop Project Team and Manage Project Team processes.

Memorize

◆ Team development goes through five progressive stages: forming, storming, norming, performing, and adjourning.

◆ Strategies used to resolve conflicts include avoidance, competition, compromise, accommodation, confrontation, and collaboration. Collaboration is the best strategy because it offers a win/win resolution.

◆ The project management plan is an input item to the Acquire Project Team, Develop Project Team, and Manage Project Team processes because it contains the human resource plan.

Key Terms and Definitions

◆ **asynchronous communication.** A communication in which the two communicating entities do not have to be present on both ends of the communication line at the same time. E-mail is an example of asynchronous communication because when the sender of the e-mail pushes the send button, the intended recipient of the e-mail message does not have to be logged on to the e-mail server.

◆ **corrective actions.** Directions for executing the project work to bring expected project performance in conformance with the project management plan. This is an output item of the QA process.

◆ **issue log.** A notebook or a database to track and manage issues. This process includes entering the issue, modifying its status, and closing the issue.

◆ **preventive actions.** Directions to perform an activity that will reduce the probability of negative consequences associated with project risks. These preventive actions are recommended by the QA process during process analysis.

◆ **virtual team.** A team of members working on the same project with few or no face-to-face meetings. Various technologies, such as e-mail, video conferencing, and the World Wide Web, are used to facilitate communication among team members.

◆ **war room.** A conference room used for project team meetings.

Review Questions

1. Which of the following is generally the best conflict-resolution technique in most situations?

   A. Avoidance

   B. Compromise

   C. Accommodation

   D. Collaboration

2. Karl, one of your team members, is arguing with you over how to perform a specific task. At the end of a long discussion, you say, "Karl, please do me a favor and do it this way for my peace of mind." Which conflict resolution technique are you using?

   A. Avoidance

   B. Compromise

   C. Accommodation

   D. Forcing

3. Which of the following is not a situation well suited for team development efforts?

    A. The kickoff meeting

    B. A conflict between two groups within the team

    C. Low team morale

    D. Changes in the budget

4. You are in the beginning of executing your project, and you need to make assignments to individuals who will do the project work. Which process should you perform?

    A. Develop Human Resource Plan

    B. Develop Project Team

    C. Acquire Project Team

    D. Make Staff Assignments

5. Virtual teams are a tool and technique used in which of the following processes?

    A. Develop Human Resource Plan

    B. Develop Project Team

    C. Acquire Project Team

    D. Manage Project Team

6. You heard in the hallway that the project manager of The Da Vinci Code project, named Pappu Gloria, has very poor soft skills. If this is true, Pappu Gloria needs to improve his:

    A. Software skills

    B. Interpersonal skills

    C. Ways of handling equipment

    D. Capability to use scheduling software

7. Which of the following is usually not the tool or technique you need to acquire a project team?

    A. DELPHI technique

    B. Negotiations

    C. Virtual teams

    D. Acquisition

286 Part III **EXECUTING THE PROJECT**

8. Shilpa Bedi, the engineering manager, receives daily progress reports from all the engineers she manages. She also visits the cubicles of the engineers several times a day to ensure that they are working and not just browsing the web. Most of the engineers agree that she is a micromanager. What kind of management theory is she applying?

   A. Theory Alpha

   B. Theory X

   C. Theory Y

   D. McClelland's achievement motivation theory

9. Gary Travis, the engineering manager, receives weekly progress reports from all engineers he manages. He encourages them to take ownership of their assignments. Most of the engineers agree that he trusts his engineers. What kind of management theory is he applying?

   A. Theory Alpha

   B. Theory X

   C. Theory Y

   D. McClelland's achievement motivation theory

10. Lois Travis, the project manager, receives weekly progress reports from all engineers she manages. She rewards the achievements of her employees and always gives the credit to her employees for their accomplishments. She is always interested in mentoring her team members and putting them on a career path. She also helps the good performers get the assignments and projects of their choice. What kind of management theory is she applying?

   A. Theory Alpha

   B. Theory X

   C. Theory Y

   D. McClelland's achievement motivation theory

Chapter 9

Managing the Stakes

PMP Exam Objectives

Objective	*What It Really Means*
3.2 Ensure Common Understanding and Set Expectations	You must understand that during the process of directing and managing project execution, you need to manage the expectations of the stakeholders, and you need to ensure what your expectations of the project team members are. You should also understand the role of collecting stakeholder requirements and distributing information in managing the expectations. This requires understanding the Manage Stakeholder Expectations and Distribute Information processes. Expectations regarding the team members were covered in Chapter 8.

Introduction

Even if your project succeeded according to the project management plan, it can be deemed as a failure if you did not do one thing right: managing project stakeholders. That is how important it is to manage project stakeholders effectively, which includes understanding and managing the influences and expectations of the stakeholders. The core element of managing stakeholders is to manage their expectations to keep them in line with the project management plan. To accomplish that, you need to distribute the right information to the right stakeholders at the right time by using the right communication method. The right stakeholders can be identified from the stakeholder register developed during project initiation. You must also perform the management according to the stakeholder management strategy developed during the project initiation stage and communicate with the stakeholders according to the communication management plan developed during project planning.

So, the core question in this chapter is how to effectively manage stakeholders. In search of an answer, we will explore three avenues—the big picture of stakeholder management, managing stakeholder expectations, and distributing information.

Stakeholder Management: Big Picture

As shown in Figure 9.1, managing stakeholders includes the following processes:

- ◆ **Identify Stakeholders.** This is the process of identifying all the stakeholders, positive and negative, during the project initiation. In this process, you develop a stakeholder register and a stakeholder management strategy.
- ◆ **Collect Requirements.** As part of scope planning, this is the process of collecting project and product requirements that will meet the stakeholders' needs and expectations. In this process you generate the stakeholder requirements document and the requirements management plan.
- ◆ **Manage Stakeholder Expectations.** This is the process of staying on the same page with the stakeholders on requirements by addressing their needs and issues.
- ◆ **Distribute Information.** This is the process of distributing relevant information to the right stakeholders at the right time by using the right methods.

 NOTE

The processes Manage Stakeholder Expectations and Distribute Information discussed in this chapter belong to communication management, introduced in Chapter 4.

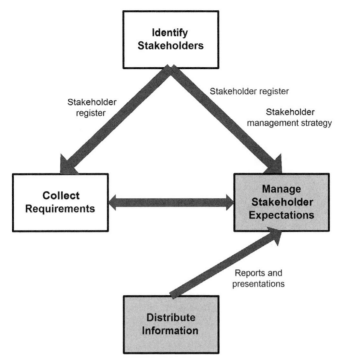

FIGURE 9.1 *Big picture of managing stakeholders.*

The Identify Stakeholders process, discussed in Chapter 2, is performed during project initiation, and the Collect Requirements process, discussed in Chapter 3, is performed during project planning. In this chapter, we explore two other components of stakeholder management: managing stakeholder expectations and distributing information.

Managing Stakeholder Expectations

Managing stakeholder expectations means communicating and working with stakeholders to stay on the same page with them on the project requirements by addressing their needs and issues as they arise. What do you really do when you manage stakeholder expectations? This is a three-pronged task:

1. **Containment.** Monitor and keep the expectations of the stakeholders within the project scope and project management plan through active communication.
2. **Concerns.** Address the stakeholder concerns that have not become issues yet—for example, anticipate problems in the near future. Addressing such concerns may uncover some potential risks that will need to be addressed. An issue is an item or a matter that is under discussion or dispute, and there are most likely opposing views and disagreements about it among the stakeholders.

3. **Issues.** Understand, clarify, and resolve issues raised by the stakeholders. Some of the resolutions can give rise to change requests; other issues may be postponed to the next project or the next phase.

CAUTION

The importance of resolving issues in a timely fashion cannot be overstated. An unresolved issue can grow into a major source of conflict and a delay in completion of project activities.

You can see that managing stakeholders' expectations will keep them on the same page with you by ensuring that they understand the internal dynamics and realities of the project, such as risks and interdependencies. Keeping them in touch with the project reality and on the same page with you will increase the probability of project success. It's the responsibility of the project manager to manage stakeholder expectations by using the process illustrated in Figure 9.2. Most of the items in the input and tools and techniques listed in this figure were already discussed in this book. Some information regarding these items and relevant to this process will be discussed in this section.

TIP

Managing stakeholders' expectations is crucial for project success because it keeps their expectations in line with the project goals, objectives, and requirements in the project management plan. Otherwise, their definition of success will be different from your definition of success, and the project will fail in their eyes even if it succeeded according to the project management plan.

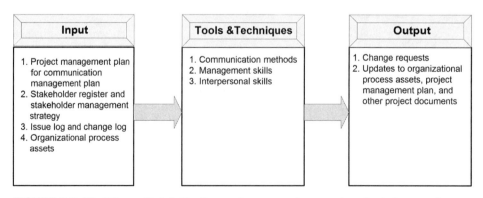

Input	**Tools &Techniques**	**Output**
1. Project management plan for communication management plan 2. Stakeholder register and stakeholder management strategy 3. Issue log and change log 4. Organizational process assets	1. Communication methods 2. Management skills 3. Interpersonal skills	1. Change requests 2. Updates to organizational process assets, project management plan, and other project documents

FIGURE 9.2 *The Manage Stakeholder Expectations process: input, tools and techniques, and output.*

Earlier I mentioned that managing stakeholder expectations is a three-pronged task. That was the *what* of managing stakeholder expectations. But how do you perform this task? The *how* of the task also has three dimensions to it:

1. **Manage stakeholders according to a strategy.** This strategy is documented in the stakeholder management strategy that you developed in the stakeholder identification process during project initiation.

2. **Identify the right stakeholders to communicate with.** A list of stakeholders and information about them is in the stakeholder register that you created during the initiation stage when you were identifying stakeholders.

3. **Communicate with the stakeholders according to the communication management plan.** This plan was developed during project planning. That means you are communicating the right information at the right time to the right stakeholders by using the right methods.

You can use the issue log, also called the *action item log*, to open the issue, monitor it, resolve it, and close it. Issues should be clearly stated, categorized, and prioritized. An action item (or issue) log is a tool used to document and monitor actions that need to be taken or issues that need to be resolved. This is an essential tool to ensure that important items do not fall through the cracks of communication.

Similarly, you can maintain a change log to document the changes that are requested, have occurred, or have been implemented during the project lifecycle.

 NOTE

> Rarely does an issue grow to become a project or a project activity. It is your responsibility to resolve issues in a timely fashion in order to maintain a constructive relationship with stakeholders. However, the resolution may cause change requests for the project, which should go through the proper evaluation and approval process before they are implemented.

The organizational process assets that can affect managing stakeholders' expectations include the following:

♦ **Organizational change control procedures.** These are important because some change requests may arise in the process of managing stakeholder expectations.

♦ **Issue management procedures.** You should comply with these procedures while managing stakeholder issues.

♦ **Organizational communication requirements.** These requirements must be met while communicating with the stakeholders.

♦ **Information from previous projects.** It's always useful to learn from the experience in order to do better.

The tools and techniques that you can use in managing stakeholder expectations include the following:

♦ **Management skills, including interpersonal skills.** You will need these skills to manage change, resolve conflicts, and build trust. These skills include presentation, writing, and public speaking skills. These skills were discussed in Chapters 1 and 4.

♦ **Communication methods.** You will use the appropriate communication methods as described in the communication management plan. These methods were discussed in Chapter 4.

As a result of managing stakeholder expectations, some changes can occur. For example, you may need to make some changes to the stakeholder management strategy in order to accommodate unexpected situations and needs. Furthermore, you may find a communication method ineffective and want to replace it with a more effective method, which will cause an update to the communication management plan. You may end up identifying a new stakeholder, and that will require a change in the stakeholder register, and so on. Obviously, you will be updating the issue log as the issue proceeds toward resolution. The point here is that when a change occurs, you should think through it and update all the documents and plans that need to be updated to ensure consistency after the change has been accommodated.

STUDY CHECKPOINT 9.1

True or False: A stakeholder is proposing something that is not within the planned scope of the project. The appropriate response to this proposal is to oppose it.

You should also document your experience of managing stakeholder expectations, which includes causes of issues, how the issues were resolved, lessons learned, and so on. This will add to the organizational process assets and will be useful for upcoming projects and as a record through the lifecycle of the current project.

To stay on the same page with stakeholders, it's important to distribute relevant information at the right time.

Distributing Information

Throughout the project lifecycle, you need to continually distribute relevant information to the right stakeholders at the right time by using appropriate methods. The information is distributed according to the communication management plan developed during the planning stage and by using the process illustrated in Figure 9.3.

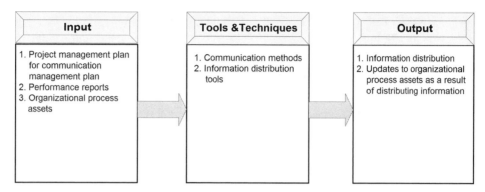

FIGURE 9.3 *The Distribute Information process: input, tools and techniques, and output.*

Input to Information Distribution

The information distribution process is used to distribute information according to the communication management plan. Therefore, the information to be distributed and the communication management plan are the obvious input items to the information distribution process. These and other input items are discussed here.

TIP

Information about project performance at status can be distributed in the form of performance reports, which should be made available before the status or performance evaluation meeting.

The distributed information includes performance reports, which contain items such as the following:

◆ Performance information, including cost and schedule
◆ Status information
◆ Results from risk analysis and risk monitoring
◆ Any other useful information
◆ Current forecasts

The performance reports are generated by using a monitoring and controlling process called Report Performance. In addition to the communication management plan and performance reports, the following organizational process assets can also affect the information distribution process:

◆ Information and lessons learned from past projects

◆ Organizational policies, procedures, and guidelines for distributing information

◆ Templates to facilitate information distribution

With this input in place, you use some tools, such as communication technology, to generate the output of this process—that is, to distribute the information.

Tools and Techniques for Information Distribution

Communication skills are necessary for successful information distribution. This and other tools and techniques for information distribution are discussed in the following paragraphs.

Communication skills. Communication is the exchange of information, so communication skills are a necessary requirement for information distribution. Communication skills, an essential part of general management skills, are used to ensure the following:

◆ The right stakeholders get the right information at the right time.

◆ The communication requirements and expectations of stakeholders are properly managed.

As discussed in Chapter 8, the communication line has two ends. There is a sender on one end and a receiver on the other. Both the sender and the receiver need to have communication skills. The sender has the following responsibilities:

◆ Ensure that the information is clear and complete.

◆ Confirm that the information is received and properly understood.

The receiver has the following responsibilities:

◆ The information is received in its entirety.

◆ The information is correctly understood.

So, the success of information distribution depends on both the sender and the receiver. Communication has two flavors in each of the following dimensions:

◆ **Media.** These flavors are writing and speaking on the sender's end and reading and listening on the receiver's end.

◆ **Place.** These flavors are internal to the project—that is, within the project—and external to the project—that is, communicated to entities external to the project, such as the customer, the media, and the public.

◆ **Format.** These flavors are formal, such as reports and briefings, and informal, such as memos and ad hoc conversation.

◆ **Hierarchy.** A horizontal hierarchy means communication among peers, whereas vertical means communication between different levels of the organizational hierarchy—for example, a manager communicating to the team that reports to the manager.

The information that needs to be communicated also needs to be gathered, stored, and retrieved.

Information distribution methods. The information can be distributed in a number of ways that fall into the following two categories:

◆ **Synchronous.** Both the sender and the receiver have to be present at the same time, such as at face-to-face project meetings and teleconferencing.

◆ **Asynchronous.** The sender and receiver don't have to be present at the same time, such as with written paper or electronic documents, online bulletin boards, e-mail, and the World Wide Web in general.

The communication methods and models were discussed in Chapter 8.

Information distribution tools. You can use one or more appropriate tools to distribute information. These sets of tools include the following:

◆ **Document format.** Hard copy or electronic.

◆ **Messages.** E-mail, fax, voicemail, Internet bulletin boards, blogs.

◆ **Meetings.** Face-to-face meetings, video conferences, and teleconferences.

◆ **Management tools.** Project scheduling tools.

You use these tools and techniques to generate the output of the information distribution process.

STUDY CHECKPOINT 9.2

The Distribute Information process uses performance reports as an input. Which process do these reports come from?

Output of Information Distribution

The output of the information distribution process is, well, the distribution of information. This distribution (or communication) of information falls into two categories:

◆ **Formal distribution.** This distribution refers to communicating the information as planned, such as regular status and progress information updates at scheduled times, such as once a week every Wednesday.

◆ **Informal distribution.** This refers to the communication of information on an as-needed basis. For example, the project sponsor can ask you for information that is not part of the regular schedule of distributing information.

The process of distributing information will create some items that can be added as a record to the organizational process assets. Here are some examples:

◆ Project reports and status reports

◆ Stakeholder notifications about resolved issues and approved changes

◆ Project presentations

◆ Project records, such as memos, meeting minutes, and project files, such as plans and schedules

◆ Feedback from stakeholders

◆ Lessons learned

The three most important takeaways from this chapter are the following:

◆ Managing stakeholder expectations through distributing information is crucial to the success of the project.

◆ Managing stakeholder expectations includes keeping those expectations in line with the project management plan and working with stakeholders to meet their needs and to resolve issues as they arise.

◆ Distributing information means making the right information available to the right stakeholders at the right time by using the right communication methods.

Summary

It is crucial to the success of the project that stakeholder expectations be managed through distribution of the right information to the right stakeholders at the right time by using the right communication methods. Processes of managing stakeholder expectations and distributing information are called Manage Stakeholder Expectations and Distribute Information, and they belong to communication management. The communication management plan, a part of the project management plan, and performance reports are the major input items to the Distribute Information process. The information can be distributed by using various methods, such as reports and presentations. The communication management plan and stakeholder management strategy are major inputs to managing stakeholder expectations. Management and interpersonal skills are crucial to successfully managing stakeholder expectations.

Performance reports, a major input to the Distribute Information process, come from monitoring and controlling the project, which is the subject of the next part of this book.

Exam's Eye View

Comprehend

◆ Managing stakeholders includes identifying stakeholders, collecting requirements from the stakeholders, managing stakeholder expectations, and distributing information to the stakeholders.

◆ Resolving issues in a timely fashion helps maintain a constructive relationship with the stakeholders.

◆ The communication management plan and performance reports are the major input items to the Distribute Information process.

◆ The communication management plan and stakeholder management strategy are major inputs to managing stakeholder expectations.

Look Out

◆ Managing stakeholder expectations is crucial to the success of the project by keeping these expectations in line with the project management plan.

◆ Unresolved issues can grow to become a source of conflict.

◆ Communication methods are the tools used in both the Distribute Information and Manage Stakeholder Expectations processes.

◆ The project management plan is used as an input to both distributing information and managing stakeholder expectations because it contains the communication management plan.

Memorize

◆ Distributing the right information to the right stakeholders at the right time by using the right communication methods helps manage stakeholder expectations.

◆ Performance reports are important, but they are not the only way to distribute information to stakeholders.

◆ Performance reports, input to the Distribute Information process, come from monitoring and controlling the project.

◆ The process of distributing information significantly adds to the organizational process assets in the form of project reports, status reports, project presentations, stakeholder notifications, project records, and lessons learned.

Key Terms and Definitions

◆ **asynchronous communication.** Communication in which the sender and receiver don't have to be present at the same time, such as written paper or electronic documents, online bulletin boards, e-mail, and the World Wide Web in general.

◆ **distribute information.** The process of making information available to stakeholders according to the project management plan.

◆ **issue.** An item or a matter that is under discussion or dispute and for which there are most likely opposing views and disagreements among the stakeholders.

◆ **issue log.** A tool used to manage issues that includes opening, modifying, tracking, documenting, and resolving issues.

◆ **managing stakeholder expectations.** A process used for communicating and working with stakeholders to stay on the same page with them on the project requirements by addressing their needs and issues as they arise.

◆ **performance report.** A document or a presentation that provides information about the performance, progress, and status of the project.

◆ **synchronous communication.** Communication in which both the sender and the receiver have to be present at the same time, such as face-to-face project meetings and teleconferencing.

Review Questions

1. Which of the following is not an output of the Distribute Information process?

   A. Performance reports

   B. Project reports and status reports

   C. Updates to project records

   D. Project presentations

2. The issue log is an input used in the following process:

   A. Distribute Information

   B. Manage Stakeholder Expectations

   C. Identify Stakeholders

   D. Resolve Issues

3. The change log is used in the following process:
- **A.** Distribute Information
- **B.** Manage Stakeholder Expectations
- **C.** Identify Stakeholders
- **D.** Perform Integrated Change Control

4. Manage Stakeholder Expectations is a process that belongs to which knowledge area?
- **A.** Human resource management
- **B.** Procurement management
- **C.** Stakeholder management
- **D.** Communication management

5. Whose responsibility is it to manage stakeholder expectations?
- **A.** The project sponsor
- **B.** The project team
- **C.** The project manager
- **D.** Both the sponsor and the project manager

6. You have created the performance report about the project that you are managing. Which process will you use to distribute the report among the stakeholders?
- **A.** Report Performance
- **B.** Distribute Reports
- **C.** Distribute Information
- **D.** Manage Stakeholder Expectations

7. Which of the following communication processes are in the executing process group?
- **A.** Distribute Reports and Manage Stakeholder Expectations
- **B.** Distribute Information and Manage Stakeholder Expectations
- **C.** Report Performance and Manage Stakeholder Expectations
- **D.** Distribute Information and Identify Stakeholders

PART IV

Monitoring and Controlling the Project

You need to continually monitor and control your project. In general, monitoring means watching the course, and controlling means taking action to either stay the course or change the wrong course. Applied to project management, you monitor the project by activities such as making performance measurements to ensure that it is on the track set by the project management plan, and you control the project to keep it on track and to bring it back on track if it falls off. The core of monitoring and controlling the project includes collecting the work performance information, the raw data, from the project execution and analyzing it for performance, which includes comparing it to the accepted performance baseline that consists of the scope baseline, schedule baseline, and cost baseline. This comparison generates the performance measurements, which may generate some change requests. The change requests must be processed through an integrated change control system for approval, and only the approved changes should be implemented. The performance measurements may also expose some previously undetected risks.

Chapter 10

Monitoring and Controlling the Project Work

PMP Exam Objectives

Objective	What It Really Means
4.1 Measure Project Performance	You must understand how to measure project performance against cost, schedule, and scope baselines. You must also understand the terms involved in cost and schedule performance analysis, such as BAC, EV, AC, CV, SV, CPI, SPI, ETC, EAC, and TCPI, covered in Chapter 12. Understand that the performance reports are used by the Monitor and Control Project Work process to generate necessary change requests. This process is covered in this chapter.
4.2 Verify and Manage Changes to the Project	You should know how to manage changes to various aspects of the project, such as project scope, project schedule, and project cost. That means you must understand the processes related to monitoring and controlling the project work, which include Monitor and Control Project Work, Perform Integrated Change Control, and Administer Procurements. These processes are covered in this chapter. You must also understand other monitoring and controlling processes covered in Chapters 11 and 12. You also must understand the impact of a change across the project—for example, the triple constraint covered in Chapter 12.

Introduction

You need to continually monitor and control your project—that is, monitor and control the project activities against the project management plan and project performance baseline. This is because executing a project means executing the project work according to the project management plan based on some baselines, such as a schedule baseline, a scope baseline, and a cost baseline. In general, monitoring means watching the course, and controlling means taking action to either stay the course or change the wrong course. You monitor the project by generating, collecting, and distributing information about project performance against the baselines. Performance reports are used to monitor and control the project work. Deviations of performance results from the plan might indicate that some changes to the original project plan are required. Other change requests might come from stakeholders, such as expanding the project scope by adding new requirements. You control all these changes by influencing the factors that generate them, processing them through a system called the *integrated change control system* that contains a process called the *Perform Integrated Change Control* process, evaluating their impact across the project, and ensuring the implementation of the approved change requests.

In addition to the schedule activities that need to be executed, the project management plan also contains a list of risks and the risk management plan. You monitor the risks by looking out for the risk triggers (the alerts that tell you a risk has occurred or is about to occur) for the already identified risks and by identifying new risks as the project progresses. You control the risks by executing the risk response plan and taking corrective and preventive actions. Quality is an integrated part of any project. Therefore, monitoring and controlling the project work includes controlling the quality. All these aspects of the project are monitored and controlled by using two high-level processes that belong to integration management: the Monitor and Control Project Work process and the Perform Integrated Change Control process. This also includes administering the procurement part of the project, which is another high-level process by its virtue.

So, in this chapter, we will explore the big picture of monitoring and controlling the project while venturing through three avenues: monitoring and controlling project work, performing integrated change control, and administering procurements.

Monitoring and Controlling the Project: Big Picture

You monitor and control your project by monitoring and controlling the project performance, changes, and risks. Monitoring includes measuring project performance, collecting information about project performance, and evaluating performance information to see the trends. Continuous monitoring helps the project management team identify the areas that need to be controlled closely by, for example, taking corrective or preventive actions.

 NOTE

Monitoring and controlling does not start only after the project starts execution. Rather, the project needs to be monitored and controlled all the way from initiation through closing.

A project is monitored and controlled using the Monitor and Control Project Work and Perform Integrated Change Control processes, which are high-level processes performed by executing more specific processes, such as cost control, schedule control, and scope control, as shown in Figure 10.1. All these processes are in the monitoring and controlling process group except the Direct and Manage Project Execution process, which belongs to the executing group.

As illustrated in Figure 10.1, work performance information generated by the Direct and Manage Project Execution process is used by most of the monitoring and controlling processes. The Control Scope, Control Schedule, and Control Cost processes analyze this information to generate work performance measurements, which are used by some other processes, such as Perform Quality Control and Report Performance. The Report Performance process generates performance reports, which are used by the Monitor and Control Risks and Administer Procurements processes. One obvious output of most of these processes is the change requests, including recommended corrective and preventive actions, which go through the Perform Integrated Change Control process for approval. If approved, the execution of these actions and changes is managed using Direct and Manage Project Execution, a process in the executing process group.

STUDY CHECKPOINT 10.1

Name three processes that convert work performance data into work performance measurements.

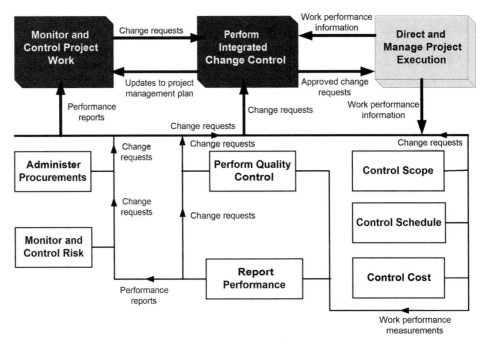

FIGURE 10.1 *Big picture of the monitoring and controlling process group.*

In the monitoring and controlling process group, the Monitor and Control Project Work process and the Perform Integrated Change Control process belong to project integration management.

Monitoring and Controlling Project Work

Monitor and Control Project Work is a high-level process for monitoring and controlling project progress to ensure that the project is on its way to meet its objectives laid out in the project management plan. Some of the major tasks performed during this process include the following:

◆ Monitoring project performance by measuring it against the project management plan in terms of parameters such as cost, schedule, and scope

◆ Monitoring the project by collecting information to support status reporting, progress measurement, and predictions

◆ Evaluating performance to determine whether it needs to be controlled by taking corrective or preventive actions

◆ Monitoring risks by tracking and analyzing the already identified project risks and by identifying new risks

◆ Controlling risks by managing the execution of risk response plans when the risks occur

◆ Maintaining an accurate and timely information base regarding the project as it progresses

◆ Monitoring and controlling changes and monitoring the implementation of approved changes

◆ Monitoring and controlling quality and administering procurements

The Monitor and Control Project Work process is illustrated in Figure 10.2. The major input to this process is the performance reports, which are compared to the performance baseline in the project management plan. From this comparison, some changes may be requested as an output of this process, which may include recommendations for corrective actions, preventive actions, and defect repairs. The performance report consists of current project status, accomplishments, scheduled activities, forecasts, and current issues. This report is generated by using the Report Performance process discussed in Chapter 11.

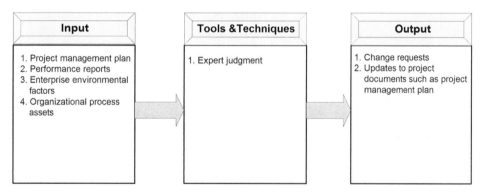

FIGURE 10.2 *The Monitor and Control Project Work process: input, tools and techniques, and output.*

Enterprise environmental factors used as input to this process include project management information systems, work authorization systems of the performing organization, risk tolerance level of the stakeholders, and industry and government standards. The organizational process assets that can be used to perform this process include financial control procedures, the company's communication requirements, management procedures regarding issues and defects, risk control procedures, process measurement database, and lessons learned from past projects.

As a result of performing this process, you may need to update some parts of the project management plan, such as scope baseline, schedule baseline, cost baseline, schedule management plan, cost management plan, and quality management plan. These updates often result from change requests made by various monitoring and controlling processes.

CAUTION

Monitor and Control Project Work is a high-level umbrella process. Most of its tasks are actually performed by using the lower-level, more specific processes discussed in this and upcoming chapters.

STUDY CHECKPOINT 10.2

Name an element for which the project management plan is used to perform the Monitor and Control Project Work process.

As mentioned earlier, change requests arising from monitoring and controlling the project or originating from any other source, such as the stakeholders, must be processed through the integrated change control process formally called Perform Integrated Change Control. Actually, one of the important tasks of monitoring and controlling the project is to influence the factors that tend to circumvent the integrated change control process and ensure that only those changes that are approved through the integrated change control process are implemented.

Integrating Change Control

The Perform Integrated Change Control process is used to manage changes to the project from project initiation through project closure. A project rarely runs exactly according to the project management plan, and therefore changes will inevitably appear. Change requests can come from evaluating project performance to bring the project in line with the project management plan, or they can come from other sources, such as the stakeholders. Regardless of where they originate from, all changes need to be managed (monitored and controlled), which includes getting the changes rejected or approved, seeing the approved changes implemented, and changing the affected plans accordingly. You, the project manager, must manage changes proactively, which includes the following activities:

◆ **Identify changes.** Identify a change that has occurred and receive a change request.

◆ **Process changes.** Get the requested changes approved or rejected. Depending on the project and the performing organization, the authority to determine whether a change is eventually rejected or approved might lie with the project manager, a customer, a sponsor, or a committee.

◆ **Manage approved changes.** Monitor and control the flow of approved changes, which includes:

    ◆ Making sure they are implemented.

    ◆ Maintaining the integrity of the project baseline (cost, schedule, and scope) by updating it to incorporate the approved changes.

    ◆ Coordinating changes and their impact across the project and updating the affected documentation. For example, an approved schedule change might impact cost, quality, risk, and staffing.

    ◆ Documenting the complete impact of the changes across the project.

◆ **Protect the integrity of the process.** Make sure that only the approved changes are implemented.

TIP

Especially in a startup organization, quite often you will notice changes making their way through the back door—for example, a product manager talking to an engineer directly and introducing changes. Do not consider yourself an opponent of changes by default, but you do need to manage changes and make sure each change goes through the integrated change control process. So, when it comes to changes, the key word is *control*, and not necessarily *oppose*.

At this point, you can ask a question: Who will actually approve or reject a change request? The answer to this question will be determined during project planning. Depending on the project and the performing organization, different possibilities exist. For example, there will be a category of change requests that the project manager may be authorized to approve or disapprove. Other types of changes may be reviewed by a change control board (CCB) that may consist of individuals from upper management and other stakeholders. The roles and responsibilities of the CCB should be clearly spelled out in the change control and configuration control procedures.

Figure 10.3 shows the integrated change control process. The change requests that need to be approved are the obvious input to this process.

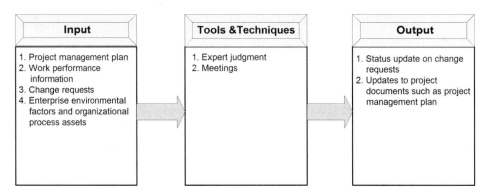

FIGURE 10.3 *The Perform Integrated Change Control process: input, tools and techniques, and output.*

Input to Integrated Change Control

Each requested change and recommended action must be processed through the integrated change control process. The approved changes have their effects on the project management plan, and therefore the plan needs to be updated accordingly. Following are the input items to the integrated change control process.

Project management plan. This is needed to help identify the changes and make updates after the changes have been approved.

Work performance information. The performance information is input because performance deviations from the plan will trigger change requests or recommended corrective or preventive actions to improve the situation.

Change requests. This is the obvious input. A requested change goes through an approval process in which it can be approved, rejected, or delayed. These change requests come from various monitoring and controlling processes or from the stakeholders. The change requests may include the following types of recommendations:

- Recommended corrective actions
- Recommended preventive actions
- Recommended defect repairs

These recommendations might arise from performance evaluations, and they are the output of various processes discussed in this chapter.

Enterprise environmental factors. The enterprise environmental factors that can influence the integrated change control process include the project management information system. This is a collection of tools and techniques (manual and automated) used to gather, integrate, and disseminate the output of project management processes. This system is used to facilitate processes from the initiation stage all the way to the closing stage. Microsoft Project, a product that lets you create a project schedule, is an example of such a tool. Another example of a component of the project management information system could be a document management system to create, review, change, and approve documents to facilitate the change control procedure.

The project management information system may include scheduling software, an information collection and distribution system, a configuration management system, and web interfaces to other automated information systems. A configuration management system can be used to monitor and control changes, and it may have some knowledge base that can also be used.

Organizational process assets. The following items in the organizational process assets can influence the change control process.

- ◆ **Organizational procedures.** Your organization may have proper procedures related to change control—for example, how to modify documents, such as plans; how to process (evaluate, approve, or reject) changes; and how to implement the approved changes.
- ◆ **Measurements.** A database of process measurements.
- ◆ **Project files.** Project files from previous projects may be a useful input to the change control process in order to learn from the past.
- ◆ **Change knowledge base.** This is the knowledge base that can be used for configuration management, such as official company standards and policies and project documents.

So what tools and techniques are available to process these requests and recommendations? Read on....

Tools and Techniques for Integrated Change Control

Expert judgment and meetings are the two main tools for the integrated change control process. You can also use the technical expertise of the stakeholders to evaluate change requests. The project management team can also use the experts on the change control board to evaluate change requests and to make approval or rejection decisions about change requests. If there is a formal change control board for the project, it will conduct meetings to review, evaluate, approve, reject, or delay the change requests.

Rejection or approval of the change request is an obvious output of the integrated change control process.

Output from Integrated Change Control

The changes that are processed through the integrated change control process will either be rejected or approved. As a result of the approved changes, the project management plan might need to be updated. Accordingly, following are the output items of the integrated change control process.

Change request status updates. The items processed through the integrated change control process will ultimately be either approved or rejected. In the meantime, each change request must have some status that can be reported. Here are some examples of status:

◆ Being processed
◆ Approved
◆ Rejected
◆ Implemented
◆ Implementation validated

Document updates. As a result of approved changes, items such as the project management plan and the project scope statement might need to be updated. The baselines in the project management plan and any subsidiary plans may need to be updated as a result of the change.

STUDY CHECKPOINT 10.3

Many processes in the monitoring and controlling process group generate change requests. Name a process in this process group that takes change requests as an input.

Administering Procurements

Administering procurements is the process of monitoring and controlling the procurement part of the project. It's a three-pronged process:

1. Manage procurement-specific relationships
2. Monitor the performance of the procurement part of the project
3. Monitor and control the procurement-related changes

Administering procurements has a two-pronged goal: The seller performance meets the procurement requirements, and the buyer meets its agreed-upon contractual obligations. Depending on the size and complexity of the project and the structure of the performing organization, procurement administration may be treated by a group outside of the project organization. But you will still need to integrate this function with the project and act as a communicator and coordinator to ensure that this function is performed smoothly without adversely affecting the other aspects of the project. The project management processes that can be used for administering procurements include Perform Quality Control, Report Performance, Direct and Manage Project Execution, Monitor and Control Risks, and Perform Integrated Change Control. In that sense, it's a high-level process illustrated in Figure 10.4. The major input items are the procurement management plan, work performance information, performance reports, contracts, and approved change requests. The tools and techniques used in administering procurements include the contract change control system, the payment system, claims administration, and inspections and audits. Administering procurements may generate change requests.

FIGURE 10.4 *The Administer Procurements process: input, tools and techniques, and output.*

STUDY CHECKPOINT 10.4

Name an input item that is common to all three processes: Monitor and Control Project Work, Perform Integrated Change Control, and Administer Procurements.

The three most important takeaways from this chapter are as follows:

◆ Work performance reports are compared to the project management plan to monitor and control the project work and to make recommendations for changes accordingly.

◆ All change requests must go through the integrated change control process, and only the approved changes should be implemented.

◆ Administering procurements is a high-level process that can be executed by performing multiple project management processes, such as Perform Quality Control, Report Performance, Direct and Manage Project Execution, Monitor and Control Risks, and Perform Integrated Change Control.

Summary

You need to monitor and control your project throughout its lifecycle, which includes monitoring and controlling project work, including procurements, performance, changes, quality, and risks. All these aspects of the project are monitored and controlled by using two high-level processes that belong to integration management: Monitor and Control Project Work and Perform Integrated Change Control. This also includes administering the procurement part of the project, which is another high-level process by its virtue. The Monitor and Control Project Work process takes performance reports as input, compares them to the planned performance (baselines) in the project management plan, and, if needed, makes recommendations for changes to bring the project back on track. The change requests from this and other processes are run through the Perform Integrated Change Control process. Only the change requests approved through this process are implemented. Project procurements are administered by using many processes, including Perform Quality Control, Report Performance, Direct and Manage Project Execution, Monitor and Control Risks, and Perform Integrated Change Control.

We discussed three high-level processes in this chapter, out of which two belong to project integration management. These processes are actually performed by executing a number of low-level processes. Quality control and risk control are two of these low-level processes, and they are discussed in the next chapter.

Exam's Eye View

Comprehend

- You monitor and control the project by monitoring and controlling project work, performance, changes, quality, and risks.

- All the individual control processes, such as risk control and quality control, can generate change requests and recommended actions, which must be processed through the integrated change control process, in which each of these requests and recommendations will either be rejected or approved.

- The approved change requests and recommendations for actions will be processed through the Direct and Manage Project Execution process for implementation.

- The Monitor and Control Project Work process and the Perform Integrated Change Control process belong to project integration management.

Look Out

- One of the important tasks of monitoring and controlling the project is to influence the factors that tend to circumvent the integrated change control process and ensure that only those changes are implemented that are approved through the integrated change control process.

- The performance reports generated by the Report Performance process are an input to the Monitor and Control Project Work process.

- Most of the processes of the monitoring and controlling group generate change requests, which must be approved or rejected by performing the integrated change control process.

- Approved change requests must be implemented by performing the Direct and Manage Project Execution process.

Memorize

◆ Work performance is an input to the Perform Integrated Change Control process and the Administer Procurements process.

◆ Performance reports are an input to the Monitor and Control Project Work process and the Administer Procurements process.

◆ Change requests are an output of Monitor and Control Project Work process and the Administer Procurements process.

◆ The Perform Integrated Change Control process generates updates to change requests as an output—that is, it approves, rejects, or postpones a change request.

Key Terms and Definitions

◆ **change control board.** A formal group of stakeholders with the authority to process change requests, which includes reviewing, approving, rejecting, and delaying change requests.

◆ **change request.** A request for deviating from the project plan or related policies or procedures, such as modifying scope, schedule, or cost. Change requests may include recommendations for corrective and preventive actions.

◆ **claim.** An assertion, demand, or request made by a buyer against the seller or vice versa for consideration or compensation under the terms of a legal contract.

◆ **control.** To analyze the performance and make and implement recommendations for corrective actions or other changes to bring the project back on track.

◆ **corrective actions.** Actions recommended for execution in the future in order to bring project performance back in line with the project management plan.

◆ **monitor.** To collect project performance information/data as planned, convert the information to performance measurements, and report the performance.

◆ **preventive actions.** Actions to be executed to keep the project from getting off track—for example, to avoid risks or poor performance.

◆ **project performance.** Measure of actual project progress against planned progress.

Review Questions

1. The integrated change control process is used to manage changes to the project at which stage?

    A. From initiating through closing

    B. Planning only

    C. Executing only

    D. Executing and closing only

2. A project manager is getting the risk-related recommended corrective actions approved. Which of the following processes is the project manager involved in?

    A. Integrated change control

    B. Risk response planning

    C. Risk identification

    D. Qualitative risk analysis

3. You have just submitted a few important change requests to the change control board for their evaluation and recommendations. What process are you executing?

    A. No process

    B. Direct and Manage Project Execution

    C. Perform Integrated Change Control

    D. Monitor and Control Project Work

4. Walking down the hallway, you heard a program manager saying to a project manager, "You need the performance reports to run this process." Which process is the program manager referring to?

    A. Monitor and Control Project Work

    B. Perform Integrated Change Control

    C. Direct and Manage Project Execution

    D. Evaluate Performance

5. The process to monitor and control procurements is called:

    A. Monitor and Control Procurements

    B. Administer Procurements

    C. Contract Administration

    D. Administer Contracts

6. Which of the following is the correct order in which to perform the listed processes for the first time?

   A. Report Performance, Administer Procurements, Perform Integrated Change Control

   B. Administer Procurements, Perform Integrated Change Control, Report Performance

   C. Perform Integrated Change Control, Administer Procurements, Report Performance

   D. Perform Integrated Change Control, Report Performance, Administer Procurements

7. The sponsor of your project wants to look at the raw data from executing the project—that is, the work performance information. Which process should you run to get this information?

   A. Report Performance

   B. Distribute Information

   C. Direct and Manage Project Execution

   D. Control Scope

8. The sponsor of your project wants to look at the work performance measurements. Which process should you run to get this information?

   A. Report Performance

   B. Distribute Information

   C. Direct and Manage Project Execution

   D. Control Scope, Control Schedule, and Control Cost

Chapter 11

Monitoring and Controlling Quality and Risk

PMP Exam Objectives

Objective	What It Really Means
4.1 Measure Project Performance	You must understand how to measure project performance against cost, schedule, and scope baselines. You must also understand the terms involved in cost and schedule performance analysis, such as BAC, EV, AC, CV, SV, CPI, SPI, ETC, EAC, and TCPI, covered in Chapter 12. You must understand how the Report Performance process is used to prepare performance reports that are used in monitoring and controlling the project work and in controlling risks.
4.3 Ensure Project Deliverables Conform to Quality Standards	You must understand how to use the Perform Quality Control process to ensure conformance to quality standards included in the project management plan. You must understand all the quality control tools, such as control charts, flowcharting, Pareto diagrams, statistical sampling, and inspection.
4.4 Monitor All Risks	You need to know that you must actively monitor the identified risks and identify and respond to new risks as they appear. You must understand the risk monitoring and controlling process called Monitor and Control Risks. You should also be familiar with risk response techniques, such as acceptance, transference, and mitigation, discussed in Chapter 6.

Introduction

At any given point in time, the project is in a certain state called the *project status*, and the difference between two states in time is called the *project progress*. Your success as a project manager is directly proportional to successfully communicating the project performance, including the project status and progress, to the right stakeholders at the right time by using the right methods. It is not a matter of chance that I have used the two words *communication* and *performance* in the same sentence; they are intimately connected and highly correlated concepts in project management. Communicating performance to the right stakeholders at the right time by using the right methods is called *performance reporting*, or *reporting* for brevity. Effective reporting is the oxygen for a project. Among many other benefits, reporting helps control project risks—the enemies within.

Quality is an integrated part of any project. Therefore, monitoring and controlling project work includes controlling quality. If you do not monitor and control risks, the quality will be affected. You monitor the risks by looking out for risk triggers (alerts that tell you a risk has occurred or is about to occur) for the already identified risks and by identifying new risks as the project progresses. You control risks by executing the risk response plan and taking corrective and preventive actions.

Therefore, the core question in this chapter is, how do you monitor and control performance communication, quality, and risk? In search of an answer, we will explore three avenues in the area of monitoring and controlling: controlling quality, controlling risks, and reporting performance.

Controlling Quality

Quality is controlled by using the Perform Quality Control process, a process of monitoring and recording results from the execution of projects, including quality activities. The goal is to evaluate quality performance and recommend necessary changes. The quality control process in the context of a big picture is shown in Figure 11.1, which relates the quality management processes to one another and also to integrated change control and project execution.

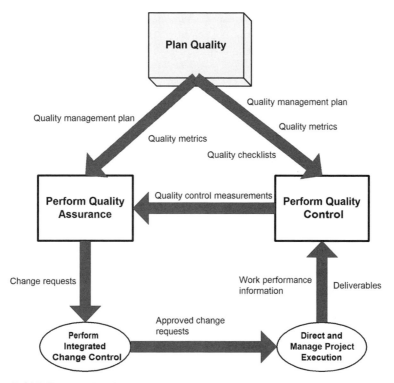

FIGURE 11.1 *Quality management in the big picture.*

STUDY CHECKPOINT 11.1

A. Which quality process generates quality control measurements?

B. Which quality process uses quality control measurements?

Controlling quality involves monitoring specific results to determine whether they comply with the planned quality standards, which include project processes and product goals, and controlling the results by taking actions to eliminate unsatisfactory performance. In other words, the Perform Quality Control process is used to monitor and control quality by accomplishing the following goals:

◆ Monitor specific project results, such as cost performance and schedule performance, to determine whether they comply with the planned quality standards, which include project processes and product goals.

◆ Identify ways to eliminate the causes of unsatisfactory performance.

The results under scrutiny include both deliverables and performance measurements by the project management team. Quality control is performed throughout the project. While dealing with quality control, you must be able to distinguish between the two terms in each of the following pairs:

◆ **Prevention and inspection**

    ◆ Prevention is a direction to perform an activity that will keep an error from entering the product and the process.

    ◆ Inspection is a technique to examine whether an activity, component, product, result, or service complies with planned requirements. The goal of inspection is to ensure that errors do not reach the customer.

◆ **Attribute sampling and variable sampling**

    ◆ Attribute sampling is a technique to determine whether a result conforms to the specified standard.

    ◆ Variable sampling is a technique to rate a result on a continuous scale that measures the degree of conformity.

◆ **Common cause and special cause**

    ◆ Common cause is a source of variation that is inherent to the system and is predictable. Such variations are also called *normal variations*, and the common causes for them are also called *random causes*.

    ◆ Special cause is a source of variation that is not inherent to the system and is removable. It can be assigned to a defect in the system.

◆ **Control limits and tolerances**

    ◆ Control limits is the area occupied by three standard deviations on either side of the central line or the mean of a normal distribution of data plotted on a control chart that reflects the expected variation of the data. If the results fall within the control limits, they are within the quality control.

    ◆ Tolerance is the range within which a result is acceptable if it falls within the limits of the range.

Figure 11.2 shows the Perform Quality Control process.

 TIP

QC can be performed by the QA department or by the QC department if the performing organization has one. Nevertheless, the project management team should have a working knowledge of statistical aspects of quality control, such as sampling and probability. This will help evaluate the QC output.

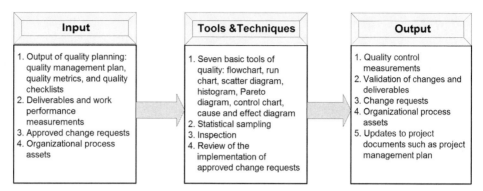

Input	Tools &Techniques	Output
1. Output of quality planning: quality management plan, quality metrics, and quality checklists 2. Deliverables and work performance measurements 3. Approved change requests 4. Organizational process assets	1. Seven basic tools of quality: flowchart, run chart, scatter diagram, histogram, Pareto diagram, control chart, cause and effect diagram 2. Statistical sampling 3. Inspection 4. Review of the implementation of approved change requests	1. Quality control measurements 2. Validation of changes and deliverables 3. Change requests 4. Organizational process assets 5. Updates to project documents such as project management plan

FIGURE 11.2 *The Perform Quality Control process: input, tools and techniques, and output.*

Input to Quality Control

The goal of quality control is to ensure that the performance from the project execution meets the planned quality standards. Therefore, the outputs from project execution and from quality planning are the obvious inputs to the Perform Quality Control process. These and other input items are discussed here:

- **Quality planning output.** The following items from the output of the quality planning process, discussed in Chapter 6, are the input to the Perform Quality Control process:
  - The quality management plan lets you know what quality standards are supposed to be implemented and how.
  - Quality metrics specify which quality features to monitor and how to measure them.
  - Quality checklists show which quality steps need to be performed.
- **Output from the Direct and Manage Project Execution process.** The following items from the output of the Direct and Manage Project Execution process, discussed in Chapter 7, are input to the Perform Quality Control process:
  - A list of deliverables from the project execution to ensure that all the required deliverables are produced before project completion
  - Work performance measurements to monitor performance. These measurements are made from the work performance information received from project execution by processing it through scope control, schedule control, and cost control.
- **Approved change requests.** You need this list to ensure that all the approved changes are implemented in a timely fashion. The list of approved change requests also includes modifications, such as revised work methods and a revised schedule.
- **Organizational process assets.** These include quality policies and procedures, work guidelines, change control procedures, communication policies, and quality-related historical data. These items will be used in the quality control process.

STUDY CHECKPOINT 11.2

Project deliverables are an input to which quality process?

Quality control is a very involved process and has a plethora of tools and techniques, discussed next.

Tools and Techniques for Quality Control

The tools and techniques used for quality control include inspection, defect repair reviews, and the so-called seven basic tools of quality.

Seven Basic Tools of Quality

Table 11.1 shows the seven kinds of charts and diagrams used in quality control, also known as the seven basic tools of quality. These tools are further described in the following list.

Table 11.1 Seven Basic Tools of Quality

Chart	Purpose
Flowchart	To anticipate what quality problems might be and where they might occur
Run chart	To perform trend analysis—that is, to predict future results based on past performance
Scatter diagram	To find the relationship between two variables, such as cause and effect, or two causes
Histogram	To display the relative importance of different variables
Pareto diagram	To identify and rank errors based on the frequency of defects caused by them
Control chart	To monitor whether the variance of a specified variable is within the acceptable limits dictated by quality control
Cause and effect diagram	To explore all the potential causes of a problem, not just the obvious ones

Flowcharts

A flowchart is a diagram that depicts inputs, actions, and outputs of one or more processes in a system. Flowcharts, commonly used in many disciplines of knowledge, show the activities, decision points, and order of processing. They help to understand how a problem occurs. You can also use flowcharts to anticipate what quality problems might be, where they might occur, and how you might deal with them.

Run Charts

A run chart is a chart that shows the history and pattern of variations. Therefore, run charts are used to perform trend analysis, which is the science of predicting future performance based on past results. In quality control, trend analysis can be used to predict such things as the number of defects and the cost to repair them. You can use the results of trend analysis to recommend preventive actions if needed. Run charts or trend analysis can be used to monitor cost performance, schedule performance, and technical performance. An example of technical performance is how many defects have been identified and how many of them remained unrepaired.

Scatter Diagrams

A scatter diagram is used to show the pattern of the relationship between two variables—an independent variable and another variable that depends on the independent variable. The dependent variable is plotted corresponding to the independent variable. For example, a variable representing a cause can be the independent variable, and a variable representing the effect can be a dependent variable. The closer the data points are to a diagonal line, the stronger the relationship (called the *correlation*) is between the two variables.

Histograms

A histogram is a bar chart that shows a distribution of variables. Each bar can represent an attribute, such as defects due to a specific cause, and its height can represent the frequency of the attribute, such as number of defects. This tool helps to identify and rate the causes of defects. You also use a histogram to identify and illustrate the most common cause of a problem, such as a cause behind defects.

You might wonder how defects can be repaired efficiently. Pareto diagrams, which are examples of histograms, have the answer for you.

Pareto Diagrams

A Pareto diagram is used to rank the importance of each error (problem) based on the frequency of its occurrence over time in the form of defects. A defect is an imperfection or deficiency that keeps a component from meeting its requirements or specifications. A defect is caused by an error (problem) and can be repaired by fixing the error. An error in a product can give rise to multiple defects, and by fixing the error you repair all the defects caused by that error.

However, all errors are not equal. Some errors cause more defects than others. According to Pareto's law, which is also known as the *80/20 rule*, 80 percent of project defects are caused by 20 percent of errors (or types of errors). Qualitatively, it means that most defects are caused by a small set of errors. The Pareto diagram lets you rank errors based on the frequency of defects they cause. You begin by having the error that causes most of the defects fixed and make your way to other errors that cause lesser numbers of defects. This way, the efforts of the project team are optimized: You get the maximum number of defects repaired with minimal effort.

The advantages of a Pareto diagram are twofold:

◆ It ranks errors according to the frequency of defects they cause.

◆ It optimizes efforts to repair the defects by working on the errors that cause most of the defects.

As an example, Table 11.2 presents data on the frequency of defects caused by certain errors. The data is displayed in Figure 11.3 in form of a Pareto diagram. In this example, 200 defects are caused by seven errors, and Error A alone causes 75 defects, which is 37.5 percent of all the defects. Similarly, you can understand the impact of other errors by looking at Table 11.2 and Figure 11.3. The Pareto diagram tells you that you should address Error A first, Error B second, and so on.

Table 11.2 Example of Frequency of Defects Corresponding to Errors Causing the Defects

Error Causing the Defects	Number of Defects	Percentage of Defects Caused by This Error	Cumulative Percentage
A	75	37.5	37.5
B	50	25.0	62.5
C	30	15.0	77.5
D	20	10.0	87.5
E	15	7.50	95.0
F	7	3.5	98.5
G	3	1.5	100.0

 NOTE

Pareto's law, in its original form, was presented as an economic theory by Vilfredo Pareto, a 19th-century Italian economist, and it states that 80 percent of income is earned by 20 percent of the population. Since then, it has been applied to other fields, such as project management.

You might ask: How many defects are acceptable? To find an answer to this question, you need to understand another tool, called the *control chart*.

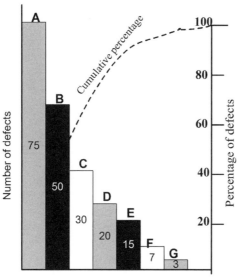

FIGURE 11.3 *An example of a Pareto diagram.*

Control Charts

Control charts are used to monitor whether the variance of a specified variable is within the acceptable limits dictated by quality control. A variance is a measurable deviation in the value of a project variable, such as cost from a known baseline or expected value. This is a way to monitor the deviations and determine whether the corresponding variable is in or out of control. The values are taken at different times to measure the behavior of a variable over time. The mean value in the control chart represents the expected value, and a predetermined spread from the mean value (usually ±3 σ) is used to define the limits within which an acceptable value can fall.

Control charts can be used to monitor the values of any type of output variables. To illustrate their main features, consider the example of a control chart shown in Figure 11.4. In this example, assume that a manufacturer produces 100 units of a product each day, and it is expected that 95 out of 100 units should have no defect—that is, the expected number of defective units is equal to five. The control limits are set to ±3. In other words, 95 units out of 100 must be correct, give or take three. That puts the lower limit at 92 and the upper limit at 98. Crossing the lower limits is not acceptable to the customer, and crossing the upper limits might require an unjustifiable cost.

Controlling quality includes dealing with defects and problems that cause them. So, studying causes of a problem is critical to quality control.

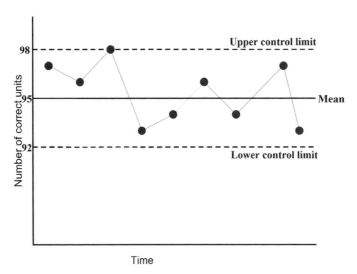

FIGURE 11.4 *An example of a control chart.*

Cause and Effect Diagram

A cause and effect diagram is used to explore all the potential causes (inputs) that result in a single effect (output), such as a problem or a defect. This type of diagram is the brainchild of Kaoru Ishikawa, who pioneered quality management processes in the Kawasaki shipyards, and therefore these diagrams are also called *Ishikawa diagrams*. Due to the shape of these diagrams, they are also known as *fishbone diagrams*. To construct and use cause and effect diagrams effectively, perform the following simple steps:

1. **Identify the problem.** Write down the problem in a box drawn on the right side of a large sheet of paper. This represents the head of the fish. Starting from the box, draw a horizontal line across the paper. This represents the spine of the fish.

2. **Identify the possible areas of causes.** Identify the areas or factors from where the potential causes of the problem might come. Environment, people, materials, measurements, and methods are some examples of areas (factors) of causes. For each factor relevant to the problem under study, draw a line off the spine and label it with the name of the factor. These lines represent the fish bones.

3. **Identify the possible causes.** For each factor, identify possible causes. Represent each possible cause with a line coming off the bone that represents the corresponding factor.

4. **Analyze the diagram.** Analyzing the diagram includes narrowing down the most likely causes and investigating them further.

Figure 11.5 shows an example of a cause and effect diagram. The problem in this example is the delay in the release of a website. The factors considered are environment, methods, people, and time. Of course, the diagram is incomplete in the sense that more factors and related causes can be explored, and causes for each factor can be explored further. But you get the point.

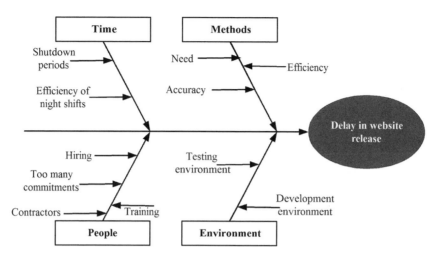

FIGURE 11.5 *An example of a cause and effect diagram: Explore the causes for a delay in a web-site release.*

 TIP

While constructing the cause and effect diagram, you can use the brainstorming method for identifying the potential factors of causes and the potential causes for each factor.

A cause and effect diagram offers a structured way to think through all possible causes of a problem. You can use these diagrams to carry out a thorough analysis of a problematic situation. This kind of analysis is useful in complex situations when, to discover the real causes, you need to explore all the potential causes and not just the obvious ones.

In addition to the seven quality tools we have discussed, there are some other tools that you can use for quality control.

Other Quality Control Tools

In addition to the seven quality tools, the following tools can also be used for controlling quality:

◆ **Statistical sampling.** Statistical sampling involves randomly selecting a part of the population for study. In quality control, you can select a subset of features for inspection. This can save a substantial amount of resources.

◆ **Inspection.** This is a technique to examine whether an activity, component, product, service, or result conforms to specific requirements. Inspections can be conducted at various levels of project execution. For example, you can inspect the results of a single activity, or you can inspect the final product of the project. Nevertheless, inspection generally includes measurements. There are various forms of inspections, such as reviews, peer reviews, audits, and walkthroughs.

◆ **Review of approved defect repairs.** This review is conducted by the QC department or body to ensure that the defects approved for repair are actually repaired to bring the defective product, service, or results in conformance with the specified requirements.

STUDY CHECKPOINT 11.3

What other process uses the tools and techniques used in the Perform Quality Control process?

These tools can be used to make quality control measurements, which in turn can be used to recommend preventive and corrective actions: the output of quality control.

Output of Quality Control

The quality control measurements and the recommendations based on those measurements are the obvious output items of the quality control process. These and other output items are discussed in the following list.

Quality control measurements. These are the results of the QC activities and are fed back to the QA process. They are also used to make recommendations for corrective and preventive actions. These measurements function as feedback for the quality assurance process.

Validated items. These are the items that have been validated through the QC process:

◆ **Validated defect repair.** Once a component has been repaired from a defect, it needs to be inspected so the repair will be accepted or rejected. The rejected items might need to be repaired again. The accepted repair is a validated defect repair.

◆ **Validated deliverables.** This refers to verifying the correctness of project deliverables. A deliverable accepted through a QC process is a validated deliverable.

Change requests. The quality control process can generate the following kinds of change requests:

◆ **Recommended corrective actions.** These actions are recommended as a result of the QC process to meet the established quality goals.

◆ **Recommended preventive actions.** These actions are recommended as a result of the QC process to avoid future failure to meet the established quality goals.

◆ **Recommended defect repair.** A defect is an imperfection or deficiency that keeps a component from meeting its requirements or specifications. Such a component needs to be repaired or replaced.

◆ **Other change requests.** These requests may arise from recommended corrective or preventive actions that might require changes to the project, or they may be needed independent of these recommendations. The changes are requested and processed through the integrated change control process.

Updates. The quality control process might generate updates to the following items:

◆ **Organizational process assets.** The completed checklists become part of the project record. Furthermore, you can update the lessons-learned database and documentation. These might include the causes of variances, the reasons for corrective and preventive actions, and the actions that worked and those that did not.

◆ **Project management plan.** The project management plan should be updated to reflect changes to the quality management plan resulting from the QC process. The quality baseline might need to be updated to reflect changes to the quality plan resulting from the QC process.

STUDY CHECKPOINT 11.4

In the following table, write the name of a quality management process in the second column corresponding to each activity listed in the first column.

Activity	Quality Management Process
You managed a quality audit of your project and found an enormous number of defects.	_____
You are looking at a diagram to pinpoint the root cause of a number of defects appearing in the project product. You write down your observations and recommend a corrective action.	_____
You are determining the cost of quality to present a case for quality assurance and quality control to your supervisor.	_____
You are examining the product to ensure that a defect has actually been repaired.	_____
You are looking at a diagram to pinpoint the root cause of a number of defects appearing in the project product. This leads you to analyze some processes and procedures for their effectiveness.	_____

Let's say you are doing a fine job in controlling quality. However, if an unidentified risk suddenly strikes or an already identified risk event has occurred but the planned response is not being implemented in a timely fashion, quality is one of the possible victims. So controlling risks is as important as controlling quality.

Monitoring and Controlling Risks

Risks are monitored and controlled by using the Monitor and Control Risks process. This process is shown in Figure 11.6, which presents the big picture of risk management.

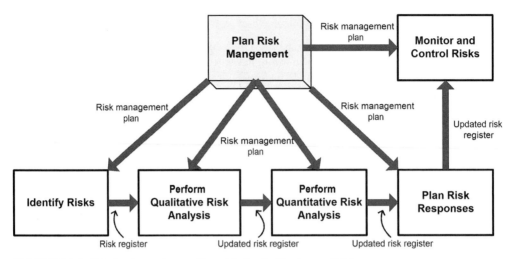

FIGURE 11.6 *Monitoring and controlling risks in the big picture of risk management.*

You must actively monitor the identified risks and identify and respond to new risks as they appear. The risk monitoring and controlling process is used to monitor and control risks and includes the following goals:

◆ Tracking identified risks

◆ Monitoring residual risks (risks that remain after risk responses have been implemented)

◆ Identifying new risks and preparing responses for them

◆ Executing the risk plan and evaluating its effectiveness

However, the risk situation can change with time. Therefore, monitoring and controlling risks also includes monitoring risk dynamics, which involves the following:

◆ Ensuring that the project execution is conforming to the risk management policies and procedures.

◆ Determining whether the project assumptions are still valid. If an assumption becomes invalid, it may eliminate a risk or may give rise to a new risk.

◆ Determining whether the current analysis has changed the risk assessment. The change in the risk assessment may require changes in other aspects of the project, such as cost, schedule, and contingency reserves.

Figure 11.7 illustrates the Monitor and Control Risks process. The risk register and risk management plan contain the list of risks you identified during risk planning and the responses you will execute if the risks occur. Work performance information from project execution and performance reports is also useful in monitoring risks. These items can help you determine whether risk response plans are being implemented, if those implementations are producing the desired results, and if there are signs of new risks.

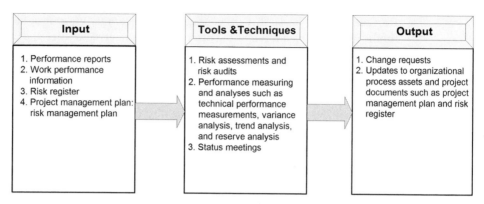

Input	Tools &Techniques	Output
1. Performance reports 2. Work performance information 3. Risk register 4. Project management plan: risk management plan	1. Risk assessments and risk audits 2. Performance measuring and analyses such as technical performance measurements, variance analysis, trend analysis, and reserve analysis 3. Status meetings	1. Change requests 2. Updates to organizational process assets and project documents such as project management plan and risk register

FIGURE 11.7 *The Monitor and Control Risks process: input, tools and techniques, and output.*

To monitor and control risks, you must have a list of identified risks, a plan to deal with the risks, and the signs of risk occurrence. Accordingly, the input items to risk monitoring and controlling are risk management plans, risk registers, approved change requests, and work performance information. These items were discussed in Chapter 6. The tools and techniques for risk monitoring and the output from it are discussed in the following sections.

Tools and Techniques for Risk Monitoring and Controlling

There are some tools and techniques available to detect risk triggers, to respond effectively to the risks that have occurred, and to identify new risks.

Risk reassessment. Risks should be continually reassessed as the project progresses. For example, a risk on the watch list might become important enough that you might need to prepare a response plan for it. On the other hand, a risk may disappear and should then be closed.

Risk audits. A risk audit is conducted to examine the following:

◆ Root causes of the identified risks

◆ Effectiveness of responses to the identified risks

◆ Effectiveness of risk management processes

The project manager is responsible for ensuring that risk assessments and risk audits are conducted with needed frequency.

Risk analyses. Risk analyses are necessary to effectively respond to risks that have occurred, to detect risk triggers, and to identify new risks. The following two kinds of analyses are appropriate for risk monitoring:

◆ **Variance and trend analysis.** Trends in project performance should be reviewed on a regular basis as the project execution progresses. These trends can be determined by analyzing the performance data based on various performance control techniques, such as variance and earned value analysis, discussed earlier in this chapter. This analysis can help in detecting new risks.

◆ **Reserve analysis.** Recall that the contingency reserve is the amount of funds or time (in the schedule) in addition to the planned budget reserved to keep the impact of risks to an acceptable level when the project is executing. The risks occurring during project execution can have positive or negative effects on contingency reserve. You perform reserve analysis at a given time to compare the remaining reserve amount to the remaining risk to determine whether the remaining reserve amount is adequate.

Technical performance measurement. Technical performance measurements compare actual versus planned parameters related to the overall technical progress of the project. The deviation determines the degree to which system requirements are met in terms of performance, cost, schedule, and progress in implementing risk handling. The parameters chosen to measure technical performance could be any parameters that represent something important related to the project objectives and requirements; software performance, human resource performance, and system test performance are some examples.

Status meetings. You should always put risk management as an agenda item at project status meetings. The time spent on this item will depend on the number of identified risks, their priorities, and the complexity of the responses planned for them. Nevertheless, keeping risk on your agenda and discussing risks with the team on a regular basis helps make risk management smoother and more effective.

These tools and techniques are used to monitor risks that might generate recommendations for actions, which are parts of the output of the risk monitoring and controlling processes.

Output from Risk Monitoring and Controlling

The output of monitoring risks includes recommendations for actions and requests for changes to control the risks. These and other output items are discussed in the following paragraphs.

Change requests. You will need to make some change requests as a result of risk monitoring and controlling. The change requests may arise from recommended actions. For example, recommended actions, such as contingency plans and workarounds, might result in requirements to change some elements of the project management plan to respond to certain risks. Of course, the change requests will need to go through the integrated change control process for approval, and the approved change requests will become the input to the Direct and Manage Project Execution process for implementation.

There are two kinds of actions recommended as a result of risk monitoring: corrective actions and preventive actions. Corrective actions include contingency plans and workaround plans. A workaround is a response to a negative risk that has occurred. A workaround is based on a quick solution and is not planned in advance of the risk occurrence event. Preventive actions are recommended to bring the project into compliance with the project management plan. Recommended corrective and preventive actions are input to the integrated change control process.

Updates. The risk monitoring and controlling processes might require updates to the following items:

- ◆ **Risk register.** You might need to include the following updates to the risk register:
  - ◆ Outcomes of risk reassessments, risk reviews, and risk audits
  - ◆ Outcomes of risks and responses to risks
- ◆ **Project management plan.** The project management plan might need to be updated as a result of risk monitoring and controlling. For example, change requests might change the risk management processes, which in turn will change the project management plan.
- ◆ **Organizational process assets.** As a result of the risk monitoring and controlling processes, some organizational process assets might need to be updated, such as templates for the project management plan, the historical information database for such information as actual costs and durations of project activities, the lessons-learned knowledge database, and checklists.

Performance reports used as input in risk controlling are generated during performance reporting.

Performance Reporting

Figure 11.8 presents performance reporting in the context of the big picture. While you are directing and managing the project execution, the work results and the progress toward creating the project results are generated. Just producing the results is no guarantee of success. Success is determined by the performance with which the results are being produced. You need to know the performance to keep the project on the right track. Furthermore, the stakeholders need to know with what rate, efficiency, and work quality the resources are being used to deliver the project output. For this, you need to collect the project performance data and use this data to make performance measurements while controlling the scope, schedule, and cost. You use this data and performance measurements to prepare performance reports, which in turn are used for distributing information and controlling risks.

Performance reporting is the process of collecting performance information, putting it into the distribution format, and distributing it. Performance reporting, for brevity, is also called *reporting* and is focused on the following components:

- ◆ **Project status.** The current state of the project.
- ◆ **Project progress.** The progress made with some previous state as a reference.
- ◆ **Forecast.** The prediction of the progress in the future based on the progress in the past.

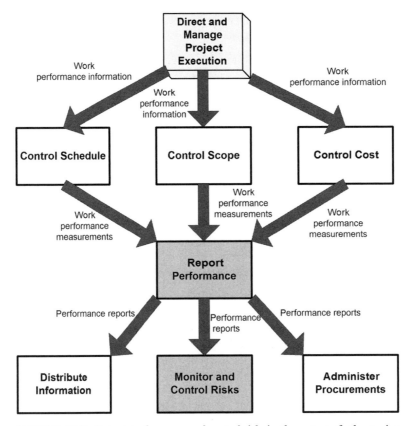

FIGURE 11.8 *Report performance and control risks in the context of other project management processes.*

 CAUTION

Do not confuse the Report Performance process with the Distribute Information process discussed in Chapter 9, even though you must recognize the overlap. Distributing information means distributing all the relevant information, whereas performance reporting focuses on the performance part of the information. You can use the information distribution system to report performance.

The formal name for the process used for performance reporting is Report Performance, and it is illustrated in Figure 11.9.

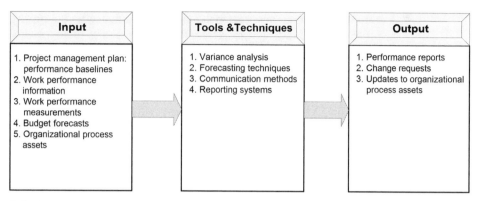

FIGURE 11.9 *The Report Performance process: input, tools and techniques, and output.*

What Goes into Performance Reporting

The core of performance reporting is to use performance measurements to prepare performance reports. To serve this core, the following items are needed as an input to the performance reporting process:

Performance measurements. These measurements are mostly made in other monitoring and controlling processes, such as control scope, control schedule, and control cost. However, you may need to make some measurements during the performance reporting process.

Work performance data. To make performance measurements and to put them in the right perspective, you need the work performance data that you collected during monitoring and controlling project execution.

Project management plan. This plan has project baselines, such as scope baseline, schedule baseline, and cost baseline. The work performance data is compared to these baselines to make performance measurements.

Organizational process assets. The organizational process assets that may come in handy in preparing the performance reports include report templates, measurement guidelines, and variance limits accepted in the organization.

Tools and Techniques for Performance Reporting

Tools and techniques used in performance reporting include communication methods, variance analysis, forecasting techniques, and reporting systems. Communication methods were discussed in Chapter 4, and variance analysis will be discussed in Chapter 12. Forecasting techniques include the following:

◆ **Earned value forecasting techniques.** The forecasting techniques based on the earned value analysis are discussed in Chapter 12.

- ◆ **Extrapolation techniques.** Extrapolation is a scientific method to predict future results based on past data. It makes use of concepts such as trend, growth, and decay. These techniques are also called *time series methods.*

- ◆ **Causal methods.** These techniques are based on predicting the behavior of a variable by identifying the underlying causes of that behavior. Regression analysis is an example of such methods.

- ◆ **Judgmental techniques.** These techniques use intuitive judgment in making predictions and can also use other methods, such as analogy and the Delphi technique.

Reporting systems. A reporting system is used to collect, store, maintain, and distribute information. Modern reporting systems often include software tools. There can be specialized reporting systems to support performance reporting, including the following:

- ◆ **Cost reporting system.** This system can store and report the cost expended on the project and on its different activities and aspects.

- ◆ **Time reporting system.** This system can store and report how much time has been expended on the project and on its different activities and aspects.

These tools and techniques can be used to generate the output of performance reporting.

What Comes Out of Performance Reporting

Performance reports are an obvious output of performance reporting. This and other output items are discussed in the following paragraphs.

Project performance reports. Performance reports present relevant information from work performance data and performance measurements in a suitable format. The relevancy and suitability depend on the audience—the stakeholders that are the consumers of these reports. The report format may include presentation elements such as tables, bar charts, and histograms in order to make the information easy to understand. The performance reports can contain the following:

- ◆ **Summary of work performance information.** Results from the comparison of the actual work results to the planned performance—that is, the performance baseline.

- ◆ **Current status.** The current state in which the project is right now.

- ◆ **Progress.** Progress made from some reference point in the past. The status refers to where the things are right now, and the progress refers to what has been accomplished since a previous status.

Forecasts. Performance reporting includes making forecasts based on past performance. These forecasts include estimates such as what the total cost incurred at project completion will be—called *estimate at completion (EAC)*—and how much cost will be incurred to complete the remaining project—called *estimate to complete (ETC)*. These forecasts can be updated as more performance information comes in.

Change requests. Measuring and communicating performance may generate change requests, which must be processed through integrated change control before implementation. For example, performance reporting may expose that certain aspects of the project are not on the right track or the project is not performing as expected by the stakeholders. The forecasting may expose danger ahead. All this can generate recommendations for corrective and preventive actions.

Updates to organizational process assets. During performance reporting, there will be lots of revelations by performance measurements and feedback from the stakeholders. This will result in updating the organizational process assets, such as lessons learned.

The three most important takeaways from this chapter are the following:

◆ Quality control is the process of monitoring and controlling specific project results to ensure the implementation of the quality plan and recommending changes or actions in case of poor implementation.

◆ The risk monitoring and controlling processes are used to monitor and control the identified risks and to look out for new risks.

◆ Work performance measurements made during monitoring and controlling scope, schedule, and cost are the raw data for performance reporting. The core of performance reporting is to prepare and distribute performance reports to the right stakeholders at the right time by using the right methods and formats.

Summary

You need to monitor and control your project throughout its lifecycle, which includes monitoring and controlling quality, risks, and performance communication—the three interrelated processes. Quality is controlled by using the Perform Quality Control process, a process of monitoring and recording the results from the execution of projects, including the quality activities. The goal is to evaluate quality performance and recommend necessary changes. To ensure quality, you must control risks as well. Risks are monitored and controlled by using the Monitor and Control Risks process, which uses the risk register and performance reports as major input items. The performance reports are prepared by using the Report Performance process, which uses work performance information and work performance measurements as input. The goal here is to prepare and distribute the performance reports to the right stakeholders at the right time by using the right methods and formats.

High-quality projects deliver the promised product, service, or result within the planned cost, schedule, and scope. Therefore, it is necessary to monitor and control changes to these three parameters discussed in the next chapter: cost, schedule, and scope.

Exam's Eye View

Comprehend

- The Report Performance process generates performance reports, which are used as input to the Monitor and Control Risks process.

- Work performance measurements generated by controlling scope, schedule, and cost are used as input to prepare performance reports and to control quality.

- Work performance information generated by the Direct and Manage Project Execution process is used as an input to prepare performance reports and to control risks.

- Like most of the monitor and control processes, the Perform Quality Control, Monitor and Control Risks, and Report Performance processes generate change requests.

Look Out

- The Report Performance process belongs to the monitoring and controlling process group and not to the executing process group.

- Deliverables are an important input to the Perform Quality Control process.

- Approved change requests, and not all change requests, are an input to the Perform Quality Control process.

- Both change requests and validation of changes are output of the Perform Quality Control process.

Memorize

- The processes to monitor and control quality, risk, and performance communication are Perform Quality Control, Monitor and Control Risks, and Report Performance.

- The Report Performance process belongs to the project communication management knowledge area.

- Budget forecasts are an input to the Report Performance process.

- Validation of deliverables is an output of the Perform Quality Control process.

Key Terms and Definitions

◆ **cause and effect diagram.** A diagram used to explore all the potential causes (inputs) that result in a single effect (output), such as a problem or a defect.

◆ **control chart.** A chart or diagram used to monitor whether the variance of a specified variable is within the acceptable limits dictated by quality control.

◆ **defect.** An imperfection or deficiency that keeps a component from meeting its requirements or specifications. A defect is caused by an error (problem) and can be repaired by fixing the error.

◆ **flowchart.** A diagram that depicts inputs, actions, and outputs of one or more processes in a system.

◆ **histogram.** A bar chart that shows a distribution of variables.

◆ **inspection.** A technique to examine whether an activity, component, product, service, or result conforms to specific requirements.

◆ **monitor and control risks.** To track identified risks, identify new risks, monitor residual risks, implement risk response plans, and evaluate risk management processes.

◆ **Pareto diagram.** A diagram used to rank the importance of each error (problem) based on the frequency of its occurrence over time in the form of defects.

◆ **performance report.** A document or a presentation that presents the project progress in terms of some parameters, such as earned value management parameters, based on the analysis of performance information/data.

◆ **quality control.** Monitoring results of executing quality-related activities and recommending necessary changes and actions to conform with the quality plans.

◆ **risk trigger.** An alert that indicates a risk event has occurred or is about to occur.

◆ **run chart.** A chart that shows the history and pattern of variations.

◆ **scatter diagram.** A diagram used to show the pattern of the relationship between two variables—an independent variable and another variable that depends on the independent variable.

◆ **statistical sampling.** Randomly selecting a part of the population for study.

◆ **workaround.** A response to a negative risk that has occurred. A workaround is based on a quick solution and is not planned in advance of the risk occurrence event.

Review Questions

1. You are using an Ishikawa diagram to find real causes of a problem by exploring all the possible causes. Which quality process are you performing?

    A. Assure Quality

    B. Plan Quality

    C. Perform Quality Control and Perform Quality Assurance

    D. Auditing and inspection

2. You want to examine the results of a process to determine whether the process is in or out of control. Which of the following is the most suitable tool to use?

    A. Control chart

    B. Cause and effect diagram

    C. Pareto diagram

    D. Scatter diagram

3. You are managing a software project with limited development resources. The QA department has discovered a large number of defects in the product, and the project sponsor is very concerned about this. You want to get the maximum number of defects repaired with minimal effort. Which quality-control tool are you going to use before you direct the efforts of the project team to fix specific problems?

    A. Control chart

    B. Cause and effect diagram

    C. Pareto diagram

    D. Scatter diagram

4. You are the project manager for a software development project that has limited resources. The customer is concerned about the quality of the code developed and wants you to conduct the code review. The product contains a large body of code with millions of lines. Which approach will you take?

    A. Tell the customer it's not possible.

    B. Use statistical sampling.

    C. Use automated testing tools.

    D. Arrange to review each line of the code.

5. A project manager is recommending corrective actions related to risk. In which of the following processes is the project manager involved?

    A. Perform Integrated Change Control

    B. Plan Risk Responses

    C. Identify Risks

    D. Monitor and Control Risks

6. A project manager is getting the risk-related recommended corrective actions approved. In which of the following processes is the project manager involved?

    A. Perform Integrated Change Control

    B. Plan Risk Responses

    C. Identify Risks

    D. Monitor and Control Risks

7. Which of the following is not an input to controlling quality?

    A. Project deliverables

    B. Work performance measurements

    C. Quality control measurements

    D. Quality checklists

8. A project manager is looking for approved change requests in order to perform a process. Which process is he preparing for?

    A. Perform Integrated Change Control

    B. Perform Quality Control

    C. Report Performance

    D. Monitor and Control Risks

9. Which of the following is not a tool or technique used in the Perform Quality Control process?

    A. Statistical sampling

    B. Inspection

    C. Histograms

    D. Technical performance measurements

10. Which of the following is not an input to the Monitor and Control Risks process?

    A. Performance reports

    B. Technical performance measurements

    C. Work performance information

    D. Risk management plan

Chapter 12

Monitoring and Controlling the Golden Triangle

PMP Exam Objectives

Objective	What It Really Means
4.1 Measure Project Performance	You must understand how to measure project performance against cost, schedule, and scope baselines. You must also understand the terms involved in cost and schedule performance analysis, such as BAC, EV, AC, CV, SV, CPI, SPI, ETC, EAC, and TCPI.
4.2 Verify and Manage Changes to the Project	You should know how to manage changes to the project scope, project schedule, and project cost. That means you must understand the processes for monitoring and controlling scope, schedule, and cost: Control Scope, Control Schedule, and Control Cost. You also must understand the impact of a change across the project—for example, the triple constraint.

Introduction

High-quality projects deliver the promised product, service, or result within the planned budget, schedule, and scope. This is also a very important and basic criterion of success: Complete the project with complete scope, on schedule, and within budget. So, it should not come as a surprise when the project performance is largely measured by making integrated measures of scope, schedule, and cost and comparing them to the scope, schedule, and cost baselines. Cost and time are the underlying fundamental parameters that determine budget and schedule, respectively. So, the three fundamental parameters that we are talking about here are scope, time, and cost. You will see in this chapter that these three project parameters are intrinsically connected by a triangular relationship. Because the success of the project depends largely on how you manage this triangle, we call it the *golden triangle*.

So, the core issue in this chapter is how to monitor and control the golden triangle. In search of an answer, we will explore three avenues: scope control, schedule control, and cost control.

Controlling Scope, Schedule, and Cost: Big Picture

The nutshell of running a project is delivering the scope according to some schedule, which will cost someone. Completing a project successfully includes delivering the planned scope according to the planned schedule and within the planned budget. The fundamental parameters for budget and schedule are cost and time, respectively. Budget is the cost with a timeline, and schedule is determined from the time estimates for completing the schedule activities. So scope, time, and cost make the heart of any project. These three project parameters comprise a triple constraint that is a framework for evaluating competing demands. A triple constraint is often depicted as a triangle, with each side representing one of these three parameters. Figure 12.1 shows the triple constraint for scope, time, and cost. This means if one of these parameters changes, at least one of the other two must change as well.

CAUTION

Don't be confused if you see the triple constraint referred to as *scope, schedule, and cost constraint* as well as *scope, time, and cost constraint*. Time and schedule are intrinsically connected.

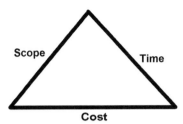

FIGURE 12.1 *Triple constraint: scope, time, and cost. You cannot change one side of the triangle without changing at least one of the other two sides.*

For example, assume you are being interviewed by a functional manager for a project manager position. Don't be surprised if you are asked a question based on the following situation:

1. The project is way behind the schedule.

2. No extra resources, such as money or project team members to perform activities, are available.

3. You have to implement all the planned features.

The question is, what will you do to meet the deadline that is approaching within a week? From a project management viewpoint, this situation is a good example of the triple constraint. The project is behind schedule, which means there is a schedule change (or a change in time available to finish the remaining project). Therefore, at least one of the other two parameters must change. If you want to meet the deadline, either you should be allotted more funds to hire more human resources or the scope of the project should be changed, which means some of the features would be left out. Depending upon the knowledge level of the functional manager about project management, this answer might not get you the job, but as a project manager, you must stand your ground. Project management is not magic; it involves dealing with cold, hard reality in a realistic way, thereby establishing clear and achievable objectives.

 NOTE

While considering the cost-schedule-scope constraint, you should also remember the schedule compression techniques, such as crashing and fast tracking, discussed in Chapter 4. Also, remember that those techniques do not guarantee that no additional cost (or resources) will be required.

You can see the relationship of triple constraint to quality by recalling that a high-quality project delivers the required product on time and within the planned scope and budget. Therefore, while balancing between these three constraints, the quality (and as a result, customer satisfaction) might be affected. The triple constraint is also a good example of how one change can give rise to other changes across the project. This highlights the importance of managing and controlling changes.

Changes to scope, schedule, and cost are controlled using the Control Scope, Control Schedule, and Control Cost processes, respectively, which are discussed in this chapter. These three processes are at the center of the project action. As Figure 12.2 illustrates, they take work performance information from the project execution and generate work performance measurements that are used by the quality control process to generate quality control measurements and by the report performance process to generate performance reports.

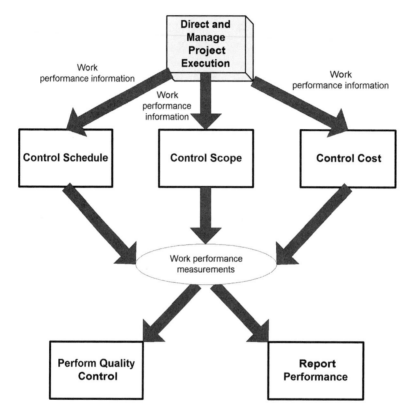

FIGURE 12.2 *The processes to control scope, schedule, and cost in a big picture.*

Cost is incurred in executing a schedule, which depends on the scope.

Controlling Scope

Controlling the project scope includes influencing factors that create changes to the scope, as well as managing change requests and controlling their impact when the change actually occurs.

While controlling the scope, you focus on the following tasks:

◆ Watch out for scope creep. Determine whether it has happened and correct the situation. Scope creep refers to scope changes applied without processing them though the change control process.

◆ Process the scope change requests through the integrated change control process for approval.

◆ Manage the implementation of scope changes after approval, as well as their impact across the project.

 TIP

In real life, scope creeps occur for various reasons. For example, perhaps a development engineer thought something was a cool feature to implement, or the customer spoke directly with the engineer to make a request for a minor additional feature, or various other similar situations occurred. If scope creep has taken your project off track, you need to take corrective actions to get the project back on the track. You should also investigate how the scope creep happened and take steps to prevent it in the future—for example, by educating team members about the proper scope change process.

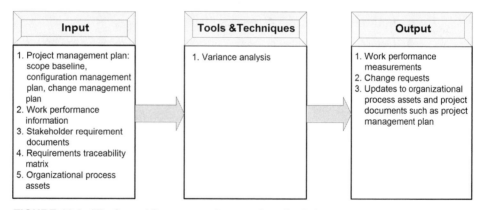

Input	Tools &Techniques	Output
1. Project management plan: scope baseline, configuration management plan, change management plan 2. Work performance information 3. Stakeholder requirement documents 4. Requirements traceability matrix 5. Organizational process assets	1. Variance analysis	1. Work performance measurements 2. Change requests 3. Updates to organizational process assets and project documents such as project management plan

FIGURE 12.3 *The Control Scope process: input, tools and techniques, and output.*

The obvious input items to the scope control process are the elements that define the scope, such as the project scope statement, the scope baseline, the WBS, the WBS dictionary, and a scope management plan that describes how to manage the scope. The performance reports might help to detect a scope change, and some change requests in other areas can result in scope change, as well.

The main output of the scope control process is the update to scope-related input elements, such as the project scope statement, the WBS, the WBS dictionary, and the scope baseline. The components of the project management plan affected by these changes might also need to be updated. Change requests and recommendations for corrective actions are other obvious output items from the scope control process.

The main tools used in the scope control process are the change control system and the project performance analysis, including the scope variance and the schedule variance. Schedule variance can have an effect on the scope if you want to finish the project on time and there are no additional resources available. The change control system of an organization is a collection of formal documented procedures that specify how the project deliverables and documents will be changed, controlled, and approved.

You monitor the project by watching its progress, which is a measure of its performance. Therefore, performance measurement and analysis make up an important category of tools and techniques in monitoring and controlling the project.

Controlling Schedule

Schedule control has a two-pronged goal—to ensure that the project is progressing on time as planned and to monitor any changes to this progress. As a project manager, you should be out in front of the project, performing the following tasks on a regular basis:

- Determining the current status of the project schedule
- Influencing the factors that generate schedule changes
- Determining whether the project schedule has changed—for example, if some activities are running late
- Managing changes as they occur

You detect a schedule change by comparing the execution time to the time in the schedule baseline, which is a major input item into the schedule control process. This is formally called Control Schedule and is illustrated in Figure 12.4.

Input to Schedule Control

To control the project schedule, you need to know what the schedule baseline (that is, the expectation) is, how the project is performing from the perspective of schedule, and what the plans are to monitor the schedule. Accordingly, the input items to the schedule control process are the following:

- **Schedule management plan.** This plan specifies how to monitor and control the project at hand.
- **Schedule baseline.** This is the approved version of the schedule, against which the schedule performance of the project will be measured.

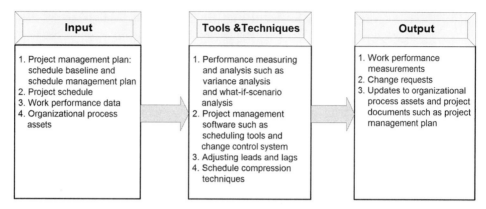

FIGURE 12.4 *The Control Schedule process: input, tools and techniques, and output.*

- ◆ **Performance reports.** These reports provide information on the schedule performance of the project, such as missed and met planned dates.
- ◆ **Approved change requests.** These are requests to change the schedule or other change requests that will affect the schedule. Approved change requests can update the schedule baseline.

Tools and Techniques for Schedule Control

The schedule is monitored by progress reporting and performance measurements and is controlled using the schedule control system. These and other tools and techniques are discussed in this section.

Progress reporting. Progress reports and current schedule status are key items to monitor the schedule. They can include finished activities, the percent of in-progress activities that have been completed, and remaining durations for unfinished activities.

Schedule change control system. This is the system you use to receive, evaluate, and process schedule changes. It can include forms, procedures, approval committees, and tracking systems.

Performance measurement and analysis. The following tools and techniques can be used to measure and analyze the schedule performance of the project:

- ◆ **Performance measurement techniques.** These techniques are used to calculate the schedule variance and schedule performance index and are discussed in the "Measuring Performance" section later in this chapter. The schedule variance discussed there is in terms of cost, but you can also perform a barebones schedule variance analysis based on the start and end dates of the schedule activities.
- ◆ **Variance analysis.** Performing a barebones schedule variance analysis is crucial to schedule monitoring because it reveals the deviation of the actual start and finish dates from the planned start and finish dates of schedule activities. It might suggest corrective actions to be taken to keep the project on the track.

◆ **Schedule comparison bar charts.** Bar charts can be used to facilitate the schedule variance analysis. You can draw two bars corresponding to one schedule activity—one bar shows the actual progress, and the other bar shows the expected progress according to the baseline. This is a great tool to visually display where the schedule has progressed as planned and where it has slipped.

TIP

A schedule variance does not necessarily mean that a schedule change is required. For example, a delay on a schedule activity that is not on the critical path might not trigger any schedule change.

Project management software. You can use project management software for scheduling to track planned start/finish dates versus actual dates for schedule activities. This software also enables you to predict the effects of project schedule changes. These are important pieces of information for monitoring and controlling the schedule.

Output of Schedule Control

Schedule performance measurements and recommendations for actions based on the measurements and progress reports are the important output items of the schedule control process.

Performance measurements. The results from schedule performance measurements, such as the schedule variance (SV) and schedule performance index (SPI), should be documented and communicated to stakeholders. These measurements might trigger recommendations for corrective actions and change requests.

Recommended corrective actions. The goal of schedule-related corrective actions is to bring the future schedule performance in line with the schedule baseline—that is, the approved version of the planned schedule. To that end, the following actions can be taken:

◆ Expedite the execution to ensure that schedule activities are completed on time or with minimal delay.

◆ Perform a root cause analysis to identify the causes of the schedule variance.

◆ Make plans to recover from the schedule delay.

TIP

Remember that corrective actions are not about going back and fixing past mistakes. Rather, they're about ensuring that future results match with the plan. You can do this by influencing future results, such as expediting the execution, or by changing the plan.

Updates. The following updates can result from the schedule control process:

◆ **Schedule updates.** Schedule changes can happen at the activity level (the start/end date of an activity has changed) or at the project level (the start/end date of the project has changed). A schedule change at the project level is called a *schedule revision*. For example, when the schedule scope is expanded, the project end date might have to be changed to allow the extra work. All significant schedule changes must be reported to the stakeholders.

◆ **Activity updates.** The schedule changes and the project progress will cause changes in the activity list and in the list of activity attributes. These changes must be documented.

◆ **Project management plan.** The schedule management plan, a component of the project management plan, is updated to reflect the changes that occur during the schedule control process.

◆ **Organizational process assets.** The lessons learned from the schedule control process can be documented to the historical database. Following are some examples:

    ◆ The causes of schedule variance

    ◆ The reasons for choosing the corrective actions that were taken

    ◆ The effectiveness of the corrective actions

    Future projects can make use of this information.

Change requests. The schedule performance analysis and progress report review can result in requests for changes to the project schedule baseline. These changes must be processed through the integrated change control process for approval. As with any other change, you must think through whether a change to the schedule baseline has any other effect across the project. If it does, you might need to update the corresponding component of the project management plan accordingly.

The project schedule is there to execute the project work within the planned scope and cost of the project. So, the project cost must be controlled as well.

Controlling Cost

Controlling cost means monitoring and controlling updates and changes to costs, budget, and the cost baseline of the project. Monitoring and controlling costs has two dimensions to it: expenditure of project funds and the work performed as a result of those expenditures. One major aspect of cost monitoring and controlling is to determine the relationship between the expenditures and the accomplishments. The cost performance lays in this relationship. The other main aspect is to control the changes to the approved cost performance baseline.

CAUTION

Like any other change, change in cost and budget must also be processed through the integrated change control process and should only be implemented after its approval.

To be more specific, monitoring and controlling the project cost includes the following tasks:

◆ **Influence** the factors that can create changes to the approved cost baseline.

◆ **Monitor** the following:

  ◆ Work performed against the funds expended

  ◆ Variance of cost performance from the approved baseline

◆ **Prevent** unapproved changes from creeping into cost reports and expenditures.

◆ **Act** to keep cost overruns within the planned acceptable limits.

◆ **Ensure** the following:

  ◆ Change requests are dealt with in a timely fashion and managed as they occur.

  ◆ Expenditures do not exceed the approved budget by period or by total amount. Any change to the budget must be approved before implementation.

◆ **Communicate** with the appropriate stakeholders about the cost associated with the approved changes.

Cost is monitored and controlled by using the Control Cost process illustrated in Figure 12.5.

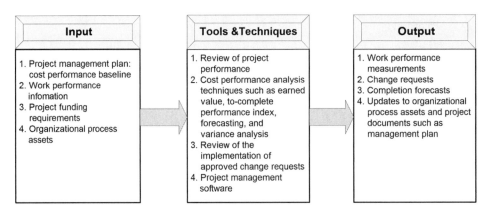

FIGURE 12.5 *The Control Cost process: input, tools and techniques, and output.*

The input items to this process are the project management plan, work performance information, project funding requirements, and organizational process assets. The items in the project management plan useful for controlling cost are the cost management plan and the cost performance baseline. The cost management plan describes how the cost will be monitored and controlled. The cost performance baseline—or *cost baseline* for short—is an approved budget; that is, the cost with the timeline for the project attached to it. Work performance information contains performance-related data from the execution of the project, including how much cost has been incurred in performing certain tasks. This cost can be compared to the planned cost to make the cost performance measurements. Project funding requirements are part of the cost baseline. Organizational process assets that can influence the cost control include cost control–related policies, procedures, and guidelines; monitoring and reporting methods; and tools used in controlling cost.

The Control Cost process converts the cost-related project performance information into project performance measurements by using some tools and techniques, such as the earned value technique, variance analysis, and forecasting. These tools and techniques are discussed in the next section. Performance reviews compare the actual progress to the planned progress. Project management software can be used for earned value management.

Work performance measurements made by comparing the work performance information to the planned performance are the obvious output of the Control Cost process. The analysis of the project performance can result in making some change requests to keep the project on track. The budget forecasts can be made from the earned value analysis. The causes of the variance of the progress from the planned progress and the lessons learned become part of the organizational process assets that can be used in future projects.

A common input to controlling scope, schedule, and cost is work performance information, and a common output is work performance measurements. That means these three processes use work performance information to make performance measurements.

Measuring Performance

Project performance is measured by comparing the project execution to the performance measurement baseline, which is an approved integrated plan for scope, schedule, and cost for the project, as explained here:

- ◆ **Cost baseline.** This is the planned budget for the project over a time period, used as a basis against which to measure, monitor, and control the cost performance of the project. The cost performance is measured by comparing the actual cost to the planned cost over a time period.
- ◆ **Schedule baseline.** This is a specific version of the project schedule developed from the schedule network analysis and the schedule model data, discussed in Chapter 4. This is the approved version of the schedule with a start date and an end date, and it is used as a basis against which the project schedule performance is measured.

◆ **Scope baseline.** This is the approved project scope that includes the approved project scope statement, the WBS based on the approved project scope statement, and the corresponding WBS dictionary.

The elaborate nature of the performance measurement analysis can be seen in the cost control process.

Performance Measurement Analysis for Cost Control

As mentioned earlier, cost control includes influencing the factors that can create changes to the cost baseline. But to detect arising changes, you need to detect and understand variances from the cost baseline by monitoring cost performance.

In general, variance is a measurable deviation in the value of a project variable (or parameter), such as cost or schedule, from a known baseline or expected value. Variance analysis is a technique used to assess the magnitude of variation in the value of a variable, such as cost from the baseline or expected value, determine the cause of the variance, and decide whether a corrective action is required. A common technique to assess cost variance is called the *earned value technique (EVT)*, also called *earned value management (EVM)*. It is a commonly used method of performance measurement that has various forms. Most often, it integrates scope, schedule, and cost performance by comparing the baselines to the actual progress made. For example, you calculate the cumulative value of the budgeted cost of work performed in terms of the originally allocated budgeted amount and compare it to the following:

1. Budgeted cost of work scheduled—that is, planned
2. Actual cost of work performed

Don't worry if these terms sound confusing right now; I will go through an example soon. However, as you will see, the greatest difficulty in understanding EVT (or EVM) stems from the coupling of cost and schedule. You must realize that the project cost and the project schedule are inherently related to each other. Schedule relates to performing certain work over a certain time period, whereas cost refers to the money spent to perform the work on a project (or a project activity) over a certain period of time. The relationship between cost and schedule can be realized by understanding that it costs money to perform a schedule activity. The "time is money" principle is at work here. For example, a project activity can be looked upon in terms of an amount of work that will be needed to complete it or in terms of its monetary value, which will include the cost of the work that needs to be performed to complete the activity.

 CAUTION

As you delve into EVM, remember that there are only three parameters that need to be monitored and developed closely: planned value (PV), earned value (EV), and actual cost (AC). The rest of the parameters and the earned value analysis are largely based on these three fundamental parameters.

The EVT involves calculating some variables where you will see the interplay of schedule (work) and cost. I will work through an example to help you understand the variables. Assume you are a project manager for the construction of a 16-mile road. Further assume that the work is uniformly distributed over 12 weeks. The total approved budget for this project is $600,000. At the end of first four weeks of work, $125,000 has been spent, and four miles of road have been completed.

I will use this example to perform the cost performance analysis and the schedule performance analysis in terms of cost.

Cost Performance

Cost performance refers to how efficiently you are spending money on the project work, measured against the expectations set in the project management plan—that is, the cost baselines. The total cost approved in the baseline is called the *budget at completion (BAC)*.

 NOTE

The variables discussed here, such as BAC, EV, and AC, can be calculated either for the whole project or for a part of the project, such as a project activity.

Budget at completion (BAC). This is the total budget authorized for performing the project work (or a project activity), also called the *planned budget*. In other words, it is the cost originally estimated in the project management plan. You use this variable in defining almost all the following variables. In our example, the value of BAC is $600,000.

Earned value (EV) or budgeted cost of work performed (BCWP). This is the value of the actual performed work expressed in terms of the approved budget for a project or a project activity for a given time period. In this variable, you see the relationship of schedule (work) and cost in action. BAC represents the total value of the project. But when you perform some work on the project, you have earned some of that value, and the earned value is proportional to the fraction of the total work performed, as shown by the formula here:

$$EV=BAC\times(\text{work completed/total work required})$$

So, in our example, EV can be calculated as:

$$EV=\$600,000\times(4\text{ miles}/16\text{ miles})=\$150,000$$

This is the earned value of the work, which may or may not be equal to the actual money that you spent to perform this work.

Actual cost (AC) or actual cost of work performed (ACWP). This is the total cost actually incurred until a specific point on the timeline in performing the work for a project. In our running example, $125,000 has already been used up to this point. So the actual cost at this point in time is $125,000. This cost is to be compared to the earned value to calculate the cost variance and cost performance.

Cost variance (CV). This is a measure of cost performance in terms of deviation of reality from the plan, and it is obtained by subtracting the actual cost (AC) from the earned value (EV), as shown in the formula here:

$$CV = EV - AC$$

So, in our example, CV can be calculated as shown here:

$$CV = \$150,000 - \$125,000 = \$25,000$$

The expected value of CV is zero because we expect the earned value to be equal to the actual cost. The positive result indicates better cost performance than expected, whereas a negative result indicates worse cost performance than expected. Deviation is one way of comparison, and ratio is another.

Cost performance index (CPI). Earned value represents the portion of work completed, and actual cost represents the money spent. So, the CPI indicates whether you are getting a fair value for your money. This is a measure of cost efficiency of a project calculated by dividing earned value (EV) by actual cost (AC), as shown in the formula here:

$$CPI = \frac{EV}{AC}$$

So, the CPI for our example can be calculated as:

$$CPI = \$150,000 / \$125,000 = 1.2$$

This means you are getting \$1.20 worth of performance for every dollar spent. A value of CPI greater than one indicates good performance, whereas a value less than one indicates bad performance. The expected value of CPI is one.

So both the CV and the CPI indicate that you are getting more value for each dollar spent. Hold back a little before opening the champagne, though. If you read the text of our example again, note that four out of 12 weeks have already passed, and only four out of 16 miles of road have been built. That means that only one-fourth of the work has been accomplished in one-third of the total scheduled time. This means we are lagging behind in our schedule. Although cost performance is good, schedule performance needs to be investigated, too.

Schedule Performance in Terms of Cost

Schedule performance refers to how efficiently you are executing your project schedule as measured against the expectations set in the project management plan. It can be measured by comparing the earned value to the planned value, just like cost performance is measured by comparing the earned value to the actual cost. Planned value refers to the value that we planned to create in the time spent so far.

Planned value (PV) or budgeted cost for the work scheduled (BCWS). This is the authorized cost for the scheduled work on the project or a project activity up to a given point on the timescale. The planned value is also called the *budgeted cost for the work scheduled (BCWS)*. PV is basically how much you were authorized to spend in the fraction of schedule time spent so far, as shown in the formula here:

> PV=BAC×(time passed/total schedule time)

Therefore, the planned value for the project in our example at the end of the first four weeks is calculated as shown here:

> PV=$600,000×(4 weeks/12 weeks)=$200,000

So, PV represents the planned schedule in terms of cost. You can calculate the schedule performance by comparing the planned schedule to the performed schedule in terms of cost.

CAUTION

Note that the total planned value (PV) of the project is the same as the budget at completion (BAC).

Schedule variance (SV). This is the deviation of the performed schedule from the planned schedule in terms of cost. No confusion is allowed here because you already know that the schedule can be translated to cost. SV is calculated as the difference between EV and PV, as shown in the formula here:

> SV=EV−PV

So, the SV in our example can be calculated as:

> SV=$150,000−$200,000=−$50,000

The negative value means we are behind schedule. Deviation represented by schedule variance is one way of comparison, and ratio represented by schedule performance index is another.

Schedule performance index (SPI). Earned value represents the portion of work completed in terms of cost, and planned value represents how much work was planned by this point in time in terms of cost. So, the SPI indicates how the performed work compared to the planned work. This is a measure of the schedule efficiency of a project calculated by dividing earned value (EV) by planned value (PV), as shown in the formula here:

$$SPI = \frac{EV}{PV}$$

So, the SPI for our example can be calculated as shown here:

> SPI=$150,000/$200,000=0.75

This indicates that the project is progressing at 75% of the planned pace—not good.

You should note that all these performance variables except the BAC are calculated at a given point in time. As shown in Figure 12.6, you can maintain a graphic that presents the values of these variables against points in time as the project progresses. Note that the value of the BAC does not change with time because it is the cost at completion time. Further note that given the BAC, the PV can be calculated at any point in time, even before the project execution starts. EV and AC are accumulated as the project execution progresses.

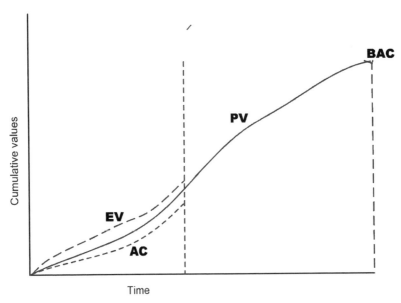

FIGURE 12.6 *The behavior of some performance variables as the project progresses in time. The variable BAC is independent of time.*

By using the variables discussed so far, you can monitor the project performance as time progresses. Not only that, you can also make predictions about future performance based on past performance.

Forecasting Techniques

Forecasting refers to predicting some information about the project in the future based on the performance in the past. The forecasting is regularly updated as the project progresses and more data from the past performance becomes available.

Estimate to complete (ETC) at budgeted rate. This is the prediction about the expected cost to complete the remaining work for the project or for a project activity. The future work is assumed to be completed at the budgeted rate. Therefore, the value of the ETC is obtained by subtracting the earned value (EV) from the budget at completion (BAC), as shown in the formula here:

$$ETC = BAC - EV$$

So, in our example, the value of ETC can be calculated as:

ETC=\$600,000–\$150,000=\$450,000

This is true if the current variances are seen as atypical and the future performance is expected to be as planned. If the current trend, however, continues, then we need to take CPI into account, as shown next.

Estimate to complete (ETC) at the present CPI. This is the prediction about the expected cost to complete the remaining work at the present CPI. Therefore, in that case, the ETC is given by:

$$ETC = \frac{BAC - EV}{CPI}$$

The next question that can be asked about the future is how much it will cost to complete the whole project.

STUDY CHECKPOINT 12.1

In our running example, calculate the ETC at the present CPI. Note that CPI is calculated as 1.2 in our running example from earlier in this chapter.

Estimate at completion (EAC) at the budgeted rate. This is the estimate made at the current point in time for how much it will cost to complete the whole project or a project activity from beginning to end. It is assumed that the future work will be performed at the budgeted rate. Therefore, the value of the EAC is obtained by adding the value of ETC at the budgeted rate to AC, as shown in the formula here:

EAC=AC+ETC (budgeted rate)

Accordingly, the value of EAC for our example can be calculated as:

EAC=\$125,000+\$450,000=\$575,000

Another useful prediction to be made is how much performance you need in the future to complete the remaining work within budget.

STUDY CHECKPOINT 12.2

Prove the validity of the following equation:

EAC=AC+BAC–EV

EAC calculated thus far is correct under the assumption that in the future the cost will be incurred as it was budgeted or performance will be made as planned. If, however, the current variance trend is assumed to continue, then EAC is calculated as discussed next.

Estimate at completion (EAC) at the present CPI. This is the estimate made at the current point in time for how much it will cost to complete the whole project or a project activity from beginning to end. It is assumed that the future work will be performed at the current CPI. Therefore, EAC is calculated as follows:

$$EAC = AC + ETC \text{ (at current CPI)}$$

$$EAC = AC + \frac{(BAC - EV)}{CPI}$$

STUDY CHECKPOINT 12.3

In our running example, calculate EAC at the present CPI. Note that CPI is calculated as 1.2 in our running example from earlier in this chapter.

As stated earlier, performance is an integrated measure of progress in the areas of scope, schedule, and cost. Just measuring one of these parameters may be misleading. For example, in our running example, we are performing better in cost but poorly in schedule. This is why sometimes EAC is measured by taking into account both CPI and SPI, as shown here:

$$EAC = AC + \frac{BAC - EV}{CPI \times SPI}$$

STUDY CHECKPOINT 12.4

In our running example, calculate EAC at the present CPI. Note that CPI is calculated as 1.2 and SPI is calculated as 0.75 in our running examples from earlier in this chapter.

To complete performance index (TCPI). This is the variable to predict the future performance needed to finish the work according to a specified goal—for example, either within the planned budget (BAC) or at the completion cost currently predicted (EAC). If the goal is to complete it within the BAC, it is calculated as the ratio of the remaining work to the remaining budget, as shown in the formula here:

$$TCPI = \frac{Remaining\ work}{Remaining\ funds} = \frac{BAC - BCWP}{BAC - ACWP} = \frac{BAC - EV}{BAC - AC}$$

Therefore, the value of TCPI in our example can be calculated as:

$$TCPI=(\$600,000-\$150,000)/(\$600,000-\$125,000)=450,000/475,000=0.95=95\%.$$

If it is realized that BAC is not attainable, then it is replaced with EAC. Accordingly, TCPI will be given by:

$$TCPI = \frac{Remaining\ work}{Required\ funds} = \frac{BAC - EV}{EAC - AC}$$

Table 12.1 summarizes most of these performance variables.

Table 12.1 Performance Variables Used in the Earned Value Technique Analysis

Variable	Abbreviation	Description	Formula
Budget at completion	BAC	Total planned cost	None
Earned value or budgeted cost of work performed	EV or BCWP	Fraction of the completed work in terms of the planned budget at a given point in time	EV=BAC×(Work completed/Total work required)
Actual cost	AC or ACWP	The money spent on the work until a given point in time	The sum of all the costs until a given point in time
Cost variance	CV	The difference between what you planned to spend and what is actually spent until a given point in time	CV=EV−AC
Cost performance index	CPI	The work performed per actual cost	CPI=EV/AC
Planned value or budgeted cost of work scheduled	PV or BCWS	The fraction of work planned to be completed at a given point in time	PV=BAC×(Time passed/Total schedule time)
Schedule variance	SV	The difference between the work actually completed and the work planned to be completed at a given point in time	SV=EV−PV
Schedule performance index	SPI	The actual work performed per planned work performed in terms of cost	SPI=EV/PV

Table 12.1 Continued

Variable	Abbreviation	Description	Formula
Estimate to complete	ETC	The estimate of what will be spent on the remaining project (or a project activity) based on the performance so far and the planned cost	ETC=BAC−EV
Estimate at completion	EAC	Estimate of what will be spent on the whole project (or a project activity) based on the performance so far and the planned cost	EAC=ETC+AC
To complete performance index	TCPI	Calculates the efficiency: remaining work per remaining funds	(BAC−EV)/(BAC−AC)

So, during the executing stage, the obvious items that need to be executed are the schedule activities, and while these activities are being executed, the attached cost, schedule, and scope need to be monitored and controlled. However, there is another important component of the project that needs to be monitored and controlled—the risk.

The three most important takeaways from this chapter are as follows:

◆ Scope, cost, and time make a triple constraint: Change in one of them changes one or both of the others.

◆ A project is monitored by continually measuring its performance as it progresses. The performance baseline to which the project progress is to be compared largely consists of scope baseline, schedule baseline, and cost baseline.

◆ In earned value management (EVM), there are several variables based on three fundamental parameters—namely, actual cost (AC), earned value (EV), and planned (PV)—that are used to compare the actual project progress to the planned progress in order to make performance measurements.

Summary

You need to monitor and control your project throughout its lifecycle, which includes monitoring and controlling performance. In an ideal world, there should be no changes to or variations from the planned baselines, such as cost, schedule, and scope baselines. A good-quality project is completed within the planned cost, schedule, and scope. However, in the real world, there are changes and variations, and therefore quality needs to be monitored and controlled, which involves monitoring certain project results by making measurements and taking actions based on those measurements.

The three project parameters—cost, scope, and schedule—are collectively known as a *triple constraint* because if one of them changes, at least one of the other two parameters must change. Therefore, project monitoring and controlling includes monitoring and controlling these three parameters, which involves measuring cost, schedule, and scope performance and taking actions based on performance. The most commonly used technique to measure cost and schedule performance is known as the *earned value technique (EVT)*, also called *earned value management (EVM)*, and it measures performance by comparing the earned value of the actual work performed to the actual cost and to the planned value that was supposed to be earned according to the plan. You incur cost in executing the scheduled work. So performance is also measured in terms of performed work or schedule performance.

After the execution of the last schedule activity is complete, you are not finished yet. You need to give proper closure to the project, which is the topic I discuss in the next section of this book.

Exam's Eye View

Comprehend

- ◆ Monitoring and controlling includes monitoring and controlling project performance.

- ◆ The three project parameters—cost, schedule, and scope—form a triple constraint, which means if one of these three parameters changes, at least one of the other two must change.

- ◆ Performance baselines and work performance information are the common inputs to monitoring and controlling the scope, schedule, and cost, and work performance measurements and change requests are the common outputs.

- ◆ Project performance is measured by comparing the work performance information from the project execution to the performance measurement baseline: scope baseline, schedule baseline, and cost baseline.

Look Out

◆ Planned value (PV), earned value (EV), and actual cost (AC) are the three key parameters that need to be monitored closely. The rest of the earned value analysis is based on these three fundamental parameters.

◆ Cost variance (CV) is calculated by subtracting the actual cost (AC) from the earned value (EV), and not from the planned value (PV).

◆ Schedule variance (SV) and schedule performance index (SPI) are calculated in terms of cost: EV and PV.

◆ It is possible for CV and SV to run in opposite directions—for example, CV has a positive value when SV has a negative value.

◆ The total planned value (PV) of the project is the same as the budget at completion (BAC).

Memorize

◆ For cost performance analysis:

EV=BAC×(Work completed/Total work required)

CV=EV−AC

CPI=EV/AC

◆ For schedule performance analysis:

PV=BAC×(Time passed/Total schedule time)

SV=EV−PV

SPI=EV/PV

EAC at the budgeted rate=AC+BAC−EV

EAC at current CPI= $AC + \dfrac{BAC - EV}{CPI}$

EAC at current CPI and current SPI= $AC + \dfrac{BAC - EV}{CPI \times SPI}$

TCPI= $\dfrac{BAC - EV}{BAC - AC}$

Key Terms and Definitions

◆ **actual cost (AC).** The total cost actually incurred until a specific point on the timescale in performing the work for a project or a project activity.

◆ **budget at completion (BAC).** The total budget authorized for performing the project work. This is the planned budget for the project, the cost that you originally estimated for the project.

◆ **change control system.** A collection of formal documented procedures that specifies how the project deliverables and documents will be changed, controlled, and approved.

◆ **cost baseline.** The planned budget for the project over a time period, used as a basis against which to monitor, control, and measure the cost performance of the project. The cost performance is measured by comparing the actual cost to the planned cost over a time period.

◆ **cost performance index (CPI).** A measure of the cost efficiency of a project calculated by dividing earned value (EV) by actual cost (AC).

◆ **cost variance (CV).** A measure of cost performance obtained by subtracting actual value (AC) from earned value (EV). A positive result indicates good performance, whereas a negative result indicates bad performance.

◆ **earned value (EV) or budgeted cost of work performed (BCWP).** The value of the actually performed work expressed in terms of the approved budget for a project or a project activity for a given time period.

◆ **earned value management (EVM) or earned value technique (EVT).** A management methodology and a technique to measure project progress by comparing integrated measures of scope, schedule, and cost with the planned performance baseline.

◆ **estimate at completion (EAC) at budgeted rate.** The estimate from the current point in time of how much it will cost to complete the entire project or an entire project activity for which the BAC is given. The value of EAC is obtained by adding the value of ETC at the budgeted rate to AC.

◆ **estimate at completion (EAC) at current CPI.** The estimate from the current point in time of how much it will cost to complete the entire project or an entire project activity for which the BAC is given. The value of EAC is obtained by adding the value of ETC at the current CPI to AC.

◆ **estimate to complete (ETC) at budgeted rate.** The expected cost, estimated by assuming the future performance will be at the budgeted rate, to complete the remaining work for the project or for a project activity.

◆ **estimate to complete (ETC) at present CPI.** The expected cost, estimated by assuming the future performance will be at the current CPI, to complete the remaining work for the project or for a project activity.

◆ **performance measurement baseline.** An approved integrated plan for scope, schedule, and cost for the project, against which the project execution is compared to measure the project performance.

◆ **project scope creep.** Changes applied to the project scope without going through the approval process, such as the integrated change control process.

◆ **schedule baseline.** A specific version of the project schedule developed from the schedule network analysis and the schedule model data. This is the approved version of the schedule with a start date and an end date, and it is used as a basis against which the project schedule performance is measured.

◆ **schedule performance index (SPI).** A measure of the schedule efficiency of a project calculated by dividing earned value (EV) by planned value (PV).

◆ **schedule revision.** An update to the project schedule that includes changing the project start date, end date, or both.

◆ **scope baseline.** The approved project scope, which includes the approved project scope statement, the WBS based on the approved project scope statement, and the corresponding WBS dictionary.

◆ **variance.** A measurable deviation in the value of a project variable, such as cost from a known baseline or expected value.

◆ **variance analysis.** A technique used to assess the magnitude of variation in the value of a variable (such as cost from the baseline or expected value), determine the cause of the variance, and decide whether a corrective action is required.

Review Questions

1. You are the project manager for a software product, and your project is in the execution stage. You have learned that Maya, a developer, has started adding some new features to the deliverable she is working on. What is the best action for you to take?

   A. Tell Maya to delete the code corresponding to these features because this is a scope creep, and scope creeps are not allowed.

   B. Learn from Maya what those features are and how much time they will take and then make necessary updates to the WBS, the WBS dictionary, and the schedule. Also tell Maya that in the future she should get approval from you before adding any new features.

   C. Determine where the request for the new features came from and process the change request through the integrated change request process.

   D. Contact Maya's functional manager and ask the manager to replace Maya with another developer.

2. Which of the following is not an output of the schedule control process?

   A. Recommended corrective actions

   B. Updates to the schedule baseline

   C. Performance measurements

   D. Budget review

3. Assume that you are the project manager for the construction of a 15-mile road. Further assume that the work is uniformly distributed over 12 weeks. The total approved budget for this project is $600,000. At the end of first three weeks of work, $160,000 has been spent, and five miles of road have been completed. What is the earned value of the project at the end of the first three weeks?

   A. $160,000

   B. $200,000

   C. $150,000

   D. $600,000

4. Assume that you are the project manager for the construction of a 15-mile road. Further assume that the work is uniformly distributed over 12 weeks. The total approved budget for this project is $600,000. At the end of first three weeks of work, $160,000 has been spent, and five miles of road have been completed. What is the planned value of the project at this point in time?

   A. $160,000

   B. $200,000

   C. $150,000

   D. $600,000

5. Assume that you are the project manager for the construction of a 15-mile road. Further assume that the work is uniformly distributed over 12 weeks. The total approved budget for this project is $600,000. At the end of first three weeks of work, $160,000 has been spent, and five miles of road have been completed. What is the cost variance?

   A. $40,000

   B. $50,000

   C. −$40,000

   D. $120,000

6. Assume that you are the project manager for the construction of a 15-mile road. Further assume that the work is uniformly distributed over 12 weeks. The total approved budget for this project is $600,000. At the end of first three weeks of work, $160,000 has been spent, and five miles of road have been completed. What is the schedule variance?

   A. $40,000

   B. $50,000

   C. Three weeks

   D. Twelve weeks

7. A CPI value of 1.25 and an SPI value of 1.33 for a project mean which of the following?

   A. The project is making slower progress and costing more than planned.

   B. The project is making faster progress and costing less than planned.

   C. The project is making slower progress and costing less than planned.

   D. The project is making faster progress and costing more than planned.

8. Project managers often talk about the triple constraint. Following are the three elements of the triple constraint:

   A. Scope, time, and, cost

   B. Scope, schedule, and quality

   C. Scope, time, and quality

   D. Schedule, time, and cost

9. An influential stakeholder has submitted a request for completing the project earlier than planned. What are the two parameters that are most likely to be affected by this time change?

   A. Schedule and deliverables

   B. Quality and risk

   C. Cost and scope

   D. Cost and budget

10. You are managing a project in biotechnology code named Mitochondria Eve. You need performance measurements to write the performance reports. Which process(es) will you run?

   A. Report Performance

   B. Control Scope, Control Schedule, and Control Cost

   C. Control Scope and Perform Quality Control

   D. Monitor and Control Project Work

PART V

Closing
the Project

To most of us, it may be common sense that every start has a finish. A project that has been started will have a finish. As I explained in Chapter 1, people have been doing projects even when there was no field of project management. The underlying philosophy of project management is to perform projects deliberately—that is, to plan them and to monitor and control them. Finishing a project deliberately means finishing it in a controlled way, not just letting it finish—even when it's cancelled.

There are three main elements of a successful project closure: final verification of the project deliverables by the project team, verification and acceptance of the deliverables that were procured, and acceptance of project deliverables by the appropriate party, such as the customer or the sponsor. This includes proper closure of all the legal contracts.

While we are talking about closure, this part of the book is also a good place to remind ourselves of our professional and social responsibilities as project management practitioners.

Chapter 13

Closing the Project

PMP Exam Objectives

Objective	What It Really Means
5.1 Obtain Final Acceptance for the Project	You must know that formal acceptance of the final product is an output of the Close Project process. You also must know that the scope of the project deliverables must be verified before the project closure begins. You must ensure that the deliverables meet the acceptance criteria.
5.2 Obtain Financial, Legal, and Administrative Closure	Understand that the project closure includes two important parts: administrative closure of the whole project and contract closure of the procurement part of the project. You must know both processes: Close Project and Close Procurements. During closure, you must follow standard accounting practices and comply with the legal procedures and laws, such as SOX.
5.3 Release Project Resources	You must know that releasing the project resources and turning over the project deliverables to another group are the essential elements of the project closure. You must also know that you should follow the policies and procedures of the performing organization to release the resources.

(continues)

PMP Exam Objectives (continued)

Objective	*What It Really Means*
5.4 Identify, Document, and Communicate Lessons Learned 5.6 Archive and Retain Project Records	You must know that documenting the lessons learned and archiving the project documents are included in the output of the Close Project process and the Close Procurements process. You should also know that identifying the lessons learned is an essential component of project review and project closure.
5.5 Create and Distribute Final Project Report 5.7 Measure Customer Satisfaction	You must know that reviewing the project is part of project closure. You must also know that measuring customer satisfaction and creating and distributing the final project report are essential components of the project review and project closure.

Introduction

The last deliverable on the project schedule has been completed, and you think that the project has been a big success. However, put that champagne bottle back into the refrigerator; the project has not ended yet. It has just reached another stage called the *project closing stage*, and, as a project manager, you need to continue monitoring and controlling the project through this stage. Also, recall that there are two kinds of project work—in house and procured. So you need to put a closure on the procured component of the project and then run the procured deliverables through the project closure process. The deliverables developed in house should be verified to check whether they meet the scope before running them through the closure process. In other words, what was planned to be done has actually been done. So that nothing falls between the cracks and for legal reasons, you need to formally close the project. This involves finalizing all the project and project management activities and giving them a proper closure. You should do this even when the project is being terminated before the planned finish line. After all the planned deliverables—developed in house and procured—have been verified, the project should be closed with the acceptance of the deliverables by the appropriate party and by archiving the appropriate documents.

So, the core issue in this chapter is how to properly close a project. In search of an answer, we will explore three avenues: verifying the scope of project deliverables, closing procurements, and closing the project.

Closing the Project: Big Picture

Project closure refers to a set of tasks that are required to formally end the project. There are two kinds of projects that you need to close formally:

- ◆ **Completed projects.** A project that has met its completion criteria falls into this category.
- ◆ **Terminated projects.** A project that was terminated before its completion falls into this category. A project can be terminated at various stages for various reasons. Following are some examples:
  - ◆ The project management plan is not approved for whatever reason.
  - ◆ The project has been executing, but you have run out of resources, and no more resources are available.
  - ◆ The project has been cancelled because it was going nowhere.
  - ◆ The project has been indefinitely postponed because there is not a large enough market for the product it would produce.

NOTE

The processes of the closing process group can be used to close a project, as well as to close a phase of a project.

A project, in general, may have in-house activities—that is, project activities being performed within the performing organization—and procurement activities. Accordingly, there are two aspects of project closure:

◆ Close the in-house activities of the project.

◆ Close the procurement part of the project.

Project closure includes the following activities:

◆ Activities to verify that all deliverables have been provided and accepted

◆ Activities to confirm that all the project requirements, including stakeholder requirements, have been met

◆ Activities to verify that the completion or exit criteria have been met

◆ Activities to ensure that the project product is transferred to the right individual or group

◆ Activities to review the project for lessons learned and archive the project records

You need to obtain final closure, such as acceptance signoffs, contract closure, or receipts for both the in-house part and the procurement part of the project and from both internal and external vendors and customers. You perform this task by using standard accounting practices and following the relevant organizational and legal procedures, such as SOX compliance.

NOTE

SOX refers to The Sarbanes-Oxley Act of 2002, also known as the Public Company Accounting Reform and Investor Protection Act of 2002. It is a United States Federal law enacted on July 30, 2002, in response to a number of major corporate and accounting scandals that affected companies such as Enron and WorldCom. These scandals cost investors billions of dollars when the share prices of affected companies collapsed and therefore shook public confidence in the nation's securities markets.

Figure 13.1 presents the big picture of project closure in a nutshell:

1. Verify the scope of the project deliverables developed in house.

2. Accept the procured deliverables through the procurement closure process.

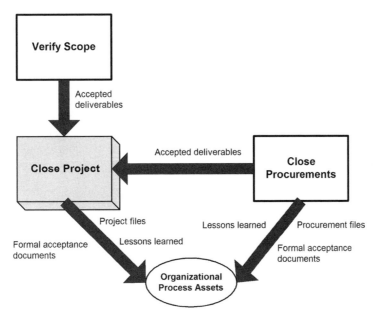

FIGURE 13.1 *Closing a project: big picture.*

3. Get the deliverables from Step 1 and Step 2 and get them accepted by the customer or sponsor to actually close the project.

4. Archive the project documents.

In the following sections we discuss details of these steps in terms of the processes shown in Table 13.1.

Table 13.1 Processes Related to Closing the Project

Process	Process Group	Knowledge Area
Verify Process	Monitoring and Controlling	Scope Management
Close Project or Phase	Closing	Integration Management
Close Procurements	Closing	Procurement Management

In a nutshell, all the aspects of the project closure should be covered, such as financial closure, legal closure, and administrative closure, with all the relevant parties, such as vendors and customers external and internal to the performing organization.

Before closure begins, the project deliverables must be checked for their scope.

Verifying the Scope of Project Deliverables

Verifying scope is the process of formally accepting the completed project deliverables. Before you hand over the project deliverables to the appropriate party mentioned in the project management plan, such as the customer or the sponsor, you need to verify that these deliverables actually meet the planned scope. So, verifying the scope of the project deliverables includes reviewing deliverables to ensure that all of them are completed as planned and therefore as expected.

CAUTION

You should perform the scope verification process even if the project is terminated—that is, ended before completion. In that case you would verify and document the level and extent of the project and product scope that was completed.

The process used to verify the scope is called Verify Scope and is illustrated in Figure 13.2. To verify the scope of deliverables, you need to pull out the project management plan and look at the sections related to the planned scope: the project scope statement, WBS, and WBS dictionary. The project scope statement includes the list of deliverables, the product scope description, and the product acceptance criteria. More scope-related details can be found in the WBS, which defines the decomposition of each deliverable into work packages. Further details, such as a description of each WBS component, the related statement of work, and technical requirements, can be found in the WBS dictionary.

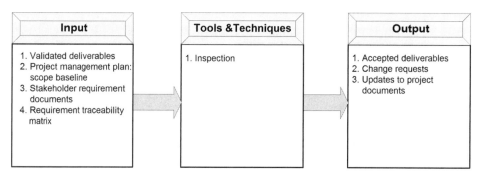

Input	Tools &Techniques	Output
1. Validated deliverables 2. Project management plan: scope baseline 3. Stakeholder requirement documents 4. Requirement traceability matrix	1. Inspection	1. Accepted deliverables 2. Change requests 3. Updates to project documents

FIGURE 13.2 *The Verify Scope process: input, tools and techniques, and output.*

STUDY CHECKPOINT 13.1

Before you begin the Verify Scope process, you look at the project scope statement, WBS, and WBS dictionary. What are these three elements collectively called?

The product requirements should be considered part of the scope and can be found in two documents: the stakeholder requirements document and the requirements traceability matrix that you prepared in the process of collecting requirements during the planning stage of the project. Finally, before you go through the process of scope verification, you should get all the deliverables validated through the quality control process. You can use inspection or auditing on the deliverables if necessary, even in the Verify Scope process.

The actual scope verification activity has different names in different organizations, such as audits, inspection, product review, and walkthrough. Nevertheless, the output of this activity is documentation of two kinds:

◆ Documentation of which deliverables have been accepted—that is, verified.

◆ Documentation of those deliverables that have not passed verification and therefore are not accepted. Also, documentation of the reasons why they failed the verification.

The scope verification process may also give rise to change requests, such as requests for defect repairs.

 CAUTION

Do not confuse scope verification with quality control. Quality control is primarily focused on checking the correctness of the deliverables and other quality requirements, whereas scope verification is primarily concerned with overall acceptance of the project deliverables. Quality control is usually performed before scope verification, but they can be performed simultaneously as well, depending on the situation.

STUDY CHECKPOINT 13.2

The Verify Scope process belongs to which process group?

The project deliverables that have been accepted through the scope verification process still need to go through final acceptance by the appropriate party, such as the customer or the sponsor.

Performing Project Closure

Closing the project means finalizing all activities across the project. You also need to determine and coordinate the procedures required for verifying and documenting the project deliverables. The items that describe what the project was planned to deliver and what it has delivered would be the obvious inputs to the process of closing the project. The formal name of the project closure process is Close Project or Phase, because it can also be used to close a phase in a multi-phase project. The process is illustrated in Figure 13.3 with its input, tools and techniques, and output.

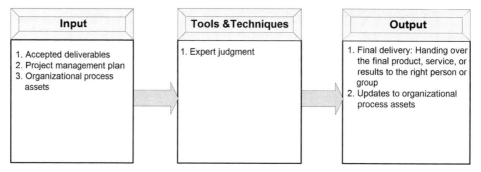

FIGURE 13.3 *The Close Project or Phase process: input, tools and techniques, and output.*

Input to the Close Project Process

You need a list of project deliverables that will go through the acceptance procedure. The project management plan contains guidelines on how to close the project. These and other input items are discussed in the following list.

◆ **Project management plan.** This defines how to close the project and will be useful in establishing the project closure procedure. The project management plan is also used in verifying and accepting the project deliverables because it explains what deliverables are expected.

◆ **Accepted deliverables.** These are the deliverables that have been verified through the scope verification process. That means these deliverables meet the scope requirements. This includes the deliverables from procurements that have been accepted through the procurement closure process.

◆ **Organizational process assets.** These can include project closure guidelines or requirements—for example, product validation and acceptance criteria, final project audits, and project evaluations. Also, you can learn from the historical information what kind of project documents you need to archive and in what detail you want to review the project to gather and store lessons learned. Your organization may also have transition criteria or a procedure on handing the product of the project to the appropriate party.

These input items provide information about what the project was supposed to deliver and what it has delivered. You use this input and some tools and techniques to carry on the project closure.

For example, you can use expert judgment in the various aspects of project closure, such as developing the closure procedures and ensuring that the closure procedures are performed to meet the appropriate standards. You can also use the project management information system to perform closure activities, such as archiving the project documents.

STUDY CHECKPOINT 13.3

What is the standard name for the process used to close a phase of a project?

You use these tools to carry on the project closure.

 CAUTION

The formal name of the process to close the project or a phase of it is Close Project or Phase. However, like other processes, we also refer to it by informal names, such as close project or project closure. You should not expect that the exam will always refer to the processes by their formal names. You should know the formal name of each process and then be able to recognize when it's being referred to in an informal way.

Output of the Close Project Process

Project closure accomplishes three main elements—completing all the closing procedures; achieving final acceptance of the project deliverables by the customer, including handing over the deliverables to the appropriate party; and archiving project-related documents. These elements are described in the following paragraphs.

Final delivery and transition. This means that the project product or output has been delivered and transitioned (handed over) to the appropriate party. This includes getting formal acceptance for the product—for example, in the form of a receipt that contains a formal statement to the effect that the requirements of the project have been met, including the terms of the contracts. One last time, make sure the following activities have been completed:

♦ Activities to define the requirements for getting approval from the stakeholders, such as customers and the sponsor, on the project deliverables and the approved changes that were supposed to be implemented

♦ Activities that are necessary to satisfy the project completion or exit criteria

◆ Activities related to the project completion, such as:
  ◆ Confirming that the project has met all requirements
  ◆ Verifying that all deliverables have been provided and accepted
  ◆ Verifying that the completion or exit criteria have been met

Updates to organizational process assets. The closure process will add the' following documents to the organizational process assets:

◆ **Acceptance documentation.** This is the documentation that proves the fulfillment of the project requirements have been confirmed, completion of the project has been verified, and the product has been formally accepted by the customer. In the case of a project termination, of course, the documentation should show that the exit criteria have been met.

◆ **Project closure documentation.** In addition to the acceptance documentation, you should also archive the other project closure documents, such as the closure procedure and the handing-over of project deliverables to an operations group. If the project was terminated, then the formal documentation indicating why the project was terminated should be included in the archive.

◆ **Project files archive.** This includes the documents from the project's lifecycle, such as the project management plan, risk registers, planned risk responses, and baselines for cost, schedule, scope, and quality.

◆ **Lessons-learned database.** The documentation on lessons learned should be saved in the organization's knowledge database so that future projects can benefit from it.

STUDY CHECKPOINT 13.4

True or False: You do not need to follow the Close Project process if the project is terminated at a rather early stage.

The deliverables that are processed through the project closure include the deliverables from procurements that are accepted through the procurement closure process. Therefore, in order to complete the project closure, you need to perform the procurement closure.

Performing Procurement Closure

A project might include work that was procured. Performing procurement closure means completing each procurement and giving it a proper closure. Project closure is not complete without procurement closure.

All the procurement contracts are closed at the end of a project or a phase by using the contract closure procedure. Procurement closure accomplishes the following two major goals:

♦ Close all the contracts applicable to the project.

♦ Receive verification (if you are a seller) or issue verification (if you are a buyer) that all the procured deliverables were received and accepted. In this respect, the contract closure process supports the administrative closure of the project.

If the project terminates without completion, you still need to go through the contract closure procedure, if there is a contract. Usually, a contract contains the contract termination clause, which contains the terms of the project termination, including the rights and responsibilities of the parties in case of the project's early termination.

The Close Procurements process is illustrated in Figure 13.4 with its input, tools and techniques, and output.

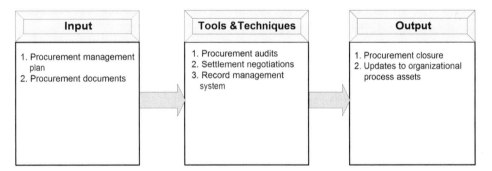

FIGURE 13.4 *The Close Procurements process: input, tools and techniques, and output.*

Input to Closing Procurements

The input items to the contract closure process are what you need to close the contract. They are discussed in the following list:

♦ **Procurement management plan.** This is needed to check whether the procurement requirements are met; it might have some procedures that you need to follow during closure.

♦ **Procurement documentation.** You need all the procurement documentation at this time for two purposes: You want to close the procurements according to the requirements in the procurement documents, and you want to archive the documentation.

The procurement management plan may contain a contract closure procedure developed to formally close all contracts associated with the project. It specifies a step-by-step methodology to execute activities needed to close the contracts. The roles and responsibilities of the team members who will be involved in the closure process are also specified.

CAUTION

A procedure and a process are not the same thing. For example, an organization may have a procedure to implement processes, such as first verify that the process is required, then collect all the input to the process before starting it, and so on.

You implement the procurement closure process by using the available tools and techniques, discussed in the next section.

Tools and Techniques for Closing Procurements

The tools and techniques for the contract closure process are the items you need to facilitate contract closure. They are discussed in the following paragraphs.

Procurement audits. This is a structured review of the procurement process with the purpose of identifying successes and failures from the planning through the executing stage of the project. The lessons learned from the audit can be applied to other phases of the same project (if it is a phase closeout) or to other projects within the same performing organization.

Settlement negotiations. Negotiations are a tool, a technique, and a skill that become very useful during the procurement closure process. Negotiations are used to give a proper closure through settlements to all outstanding claims, issues, and disputes. If direct negotiations fail, the option of some kind of mediation or arbitration should be explored. Obviously, the legal department of your organization should be involved here.

Records management system. This is a part of the project management information system and can be used to manage contract documentation and records. For example, you can use this system to archive documents, maintain an index of contract and communication documents, and retrieve documents.

Output of Closing Procurements

The obvious output of closing procurements is the closed procurements. This and other output items are discussed here.

Procurement closure. Procurement closure means the procured work is completed with all its requirements and is accepted. Generally, it is accomplished by a formal notice from the buyer to the seller, which might come, for example, through the buyer's authorized administrator. The requirements for formal contract closure are usually defined in the terms of the contract and are included in the procurement management plan.

Updates to organizational process assets. The following items should be added to the organizational process assets:

◆ **Procurement documentation.** This includes all the procurement documents, including the procurement management plan, closed contracts, and the procurement closure notice. These documents should be archived.

◆ **Acceptance notice.** This notice formally acknowledges the acceptance of deliverables through a notice from the buyer to the seller, notifying that the procurement deliverables have been accepted. This is an important document and should be preserved.

◆ **Lessons learned.** The procurement experience for this project should be analyzed, and the lessons learned should be gathered, recorded, and archived so that future projects can benefit from them.

Some important elements that are usually part of the details of project closure are discussed in more detail in the next section.

The Finishing Touch

Reviewing the project, releasing the project resources, and turning over the project deliverables to another group are the elements of the administrative aspect of project closure that need to be explored further.

Reviewing the Project

Part of the details of project closure is to analyze project success or failure. You can accomplish this by collecting and generating project evaluation information, such as what went well and what did not. Some of this information already exists in the work performance reports. However, the final information can be gathered in various ways, such as a post-project review meeting with the team or a questionnaire. The most important output (and the whole purpose) of the review is the lessons learned. The review should be comprehensive and should cover the following:

◆ Both technical and nontechnical components

◆ Both positive and negative aspects—that is, the things that went well and the things that did not go well

◆ All stages and phases of the project

 TIP

The purpose of the post-project review, also called the *post-project assessment*, is to learn lessons that can be applied to future projects to run them more effectively. Do not let the review turn into a finger-pointing show.

As part of the project review, you should also measure customer satisfaction from the customer feedback collected by using techniques such as interviews and surveys. This will help the organization establish and maintain a long-term relationship with the customer. An example of a survey is a 360-degree survey, which means feedback from all kinds of stakeholders in the project. In general, a 360-degree survey contains feedback from all around the entity being evaluated. For example, a 360-degree evaluation of an employee's performance will be based on feedback from the employee's peers, supervisors, customers that the employee deals with, other employees that this employee may be managing, and self-evaluation.

The findings of the review should be recorded in a document that might have different names in different organizations, such as the *post-project review report* or the *project assessment report*. Your organization might even have a template or standard for such a report. Depending upon the size of the project, the review report might be part of the project closure report or a separate report. The report will be distributed among the stakeholders and will be added to the project archive. The project closure report can also include the final project performance as compared to the baselines, as well as a description of the final project product.

Releasing the Resources

For effective and efficient use of the organization's resources, it is imperative that they be released in an efficient and proper manner. The release procedure might be included in the resource planning—for example, the staff management plan should address the issue of releasing the human resources. Well-planned release or transfer of team members reflects managerial professionalism, which requires that employees be treated with respect and dignity. By ensuring a well-planned release and a smooth transition to other projects, you are helping the employees focus wholeheartedly on the project toward the very end, rather than worrying about the next assignment. This will obviously improve the productivity of team members and the efficiency of the project. Following are some suggestions to consider for properly releasing human resources:

- ◆ Although it is possible that different team members will be released at different times, at the project closure you should organize some closure event to honor and thank the project team members, including the contractors, for their contributions. However, you must check your company policy regarding including contractors in company-sponsored events and giving them rewards.

- ◆ Plan ahead and do not wait until the last minute. Communicate with the functional manager ahead of time about when a staff member is going to be released.

- ◆ Work closely with your organization's human resources department, which might have some guidelines or procedures that you need to follow.

- ◆ Write (or offer to write) recommendation letters for team members who have made outstanding contributions to the project.

Once all the closure tasks are completed and the documents are finalized, the project might need to be turned over to another group in the organization—for example, to the maintenance or operations group.

Saying Goodbye: The Project Turnover

Depending upon the project, you might need to coordinate the turnover of the project deliverables to the customer or to another group in your organization, such as a maintenance or operations group. The turnover requirements, such as training help-desk employees, should have been included in the project management plan.

 TIP

Although the standard project processes are the same for each organization, the details and the manners in which they are implemented might be different for different organizations. Each organization can develop its own implementation details, which consist of items such as detailed steps for how to carry on the project processes, templates, meetings, and procedures.

The three most important takeaways from this chapter are as follows:

◆ The project deliverables validated through the quality control process must go through the Verify Scope process to ensure that the planned scope has been met.

◆ The deliverables acquired through procurement must go through the procurement closure process for acceptance by the appropriate party, such as the project manager.

◆ The deliverables verified through the Verify Scope process and the deliverables accepted through the procurement closure process must go through the project closure process for acceptance by the appropriate party.

Summary

All projects, big or small, terminated or completed, should go through the closure stage, which involves the closure of both parts of the project: in house and procurements. The project deliverables validated through the quality control process are verified for their scope through the Verify Scope process. These verified deliverables go through the project closure process for acceptance by the appropriate party, such as the customer or the project sponsor. The same process is used to close a project or a phase of it and is formally called the Close Project or Phase process. If the project has a procurement component, the products from procurement must first go through the procurement closure process for acceptance by the project manager or other authorized party, and then the accepted product must go through the project closure process for acceptance by the appropriate party, such as the customer or the project sponsor.

Like every other profession, project management has its integrity and ethics that you need to uphold. You'll explore this topic in the next chapter.

Exam's Eye View

Comprehend

◆ You, the project manager, manage the project closure. You can even recommend project closure to the project sponsor—for example, if you run out of resources and no more resources are available—but the authorization for the project closure must come from the sponsor.

◆ Before going through project closure, the deliverables must be checked for their scope through the Verify Scope process.

◆ Before going through the Verify Scope process, the project deliverables must be validated through the Perform Quality Control process.

◆ The project, in general, can have two kinds of work—in house and procured. Accordingly, there are two components of closure—project closure and procurement closure.

◆ The deliverables accepted through the procurement closure process also go through the project closure process.

Look Out

◆ Not only the completed projects, but also the terminated projects, must be formally closed using the processes of the closing process group.

◆ The Verify Scope process belongs to the monitoring and controlling process group.

◆ Verify Scope and Perform Quality Control are two different processes, even though both use inspection as a tool.

◆ The same process is used to close a phase of a project and the project itself.

Memorize

◆ The project sponsor signs the final project closure documents. The sponsor can also authorize the closure of the project at any stage.

◆ The product acceptance is carried out using the Close Project or Phase process.

◆ The contracts are closed using the Close Procurements process.

◆ The contributions to the documentation archive, including the lessons-learned database, are made by both the Close Project or Phase and the Close Procurements processes.

Key Terms and Definitions

- ◆ **360-degree survey.** A form of feedback from all around the entity being evaluated.

- ◆ **close procurements.** The process used to complete and settle each contract, which includes resolving any open item and closing each contract applicable to the project.

- ◆ **close project or phase.** A process used to finalize all activities across all of the process groups to formally close the project or a phase of it. It's also used to establish the procedures for administrative and contract closures.

- ◆ **procurement audit.** A structured review of the procurement process with the purpose of identifying successes and failures from the planning through the executing stage of the project.

- ◆ **project/product transition.** Handing over of the project output to the appropriate party.

- ◆ **SOX compliance.** Compliance with the Sarbanes-Oxley Act of 2002, also called the Public Company Accounting Reform and Investor Protection Act of 2002.

- ◆ **verify scope.** The process of formally accepting the completed project deliverables.

Review Questions

1. Which of the following scenarios will not trigger the closure stage of the project?

    A. The project plan was not accepted, and therefore the project never went to the execution stage.

    B. A schedule activity on a critical path is way behind schedule, and there is no way you can meet the project finish date.

    C. The project was cancelled when it was in the middle of the executing stage.

    D. The project sponsor has withdrawn support for the project.

2. Your project has entered the closing stage, and you are planning for the project review. Which of the following guidelines will you follow for the review?

    A. Cover all the stages of the project and both its positive and negative aspects.

    B. The emphasis in the review should be on the schedule.

    C. The focus should be on the positive aspects of the project, where the team performed well. This will boost the morale of the team, the team will perform even better in future projects, and it will also help get funding for future projects.

    D. The focus of the review should be on risk management.

3. At which stage has a successful project arrived when the closing process starts?
   A. Initiating
   B. Planning
   C. Executing
   D. Closing

4. You heard a functional manager saying, "We are going to skip the closing stage. There is no need for formalities in this project; it's a total waste of time." For which kind of projects is it appropriate to skip the closing stage?
   A. Technical projects
   B. Small and simple projects
   C. Large and complicated projects
   D. No projects

5. Which of the following stakeholders can authorize the closure of a project?
   A. Project manager
   B. Customer
   C. Project sponsor
   D. Functional manager

6. Which of the following is not an activity of the procurement closure of a project?
   A. Issuing formal acceptance of the procured products
   B. Handing over the accepted products to the appropriate parties, such as the customer or the sponsor
   C. Closing all the contracts associated with the project
   D. Archiving lessons-learned documents

7. You are preparing to close a project you have been managing. Which of the following is not an input to the Close Project or Phase process?
   A. Acceptance criteria
   B. Project management plan
   C. Project deliverables validated through the quality control process
   D. Final project audits

8. You are in the process of closing the Stem Cells Are Us project. Which of the following is not an output of the Close Project or Phase process?

   A. Lessons learned

   B. Acceptance of products

   C. Closed contracts

   D. Project closure documentation

9. Which of the following is the correct order of performing processes?

   A. Verify Scope, Perform Quality Control, Close Project or Phase

   B. Perform Quality Control, Verify Scope, Close Project or Phase

   C. Verify Scope, Close Project or Phase, Close Procurements

   D. Perform Quality Control, Close Project or Phase, Close Procurements

10. The lessons learned are an output of which closing process(es)?

   A. Close Project or Phase and Close Procurements

   B. Contract closure

   C. Work closure

   D. Administrative closure

Chapter 14

Performing Professional Responsibility

PMP Exam Objectives

Objective	*What It Really Means*
6.1 Ensure Personal Integrity and Professionalism	You must know that as a project manager, you need to ensure individual integrity and professionalism by adhering to ethical standards, legal requirements, and social norms of the locality of your project. You should know that personal integrity is based on honesty and responsibility.
6.2 Contribute to the Project Management Knowledge Base	You must know that you are expected to contribute to the project management knowledge base by sharing research, best practices, and lessons learned. The goal here is to advance the project management profession by improving the quality of project management and improving the capabilities of colleagues.
6.3 Enhance Personal Professional Competence	You must know that you are expected to continually improve your professional competence by acquiring and applying knowledge of project management and thereby improving the project management services you offer, continually enabling yourself to deliver what you promise.

(continues)

PMP Exam Objectives (continued)

Objective	*What It Really Means*
6.4 Promote Interaction among Stakeholders	You must know that you are expected to promote a collaborative project management environment by facilitating interaction among the project team members and other stakeholders. You accomplish this in a professional and cooperative manner by showing respect for personal and cultural differences. For all these objectives, you must understand the Project Management Institute's Code of Ethics and Professional Conduct based on four core values: fairness, honesty, respect, and responsibility.

Introduction

As the name of the certification suggests, you are going to become a project management professional, if you are not one already. A professional is an individual who practices an occupation with professionalism, which is a bond that binds a professional with the code of conduct for that occupation. Professionalism is not Einstein's theory of relativity. You might need to learn a few things in the beginning, but during the course of practicing a profession, professional conduct (that is, professionalism) becomes common sense. All professions share the essence of professionalism. It is as simple as doing the right thing. As a project manager, remember one golden rule: Deal with unprofessional situations directly, openly, and fairly, rather than ignoring them. Professionalism starts with individual integrity, which is based on truth, honesty, and openness.

Therefore, the key question in this chapter is, how can you practice project management with professional responsibility? In search of an answer, we will explore three avenues—individual integrity, interaction with clients and project stakeholders, and core values of ethical and professional conduct.

Ensuring Individual Integrity

Professionalism begins with individual integrity, which is a state of being complete and incorruptible. You can look at integrity as a point of reference based on truth and honesty, and you can maintain your integrity by using this point of reference as a guideline for your behavior and decision-making. Integrity identifies you as who you are. You demonstrate integrity by taking responsibility for your decisions and actions. If you don't have integrity, people won't know who you really are, and they won't trust you. So, individual integrity is a very significant part of professionalism in any profession.

 NOTE

Sometime the term *practitioner* is also used to refer to a project management professional. A project management practitioner is any individual who, as part of the project management profession, participates in an activity that contributes to the management of a project, program, or portfolio.

As a professional (the practitioner of a profession), you must set high standards, and you must aspire to meet those standards in all avenues of your life: while practicing the profession, at work, and at home. In that context, in project management, you maintain your integrity by being honest and truthful everywhere—for example, in the PMP exam, as well as while working in the project management field.

Dealing with the PMP exam and PMI. For example, while going through the process of obtaining PMP certification, individual integrity demands that it is your responsibility to adhere to the following practices:

◆ While going through the process of obtaining PMP certification, provide accurate and true information.

◆ Maintain the confidentiality of the content of the PMP examination. For example, do not disclose the questions in the exam to other PMP candidates.

◆ Cooperate with PMI concerning any ethical violation and in collecting related information.

The same honesty, truthfulness, and openness that you exhibit during the process of obtaining PMP certification also applies while you are working in the field of project management.

STUDY CHECKPOINT 14.1

Does the Code of Ethics and Professional Conduct only apply to the PMP certification and not to other certifications?

Working in the project management field. The activities that you perform as a PMP include representing yourself as a PMP, advertising your organization and your services, and running projects. To maintain your individual integrity during these activities, it is your responsibility to adhere to the following practices:

◆ Be accurate and truthful in advertising and representing your qualifications, experience, and the services you can perform.

◆ Be accurate and truthful to the public in advertising and public statements. For example, if your project is going to damage the environment, don't say it's going to help the environment.

◆ Maintain and satisfy the scope and objectives of the services promised to the customer.

◆ Follow the applicable laws, regulations, and ethical standards of the city, state, and country of your workplace. For example, don't say something like, "This is not how we do it back in Texas."

◆ Neither offer nor accept inappropriate payments in any form, such as gifts, which might qualify as bribery.

> **TIP**
>
> When you are in a foreign country, sometimes it can be tricky to figure out the right thing to do in a given situation. The trick here is if you are being asked to do something, such as pay some money to an official for getting something done, that is not legal or ethical in your country and culture, first investigate whether it is legal and ethical in the country you are in now. If you find it to be illegal and unethical there as well, but you are told it's a common practice, do not do it.

As you practice project management, you will learn lessons you can share with the community of project managers—that is, you can contribute to the project management knowledge base.

Contributing to the Knowledge Base

Professionalism demands (or encourages) that project managers (or PMPs) contribute to the project management knowledge base by publishing, teaching, and sharing lessons learned during practice. While doing so, you should adhere to the following practices:

- ◆ Share the information in an accurate, truthful, and complete manner.
- ◆ Recognize and honor the intellectual property developed or owned by others and give credit where credit is due when you use it.
- ◆ Follow the Code of Ethics and Professional Conduct by PMI and disseminate it among the PMP community.

> **CAUTION**
>
> PMI in general expects a PMP to stay engaged and help advance the project management profession by completing tasks such as contributing to the knowledge base. So participating in project management training, mentoring, sharing lessons learned, and promoting best practices are all recommendations by PMI that might appear in some exam questions, even if you don't see them literally mentioned in the Code of Ethics and Professional Conduct.

Contributing to the knowledge base is one side of the coin; the other side is obtaining knowledge or enhancing your individual professional competence.

Enhancing Individual Professional Competence

Professionalism in project management, as in any other field, demands that while practicing your profession you continue to learn and grow professionally. This is important for your individual success and for the advancement of the profession. It enables you to continue delivering what you promise to your customers.

Project management is a very involved and growing field. PMP certification and this book only introduce you to the field. For example, you can focus on any of the nine knowledge areas, such as risk management or quality management, and explore it further. Exploring the existing dimensions further is one area of learning, and adding new dimensions is another. For example, how about managing virtual teams—that is, teams that are spread out geographically? This new dimension in project management is quickly becoming an important and integral part of the project management profession, even faster than PMI can digest.

Exploring existing dimensions further and practicing new dimensions enhances your individual professional competence, as well as enables you to contribute to the knowledge base. Working in the field will also expose your professional weaknesses, which you will need to work on. This is also an integral part of enhancing your individual professional competence.

Whether you are enhancing your individual professional competence or contributing to the knowledge base, you are interacting with other members of your professional community. During the course of a project, the most important interaction is the interaction among project stakeholders.

Promoting Interaction among Stakeholders

A project manager needs to have a host of skills, and all of them are important. However, if I'm forced to name the most important skill a project manager must have and the most important activity a project manager should perform, the answer would be communication. On that note, as a project manager, it is your responsibility to facilitate interaction among the project stakeholders. You use communication for various purposes, such as to keep everybody on the same page regarding the status and issues of the project so there is no confusion or misunderstanding.

While dealing with stakeholders and facilitating interaction among them, professionalism demands that you adhere to the following practices:

◆ Treat stakeholders with respect and show respect for cultural diversity.

◆ Be accurate and truthful when presenting services and preparing estimates for costs and expected results.

◆ Be open, honest, and fair in your dealings with stakeholders, especially when you are resolving an issue.

◆ Honor confidentiality for the information you collect during your interactions with stakeholders.

◆ Disclose to stakeholders (clients, customers, owners, or contractors) significant circumstances that could be construed as conflicts of interest. It is your responsibility to ensure that a conflict of interest does not compromise the legitimate interests of a stakeholder and does not influence your professional judgments.

Dealing with Unprofessional Conduct

Working as a project manager, you will encounter minor to serious unprofessional conduct from time to time. The key here is, again, to be honest, truthful, and open.

 TIP

You might encounter small ethical violations, which might be painful to resolve. However, as a professional, you should choose to address them instead of ignoring them, and you should address them openly, fairly, and in a timely fashion. Openly, however, does not necessarily mean you go on CNN; you talk directly to the appropriate party.

As you already know, we live in a world of duality—good and bad, pleasure and pain, professionalism and unprofessionalism, and the like, all living side by side. Scary! However, if you stick to *your* professionalism, then you do not need to be afraid of a lack of professionalism in others. Do not focus on the person; focus on the conduct and remember that the only weapon you have to defeat a lack of professionalism is professionalism. If you are unprofessional, you cannot defeat a lack of professionalism; you can only promote it.

So, when you encounter a lack of professionalism, stay professional, focus on the issue and not on the person, maintain a smile on your face, and deal with the situation honestly, openly, and truthfully.

Code of Ethics and Professional Conduct: The Big Picture

In this chapter, we have discussed all the elements of being ethical and professional as a project management practitioner. In this section, we summarize our discussion into a big picture. The formal name for the standard for ethical and professional behavior issued by PMI is the

Code of Ethics and Professional Conduct. According to this standard, as shown in Table 14.1, the four pillars that make the foundation of professional conduct are fairness, honesty, respect, and responsibility. These four values, identified by PMI as the most important to the global project management community, are defined in the following list.

◆ **Fairness** is the act of making decisions and behaving impartially and objectively, free from favoritism, competing self-interest, and prejudice.

◆ **Honesty** is the policy to understand the truth based on facts and act in a truthful manner, both in communication and in conduct.

◆ **Respect** is the behavior of showing high regard for yourself, the people you are dealing with, and the resources entrusted to you. Resources entrusted to you may include human resources, money, and natural and environmental resources.

◆ **Responsibility** is an act of taking ownership for the decisions you make or fail to make, the actions you take or fail to take, and the consequences that result.

These values are not only good human and professional duties, but also help in developing a good business. For example, an environment of respect fosters trust, confidence, and mutual cooperation that lead to performance excellence. In an environment where diverse perspectives and views are encouraged and valued, better solutions will be designed, which will increase the chances of project success.

CAUTION

You should also consider the implications of the basic definitions of the four fundamental values. For example, respect for human resources also means caring about the reputation and safety of the human resources you are managing and other stakeholders.

As shown in Table 14.1, each of these four values is exercised in two dimensions: aspirational and mandatory. The aspirational standard describes the conduct that we strive to uphold in the practice of project management. The mandatory standard establishes firm requirements and in some cases limits or prohibits practitioner behavior. Practitioners who do not conduct themselves in accordance with these standards will be subject to disciplinary procedures before PMI's Ethics Review Committee.

CAUTION

Do not confuse aspirational with optional. An aspirational standard is called aspirational because adherence to this standard is not an easy measure. That said, you are expected to comply with this standard as a professional: It is not optional.

Table 14.1 Four Fundamental Values That Make the Foundation of the Code of Ethics and Professional Conduct by PMI

Value	Aspirational Standard	Mandatory Standard
Fairness	1. Constantly examine and correct yourself if necessary to ensure impartiality and objectivity. 2. Demonstrate transparency in your decision-making process. 3. Provide equal access to information for those who are authorized to have the information. 4. Make opportunities equally available to all qualified candidates.	1. Conflict of interest. Fully disclose any real or potential conflict of interest. Do not get involved in decision making and do not attempt to influence the outcome without such disclosure to all the affected stakeholders. 2. Apply the official rules without bias driven by favoritism and prejudice. 3. Do not use bribery, favoritism, or nepotism in dealing with people, such as hiring or firing, rewarding or punishing, and awarding or denying contracts. 4. Do not discriminate against people based on age, disability, gender, nationality, race, religion, or sexual orientation.
Respect	1. Listen to others including those with whom you disagree, in an attempt to understand them. 2. In a professional manner, directly approach those individuals with whom you have a disagreement or a conflict. 3. Stay professional even if the person you are dealing with is being unprofessional. 4. Be knowledgeable about and respectful to the norms and customs of other people.	1. Do not use any form of power, such as expertise, status, or position, to influence a decision or other people's actions in order to benefit at their expense. 2. Negotiate in good faith. 3. Do not act toward other people in an abusive manner. 4. Respect the property rights—including intellectual property rights—of other individuals and organizations.
Honesty	1. Always try to find the facts, be truthful in presenting the facts, and create an environment in which others feel safe to tell the truth. 2. Provide accurate information in a timely manner. 3. Make commitments and promises in good faith.	1. Do not engage in or condone behavior designed to deceive others, such as making false or misleading statements, presenting incomplete facts, providing information without context, and withholding information. 2. Do not engage in attaining personal gain at the expense of others through improper means, such as dishonesty.

Table 14.1 Continued

Value	Aspirational Standard	Mandatory Standard
Responsibility	1. Base your decisions and actions on the best interests of the environment, public safety, and society as a whole. 2. Accept only those assignments that are consistent with your background, including your qualifications, skills, and experience. And when you accept an assignment, deliver what you promised. 3. Accept responsibility for your mistakes (errors and omissions) and accountability for the consequences. Also, report errors caused by others to the appropriate party. 4. Protect proprietary or confidential information that has been entrusted to you during your assignment. 5. Hold yourself and others accountable to the Code of Ethics and Professional Conduct by PMI.	1. Know and comply with the policies, rules, regulations, and laws that govern your work activities. 2. Report any unethical or illegal conduct to an appropriate party, such as management and those affected by the conduct. 3. The ethical complaints you make must be substantiated by facts. 4. Report violations of PMI's Code of Ethics and Professional Conduct to the appropriate body for resolution. 5. Pursue disciplinary action against an individual who retaliates against a person because that person raised ethical concerns.

 NOTE

The Code of Ethics and Professional Conduct by PMI applies to anyone who meets at least one of the following criteria:

- Is a member of PMI
- Holds a PMI certification or has applied to start the certification process
- Serves PMI as a volunteer

STUDY CHECKPOINT 14.2

What are the two standards of the Code of Ethics and Professional Conduct?

So, let's conclude this final chapter with the mantra of our profession: fairness, honesty, respect, and responsibility.

The three most important takeaways from this chapter are as follows:

◆ You should practice your profession with professionalism, supported by individual integrity based on honesty, truthfulness, and openness.

◆ You should continue enhancing your professional competence and contributing to the project management knowledge base.

◆ The four values that make up the foundation of professional conduct are fairness, honesty, respect, and responsibility.

Summary

As a PMP, you must practice project management with professionalism—that is, with professional responsibility—which includes following the rules and policies of the certification process and of the organization for which you are managing the project. The key to professionalism is individual integrity based on honesty, truth, and openness. Professionalism requires that you interact with your client and with the project stakeholders with mutual dignity and respect and show respect to diversity of cultures and beliefs. If you encounter an unprofessional situation, rather than ignoring it, you deal with it honestly, openly, and truthfully. Your professional responsibility as a PMP also demands that you continue enhancing your professional competence and contributing to the project management knowledge base.

Keep in mind that while honesty, truth, and openness are essential elements of individual integrity regardless of where you are, the definitions of right versus wrong, acceptable versus unacceptable, and to some extent ethical versus unethical might vary across cultures. Sometimes you will need to think hard to do the right thing when faced with tricky situations. For example, just because bribery is a common and acceptable practice in a country, that does not make it the right thing to do, especially if it is illegal. When you are not sure which option is the right one, investigate whether it is legal and ethical in that country.

With individual integrity, you follow the Code of Ethics and Professional Conduct by PMI, which is founded on four fundamental values: fairness, honesty, respect, and responsibility.

Exam's Eye View

Comprehend

- Honesty, truthfulness, and openness define integrity, which is the key to professionalism.

- While managing a project, you will perform the selected process for the project and will not cut corners—for example, to save money. A process is in place for the overall efficiency of the project, not as a formality.

- If an option sounds sneaky, manipulative, and as if it favors one stakeholder over another, it is not the option you want to choose.

- Disclose any conflict of interest to the relevant client and don't let this conflict influence your professional judgment.

Look Out

- Do not do something that is illegal, unethical, or both in the country and culture of your workplace, even if it is legal and ethical back home.

- Do not do something that is illegal, ethical, or both, even if you are told that it is a common and acceptable practice.

- When you encounter an unprofessional attitude or situation, deal with it quickly, honestly, and openly, even when it is hard to do so and easy to ignore the problem.

- Beware of the options that offer you easier ways out or shortcuts. Those options are usually wrong.

- Showing respect to other cultures does not mean getting involved in something illegal.

Memorize

- Follow the law of the land for your workplace.

- Show respect to other individuals and cultures.

- Honor the confidentiality of information that you learn during the course of getting certified, dealing with customers, and managing projects.

- Help advance the profession of project management by enhancing your individual professional competence and by contributing to the project management knowledge base.

- The four values that make up the foundation of professional conduct are fairness, honesty, respect, and responsibility.

Key Terms and Definitions

- **abusive manner.** Conduct that hurts another person either physically or emotionally, such as creating feelings of exploitation, manipulation, fear, or humiliation.
- **fairness.** An act of making decisions and behaving impartially and objectively, free from favoritism, competing self-interest, and prejudice.
- **honesty.** The policy of understanding the truth based on facts and acting in a truthful manner both in communication and in conduct.
- **project management practitioner.** Any individual who, as part of the project management profession, participates in an activity that contributes to the management of a project, program, or portfolio.
- **respect.** A behavior of showing high regard for yourself, the people you are dealing with, and the resources entrusted to you.
- **responsibility.** An act of taking ownership for the decisions you make or fail to make, the actions you take or fail to take, and the consequences that result.

Review Questions

1. You have applied for the PMP exam, and you are attending a training session for the exam offered by a PMP who proudly poses a number of questions to the audience and claims that these are the questions in the real exam. What should you do? (Choose one.)

    A. Immediately leave the classroom and never take another course from the same training agency.

    B. Write to the president of the training agency.

    C. Report this trainer to the police.

    D. Contact PMI and inform them of the situation.

2. You are managing a project in a country foreign to you. The project sponsor asks you to write a check to a city official to get some paperwork required for the project moving forward. Such an activity in your home country would be considered bribery, which is illegal. What should you do?

    A. Investigate whether what the sponsor is suggesting is legal and ethical in this country.

    B. Report the sponsor to the police.

    C. Write the check to the city official because the project sponsor asked you to do so.

    D. Tell the sponsor that he's an unethical person and you are leaving the project.

3. You are managing a project in a country foreign to you. The project sponsor asks you to write a check to a city official to get some paperwork required for the project moving forward. She confesses that it is, as a matter of fact, bribery and is technically illegal, but it is a very common and acceptable practice in this country. What should you do?

    A. Go ahead and do it.

    B. Tell the project sponsor politely that because it is illegal, you cannot do it.

    C. Write an e-mail to the project sponsor's boss.

    D. Tell the sponsor that she's an unethical person and you are leaving the project.

4. You are managing a project in a country foreign to you, and the project is in the planning stage. The project sponsor asks you to inflate the cost estimate by 30 percent. He says, "We're not in Kansas anymore, buddy; if you want to get the license for a pistol here, you would have to apply for a machine gun." He insists that this is the only way he can get the required money because management always reduces the estimate before allotting money. Which of the following is the best step you could take?

    A. Report the project sponsor to PMI.

    B. Inflate the cost estimate as the sponsor said; after all, he is the sponsor.

    C. Prepare an accurate estimate along with a risk report that explains the risks involved if the adequate funds are not available.

    D. Prepare two cost estimates—one for the management and another one for actual implementation.

5. You are the project manager of a project that needs to procure a bunch of activities as a subproject due to the lack of skills in the organization. Your sister-in-law owns a firm that specializes in the area of the activities that need to be procured. She has shown an interest in this procurement. Which of the following steps would be the best to take?

    A. Allot this work to your sister-in-law. After all, her firm specializes in this area.

    B. Allot this work to your sister-in-law and make sure you don't let your relationship affect your professional judgment.

    C. Disclose your relationship with your sister-in-law to the stakeholders and allow multiple vendors to bid for the opportunity. Excuse yourself from the final decision-making.

    D. Insist that this is part of networking and you can get the best deal from your sister-in-law.

6. Which of the following is not expected by the PMP Code of Professional Conduct?

    A. Being honest with your customers

    B. Taking classes to improve your professional weaknesses in project management so that you can accept more assignments and deliver what you promise

    C. Going to church or temple as often as you can to learn about ethics

    D. Cooperating with PMI concerning ethics violations

7. You are the project manager for a project that involves procurement. Multiple vendors bid for the work to be procured. The cost estimate from Best Deals is significantly higher than from any other vendor. Which of the following is an appropriate action to take?

    A. Be open and ask Best Deals why their estimate is higher than that of all other vendors.

    B. Communicate with Best Deals to find out exactly how they reached this estimate and what statement of work they are using to make the estimate.

    C. Talk to other bidders to find out what's going on with Best Deals. Ask other bidders why their estimates are so low.

    D. Write to the CEO of Best Deals to complain about this outrageously high estimate.

8. You are the project manager for the Peace in the City project. You have learned that three of the stakeholders have started fighting over the scope of the project. What step will you take?

    A. Contact the stakeholder and check whether they have any question about the scope of the project. Starting this way, you will resolve the conflict.

    B. Contact senior management and report the conflict to them so they can resolve it.

    C. Contact the project sponsor and inform him of the conflict among the stakeholders so the sponsor can resolve it.

    D. Don't do anything; just keep your focus on the actual work of the project.

9. You have taken over a project that is already in the executing stage. You discover that some of the milestones still in progress have been reported as completed to the senior management by the previous project manager in the status reports. Which of the following is the best first step to take?

    A. There is no need to inform the stakeholders about it; just use schedule compression techniques to make up the difference.

    B. Immediately inform stakeholders and senior management of the discrepancy and provide them with the accurate project status.

    C. Report the previous manager to PMI.

    D. Ask the sponsor what to do now.

10. You are hired as a project manager for a company. Which of the following is *not* your responsibility?

   A. Ensuring that no project activity violates the law of the land

   B. Honoring the confidentiality of the information you collected while managing the project

   C. Determining whether company procedures are legal

   D. Contributing to the project management knowledge base

11. The four values that make the foundation of the Code of Ethics and Professional Conduct by the PMI are the following:

   A. Fairness, honesty, respect, and responsibility

   B. Fairness, openness, respect, and responsibility

   C. Fairness, honesty, contribution to the knowledge base, and responsibility

   D. Fairness, honesty, respect, and acquiring new skills

PART VI

Appendixes

Answers and Solutions to Study Checkpoint Exercises

Chapter 1

Study Checkpoint 1.1

Identify each of the following items as a project or an operation.

A. Restaurant employees serving breakfast to the customers every day
B. A bookseller processing customer orders
C. A network administrator ensuring that the network stays up and running 24×7
D. Writing and publishing a book

Answer: A, B, and C are examples of operations—ongoing and repetitive efforts. D is a project with a definitive amount of effort and a unique product.

Study Checkpoint 1.2

What is the core difference between knowledge areas and process groups? Try to answer this question in one sentence.

Answer: Knowledge areas are disciplines of management that represent management knowledge in a certain topic, such as cost and time, whereas process groups are about the application of that knowledge—that is, where and when to apply that knowledge, for example during initiating or during planning, and so on.

Okay, that was a long sentence. Here is the short answer: Knowledge areas are about knowledge on project management topics, and process groups are about applying that knowledge.

Study Checkpoint 1.3

In the following table, match each item in the first column with a corresponding item in the second column:

Knowledge Area   *Action*

A. Scope   1. Manage interdependencies among different processes belonging to different knowledge areas.

B. Cost   2. Ensure the project includes the work required to complete the project successfully and no extra work.

C. Time   3. Plan the schedule and complete the project within the planned schedule.

D. Quality   4. Plan the budget, track what you are spending, and complete the project within budget.

E. Risk   5. Be sure to develop the right product that will satisfy the needs for which the project is undertaken.

F. Procurement   6. Obtain the team to do the project work and lead and motivate the team to keep working in the right direction in an efficient and effective way.

G. Human Resources   7. Generate and distribute required project information to the right stakeholders at the right time by using the right method.

H. Communication   8. Plan for uncertain events that could happen and deal with them when they do happen in such a way that possible benefit is maximized and damage is minimized.

I. Integration   9. Identify the project work that needs to be contracted out of the performing organization and contract it out.

Answer:

A. 2
B. 4
C. 3
D. 5
E. 8
F. 9
G. 6
H. 7
I. 1

Study Checkpoint 1.4

What is the core difference between enterprise environmental factors and organizational process assets?

Answer: Enterprise environmental factors are about how the performing organization does its business, whereas organizational process assets are about how the organization runs its projects.

Explanation: Enterprise environmental factors are the factors of the overall environment in which the organization is operating, doing its business. Organizational process assets are the process-related assets, and the projects are made of processes; therefore, the organizational process assets speak more to how the organization performs its projects.

Study Checkpoint 1.5

Match each item in the first column of the following table with one or more suitable items in the second column.

Entity	May Contain
A. Operation	1. Non-project work
B. Project	2. Projects
C. Program	3. Programs
D. Portfolio	4. Portfolios
	5. Activities to create a well-defined, unique product

Answer:

A. 1
B. 5
C. 1, 2, 3
D. 1, 2, 3

Study Checkpoint 1.6

You are about to throw a quarter and a dime several times. What is the probability that the following will happen?

A. The quarter will land heads up on the first try.
B. The dime will land tails up on the first try.
C. The quarter will land heads up and the dime will land tails up on the first try.
D. Both the quarter and the dime will land heads up on the first try.
E. The quarter will land heads up on the first try and also heads up on the second try.

Answer:

The quarter has a probability of 0.5 to land either way: heads up or tails up. The same is true for the dime.

Considering that, Answers A and B are 0.5, and Answers C, D, and E are 0.25. (0.5×0.5=0.25).

Study Checkpoint 1.7

In the following table, match each item in the first column with the corresponding item in the second column.

Project Variable	Value
A. Level of staff	1. Highest in the beginning and end of the project and lowest when the project is being executed.
B. Risk	2. Highest in the beginning and decreases as the project progresses.
C. Ability to influence the characteristics of the project product without significantly impacting the project cost	3. Low in the beginning and maximum when the project is being executed.
D. Cost	4. Uniform throughout the project

Answer:

  A. 3
  B. 2
  C. 2
  D. 3

Chapter 2

Study Checkpoint 2.1

You have been offered a project B that will earn you a profit of $100,000 in three months. You already have an offer of a project A that will earn you a profit of $70,000 in three months. You can only do one project during these three months, and the project requesters are unable to move the project durations.

  A. What is the opportunity cost of project A?
  B. What is the opportunity cost of project B?
  C. Just based on the opportunity cost, which project will you select?
  D. Describe what can change your decision based just on the opportunity cost.

Answers:

A. $100,000, because this is the opportunity that you are missing when you take on project A.

B. $70,000, because this is the opportunity that you are missing when you take on project B.

C. Project B will be selected because it has a smaller opportunity cost.

D. Opportunity cost is only one of several criteria that are used to select projects. It may be that some other criteria, such as a scoring model, produce different results. You have to see which method is more relevant for your case.

Study Checkpoint 2.2

A. What is the first process you perform in managing a project?

B. What do you need before you can begin initiating your project?

Answers:

A. Develop Project Charter

B. The input to the Develop Project Charter process: business case, including business need, statement of work, contract, and so on.

Study Checkpoint 2.3

In the following table, match each item in the first column to one or more items in the second column to describe its role during project initiating:

Item	Role
A. Statement of work	1. Input to developing project charter
B. Project charter	2. Output of developing project charter
C. Procurement documents	3. Input to identifying stakeholders
D. Project management strategy	4. Output of identifying stakeholders

Answers:

A. 1

B. 2, 3

C. 3

D. 4

Chapter 3

Study Checkpoint 3.1

Among the following attributes, identify which are part of the product scope and which are part of the project scope.

- A. Develop software modules to support a website.
- B. The user can only access this website after logging in.
- C. The drug should not have more than two side effects.
- D. The drug must be developed within one year.
- E. The drug must be tested in-house before it goes to the Food and Drug Administration.

Answers:

Project scope: A, D, E

Product scope: B, C

Study Checkpoint 3.2

In the following table, match each item in the first column with an appropriate item in the second column.

A. The software product must run on both the Microsoft Windows and Apple Macintosh platforms.	1. Project deliverable
B. An online education website.	2. Project constraint
C. The drug must be developed within six months.	3. Product requirement
D. The software module must not have more than 10 bugs.	4. Project management requirement
E. The project manager must have a PMP certification.	5. Product acceptance criteria

Answers:

- A. 3
- B. 1
- C. 2
- D. 5
- E. 4

Study Checkpoint 3.3

   A. What is the difference between management control points and control accounts?

   B. What is the difference between control accounts and a code of accounts?

Answers:

   A. Management control points are the nodes in the WBS hierarchical structures that are selected for managing some parameters or characteristics of the project. Control accounts are those management control points that are used to manage scope, budget, actual cost, and schedule. These three quantities are integrated and compared to earned value in order to measure project performance. In other words, a control account is an example of management control points.

   B. A code of accounts is a set of numbers or a numbering system used to uniquely identify each component of the WBS. So, each component of the WBS can have a code of account, but each component is not a control account; only a few selected components are control accounts.

Chapter 4

Study Checkpoint 4.1

   A. What is the most common logical relationship used in schedule network diagrams?

   B. What is the least common logical relationship used in schedule network diagrams?

Answer:

   A. Finish to start

   B. Start to finish

Study Checkpoint 4.2

In the program evaluation and review technique (PERT), the most likely scenario is given a weight of 4 as compared to the weight of 1 for each of the pessimistic and optimistic scenarios. The pessimistic estimate for an activity is 25 days, the optimistic estimate is 5 days, and the most likely estimate is 10 days. Calculate the expected estimate by using the PERT technique.

Answer:

$T_e = (nt_m + t_o + t_p)/(n+2)$

$\quad = (4 \times 10 + 5 + 25)/(4+2)$

$\quad = 70/6 = 11.7 \text{ days}$

Study Checkpoint 4.3

Lora Nirvana is the project manager for the Sequence the DNA of a Buffalo (SDB) project. Match each item in the first column of the following table to the correct item in the second column.

Output of the Develop Schedule Process	*Description*
A. Schedule data	1. A bar chart that includes all the activities of the project and also includes milestones. Lora points to this bar chart for the project sponsor to show where they are in the execution of the project.
B. Project document updates	2. A bar chart hanging on the calendar that has never changed once it was approved. Lora compares the current bar chart with this bar chart to show the progress.
C. Schedule	3. On a bar chart, Lora points to the dates when she will have the DNA sample isolated and purified, when she will get the DNA sample run through the genetic analyzer, when she will receive the results from the analyzer, and when the results will be published on the Internet.
D. Schedule baseline	4. After realizing that their chosen vendor has a track record of sending the DNA analysis kits late, Lora writes something into the risk register.

Answers:

A. 3
B. 4
C. 1
D. 2

Study Checkpoint 4.4

Lora Nirvana is the project manager for the Sequence the DNA of a Buffalo (SDB) project. Match each item in the first column of the following table to the correct item in the second column.

Term	*Action*
A. Message	1. While developing the schedule, Lora realized that there was a risk involved in the project. So, she put her thoughts into a note that she wrote on her computer.
B. Medium	2. She sent the note to the project sponsor.
C. Encode	3. She used e-mail to send the message.

D. Noise   4. The sponsor received the message.

E. Receiver   5. The sponsor could not understand some of the acronyms and terms in the e-mail message, such as variable number of tandem repeats (VNTR and central dogma of molecular biology).

F. Feedback   6. The sponsor responded to Lora expressing his concern that he could not exactly understand her concerns.

Answers:

  A. 2
  B. 3
  C. 1
  D. 5
  E. 4
  F. 6

Chapter 5

Study Checkpoint 5.1

An activity cost estimate goes like this: It will take a programmer 20 hours to write this program. The average rate to hire a programmer is $50 per hour. Therefore, the cost of writing this program, assuming that everything else needed to write the program (such as a computer) is in place, is 20×$50=$1,000. What kind of estimation technique is at work here?

Answer: Parametric estimation

Study Checkpoint 5.2

The pessimistic cost estimate for an activity is $6,000, the optimistic estimate is $3,000, and the most likely estimate is $5,000. Calculate the expected estimate by using the PERT technique.

Answer:

$C_e = (nC_m + C_o + C)/(n+2)$

$= (4 \times 5000 + 3000 + 6000)/(4+2)$

$= 29,000/6 = 4,833$

Expected cost estimate = $4,833

Study Checkpoint 5.3

Rajinder Preeti is in the process of estimating costs and preparing the budget for her project. In the following table, match each of her activities in the first column with the corresponding technique in the second column.

Activity	*Technique*
A. Rajinder discovers that there are lots of unknowns about an activity that could cost a lot more than has been estimated because it could take longer. So she puts some money aside to deal with this situation.	1. Parametric estimation
B. There is a complicated activity for which there is much disagreement among the team about its cost estimate. So, Rajinder makes an estimate by taking the average of the most optimistic estimate, the most pessimistic estimate, and the most realistic estimate.	2. Reserve analysis
C. Rajinder shows the estimate in Point B to her supervisor. The supervisor expresses her doubts about the final figure. Rajinder then splits the complex activity into smaller pieces, estimates the costs of each piece, and adds up the cost to reach the final figure.	3. Cost aggregation
D. For another activity, Rajinder just multiplies the number of work hours with the hourly rate for each team member involved in the activity and adds those numbers to reach the final cost estimate for the activity.	4. Reconciliation of funding limits
E. Rajinder adds up cost estimates for all the activities of the project in order to determine the budget.	5. Bottom-up estimating
F. Rajinder discovers that the overall budget is not consistent with the availability of funding. So, she has a careful look at the schedule to solve this problem.	6. Three-point estimate

Answers:

- A. 2
- B. 6
- C. 5
- D. 1
- E. 3
- F. 4

Study Checkpoint 5.4

Rajinder, the project manager, is now working on procurement planning for a portion of the project. She is looking at all the following options for procuring different pieces. Match each consideration in the first column of the following table to the corresponding contract type in the second column.

Consideration	*Contract type*
A. Rajinder will pay $3,000 for the use of facility and $5,000 per month for the employees working for the procured piece for the duration of work. However, there is a cap of $50,000 for the maximum cost.	1. Fixed price (FP)
B. Rajinder will pay for the cost of labor and a lump sum of $5,000.	2. Time and Material (T&M)
C. Rajinder will provide $50,000 to maintain the website for the project for two years.	3. Cost plus fixed fee (CPFF)
D. Rajinder will provide $10,000 for developing a software program and an extra $1,000 if fewer than 10 bugs are discovered in the program in the first year of its use.	4. Cost plus percentage of cost (CPPC)
E. Rajinder will pay the labor cost each month plus 5% of this cost as coffee and snacks at work and for recognition and rewards for the labor.	5. Cost plus incentive fee (CPIF)

Answers:

A. 2

B. 3

C. 1

D. 5

E. 4

Chapter 6

Study Checkpoint 6.1

You are trying out a Monte Carlo simulation program that estimates the value of a parameter by using some random variables. You know through the data that the exact value should be 50. You ran the program three times, and it gave you three values: 60, 61, and 62. Based on these values, answer the following questions:

A. How precise is the program in making the estimates?

B. How accurate are the estimates?

C. Are the values generated by the program more accurate or more precise?

Answers:

A. The program is quite precise because the values 60, 61, and 62 are very close to each other.

Average value = 61

% uncertainty = $[(62-60)/61] \times 100\% = 3.3\%$

B. The estimates are far away from the true value, and therefore accuracy is not very good.

Average % deviation = $[(61-50)/50] \times 100\% = 22\%$

C. Comparing the errors in parts A and B, the results are more precise and less accurate.

Study Checkpoint 6.2

Perform the EMV analysis of the decision tree presented in Figure 6.10 to make a decision on which option to take.

Answers:

Option	Initial Cost	Risk Cost	Probability	EMV for Risk Cost	Total Cost
Update	$50,000	$200,000	40%	0.40×$200,000= $80,000	$50,000+$80,000= $130,000
Build from scratch	$70,000	$200,000	10%	0.10×$200,000= $20,000	$70,000+$20,000= $90,000

Study Checkpoint 6.3

You are the project manager of a movie-shooting project. The first column in the following table lists some actions you are taking to deal with risks. Match each item in the first column with one item in the second column of this table.

Action	Risk Response Type
A. One of the scenes is to be shot in a country that has enormous bureaucracy and red tape. They might create roadblocks and make it difficult for you. There isn't much you can plan about it.	1. Avoid
B. The jungle where you are going to shoot a few scenes is a wetland and very hot and humid, and the probability of damage happening to the equipment is very high. So, you have decided to buy insurance to protect you against this possible damage.	2. Accept
C. You have learned that during certain parts of the year, the locals come to the jungle in big numbers for hunting. So, you have decided not to do the shoot during that part of the year.	3. Exploit

D. Although the movie does not depend on it, it will add a lot of marketing value to the movie if your cameras could capture an endangered species of bird that lives in the jungle. You are choosing the specific time of the year for shooting and taking some other actions to increase the probability that the birds will show up.

4. Share

E. The movie has something to do with Thanksgiving Day. You have put some extra resources to ensure that the movie is completed in a timely manner for release on Thanksgiving Day.

5. Mitigate

F. You have learned that there could be mosquitoes in the area that you are going to shoot. So you have planned to take plenty of mosquito repellent and other products to prevent mosquito bites.

6. Enhance

G. You know that another movie team is going to shoot some scenes in the same jungle during a different time of the year. You have signed a contract with them to share or trade shots of the endangered bird species.

7. Transfer

Answers:

A. 2
B. 7
C. 1
D. 6
E. 3
F. 5
G. 4

Chapter 7

Study Checkpoint 7.1

List the processes of the executing process group.

Answers:

1. Direct and Manage Project Execution
2. Perform Quality Assurance
3. Acquire Project Team
4. Develop Project Team
5. Manage Project Team

6. Distribute Information
7. Manage Stakeholder Expectations
8. Conduct Procurements

Study Checkpoint 7.2

True or False: Approved change requests are processed through the Perform Integrated Change Control process.

Answer: False. The change requests are processed through the Perform Integrated Change Control process. Once they are approved, they are processed through the Direct and Manage Project Execution process for implementation.

Study Checkpoint 7.3

True or False: Quality assurance also uses the tools and techniques of quality planning and quality control.

Answer: True

Study Checkpoint 7.4

What is the main goal of the Conduct Procurements process?

Answer: To select the sellers and award procurement contracts to them.

Chapter 8

Study Checkpoint 8.1

Each comment in the first column of the following table points to a conflict resolution strategy. Match each comment with the corresponding strategy in the second column.

Comment	*Conflict Resolution Technique*
A. Let's have a face-to-face meeting and hear out both parties.	1. Avoidance/withdrawal
B. Both of you have to meet halfway; you can't get everything all the time.	2. Competition/forcing
C. I'm the one who is running the show here, and I have made the decision.	3. Compromising/smoothing
D. Okay, I see your point now. I was thinking more at a personal level; your view is more compatible with the project's objectives. I guess for that reason I can live with your approach.	4. Accommodation

E. You guys are not even listening to my argument. I feel I'm wasting my time. So, I'm not going to discuss it with you any longer.

5. Collaboration

F. Let's sit down, talk it out, and design the best solution for all parties.

6. Confronting /problem solving

Answers:

A. 6

B. 3

C. 2

D. 4

E. 1

F. 5

Study Checkpoint 8.2

In the following table, match each scenario in the first column with an appropriate theory in the second column.

Scenario

A. The management is really nice to the employees, and there are lots of perks. But I'm more concerned about my career path once I join this company.

Motivation Theory

1. Maslow's hierarchy of needs theory

B. Engineering manager Bob has a habit that employees don't like. Every time he passes by a cubicle of an employee, he always peers at the computer screen over the shoulders of the employee to see what the employee is really doing on the computer.

2. Herzberg's motivation-hygiene theory

C. Rachel Janowicz quit her project management job with the Gugu Gaga company immediately after winning the California Super Lotto. She said, "Well, my money problem is solved. Now I will do what I always wanted to do."

3. McClelland's achievement motivation theory

D. I'm not going to attend this seminar. Basically, I'll be listening to their pitches all day long. What are the odds that I'll win the door prize?

4. McGregor's X-Y theory

E. Kushal did not really like the assignment. But he did it anyway because he did not want to let his manager down.

5. Expectancy theory

Answers:

A. 2
B. 4 (X theory)
C. 1
D. 5
E. 3

Chapter 9

Study Checkpoint 9.1

True or False: A stakeholder is proposing something that is not within the planned scope of the project. The appropriate response to this proposal is to oppose it.

Answer: False. A project manager is not a de facto opponent to change; instead you should be an agent for change. Your response should be to evaluate the change for its effects on the project and then put it through the approval process, where it may be either rejected or selected.

Study Checkpoint 9.2

The Distribute Information process uses performance reports as an input. Which process do these reports come from?

Answer: Report Performance

Chapter 10

Study Checkpoint 10.1

Name three processes that convert work performance data into work performance measurements.

Answer: Control Scope, Control Schedule, and Control Cost

Study Checkpoint 10.2

Name an element for which the project management plan is used to perform the Monitor and Control Project Work process.

Answer: Performance baseline

Study Checkpoint 10.3

Many processes in the monitoring and controlling process group generate change requests. Name a process in this process group that takes change requests as an input.

Answer: Perform Integrated Change Control

Study Checkpoint 10.4

Name an input item that is common to all three processes: Monitor and Control Project Work, Perform Integrated Change Control, and Administer Procurements.

Answer: Project management plan

Chapter 11

Study Checkpoint 11.1

A. Which quality process generates quality control measurements?
B. Which quality process uses quality control measurements?

Answers:

A. Perform Quality Control
B. Perform Quality Assurance

Study Checkpoint 11.2

Project deliverables are an input to which quality process?

Answer: Perform Quality Control

Study Checkpoint 11.3

What other process uses the tools and techniques used in the Perform Quality Control process?

Answer: Perform Quality Assurance

Study Checkpoint 11.4

In the following table, write the name of a quality management process in the second column corresponding to each activity listed in the first column.

Activity	*Quality Management Process*
You managed a quality audit of your project and found an enormous number of defects.	_____
You are looking at a diagram to pinpoint the root cause of a number of defects appearing in the project product. You write down your observations and recommend a corrective action.	_____
You are determining the cost of quality to present a case for quality assurance and quality control to your supervisor.	_____
You are examining the product to ensure that a defect has actually been repaired.	_____
You are looking at a diagram to pinpoint the root cause of a number of defects appearing in the project product. This leads you to analyze some processes and procedures for their effectiveness.	_____

Answers:

Activity	*Quality Management Process*
You managed a quality audit of your project and found an enormous number of defects.	Perform Quality Assurance
You are looking at a diagram to pinpoint the root cause of a number of defects appearing in the project product. You write down your observations and recommend a corrective action.	Perform Quality Control
You are determining the cost of quality to present a case for quality assurance and quality control to your supervisor.	Plan Quality
You are examining the product to ensure that a defect has actually been repaired.	Perform Quality Control
You are looking at a diagram to pinpoint the root cause of a number of defects appearing in the project product. This leads you to analyze some processes and procedures for their effectiveness.	Perform Quality Assurance

Chapter 12

Study Checkpoint 12.1

In our running example, calculate the ETC at the present CPI. Note that CPI is calculated 1.2 in our running example from earlier in this chapter.

Answer:

$$ETC = \frac{BAC - EV}{CPI} = \frac{\$600,000 - \$150,000}{1.2} = \$375,000$$

Study Checkpoint 12.2

Prove the validity of the following equation:

EAC=AC+BAC−EV

Answer:

The definition of EAC: EAC=AC+ETC (1)

The definition of ETC: ETC=BAC−EV (2)

Substitute the value of ETC from Equation (2) into Equation (1) to obtain:

EAC=AC+BAC−EV

Study Checkpoint 12.3

In our running example, calculate EAC at the present CPI. Note that CPI is calculated as 1.2 in our running example from earlier in this chapter.

Answer:

$$EAC = AC + \frac{BAC - EV}{CPI} = \$125,000 + \frac{\$600,000 - \$150,000}{1.2} = \$500,000$$

Study Checkpoint 12.4

In our running example, calculate EAC at the present CPI. Note that CPI is calculated as 1.2 and SPI is calculated as 0.75 in our running example from earlier in this chapter.

Answer:

$$EAC = AC + \frac{BAC - EV}{CPI \times SPI} = \$125,000 + \frac{\$600,000 - \$150,000}{1.2 \times 0.75} = \$625,000$$

3.1

...ope process, you look at the project scope statement, WBS, and ...se three elements collectively called?

3.2

The Verify Scope process belongs to which process group?

Answer: Monitoring and controlling

Study Checkpoint 13.3

What is the standard name for the process used to close a phase of a project?

Answer: Close Project or Phase

Study Checkpoint 13.4

True or False: You do not need to follow the Close Project process if the project is terminated at a rather early stage.

Answer: False. Once a project has begun, it must be closed properly, regardless of whether it was completed or terminated at any stage.

Chapter 14

Study Checkpoint 14.1

Does the Code of Ethics and Professional Conduct only apply to the PMP certification and not to other certifications?

Answer: No. The Code of Ethics and Professional Conduct applies to all certifications by PMI. We have used PMP here just as an example.

Study Checkpoint 14.2

What are the two standards of the Code of Ethics and Professional Conduct?

Answer: Aspirational and Mandatory

Chapter 1

1. Answer: D

   D is the correct answer because the defining characteristics of a project are that it must be temporary (with a start and finish date), and it must produce a unique (new) product.

   A and **B** are incorrect because it's possible to have a project that will involve only one person, and there could be a project without an individual called the project manager. The only two defining characteristics of a project are that it is temporary and unique.

   C is incorrect because an operation can have a plan and a budget, too.

2. Answer: B

   B is the correct answer because building a library is temporary—that is, it will have a start and a finish date, and it will be a new library.

   A, C, and **D** are incorrect because running a donut shop, keeping a network up and running, and running a warehouse are all ongoing operations.

3. Answer: D

   D is the correct answer because the names of the five process groups are initiating, planning, executing, monitoring and controlling, and closing.

   A, B, and **C** are incorrect because there are no process groups with the names of starting, organizing and preparing, or implementing.

4. Answer: D

   D is the correct answer because team management is not a knowledge area itself; this task is part of the knowledge area called human resource management.

   A, B, and **C** are incorrect because all these are three of the nine project management knowledge areas.

5. Answer: A

A is the correct and the best answer because the project plan is developed starting from the concept and going through progressive elaboration.

B and **C** are incorrect because B includes the project lifecycle and C is the lifecycle. Progressive elaboration does not include the lifecycle of the project; its goal is to plan the project. Because the project planning can develop (or change) throughout the project lifecycle, progressive elaboration can continue through the project lifecycle, but it does not include the work of the lifecycle.

6. Answer: B

B is the correct answer because the projectized organization provides the greatest authority for the project manager.

A and **C** are incorrect because the authority of the project manager is none to low in a functional organization and low to high in a matrix organization.

D is incorrect because there is no organizational structure called leveled.

7. Answer: A

A is the correct answer because the authority of the project manager is none to low in a functional organization.

B and **C** are incorrect because the authority of the project manager is high to full in a projectized organization and low to high in a matrix organization.

D is incorrect because there is no organizational structure called leveled.

8. Answer: A

A is the correct answer because:

The probability that OTF will deliver = 3/4

The probability that ST will deliver = 1−2/3 = 1/3

The probability that both will deliver = 3/4×1/3=1/4=0.25

9. Answer: C

C is the correct answer because it is false. Stakeholder influence is at its highest in the beginning of the project and decreases as the project progresses.

A, B, and **D** are incorrect answers because all these are true statements.

10. Answer: B

B is the correct answer because it's a false statement. Operations are usually ongoing and do not have a closure or end as a project does.

A, C, and **D** are incorrect answers because these are true statements about both projects and operations.

11.   Answer: B

B is the correct answer because it sounds like a group of interrelated projects, which would nicely fit into a program.

A is an incorrect answer because a project usually has only one project manager.

C is incorrect because the undertaking is temporary and has a set of unique products.

D is incorrect because a portfolio may contain projects and programs, and this conversation is being held at the program level and not at the portfolio level.

12.   Answer: C

C is the correct answer because in addition to skills related to an application area and general management, an effective project manager must have knowledge, the ability to perform, and personal effectiveness.

A, B, and **D** are incorrect because these options do not count all three necessary skills: knowledge, performance, and personal.

13.   Answer: C

C is the correct answer because a weak matrix looks more like a functional organization in which a project manager is effectively a coordinator.

A and **B** are incorrect because a strong matrix is closer to a projectized organization in which the project manager has full authority.

D is incorrect because there is no organizational structure called hierarchical.

14.   Answer: D

D is the correct answer because a project manager is responsible for achieving the project objectives regardless of the structure of the organization.

A, B, and **C** are incorrect because the authority of the project manager may vary over structures, but the responsibility for meeting the project objectives stays with the project manager.

15.   Answer: C

C is the correct answer because environmental factors may have positive or negative impacts on the project; for example, they may expand or constrain project options.

A and **B** are incorrect because environmental factors may have positive or negative impacts.

D is incorrect because environmental factors are hardly ever neutral. You must be aware of them and try to use them for the success of the project.

Chapter 2

1. Answer: A

   A is correct because the management of the performing organization issues the project charter.

   B is incorrect because issuing a project charter is the responsibility of the performing organization, and a stakeholder does not even have to be a member of the performing organization.

   C is incorrect because issuing a project charter is the responsibility of the performing organization, and a customer does not even have to be a member of the performing organization.

   D is incorrect because the charter authorizes the project manager and not vice versa.

2. Answer: B

   B is the correct answer because the project charter and stakeholder register are two documents that are the output of the initiating process group.

   A is incorrect because the statement of work is an input to the initiating process group and not a result (output) of it.

   C and **D** are incorrect because there are no standard documents called the scope plan or the preliminary project scope statement that are output of the initiating process group.

3. Answer: B

   B is the correct answer because the project charter names the project manager and provides the project manager the authority to use organizational resources to run the project.

   A is incorrect because the sponsor is not authorized by the project charter; the opposite might be true.

   C and **D** are incorrect because these tasks are performed in the Identify Stakeholders process.

4. Answer: D

   D is the correct answer because the project schedule is developed during planning. However, some milestone schedule may be included in the project charter.

   A, B, and **C** are incorrect because all these items may be included in the project charter.

5. Answer: C

C is the correct answer because the approved project schedule is not available when you are performing the Identify Stakeholders process for the first time.

A is incorrect because the project charter is a major input to identifying stakeholders.

B and **D** are incorrect because a contract may be an input as part of the procurement documents, and the stakeholder register template may be an input as part of the organizational process assets.

6. Answer: A

A is correct because the statement of work is an input to developing the project charter, which in turn is an input to identifying stakeholders.

B is incorrect because the statement of work is an input to developing the project charter.

C and **D** are incorrect because the project charter is an input to identifying stakeholders.

7. Answer: B

B is the correct answer because a hard deadline imposed on a project is an example of a constraint.

A is incorrect because an assumption is a factor that you believe to be true; it is not a condition, such as a hard deadline.

C is incorrect because a hard deadline tells very little about the actual schedule.

D is incorrect because crashing is the process of assigning more resources to finish a project by a given deadline. Just because a deadline is given, that does not necessarily mean you need crashing.

8. Answer: B

B is correct because assumptions represent uncertainty and hence risk. Assumptions must be validated and analyzed as part of risk management at various stages of the project.

A is incorrect because assumptions by definition represent uncertainty, and as a project manager, it is your responsibility to validate the assumptions at various stages of the project.

C is incorrect because it is not the correct definition of assumption.

D is incorrect because you can start the project with the assumptions. All you have to do is validate them at various stages of the project and analyze them as part of risk management.

9. Answer: A

A is the correct answer because enterprise environmental factors are input to various processes, but they do not constitute a specific project selection method.

B, C, and D are incorrect because scoring models, benefit cost ratio, and constrained optimization methods are all project selection methods.

10. Answer: A

A is the correct answer because adding parental guide notices is a business (legal) requirement.

B is incorrect because adding these notices is not an opportunity to make revenue; it is a requirement that must be met to keep the website up without offending customers or the legal system.

C and D are incorrect because the project at hand does not solve any organizational problem and is not launched to meet any internal organizational need.

11. Answer: D

D is correct because the SOW references the business need, product scope description, and strategic plan.

A is incorrect because the SOW refers to product scope, which is not the same as project scope.

B is incorrect because the SOW does not have to refer to human resources, and it may or may not refer to the contract.

C is incorrect because the project manager may not even exist when the project charter is being developed.

12. Answer: B

B is the correct answer because the initiating process group generates the project charter, stakeholder register, and stakeholder management strategy.

A is an incorrect answer because there is no standard document called the preliminary project scope statement that is generated during project initiating.

C and D are incorrect answers because there are no standard documents called the detailed project scope statement and strategic plan that are generated during project initiating.

13. Answer: A

A is the correct answer because the Develop Project Charter process generates the project charter, and the Identify Stakeholders process generates the stakeholder register and stakeholder management strategy.

B is incorrect because these are input items to the initiating process group.

C is incorrect because there is no standard document named the preliminary scope statement that is produced during initiation.

Chapter 3

1. Answer: D

   D is the correct answer because work packages don't have to appear in the order the work will be performed. This sequencing will be done later.

   A, **B**, and **C** are incorrect answers because these are the characteristics of the WBS.

2. Answer: D

   D is correct because the project charter is created in the initiation stage, and it is an input item to creating the requirements documentation and the scope statement.

   A is incorrect because the project charter is an input item into creating the project scope statement.

   B is incorrect because the project scope statement is an input item into creating the WBS.

   C is incorrect because the project charter is an input into creating the requirements documentation.

3. Answer: A

   A is correct because the Create WBS process is used to create the WBS.

   B is incorrect because the Define Scope process is used to create the project scope statement.

   C is incorrect because there is no standard process named Develop WBS.

   D is incorrect because project initiating is a process group that includes two processes to develop the project charter and to identify stakeholders.

4. Answer: B

   B is correct because the Define Scope process is used to create the project scope statement.

   A is incorrect because the Create WBS process is used to create the WBS.

   C is incorrect because there is no such standard process named Create Project Scope.

   D is incorrect because project initiating is a process group that includes two processes to develop the project charter and to identify stakeholders.

5. Answer: C

   C is the correct answer because the scope statement, the WBS document, and the WBS dictionary combined make the scope baseline against which all change requests will be evaluated.

   A, **B**, and **D** are incorrect because all these are true statements about the project scope management plan.

6. Answer: A

   A is correct because the components in the lowest level of the WBS hierarchy are called *work packages*.

   B is incorrect because a milestone might consist of more than one work package.

   C is incorrect because if a phase is represented in the WBS, it will be represented at a much higher level.

   D is incorrect because a feature does not necessarily correspond to one work package.

7. Answer: D

   D is correct because the four limited resources, pre-imposed deadlines, and schedule milestones are good examples of common project constraints, and skill set is not.

   A, **B**, and **C** are incorrect because these are good examples of common constraints.

8. Answer: D

   D is correct because the scope statement, the WBS document, and the WBS dictionary combined make the scope baseline for the project.

   A is incorrect because the WBS dictionary is missing from the list.

   B is incorrect because you must include the WBS document and the WBS dictionary in the scope baseline.

   C is incorrect because you must include the scope statement and the WBS dictionary in the scope baseline.

9. Answer: D

   D is correct because you, the project manager, create the WBS with help from the project team.

   A is incorrect because the project manager creates the WBS with the help from the team.

   B and **C** are incorrect because neither the customer nor the upper management of the performing organization creates the WBS.

10. Answer: B

    B is correct because the WBS is not part of the project statement; it is an output of the Create WBS process, to which the scope statement is an input item.

    A, **C**, and **D** are incorrect because all these items are parts of the scope statement.

11. Answer: C

C is the correct answer because according to the PMBOK Guide Fourth Edition, the scope management plan is developed as part of the effort of developing the project management plan; there is no formal separate process for it.

A is incorrect because the scope planning process does not exist in the Fourth Edition.

B is incorrect because you need the scope management plan before you can perform the Define Scope process.

D is incorrect because the scope management plan is developed during project planning and not during project initiating.

12. Answer: B

B is the correct answer because job shadowing is another name for the observations technique for collecting requirements.

A, C, and **D** are incorrect because job shadowing is not a standard tool or techniques for these processes.

13. Answer: D

D is the correct answer because the requirements documentation is an input to both the Define Scope process that generates the scope statement and the Create WBS process that generates the WBS.

A, B, and **C** are incorrect because you must have the stakeholder register and the project charter before you can collect requirements.

14. Answer: A

A is the correct answer because the project charter is an input to collecting requirements, and the requirements are an input to creating the WBS.

B is incorrect because the project charter is an input to collecting requirements.

C is incorrect because requirements are an input to defining scope.

D is incorrect because scope statement created by the Define Scope process is an input to creating the WBS.

15. Answer: B

B is the correct answer because the control account is the node in the WBS that is used to measure project performance by comparing the integrated schedule, scope, budget, and actual cost with the earned value.

A is incorrect because the code of account is the number system used to uniquely identify each component of the WBS.

C and **D** are incorrect because there are no standard terms called management account and performance node to refer to any node in the WBS.

Chapter 4

1. Answer: C

   C is the correct answer because the precedence diagramming method is the most commonly used network diagramming method that can be used in the activity sequencing process to represent any of the four kinds of dependencies.

   A and **B** are incorrect because CPM and CCM are the network diagram analysis methods that are used in the schedule development process.

   D is incorrect because the arrow diagramming method is not the popular method.

2. Answer: B

   B is the correct answer because crashing is used to compress the schedule by adding more resources to the project.

   A and **D** are incorrect because the network diagramming method and the sequencing method do not need crashing.

   C is incorrect because crashing does not reduce cost. It may well increase cost when you commit additional resources.

3. Answer: A

   A is the correct answer because there are no float times on the critical path.

   B and **C** are incorrect because the critical path controls the finish date for a given start date and vice versa.

   D is incorrect because the critical path is the longest sequence, not the shortest.

4. Answer: B

   B is the correct answer because an activity has external dependency when it relies on factors outside the project.

   A is incorrect because Activity Y has a mandatory dependency on Activity X when Y inherently depends on X.

   C is incorrect because there is no such dependency called internal.

   D is incorrect because we have an external dependency here.

5. Answer: B

   B is the correct answer because finish-to-start dependency means that the successor (B) activity cannot start until the predecessor (A) activity is finished.

   A is incorrect because the start-to-finish relationship means that the successor activity cannot finish until the predecessor activity is started.

   C is incorrect because we do not have enough information to say that this dependency is mandatory.

   D is incorrect because although there is a dependency between two activities, that does not mean they are on the critical path.

6. Answer: A

A is the correct answer because each activity on the critical path has a zero float time, and therefore if an activity is delayed, it will delay the entire project.

B, C, and **D** are incorrect because these are incorrect statements about the activities on the critical path.

7. Answer: C

C is the correct answer because the analogous estimating technique estimates the duration of an activity based on the duration of a similar activity in a previous project.

A is incorrect because parametric estimating uses parameters such as the productivity rate of the resource assigned to the activity.

B is incorrect because the individual in this example used the analogous method and not the expert judgment method, even though he happened to be an expert—we don't know in which field.

D is incorrect because the Delphi technique is used for risk identification, not for activity duration estimating, and also there are multiple experts involved in the Delphi technique.

8. Answer: C

C is correct because the team member is offering a valid reason for the change, and it does not affect the finish date of the project. However, you must change the schedule to reflect the new duration estimate.

A is incorrect because you do not need to consult with the functional manager in making this decision because the team member is offering a valid reason for the change, and it does not affect the finish date of the project.

B is incorrect because if you accept the change, you must modify the schedule accordingly.

D is incorrect because this change does not qualify to be processed through the integrated change control process.

9. Answer: A

A is the correct answer because float time is the positive difference between the allowed late start date and the early start date of a schedule activity, without changing the schedule finish date.

B, C, and **D** are incorrect because these are not valid terms used to describe delaying an activity without changing the schedule finish date.

10. Answer: B

B is the correct answer because by doing some activities in parallel (fast tracking), you might be able to compress the schedule without adding cost.

A is incorrect because crashing usually results in increased cost because it involves adding extra resources.

C is incorrect because the project sponsor is sponsoring (paying for) the project. So, asking for a new sponsor does not make sense; it can only trigger the sponsor to ask for a new project manager.

D is incorrect because you do not want to bypass the sponsor on budgetary matters because the budget will need the sponsor's approval.

11. Answer: C

C is the correct answer because it has the longest sequence: 8+6+8=22.

A is incorrect because this path is only 20 units long.

B is incorrect because there is no such path as Start-I-G-E-Finish in this network diagram.

D is incorrect because this path is only 21 units long, which is less than 22.

E is incorrect because there is no such path as Start-I-G-H-E-Finish in this network diagram.

12. Answer: D

D is the correct answer because the float time for G is zero because it is on the critical path.

A, **B**, and **C** are incorrect because G is on the critical path and must have a float time of zero.

13. Answer: C

C is the correct answer because if you consider all the paths in the network diagram, the path Start-F-G-H-Finish adds up to 22, which is longer than any other path in the diagram.

A, **B**, **D**, and **E** are incorrect because they do not add up to the correct total for the path.

14. Answer: B

B is the correct answer because in the three-point method with the PERL technique, the duration estimate is the weighted average: (9+18+4×12)/6=12.5.

A is incorrect because in the PERL technique, a weight of 4 is assigned to the most likely scenario as compared to the weight of 1 for each of the optimistic and pessimistic scenarios.

C and **D** are incorrect because the duration estimate should be the weighted average of the three points.

15. Answer: B

    B is the correct answer because the activity duration is calculated after an activity has been defined.

    A, C, and **D** are incorrect because the WBS, project scope statement, and WBS dictionary (as parts of the scope baseline) are valid input items to the Define Activities process.

16. Answer: A

    A is the correct answer because by trying to understand the phrases and terms, you are trying to decode the message, and those phrases and terms are acting as noise.

    B and **C** are incorrect because this is a message sent by the team member and is not a response.

    D is incorrect because we don't know in which language the message is written.

17. Answer: D

    D is the correct answer because stakeholder management is an input to communication planning.

    A, B, and **C** are incorrect because all these items are part of the communication management plan, an output of communication planning.

Chapter 5

1. Answer: D

    D is the correct answer because a chart that displays the resource requirements for each activity is an example of a resource assignment matrix (RAM).

    A is incorrect because a project organization chart represents the relationships between the different roles in the project, and that is not what management wants.

    B is incorrect because the WBS contains the work packages, not the activities and the resource requirements.

    C is incorrect because management wants the resource requirements for each activity, not just a list of roles and responsibilities.

2. Answer: C

    C is the correct answer because the project schedule is the output of the Develop Schedule process.

    A, B, and **D** are incorrect because all these items are the output of the human resource planning process.

3. Answer: C

C is the correct answer because the project manager (along with the project management team) is responsible for the staff management plan, and it is created as an output of the human resource planning efforts in a process called Develop Human Resource Plan.

A, B, and **D** are incorrect because these are false statements about the staff management plan.

4. Answer: A

A is the correct answer because the cost baseline is an output of the Determine Budget process.

B and **D** are incorrect because there are no standard processes with these names.

C is incorrect because the Estimate Costs process is used to estimate the costs, and these estimates needs to be aggregated to determine the budget.

5. Answer: B

B is the correct answer because the human resource plan is an input into estimating costs.

A and **C** are incorrect because you cannot estimate costs until you have a human resource plan, and you cannot determine budget until you have cost estimates.

D is incorrect because there is no standard process with this name.

6. Answer: D

D is the correct answer, and the other answers are incorrect because the project schedule is an input to estimating costs, cost estimates are an input to determining the budget, and the project schedule and budget (cost baseline) are an input to planning procurements.

7. Answer: A

A is the correct answer because contingency reserve is applied both to activity durations (time) and cost estimates.

B, C, and **D** are incorrect answers because these are true statements about contingency reserve.

8. Answer: D

D is the correct answer because the cost overrun is borne by the seller.

A is incorrect because in cost plus incentive fee (CPIF) cost overrun is paid by the buyer.

B is incorrect because in time and materials (T&M), the increased cost due to the increased quantity of resources, such as work hours by a contractor, is borne by the buyer.

C is incorrect because in cost plus percentage of cost (CPPC), cost overrun is paid by the buyer.

9. Answer: A

    A is the correct answer because it's only the rates for labor and material that are fixed.

    B, C, and **D** are incorrect because the given scenario does not match the definitions of these contract types.

10. Answer: B

    B is the correct answer because contract types are a tool and not an input to planning procurements.

    A, C, and **D** are incorrect answers because all of these are true statements.

11. Answer: C

    C is the correct answer because cost overrun is paid by the buyer, and the fee increases with the increase in cost as well.

    A is incorrect because the firm fixed price presents risk to both buyer and seller because the fixed price might turn out to be above or below the actual cost.

    B and **D** are incorrect because the fee in these cases does not rise with the increase of the actual cost.

12. Answer: A

    A is the correct answer because you can fairly estimate the cost for one program, and you do not know the number of programs required.

    B and **C** are incorrect because the reimbursable cost does not make sense in this case, and you don't have to add a fee to the cost.

    D is incorrect because you cannot correctly estimate the total price because you do not know how many programs are required.

Chapter 6

1. Answer: B

    B is the correct answer because a risk can have a negative or a positive effect on a project.

    A, C, and **D** are incorrect answers because these are true statements about project risks.

2. Answer: A

    A is correct because the risk register is the output of the risk identification process, but it is not used as an input because it does not exist before this process.

    B, C, and **D** are incorrect because the risk register is an input item to qualitative risk analysis, quantitative risk analysis, and risk response planning, whereas the updated risk register is an output from each of these processes.

3. Answer: D

   D is the correct answer because you cannot identify risks in your specific project based on the information collected from the Web.

   A, B, and **C** are incorrect answers because brainstorming, Delphi technique, and SWOT analysis are valid information-gathering techniques used for identifying risks.

4. Answer: A

   A is the correct answer because depending upon the experience of the team, a risk can be moved directly after the identification process to the quantitative analysis process without performing the qualitative analysis.

   B, C, and **D** are incorrect answers because these are true statements.

5. Answer: B

   B is correct because building redundancy into a system is an example of mitigating the risk.

   A is incorrect because the risk can still happen because you have not changed the plan, such as moving the server center to some other city.

   C is incorrect because accepting a risk means no action or a conditional action.

   D is incorrect because you have not transferred the risk to a third party.

6. Answer: D

   D is correct because the risk has been transferred to a third party.

   A is incorrect because the risk can still happen because you have not changed the plan, such as eliminating the need for that part of the system.

   B is incorrect because mitigating the risk does not involve transferring the risk to a third party.

   C is incorrect because accepting a risk means no action or a conditional action.

7. Answer: C

   C is correct because the numerical analysis of a risk is called *quantitative risk analysis*.

   A is incorrect because assigning numbers does not necessarily mean you are performing a Monte Carlo simulation, although it is one of the tools to perform quantitative analysis.

   B is incorrect because qualitative analysis does not involve numerical analysis, such as EMV calculations.

   D is incorrect because risk response planning will be based on the results of risk analysis.

8. Answer: D

D is correct because the probability of the risk is 50%, and the probability of the positive impact is 40%, so the total probability for the positive impact to happen is 0.5×0.4=0.2.

EMV=Probability×Value of the outcome=0.2×$200,000=$40,000

A, **B**, and **C** are incorrect because they show wrong values for EMV.

9. Answer: A

A is correct because the probability of the risk is 50%, and the probability of the positive impact is 40%, so the total probability for the positive impact to happen is 0.5×0.4=0.2.

EMV=Probability×Value of the outcome=0.2×$200,000=$40,000

Similarly, EMV for threat=0.3×$50,000=−$15,000

Therefore, EMV for the risk=$40,000−$15,000=$25,000

B, **C**, and **D** are incorrect because they show wrong values for EMV.

10. Answer: D

D is correct because secondary risks are those risks that arise as a result of risk responses.

A is incorrect because a residual risk is a risk that remains after a response has been performed.

B is incorrect because depending upon the nature of the secondary risk, it may have any priority.

C is incorrect because the risk response will depend upon the analysis results of the risk.

11. Answer: D

D is the correct answer because there is no such risk response named risk rejection.

A, **B**, and **C** are all incorrect answers because these are valid risk responses.

12. Answer: A

A is correct because SWOT is a risk identification technique that identifies the risks by examining the strengths, weaknesses, opportunities, and threats (SWOT) of a given project.

B is incorrect because this is a wrong statement about SWOT.

C and **D** are incorrect because SWOT is a technique used in risk identification, not in risk response planning, nor in quantitative risk analysis.

13. Answer: C

C is the correct answer because you need to perform quantitative risk analysis to create a list of risks prioritized based on the total effect of each risk on the overall project objectives.

A, B, and D are incorrect because these are the possible output items from the qualitative risk analysis.

14. Answer: D

D is the correct answer because the decision about a risk-related contractual agreement can be an output of risk response planning, not the quantitative risk analysis.

A, B, and C are incorrect because all these are the possible output items from the quantitative risk analysis.

15. Answer: B

B is the correct answer because benchmarking is a quality planning technique that compares practices, products, or services of a project with those of some reference projects for the purpose of learning, improving, and creating the basis for measuring performance.

A is incorrect because you can always brainstorm, but it does not have to compare the results of similar activities.

C is incorrect because although it is a quality planning technique, it involves striking a balance between cost and benefit (which are not similar).

D is incorrect because quality metrics are not quality planning techniques; these are output items of the quality planning process.

16. Answer: A

A is the correct answer.

B is incorrect because Shewhart defined the plan-do-check-act cycle of quality management and Deming modified it.

C and D are incorrect because Crosby and Juan have contributions to the knowledge base of quality management, but they did not define the plan-do-check-act cycle.

17. Answer: D

D is the correct answer because one of the tenets of modern quality management is that quality is planned, designed, and built in, and not inspected in.

A, B, and C are incorrect answers because there are no such tenets in modern quality management.

Chapter 7

1. Answer: D

    D is the correct answer because corrective actions are recommended by the QA process.

    A, B, and **C** are incorrect answers because deliverables and work performance information (status) are generated, and defect repairs are implemented by the Direct and Manage Project Execution process.

2. Answer: D

    D is the correct answer because corrective actions are an output item of the QA process.

    A, B, and **C** are incorrect answers because quality metrics generated by quality planning, quality control measurements generated by quality control, and work performance information (status) generated by the Direct and Manage Project Execution process all become input to the QA process.

3. Answer: C

    C is the correct answer because buy-or-make analysis is a technique used in the procurement planning process called *Plan Procurements.*

    A is incorrect because buy-or-make decisions are input to the Conduct Procurements process.

    B is incorrect because there is no standard process called Select Sellers.

    D is incorrect because Estimate Costs is not the process in which make-or-buy decisions are made.

4. Answer: D

    D is the correct answer because the procurement documents should be rigorous enough to ensure consistent responses from different sellers that can be fairly compared to one another and flexible enough to allow sellers to offer suggestions on better ways to satisfy the requirements.

    A is incorrect because it does not allow sellers to be creative in offering solutions.

    B is incorrect because documents must be rigid enough that each seller understands the requirements.

    C is incorrect because the requirements are set by the buyer and not by the seller.

5. Answer: C

    C is the correct answer because the amount of work and hence the cost cannot be determined at this point.

    A is incorrect because the amount of work and hence the cost cannot be determined at this point.

B is incorrect because a time and materials contract is used when the cost of an item can be fairly estimated but the number of needed items is unknown. This is not the case here.

D is incorrect because there is no such contract type as cost plus time.

6. Answer: B

   B is the correct answer because quality planning is the process to plan for quality, which is the degree to which the project requirements are met.

   A is incorrect because quality control is the process to monitor specific project results to ensure they meet the planned quality standards.

   C is incorrect because quality assurance is the process of applying (not planning) the planned quality activities to ensure (and verify) that the requirements are met.

   D is incorrect because this answer is not relevant to the given scenario.

7. Answer: A

   A is the correct answer because the quality audit is a technique for performing quality assurance.

   B and **C** are incorrect because the quality audit is a technique for performing quality assurance, whereas quality planning is about determining which quality standards are relevant to the project and how to satisfy them. Quality assurance is about applying the planned quality activities.

   D is incorrect because there is no such quality management process as quality inspection.

8. Answer: B

   B is the correct answer and **A**, **C**, and **D** are incorrect because quality assurance uses the output of quality planning and quality control as its input.

9. Answer: A

   A is the correct answer because only approved change requests should be implemented.

   B is incorrect because the project manager, not the QA department, is responsible for dealing with change requests.

   C is incorrect because the project manager is an agent of change, a manager of change, and not an opponent of change by default.

   D is incorrect because any change request must go through the approval process.

10. Answer: D

    D is the correct answer because auditing (inspecting) is part of the quality assurance process.

    A and **B** are incorrect because auditing is a tool used in quality assurance.

    C is incorrect because there is no standard process called Inspect Quality.

Chapter 8

1. Answer: D

   D is the correct answer because collaboration offers a win/win resolution.

   A is incorrect because avoidance ignores the problem rather than solving it.

   B is incorrect because in compromising, both parties give up something and might look at the resolution as a lose/lose proposition.

   C is incorrect because accommodation offers a win/lose resolution; one party gives up something to accommodate the interests of the other party.

2. Answer: D

   D is the correct answer because you are forcing your way on the other party.

   A and **B** are incorrect because you are neither ignoring the problem nor compromising.

   C is incorrect because you are not accommodating the other side.

3. Answer: D

   D is the correct answer because change in budget has very little to do directly with team development.

   A and **B** are incorrect answers because the project kickoff meeting is an indirect method to start team development, and an effective resolution of a conflict does contribute to team building.

   C is also incorrect because during times when the team is in a low-morale mode, you should be able to lift the team morale and thereby contribute to team development.

4. Answer: C

   C is the correct answer because staff assignments are an output of the Acquire Project Team process.

   A is incorrect because the human resource plan contains roles and responsibilities and not all the staff assignments.

   B is incorrect because staff assignments are an input to the Develop Project Team process.

   D is incorrect because there is no standard process named Make Staff Assignments.

5. Answer: C

   C is the correct answer because a virtual team is one of the options, depending on the project when you are acquiring the team.

   A, B, and **D** are incorrect answers because virtual teams are a tool in acquiring the team.

6. Answer: B

B is the correct answer because the term *soft skills* refer to interpersonal skills.

A, C, and **D** are incorrect because these skills are not referred to as soft skills.

7. Answer: A

A is the correct answer because the Delphi technique is the information-gathering technique used for experts to reach consensus on a topic. However, in acquiring the team, you want to use all the influence and negotiations to get the best team.

B, C, and **D** are incorrect because these are valid techniques to be used for acquiring the team.

8. Answer: B

B is the correct answer because Theory X managers think that employees dislike their work and will try to avoid it.

A is incorrect because there is no standard management theory called Theory Alpha.

C is incorrect because Theory Y managers trust their employees.

D is incorrect because McClellands's theory states that the need for achievement, affiliation, and power motivates employees.

9. Answer: C

C is the correct answer because Theory Y managers trust their employees.

A is incorrect because there is no standard management theory called Theory Alpha.

B is incorrect because Theory X managers think that employees dislike their work and will try to avoid it.

D is incorrect because McClellands's theory states that the need for achievement, affiliation, and power motivates employees. C is the more appropriate answer in this case.

10. Answer: D

D is the correct answer because McClelland's theory states that the need for achievement, affiliation, and power motivates employees.

A is incorrect because there is no standard management theory called Theory Alpha.

B is incorrect because Theory X managers think that employees dislike their work and will try to avoid it.

C is incorrect because Theory Y managers trust their employees. D is the more appropriate answer in this case.

Chapter 9

1. Answer: A

   A is the correct answer because performance reports are an input to the Distribute Information process.

   B, C, and **D** are incorrect answers because all these items are part of the output of the Distribute Information process.

2. Answer: B

   B is the correct answer because issue logs are used to track and manage stakeholder issues in the process of managing stakeholder expectations.

   A and **C** are incorrect answers because these processes do not use the issue log as input.

   D is incorrect because there is no standard process named Resolve Issues.

3. Answer: B

   B is the correct answer because the change log is used to document changes that occur during the project, and it works as an input to managing stakeholder expectations.

   A and **C** are incorrect answers because these processes do not use the change log as an input.

   D is incorrect because the Perform Integrated Change Control process is the high-level process that is used to review change requests and approve or reject them.

4. Answer: D

   D is the correct answer because both the Distribute Information and Manage Stakeholder Expectations processes belong to communication management.

   A is incorrect because you are not really managing the stakeholders as resources; you are managing their expectations.

   B is incorrect because stakeholders belonging to the procurement part are only a subset of all stakeholders.

   C is incorrect because there is no standard knowledge area called stakeholder management.

5. Answer: C

   C is the correct answer because it is the responsibility of the project manager to manage stakeholder expectations.

   A, B, and **D** are incorrect answers because the project manager can ask for help from anyone in managing the stakeholder expectations, but the responsibility of managing stakeholder expectations falls upon none other than the project manager.

6. Answer: C

    C is the correct answer because you use the Distribute Information process to distribute information, such as performance reports, among the stakeholders.

    A is incorrect because the Report Performance process is used to create performance reports.

    B is incorrect because there is no standard process called Distribute Reports.

    D is incorrect because Manage Stakeholder Expectations is a more general process; it is not the process used specifically to distribute information.

7. Answer: B

    B is the correct answer because the executing process group contains two communication processes: Distribute Information and Manage Stakeholder Expectations.

    A is incorrect because there is no standard process called Distribute Reports.

    C is incorrect because Report Performance belongs to the monitoring and controlling process group.

    D is incorrect because Identify Stakeholders belongs to the initiating process group.

Chapter 10

1. Answer: A

    A is the correct answer because changes can happen and need to be managed throughout the lifecycle of a project.

    B, C, and **D** are incorrect because changes can happen and need to be managed throughout the lifecycle of a project.

2. Answer: A

    A is the correct answer because the recommendations for corrective and preventive actions and change requests must be processed through the integrated change control process for approval.

    B, C, and **D** are incorrect because changes and recommendations are approved through the integrated change control process.

3. Answer: C

    C is the correct answer because all change requests are processed through the integrated change control process.

    A is incorrect because project management is performed through processes.

    B is incorrect because the Direct and Manage Project Execution process can generate change requests, but this process is not used to evaluate change requests.

    D is incorrect because the Monitor and Control Project Work process can generate change requests, but this process is not used to evaluate change requests.

4. Answer: A

    A is the correct answer because project work is monitored largely by comparing project performance to planned performance.

    B and **C** are incorrect because the Perform Integrated Change Control process uses work performance information (the raw data for the performance reports) and not the performance reports as input.

    D is incorrect because there is no standard process with this name.

5. Answer: B

    B is the correct answer because the name of the standard process to monitor and control procurements is called Administer Procurements according to the latest (Fourth Edition) PMI Standard.

    A and **D** are incorrect because there are no standard processes with these names.

    C is incorrect because Contract Administration was the name of the process in the Third Edition of the Standard, not in the current edition.

6. Answer: D

    D is the correct answer because the Administer Procurements process uses performance reports generated by the Report Performance process and approval of change requests generated by the Perform Integrated Change Control process.

    A is incorrect because the Administer Procurements process will need approved change requests from the Perform Integrated Change Control process, which therefore must be run first.

    B and **C** are incorrect because Report Performance must be run before Administer Procurements, as it uses performance reports generated by the Report Performance process.

7. Answer: C

    C is the correct answer because work performance information is the output of the Direct and Manage Project Execution process.

    A is incorrect because Report Performance uses work performance measurements to create performance reports.

    B is incorrect because the Distribute Information process is used to distribute the information.

    D is incorrect because the Control Scope, Control Schedule, and Control Cost processes are used to convert work performance information into work performance measurements.

8. Answer: D

   D is the correct answer because the Control Scope, Control Schedule, and Control Cost processes are used to convert work performance information into work performance measurements.

   A is incorrect because Report Performance uses work performance measurements to create performance reports.

   B is incorrect because the Distribute Information process is used to distribute the information.

   C is incorrect because it is work performance information and not performance measurements that are the output of the Direct and Manage Project Execution process.

Chapter 11

1. Answer: C

   C is the correct answer because the Ishikawa diagram is a tool used in the Perform Quality Control process to explore all the potential causes of a problem. Also, Perform Quality Assurance processes use all the tools and techniques of the Perform Quality Control processes.

   A is incorrect because there is no standard process called Assure Quality.

   B is incorrect because an Ishikawa diagram is a tool used during the Perform Quality Control process and not during the Plan Quality process.

   D is incorrect because auditing and inspection are tools and not processes.

2. Answer: A

   A is the correct answer because a control chart is used to plot the results to determine whether they are within the acceptable limits.

   B is incorrect because a cause and effect diagram, also called an *Ishikawa diagram* or a *fishbone diagram*, is used to explore all the possible causes of a problem.

   C is incorrect because a Pareto diagram is used to identify and rank errors based on the frequency of defects caused by them.

   D is incorrect because a scatter diagram is used to find the relationship between two variables, such as cause and effect, or two causes.

3. Answer: C

   C is the correct answer because a Pareto diagram can be used to rank problems based on the frequency of defects caused by them. Then, you will direct the team effort to fix those problems that caused most of the defects.

   A is incorrect because a control chart is used to plot the results to determine whether they are within the acceptable limits.

B is incorrect because a cause and effect diagram, also called an *Ishikawa diagram* or a *fishbone diagram*, is used to explore all the possible causes of a problem.

D is incorrect because a scatter diagram is used to find the relationship between two variables, such as cause and effect, or two causes.

4. Answer: B

B is the correct answer because by using statistical sampling, you will pick up a few samples of the code at random and get them reviewed. The results will represent the quality of the whole code, statistically speaking.

A is incorrect because this is not an unreasonable demand.

C is incorrect because testing tools cannot serve the purpose of a code review, and the customer wants the code review.

D is incorrect because you have limited resources.

5. Answer: D

D is the correct answer because the risk-related recommendations for corrective actions are the output of the risk monitoring and controlling process.

A, B, and **C** are incorrect because the outputs of these processes do not include recommended corrective actions.

6. Answer: A

A is the correct answer because the recommendations for corrective and preventive actions and change requests must be processed through the integrated change control process for approval.

B, C, and **D** are incorrect because changes and recommendations are approved through the integrated change control process.

7. Answer: C

C is the correct answer because quality control measurements are an output of quality controlling.

A, B, and **D** are incorrect because all these items are included in the input to quality control.

8. Answer: B

B is the correct answer because an approved change request is an input to the Perform Quality Control process. You need to monitor this list to ensure that all the changes on this list are implemented.

A is incorrect because Perform Integrated Change Control can have approved change requests as output, not as input.

C and **D** are incorrect because these processes do not use approved change requests as input.

9. Answer: D

> **D** is the correct answer because technical performance measurements are a technique used in the Monitor and Control Risks process but not in the Perform Quality Control process.
>
> **A, B,** and **C** are incorrect because all of these are tools and techniques for the Perform Quality Control process.

10. Answer: B

> **B** is the correct answer because measuring technical performance is a technique—and not an input—used in monitoring and controlling risks.
>
> **A, C,** and **D** are incorrect because these items are included in the input of monitoring and controlling risks.

Chapter 12

1. Answer: C

> **C** is the correct answer because the right action here is to find the source of the change requests and process the request through the integrated change control process.
>
> **A** is incorrect because you are taking action without doing your homework: investigation.
>
> **B** is incorrect because you should not let anyone apply the changes without the changes having been approved.
>
> **D** is incorrect because the right course of action here is to find out the source of the change request and ensure that the request goes through the approval process.

2. Answer: D

> **D** is the correct answer because a budget review is not an output item from the schedule control process.
>
> **A, B,** and **C** are incorrect because all these items are the output of the schedule control process formally called Control Schedule.

3. Answer: B

> **B** is the correct answer because the formula for earned value is:
>
> EV=BAC×(work completed/total work required)
>
> which means
>
> EV=$600,000×(5 miles/15 miles)=$200,000
>
> **A** is incorrect because $160,000 is the actual cost (AC) and not the earned value (EV).

C is incorrect because earned value is proportional to the fraction of work performed and not the fraction of time passed.

D is incorrect because $600,000 is the budget at completion (BAC), not the EV.

4. Answer: C

    C is the correct answer because the formula for planned value is:

    PV=BAC×(time passed/total schedule time)

    which means

    PV=$600,000×(3 weeks/12 weeks)=$150,000

    A is incorrect because $160,000 is the actual cost (AC) and not the planned value (EV).

    B is incorrect because planned value is proportional to the fraction of time passed, not the fraction of work performed.

    D is incorrect because $600,000 is the budget at completion (BAC), not the PV.

5. Answer: A

    A is the correct answer because the formula for cost variance is:

    CV=EV−AC

    which means

    CV=$200,000−$160,000=$40,000

    B is incorrect because CV is equal to EV−AC, not EV−PV.

    C is incorrect because it calculates the total cost for 12 weeks based on AC for three weeks and then subtracts it from BAC, which is the wrong method to calculate CV.

    D is incorrect because it calculates the total cost for 15 miles based on AC for five miles and then subtracts it from BAC, which is the wrong method to calculate CV.

6. Answer: B

    B is the correct answer because the formula for schedule variance is:

    SV=EV−PV

    which means

    SV=$200,000−$150,000=$50,000

    A is incorrect because SV is equal to EV−PV, not EV−AC.

    C and **D** are incorrect because SV is measured in units of cost, not in units of time.

7. Answer: B

    B is the correct answer because a CPI value greater than one means the cost performance of the project is better than planned, and an SPI value of greater than one means the schedule performance of the project is better than planned.

    A, C, and **D** are incorrect because a CPI value greater than one means the cost performance of the project is better than planned, and an SPI value of greater than one means the schedule performance of the project is better than planned.

8. Answer: A

   A is the correct answer because the three elements of the triple constraint are scope, time, and cost.

   B and **C** are incorrect because quality is not considered one of the three elements of the triple constraint, even though it may be affected by the triple constraint.

   D is incorrect because scope is missing from the list.

9. Answer: C

   C is the correct answer because cost and scope are the two elements of the triple constraint in addition to time. If one of these three elements changes, one or both of the other two will change.

   A and **B** are incorrect because none of deliverables, quality, and risk is included in the triple constraint.

   D is incorrect because cost and budget make one element in the triple constraint.

10. Answer: B

   B is the correct answer because controlling scope, schedule, and costs generates work performance measurements.

   A is incorrect because the Report Performance process is used to generate the performance reports and uses work performance measurements as input.

   C is incorrect because the Perform Quality Control process uses work performance measurements as an input and does not generate them.

   D is incorrect because the Monitor and Control Project Work process does not generate work performance measurements.

Chapter 13

1. Answer: B

   B is the correct answer because if the project is behind the planned schedule, it does not mean it should be closed. You can bring it back on schedule, or you can change the plan accordingly.

   A, C, and **D** are incorrect because all these scenarios will cause the project to close, and when a project is closed, it must be closed by using the processes in the closing process group.

2. Answer: A

   A is the correct answer because future projects can benefit the most from the review if all the stages of the project are covered with both positive and negative aspects.

B and **D** are incorrect because all the stages and aspects of the project should be reviewed.

C is incorrect because both positive and negative aspects should be covered with equal emphasis.

3. Answer: D

D is the correct answer because if the project is to be successful, it must have been executed and controlled successfully before the closure begins.

A, B, and **C** are incorrect because if a project has not made it to the closing stage by the time closing begins, the project is being terminated without completion.

4. Answer: D

D is the correct answer because no project, small or large, should skip the closing stage.

A, B, and **C** are incorrect because no project should skip the closing stage. Each project must go through a proper closure.

5. Answer: C

C is the correct answer because it is the project sponsor who signs the final closure documents and can send the project to closure at any stage of the project.

A is incorrect because the project manager is responsible for managing all the activities needed to close the project, but the closure must be authorized by the sponsor.

B and **D** are incorrect because neither the customer nor the functional manager can authorize the project closure.

6. Answer: B

B is the correct answer because the deliverables accepted through procurement closure must go through project closure for handing them over to the customer or the sponsor.

A, C, and **D** are incorrect because all these activities are part of the procurement closure.

7. Answer: C

C is the correct answer because the deliverables accepted through the quality control process must go through the Verify Scope process before they can become an input to the Close Project process.

A and **D** are incorrect because these items are included in the organizational process assets used to close the project.

B is incorrect because the project management plan is a valid input to the Close Project process.

8. Answer: C

C is the correct answer because the closed contracts are the output of the Close Procurements process.

A, B, and D are incorrect because all these items are the output of the Close Project process.

9. Answer: B

B is the correct answer because the deliverables must go through the Verify Scope process before going through the Close Project process, and before the scope can be verified, they must be validated through the quality control process.

A is incorrect because the deliverables must be validated through the quality control process before their scope can be verified.

C and D are incorrect because the Close Procurement process must be performed before you have all the accepted products that will go through the Close Project process.

10. Answer: A

A is the correct answer because you can review the project work as well as the procurement work and procedure and learn from both.

B, C, and D are incorrect because these are no closing processes with these names.

Chapter 14

1. Answer: D

D is the correct answer because the Code of Ethics and Professional Conduct by the PMI states that if you can substantiate it with facts, it is your responsibility to report possible violations of the Code of Ethics and Professional Conduct by individuals in the field of project management.

A and B are incorrect because you can do it if you feel like it, but this is not the best answer.

C is incorrect because you don't know whether a law was violated, and according to the Code of Conduct statement, D is the best answer.

2. Answer: A

A is the correct answer because if in a foreign land you are being asked to do something that is unethical and illegal in your home country, you are supposed to investigate whether it is illegal and unethical there as well.

B and D are incorrect because you don't know yet whether the sponsor is asking you to do something illegal.

C is incorrect because you think it is unethical and illegal, so you must investigate it.

3.   Answer: B

B is the correct answer because you should share your findings that this is an illegal activity with the project sponsor.

A is incorrect because it clearly disobeys the law of the land.

C is incorrect because you are supposed to directly approach the person with whom you have a disagreement or conflict.

D is incorrect because you are supposed to deal with the problem head on, not walk away from it.

4.   Answer: C

C is the correct answer because honesty, openness, and truthfulness are part and parcel of professional behavior, and this is true inside and outside of Kansas. Regardless of where you are, the professional code of conduct is the same.

A is incorrect because you do not have enough information to take this step.

B and **D** are both incorrect because you are not being truthful, honest, and open.

5.   Answer: C

C is the correct answer because this is a case of a possible conflict of interest, and option C is the right thing to do.

A and **B** are incorrect because you are not disclosing a possible conflict of interest.

D is incorrect because this is a possible conflict of interest or can be looked upon as such by others, rather than as mere networking.

6.   Answer: C

C is the correct answer because this is not part of the Code of Ethics and Professional Conduct by PMI.

A, B, and **D** are all incorrect because these activities are included in the PMP Code of Professional Conduct.

7.   Answer: B

B is the correct answer because you want to make sure that Best Deals is making the estimate based on the same information about the work that the other vendors are.

A and **C** are incorrect because you are violating confidentiality.

D is incorrect because it is an unnecessary activity.

8.   Answer: A

A is the correct answer because as a project manager, it is your responsibility to facilitate interaction among the stakeholders and resolve conflicts.

B, C, and **D** are incorrect because it is your responsibility to resolve this conflict.

9. Answer: B

   B is the correct answer because as a project manager, it is your responsibility to keep the stakeholders informed of the project status.

   A is incorrect because you are not performing your responsibility to provide the true project status to the stakeholders.

   C is incorrect because you don't have enough information to take this action.

   D is incorrect because it is your responsibility to investigate the situation and propose a solution.

10. Answer: C

    C is the correct answer because it is not your job to investigate the legality of the company procedures.

    A, B, and **D** are incorrect because all these are parts of the professional responsibility of a project manager.

11. Answer: A

    A is the correct answer because fairness, honesty, respect, and responsibility are the four fundamental values in the Code of Ethics and Professional Conduct by the PMI.

    B, C, and **D** are incorrect because one fundamental value is missing from each of these options.

Final Exam

Questions

1. The CEO of your company has invited you to her office. She is swamped with project proposals from the employees of the company. She is excited that employees are being creative. However, she is finding it very challenging to make selections out of a large pool of proposals. So, she needs your help. Which of the following is not a project selection method?

    A. Expert judgment

    B. Scoring models

    C. Cost/benefit ratio

    D. Cost variance

2. You are starting a project in your company and are identifying the stakeholders. The CEO of your company is not directly involved in the project. Which of the following is not a stakeholder in this project?

    A. Operations managers and functional managers

    B. CEO

    C. Project manager and project team

    D. All of the above are stakeholders

3. Which of the following statements is true about the initiating process group?

    A. It establishes the need for the feasibility study about the project.

    B. It is where you put together a project schedule.

    C. It is where you facilitate the formal approval for starting the new project or a project phase.

    D. It is where you develop a complete project management plan.

4. Which of the following officially starts a project?

   A. The project charter

   B. The project scope statement

   C. The process initiation plan document

   D. The project management plan

5. You are the project manager of the Golden Arches project, which will generate a software product. A critical bug is discovered in the software by the QA team. You meet with the experts and determine a workaround for this bug to keep the project on track. Which process were you performing to make this determination?

   A. Testing

   B. Plan Quality

   C. Plan Risk Responses

   D. Perform Quality Control

6. Your organization is involved in so many activities. You want to organize some of those activities into projects. Which of the following best defines a project?

   A. A set of schedule activities performed by a team that has a project manager

   B. A set of sequential activities performed by using project management processes

   C. A temporary endeavor undertaken to create a unique product, service, or result

   D. An ongoing operation being performed to meet customer requirements

7. Which of the following statements best defines a program?

   A. A project with a large budget exceeding a minimum threshold value

   B. A set of processes used to perform a sophisticated project

   C. A set of projects coupled together to save money

   D. A set of related projects managed in a coordinated way to gain benefits and control not available by managing them individually

8. You are the project manager of the Mind the Gap project, which involves providing Internet access to an underprivileged community in your city. You have to get some of the schedule activities of the project finished by an external vendor. You have written the statement of work, and you have gathered or prepared all the documents that will be given to the bidders. What process were you performing while you were engaged in these activities?

   A. Plan Purchases and Acquisitions

   B. Plan Procurements

   C. Solicitation Planning

   D. Close Procurements

9. You are the project manager of the Mind the Gap project, which involves providing Internet access to an underprivileged community in your city. You have to get some of the schedule activities of the project finished by an external vendor. You have written the statement of work, and you have gathered or prepared all the documents that will be given to the bidders. What process will you perform next to select sellers and reward contracts?

   A. Plan Procurements

   B. Conduct Procurements

   C. Administer Procurements

   D. Request Seller Responses

10. You have just joined a stem-cell research company as a project manager and are trying to learn the ropes. In which of the following organization types does the project manager have the highest level of authority?

    A. Functional

    B. Strong matrix

    C. Weak matrix

    D. Projectized

11. You have just joined a stem-cell research company as a project manager and are trying to learn more about the structure of this organization. In which of the following organization types does the project manager have the lowest level of authority?

    A. Functional

    B. Strong matrix

    C. Weak matrix

    D. Projectized

12. You are the project manager of the DNA Sequencing project, and you are evaluating the project performance measured against the project baseline on a regular basis. In doing so, you are performing processes that belong to which of the following process groups?

    A. Planning

    B. Executing

    C. Monitoring and controlling

    D. Evaluating

13. You are the project manager of a project that is already executing. You have just discovered that there are differences among the stakeholders over what the project objectives are and what their expectations of the project are. As a project manager, which of the following actions will you take? (Choose one.)

    A. Report the differences to the project sponsor because it is the sponsor's responsibility to resolve the differences.

    B. People are entitled to their points of view, so you should ignore the differences and honor them.

    C. You should encourage the differences because different opinions will result in the best end product.

    D. By using appropriate communication methods, you must manage the stakeholders' expectations on a regular basis and ensure that everyone is on the same page about the scope of the project.

14. You have been invited to the Department of Energy to give a seminar on process groups. Which of the following are the five process groups in project management?

    A. Initiating, planning, executing, monitoring, and controlling

    B. Initiating, planning, executing, monitoring and controlling, and closing

    C. Initiating, scoping, executing, monitoring, and closing

    D. Initiating, planning, executing, testing, and closing

15. You have been assigned to develop the project charter for the Simulate the Campbell City Economy project. Which of the following should always be included in a project charter?

    A. Name of the project manager and name of the project sponsor

    B. Statement of work

    C. Project scope statement

    D. Project management plan

16. Which of the following statements about the project management process groups is true? (Choose one.)

    A. Process groups are always executed in a serial fashion without any overlap.

    B. The execution of processes from various process groups can overlap in time.

    C. A given process group is executed with equal intensity at each phase of a project.

    D. Process groups are one-time events: You execute them only once in a project.

17. You are the project manager of a project that has finished its first phase. What is your approach toward reviewing the initiating processes at the beginning of the second phase and all subsequent phases?

    A. It should be done because it will keep the project team members employed for a longer time.

    B. It should be done to ensure that the project stays the course even if the business need for which the project is being performed changes.

    C. It should be done because it helps keep the project focused on the business need for which the project is being performed.

    D. It should not be done because it's a waste of time and human resources.

18. You are the project manager in a functional organization called Talking Heads, Inc. One of your team members, Lou Dobb, is falling behind in completing the schedule activities assigned to him. When you talked to him, he told you that too many people were asking him to do things. You want to look into this matter further. Who do you think has the authority to give assignments to Lou Dobb?

    A. A functional manager

    B. Project managers

    C. The project team

    D. The project management team

19. You are the project manager for the Find the God Particle project at CERN. The next phase of the project is to turn the collider on and collect the data at the detectors set up at the collision points. You need to get the authorization for this phase. A project phase is authorized by using a process in which of the following process groups?

    A. Initiating

    B. Phase initiating

    C. Planning

    D. Executing

20. Which of the following are not project management process groups? (Choose one letter.)

    A. Initiating and planning

    B. Designing and testing

    C. Executing and closing

    D. Monitoring and controlling

21. Which two of the following are not project management knowledge areas? (Choose two.)

    A. Integration management

    B. Team management

    C. Cost management

    D. Risk management

    E. Stakeholder management

    F. Procurement management

    G. Risk management

22. You are the project manager of a project that is executing. Several defects have been discovered in the project product. The project team does not have time to repair all the defects. Which tool will you use to prioritize the defects?

    A. Control chart

    B. Pareto diagram

    C. Decision tree analysis

    D. Variance analysis

23. You are identifying which quality standards are relevant to your project and determining how to meet those standards. To accomplish this task, you are using processes from the:

    A. Planning process group

    B. Executing process group

    C. Controlling process group

    D. Quality planning process group

24. Which of the following processes is not included in project time management?

    A. Control schedule

    B. Define activities

    C. Sequence activities

    D. Estimate time

25. You are the project manager of the Click It or Ticket project that is executing and being monitored and controlled. You want to measure the performance of the project against the baseline. Which of the following tools will you use? (Choose one.)

    A. Control chart

    B. Pareto diagram

    C. Decision tree analysis

    D. Variance analysis

26. You have heard a program manager telling a project manager, "The name of the game here is Control Schedule." What is the purpose of the control schedule process?

   A. To ensure that no changes to the schedule happen

   B. To manage schedule changes and to ensure that only approved changes to the schedule are implemented

   C. To prevent scope creep

   D. To control schedule activities on the critical path

27. You are in the process of developing the project charter for an upcoming project. Which of the following statements is not true about the project charter?

   A. It determines the scope of the project.

   B. It names the project manager for the project.

   C. It authorizes the project manager to use organizational resources to perform project activities.

   D. It provides a high-level product description.

28. Which of the following is not true about the project scope statement?

   A. It includes project assumptions and constraints.

   B. It includes an initial list of risks.

   C. It may include an initial WBS.

   D. It is an output of the scope planning process.

29. Which of the following is an output of the Define Scope process?

   A. Project charter

   B. Project scope statement

   C. Requirement documents

   D. Project schedule

30. You are the project manager of a project that is executing and being controlled. You want to make a decision on one part of the project product—whether to build it or to update an existing version. Which of the following tools will you use?

   A. Control chart

   B. Pareto diagram

   C. Decision tree analysis

   D. Variance analysis

31. You are planning for a new project called Shine Twin Cities. It's important that you document all the constraints involved in this project. Which of the following is an example of a constraint?
    A. A milestone that must be met by a certain date due to a marketing window depending on the beginning of a shopping season
    B. A quality standard that must be implemented
    C. A schedule activity on a critical path
    D. The threat of a strike at the external vendor from whom you are going to procure some items

32. You are in the process of developing the scope for the Save Our Schools project. Your program manager, Rachel Janowicz, has asked you to create a rough version of the scope management plan before you actually figure out the scope. Which of the following is not true about the project scope management plan?
    A. It describes how the project scope will be defined.
    B. It describes how the project scope will be controlled.
    C. It is the output of a process called Plan Scope.
    D. It describes how the project scope will be verified.

33. You are in the process of collecting requirements for the project assigned to you. Which of the following is an output of the Collect Requirements process?
    A. Project scope management plan
    B. Requirements management plan
    C. Project statement of work
    D. WBS

34. You are in the process of defining the scope for the Mitochondria Eve project. You need some documents before you can actually begin this process. Which of the following is not an input item to the Define Scope process?
    A. Project charter
    B. Project scope statement
    C. Requirement documents
    D. Project scope statement templates

35. Which of the following is not included in the project scope statement?
    A. Project assumptions and constraints
    B. Scope management plan
    C. Product scope description
    D. Product acceptance criteria

36. While walking down the hallway, you accidentally hear Mike, your project team member, declaring to another team member that he is not going to be able to finish his assignment on time because there was a problem he could not solve. The assignment that Mike is working on involves a schedule activity on the critical path. Which of the following actions will you take?

    A. You won't take any action until Mike speaks directly with you.

    B. You will raise this issue in the next project team meeting.

    C. You will raise the issue with Mike's functional manager.

    D. You will tell Mike that you overheard him and discuss the issue with him directly.

37. Which of the following statements correctly defines the statement of work in a case of procurement?

    A. A type of contract used to procure a product, service, or result

    B. A document that describes a product, service, or result that will be procured

    C. A document that describes each schedule activity

    D. A document written by the seller in the procurement

38. Which of the following is a tool used in the Define Scope process?

    A. Expert judgment

    B. Focus groups

    C. Interviews

    D. Project charter

39. Which of the following is not a tool used in the Define Scope process?

    A. Expert judgment

    B. Product analysis

    C. Facilitated workshops

    D. Decomposition

40. You are preparing to develop the WBS for the Singular Intelligence project. Which of the following is a true statement about the WBS?

    A. It is a deliverable-oriented hierarchical decomposition of the project work to be performed by the project team.

    B. It's a hierarchically organized set of resources needed by the project.

    C. It's a hierarchically organized set of risks identified for the project.

    D. It represents the reporting hierarchy in the performing organization.

41. The WBS is an input to which of the following processes?
    A. Define Activities
    B. Sequence Activities
    C. Define Scope
    D. Plan Human Resources

42. You are the project manager of a project that is being planned. Which of the following techniques can you use to develop the WBS?
    A. Pareto chart
    B. Analogous estimating
    C. Decomposition
    D. Bottom-up estimating

43. You have seen a program manager getting impatient with a project manager, saying, "Why haven't you performed the variance analysis?" Variance analysis is a technique used for which of the following?
    A. To measure the deviation of the actual project performance from the planned baseline and determine the cause of this variance
    B. To determine how different schedule activities vary in their importance to the final objectives of the project
    C. To determine the difference between the cost estimates for various schedule activities
    D. To determine the variance between the available resources and the required resources for a project and how this variance will affect the project results

44. You are the project manager of the Here I Come Berkeley project that is being executed. You are actively monitoring and controlling changes to the project. Which of the following is not a direct output of the Control Scope process?
    A. Updates to the scope statement
    B. Updates to the scope baseline
    C. Updates to the WBS
    D. Updates to cost estimates

45. You are in the process of creating the WBS for the Sky Over Davis project. Which process group are you using?
    A. Initiating
    B. Planning
    C. Executing
    D. Scoping

46. Which of the following does not affect the duration of a schedule activity?

   A. Resources assigned to the activity

   B. Availability of the assigned resources

   C. Whether the activity is on a critical path

   D. Experience of the human resource assigned

47. You are the project manager of a project that is running behind schedule, and the customer is not happy about the delay. You can put a limited amount of additional resources on the project. However, you want to obtain the greatest amount of schedule compression for the least increase in cost. Which schedule compression technique will you be using?

   A. Fast tracking

   B. PDM

   C. Crashing

   D. Critical path elimination

48. Which of the following is not an input to the Define Activities process?

   A. Project scope statement

   B. WBS

   C. WBS dictionary

   D. Risk breakdown structure (RBS)

49. You are the project manager of a project that is running behind schedule, and the customer is not happy about the delay. You are planning to run two phases of the project in parallel that were originally scheduled to be run in sequence. In doing so, which schedule compression technique will you be using?

   A. Fast tracking

   B. PDM

   C. Crashing

   D. Critical path elimination

50. Parametric estimating is used in:

   A. Estimating the resources for an activity

   B. Assessing the duration for an activity

   C. Sequencing the schedule activities

   D. Controlling the schedule

51. Which of the following is not an input to the activity sequencing process?
    A. Project scope statement
    B. Project schedule network diagrams
    C. Activity list
    D. Milestone list

52. The project manager of the Blue Sky Over Marysville project has left, and you have been appointed the new project manager for this project. You have discovered that there are some unaddressed change requests. You have evaluated these requests, and they all tend to change the scope of the project. You want to know who has the authority to approve these requests. Which of the following sources will you check first?
    A. The customer
    B. The project sponsor
    C. The project scope management plan
    D. The project charter

53. Which of the following is an output of the activity sequencing process?
    A. PDM
    B. Pareto charts
    C. WBS
    D. Project schedule network diagrams

54. You are the project manager of the project World Dominance. The project is almost complete when you get a request from a stakeholder for a minor change to the project that apparently will not change the schedule or the cost. The requester is not a key stakeholder. Which of the following is the appropriate action that you should take?
    A. Tell the stakeholder that this is not the time to make any changes to the project.
    B. Investigate the impact of this change across the project.
    C. Tell the appropriate team member to make the change.
    D. Submit the change request for approval.

55. Which of the following is an output of the Estimate Activity Resources process?
    A. Resource breakdown structure
    B. Risk breakdown structure
    C. WBS
    D. Activity list

56. The Delphi technique is used for:

   A. Resolving conflicts

   B. Analyzing performance

   C. Estimating resources

   D. Gathering information

57. You are on your way to UC Davis to present a seminar on project time management. The seminar organizer has asked you to present the material within the boundaries of the standards by the PMI. Which of the following sets of processes belongs to time management?

   A. Monitor and control project work, estimate activity duration, and develop schedule

   B. Activity definition, activity resource estimating, and schedule compression

   C. Define activities, estimate activity resources, and control schedule

   D. Develop project team, develop schedule, and control schedule

58. Which of the following is the correct sequence in which the processes will be performed?

   A. Create WBS, activity definition, activity resource estimating, activity duration estimating, and schedule development

   B. Activity definition, Create WBS, activity resource estimating, activity duration estimating, and schedule development

   C. Create WBS, activity definition, activity duration estimating, activity resource estimating, and schedule development

   D. Create WBS, activity definition, activity duration estimating, schedule development, and activity resource estimating

59. You are the project manager of the Good Will project. The WBS has been created, activities have been defined, and resources have been estimated. It's time to estimate the duration for each activity. Which of the following should perform the activity duration estimate?

   A. The project manager

   B. The individual or the team that will do the work

   C. The project management team

   D. The senior management

60. Which of the following is not true about the critical path?

    A. The float time for each activity on the critical path is zero.

    B. The critical path is the longest of all the paths in the network diagram on the time scale.

    C. If an activity on the critical path is delayed, the finish date for the project will be delayed.

    D. Any change request for an activity on the critical path will automatically be rejected.

61. The project manager of the Mother Nature project has left during the project execution, and you have been appointed the new project manager for this project. The project sponsor has asked you to give her a copy of the document that contains the work package descriptions. Which of the following documents will you look for?

    A. The project scope statement

    B. The WBS dictionary

    C. The project schedule

    D. The project charter

62. Which of the following is true about the critical chain method?

    A. It is a technique used in the activity duration estimating process.

    B. It is a technique used in the cost estimating process.

    C. It is a schedule development technique that involves adding duration buffers, which are not actual activities.

    D. It is a technique that involves adding duration buffers, which are actual work activities, to change the interdependencies of the activities.

63. Which of the following is true about the three-point estimating technique?

    A. It determines three values from three scenarios: optimistic, pessimistic, and most likely. The most likely value is taken as the final value.

    B. This method is used to determine the uncertainty in estimating the activity duration.

    C. It is a technique that uses the float time in duration estimating.

    D. It is a method that calculates the activity duration by taking the average of three estimates provided by the customer, the project manager, and the team member who will do the work.

64. Which of the following is true about the analogous estimating technique?

    A. It is used to assess the probability of success for a project based on the success rate for similar projects executed previously.

    B. It is bottom-up estimating: You estimate the duration for the components of an activity and sum them up.

    C. It estimates the duration of an activity based on the duration of a similar activity in the same project.

    D. It estimates the duration of an activity based on the duration of a similar activity in a previous project.

65. Which of the following is a true statement about the earned value technique?

    A. It is used in the scope control process.

    B. It is used in project performance measurements.

    C. It is used in planning for procurement.

    D. It is a project selection technique.

66. The rolling wave planning technique is used in the:

    A. Activity definition

    B. Activity sequencing

    C. Activity resource estimating

    D. Schedule development

67. Parametric estimating involves:

    A. Taking the average of duration estimates for similar activities

    B. Using a statistical relationship between historical data and other variables to calculate quantities, such as activity duration estimates and cost estimates

    C. Using previous cost estimates on similar activities to calculate the cost of an activity in the current project

    D. A technique used in quantitative risk analysis

68. Which of the following items is not used in calculating the earned value (EV)?

    A. Actual cost of the work performed: budget at completion (BAC)

    B. Originally approved budget

    C. Work completed

    D. Total work required to be completed

69. Recall actual cost (AC), planned value (PV), earned value (EV), and cost variance (CV) in the earned value technique. The CV is calculated as:
    - **A.** $PV - EV$
    - **B.** $AC - EV$
    - **C.** $EV - AC$
    - **D.** $PV - AC$

70. Recall actual cost (AC), planned value (PV), earned value (EV), cost variance (CV), budget at completion (BAC), and cost performance index (CPI) in the earned value technique. The CPI is calculated as:
    - **A.** EV / PV
    - **B.** EV / AC
    - **C.** CV / AC
    - **D.** EV / BAC

71. The activity list is an input to:
    - **A.** Activity sequencing
    - **B.** Activity definition
    - **C.** The WBS
    - **D.** Scope planning

72. Given:

    $$AC = 100$$
    $$BAC = 300$$
    $$EV = 90$$

    Assuming that the variations that have occurred so far in the project will not occur in the future, the estimate to complete (ETC) is:
    - **A.** 290
    - **B.** 200
    - **C.** 210
    - **D.** 10

73. Given:

    $$AC = 100$$
    $$BAC = 300$$
    $$EV = 90$$

    Assuming that the variations that have occurred so far in the project will not occur in the future, the EAC is:
    - **A.** 290
    - **B.** 310
    - **C.** 110
    - **D.** 400

74. You are the project manager of a project that is executing 17 percent under budget. Which of the following does this mean?

    A. EV is 100 and AC is 120.

    B. PV is 100 and EV is 120.

    C. PV is 120 and AC is 100.

    D. AC is 100 and EV is 120.

75. Which of the following is not an input to the Control Schedule process?

    A. Activity list

    B. Schedule baseline

    C. Work performance information

    D. Schedule management plan

76. In project management, the term "float" is synonymous with the term:

    A. Lag

    B. Lead

    C. Slack

    D. Critical

77. Which of the following processes uses a technique called *adjusting leads and lags*?

    A. Define Activities

    B. Control Schedule

    C. Sequence Activities

    D. Develop Schedule

78. You are preparing to perform quality planning for your project. Which of the following is an input to quality planning?

    A. Project scope statement

    B. Quality checklists

    C. Quality metrics

    D. Cost of quality

79. You are performing the Plan Quality process. You want to make sure you get all that you are supposed to from this effort. Which of the following is not an output of the quality planning process?

    A. Quality management plan

    B. Quality checklists

    C. Quality metrics

    D. Recommended preventive actions

80. Which of the following quality processes is performed first?

    A. Define Quality

    B. Plan Quality

    C. Perform Quality Control

    D. Perform Quality Assurance

81. You are the project manager of a project that is executing. You are monitoring and controlling the quality of the project. Which of the following is not an input to quality control?

    A. Quality metrics

    B. Quality checklists

    C. Pareto chart

    D. Work performance measurements

82. You are the project manager of the Reform Health Insurance project. You are working on ensuring the application of systematic quality activities that were planned in the quality planning process and ensuring that the project will employ all the processes needed to meet the requirements. Which process are you performing?

    A. Perform Quality Control

    B. Plan Quality

    C. Perform Quality Assurance

    D. Perform Testing

83. You are the project manager of a project that is executing. You are monitoring and controlling the quality of the project. Which of the following is not a technique for quality control?

    A. Flowcharting

    B. Control charts

    C. Pareto chart

    D. Benchmarking

84. You are the project manager of a project that is executing. You are working on ensuring the application of systematic quality activities that were planned in the quality planning process and ensuring that the project will employ all the processes needed to meet the requirements. Which of the following is not an output of the process you are performing?

    A. Recommended corrective actions

    B. Quality metrics

    C. Change requests

    D. Updates to the quality management plan

85. You are working with the QA team to find out the real cause of lots of problems in the product of your project. You are using a cause and effect diagram to find real causes of the problems by exploring all the possible causes. Which quality process are you performing?

    A. Quality assurance

    B. Quality planning

    C. Quality control

    D. Auditing

86. Which of the following is not a characteristic of a control chart?

    A. It reflects the expected variation of the data.

    B. It is used to monitor whether the variance of a specified variable is within the acceptable limits dictated by quality control.

    C. It is used to illustrate the behavior of a variable over time.

    D. It predicts the amount of risk associated with a variance.

87. Which of the following is not a tool of quality control?

    A. Regression diagram

    B. Run chart

    C. Scatter diagram

    D. Pareto diagram

88. Your manager has told you to use benchmarking. You have heard about benchmarking a lot in the company you are working in. Which of the following describes characteristics of benchmarking?

    A. It is used to prepare a response to an identified risk.

    B. It compares practices, products, or services of a project with those of some reference projects.

    C. It is a managerial technique used to manage the stakeholder expectations.

    D. It is used only to compare the performance of two software programs.

89. Which of the following processes will be performed first?

    A. Create WBS

    B. Activity sequencing

    C. Quality control

    D. Schedule control

90. Which of the following is not a process of quality management?
    A. Perform Quality Control
    B. Perform Quality Assurance
    C. Plan Quality
    D. Procurement Quality Planning

91. You are the project manager of the ABC project. You are in the process of identifying the project risks. Which of the following is an output of risk identification?
    A. Recommended corrective actions
    B. Risk register
    C. Risk response plan
    D. Risk dictionary

92. You are looking into strategies to deal with the negative risks in your project. Which of the following is not a strategy that you can use to deal with negative risks?
    A. Avoid
    B. Transfer
    C. Mitigate
    D. Audit

93. You are looking into strategies to deal with the negative risks in your project. Which of the following statements is not true about the risk mitigation strategy?
    A. Mitigation is used only after the risk occurs.
    B. Mitigation involves taking action to reduce the impact of the risk if it occurs.
    C. Mitigation involves taking action early on to reduce the probability of risk occurrence.
    D. Designing redundancy into a system is an example of mitigation.

94. Which of the following is not an input to risk identification?
    A. Project scope statement
    B. Risk register
    C. Risk management plan
    D. Schedule management plan

95. Which of the following is a set of risk management processes?
    A. Plan risk management, identify risks, perform qualitative risk analysis, perform quantitative risk analysis, plan risk responses, and monitor and control risks
    B. Risk management planning, risk evaluation, qualitative risk analysis, quantitative risk analysis, risk response planning, and risk monitoring and controlling
    C. Risk management planning, risk identification, risk evaluation, risk mitigation, risk response planning, and risk monitoring and controlling
    D. Risk management planning, risk transference, risk assessment, quantitative risk analysis, risk response planning, and risk monitoring and controlling

96. Activities are further decomposition of:
    A. Work packages
    B. Project charter
    C. Project scope statement
    D. Schedule network diagrams

97. You are the project manager of a project that is executing. You are looking at different ways to maximize the opportunities and minimize the threats presented by the project risks. Which process are you performing?
    A. Risk identification
    B. Quantitative risk analysis
    C. Qualitative risk analysis
    D. Risk response planning

98. You are the project manager of a project that is executing. You are looking at different options to respond to the risks. Which of the following is not an output of risk response planning?
    A. Risk-related contractual agreements
    B. Recommended corrective actions
    C. Project management plan updates
    D. Risk register updates

99. The acceptance strategy in risk response planning means the project team has decided to:
    A. Purchase insurance for the product to which the risk belongs.
    B. Take no action or take an action only if a particular event happens in the future.
    C. Take action to eliminate the risk.
    D. Accept whatever response the project manager comes up with.

100. You are the project manager of a project that is executing. You are actively monitoring and controlling the risks. Which of the following is not an output of the risk monitoring and controlling process called Monitor and Control Risks?

- **A.** Risk register updates
- **B.** Change requests
- **C.** Performance reports
- **D.** Recommended corrective actions

101. You are the project manager of a construction project. The project team has identified some project risks and wants to analyze them. Which of the following is a set of tools and techniques that can be used in the quantitative risk analysis?

- **A.** Data-gathering techniques, quantitative risk analysis and modeling techniques, and mitigation techniques
- **B.** Sensitivity analysis, expected monetary value analysis, decision tree analysis, and expert judgment
- **C.** Data-gathering techniques, quantitative risk analysis and modeling techniques, and checklist analysis
- **D.** Sensitivity analysis, expected monetary value analysis, decision tree analysis, and contingency planning

102. You have joined a project as a project manager. The project was already executing. Just before leaving, the previous project manager handed you the risk management plan and told you that the team had just finished the risk management planning. Which of the following don't you expect to see in this document?

- **A.** Probability and impact matrix definitions
- **B.** Risk response plan for each risk
- **C.** Risk categories
- **D.** Risk reporting and tracking

103. You are the project manager of a project that is in the planning stage. You are using a probability and impact matrix and other tools and techniques to prioritize the risks. Which process are you performing?

- **A.** Perform Quantitative Risk Analysis
- **B.** Perform Qualitative Risk Analysis
- **C.** Plan Risk Responses
- **D.** Monitor and Control Risks

104. You are using different tools and techniques to prioritize the risks in your project. Which of the following tools will you not be using?

    A. Probability and impact matrix

    B. Risk urgency assessment

    C. Risk audits

    D. Assessment of the risk data quality

105. You, with your project team, are performing the risk response planning process. You update the risk register as a result of this process. Which of the following is not going to be an item in the risk register after you make the updates?

    A. Risk owners and assigned responsibilities

    B. Agreed-upon risk response strategies

    C. Results from qualitative and quantitative risk analyses

    D. WBS dictionary

106. A project team member has asked you what progressive elaboration is. Which of the following is the best definition of progressive elaboration that you can give to her?

    A. Taking the project from initiating to closing

    B. Taking the project from conception to completion

    C. Taking the project from concept to project management plan

    D. Decomposing the project objectives into smaller, more manageable work pieces

107. The project charter is important due to which of the following reasons?

    A. It authorizes the sponsor.

    B. It identifies all the stakeholders.

    C. It authorizes the project manager to use the organization's resources.

    D. It identifies the project team members.

108. You had a conversation with your supervisor, Lisa Fuller, about an upcoming project. At the end of the conversation, Lisa said, "Now, be careful; you are making too many assumptions about the project." Which of the following is true about assumptions in project planning?

    A. Because assumptions are a part of the project charter that you did not write, you don't need to validate them. Just assume the assumptions are true, and if the project fails, it's not your fault.

    B. The project charter may include assumptions.

    C. An assumption is a condition that has been verified to be true, so you don't need to validate it.

    D. You must not start a project until all the assumptions have been proven to be true.

109. Which of the following is done first?
     A. Creating the scope statement
     B. Creating the project charter
     C. Schedule development
     D. Creating the WBS

110. Which of the following is not an output of human resource planning?
     A. Project staff assignments
     B. Staffing management plan
     C. List of roles and responsibilities
     D. Project organization chart

111. You are in the process of planning the scope for your project. Which of the following is a false statement about the project scope management plan?
     A. It describes how to verify the scope.
     B. It serves as the baseline for the project scope.
     C. It describes how to control the scope.
     D. It describes how to create the WBS.

112. You have joined the Project Rainbow project because the previous project manager left. The previous project manager handed you the project charter and the project scope statement before leaving. The next step, he said, is to develop the WBS. Who will do that?
     A. The project manager alone
     B. The project manager and the project sponsor
     C. The project manger with help from the project team
     D. The customer

113. Which of the following is not the tool for the project human resource planning?
     A. Resource assignment matrix (RAM)
     B. Networking
     C. Organizational theories
     D. Benchmarking

114. Which of the following is a false statement about a project risk?
     A. A risk can only have a negative effect on a project.
     B. A risk arises out of uncertainty.
     C. Identified risks are usually listed in a document called the *risk register*.
     D. Risks can be categorized by developing the risk breakdown structure (RBS).

115. Which of the following is not a process of human resource management?

   A. Develop Human Resource Plan

   B. Acquire Project Team

   C. Manage Stakeholder Expectations

   D. Develop Project Team

116. You are the project manager of the Grand Trunk Road project. With the help of the project team, you are identifying the project risks. Which of the following is not an information-gathering technique used in the risk identification process?

   A. Interviewing

   B. Delphi technique

   C. Decision tree analysis

   D. SWOT analysis

117. You are in the process of documenting all kinds of risks in the Save Route 66 project. Which of the following is a correct statement about secondary risks?

   A. These are residual risks.

   B. These are risks that have medium or low priority.

   C. These are risks that can result from responses to identified risks.

   D. These are risks that will be avoided.

118. In your Kamagata Maru moviemaking project, you must shoot a scene at a ski resort with many people skiing around. This project activity has which of the following kinds of dependencies?

   A. External

   B. Mandatory

   C. Internal

   D. Discretionary

119. You are the project manager for a software development project in a matrix organization. You have an influence on making the staff assignments. Which of the following characteristics will you not consider during these assignments?

   A. Competency

   B. Availability

   C. Lifestyle

   D. Salary requirement

120. Conflict management is a technique used in which of the following processes?

    A. Develop Human Resource Plan

    B. Acquire Project Team

    C. Develop Project Team

    D. Manage Project Team

121. Co-location is a technique used in which of the following processes?

    A. Plan Human Resources

    B. Acquire Project Team

    C. Develop Project Team

    D. Manage Project Team

122. You are the project manager of the Dream Big project. The project is executing. Which of the following tools and techniques will you not use to manage the project team?

    A. Observations and conversations

    B. Bonuses

    C. Conflict management

    D. Issue log

123. You are managing the Go Dinky Town project. In the last meeting, the term "virtual team" was mentioned. A virtual team is a tool for which of the following processes?

    A. Develop Human Resource Plan

    B. Acquire Project Team

    C. Develop Project Team

    D. Manage Project Team

124. Which of the following does not belong to the set of characteristics that makes a good recognition and reward strategy?

    A. Clear the reward criteria.

    B. Any member should be able to win the reward.

    C. Keep the reward standard high so that only the cream of the crop can reach the reward.

    D. Cultural diversity should be considered and respected.

125. Which of the following conflict resolution strategies provides a win/win resolution?

    A. Avoidance

    B. Collaboration

    C. Accommodation

    D. Compromise

126. The activity list that will be used to develop network diagrams is an output of which process?

    A. Defining activities

    B. Creating the WBS

    C. Planning the scope

    D. Developing the schedule

127. The list of risks that could affect the project is created by using which of the following processes?

    A. Define Risks

    B. Identify Risks

    C. Plan Risk Management

    D. Plan Risk Responses

128. Quality audits are being arranged for the Santana Row project. Quality audits are part of which of the following quality management processes?

    A. Plan Quality

    B. Perform Quality Control

    C. Perform Quality Assurance

    D. Perform Quality Inspection

129. A project team member asks you why you should monitor the activities on the critical path more closely. Which of the following will be your answer?

    A. Because the activities on the critical path need to be performed before the activities on other paths.

    B. Because each activity on the critical path has a zero float time and thereby poses a schedule risk.

    C. Because the activities on the critical path are very critical to the organization's strategy.

    D. Because the activities on noncritical paths depend upon the activities on the critical path.

130. Which of the following is not an output of the plan procurements process?

    A. Selected sellers list

    B. Procurement documents package

    C. Make-or-buy decisions

    D. Source selection criteria

131. To meet severe budget cuts, you have no other choice than to outsource most of the components of your Do More In Less project. So, you are planning for procurements. Which of the following is not a process of project procurement management?

    A. Select Sellers

    B. Plan Procurements

    C. Conduct Procurements

    D. Administer Procurements

132. Which of the following is not a proper name for a type of contract that can be used in procurement?

    A. Cost reimbursable

    B. Fixed price

    C. Profit shared

    D. Time and material

133. You are a project manager of a project that is executing. You need to procure a well-defined product. Which of the following will be the most suitable contract type for this procurement?

    A. Cost reimbursable

    B. Fixed price

    C. Profit shared

    D. Time and material

134. You are a project manager of a project that is executing. You need to procure a product that is not well defined. There are many grey areas. Which of the following contract types presents the highest risk?

    A. Firm fixed price

    B. Cost plus percentage of cost

    C. Cost plus fixed fee

    D. Cost plus incentive fee

    E. Time and material

135. You are the project manager of the On The Go project. Your company is procuring a part of your project and therefore preparing the procurement documents. Which of the following is true about the procurement documents?

    A. The documents should have a rigidly fixed format so that there are no variations in the responses from different sellers.

    B. The documents should be completely open-ended so that each seller has the complete freedom to suggest the requirements and present their solutions.

    C. Documents should be flexible enough to allow the sellers to be creative in offering solutions for meeting the requirements.

    D. The documents should follow the standards required by the sellers.

136. Which of the following is not true about conflict management?

    A. Successful conflict management results in an increased productivity and positive working relationships among the team members.

    B. Communication planning and clarity of roles and responsibilities can reduce the amount of conflict.

    C. Differences of opinion are harmful for the project.

    D. A conflict should be addressed in private by using a direct collaborative approach.

137. You are the project manager of a government project Uncle Sam Wants You, and you want to procure a few items. You are looking at the possibility of advertising for this procurement. Which of the following is not true about using advertising as a tool in the Conduct Procurements process?

    A. Advertising causes extra headaches and opens you up for lawsuits from the bidders, so stick with your company's list of sellers.

    B. Advertising can be placed in public newspapers or in professional journals.

    C. Advertising is sometimes required in government projects.

    D. Advertising can help you find a better seller by expanding the current list of sellers.

138. You are managing the execution of a Department of Defense project. The organizational environment is very well structured, and the management is very authoritarian. Which of the following is not an output item of the Direct and Manage Project Execution process?

    A. Implementation of corrective and preventive actions

    B. Deliverables

    C. Approved change requests

    D. Implementation of defect repairs

139. Which of the following processes does not belong to integration management?
   A. Develop Project Charter
   B. Manage Project Team
   C. Close Project
   D. Monitor and Control Project Work

140. Negotiation is a tool in which of the following processes?
   A. Develop Schedule
   B. Acquire Project Team
   C. Manage Stakeholder Expectations
   D. Develop Project Team

141. When should the administrative part of the project closure be performed?
   A. Before the product is accepted by the customer
   B. When there are risks involved in the project
   C. At the end of each project or each phase of a project
   D. At the time of signing the contracts for a procurement

142. You are about to release the project resources. Which process are you performing?
   A. Release Resources
   B. Administrative Closure
   C. Close Project or Phase
   D. Monitor and Control Project Work

143. You are using a Pareto diagram to rank the importance of each error in the product of your project. Which quality process are you performing?
   A. Quality control
   B. Quality planning
   C. Quality assurance
   D. Auditing

144. You are a project manager for the construction of a 30-mile road. Assume that the work is uniformly distributed over 12 weeks. The total approved budget for this project is $600,000. At the end of first three weeks of work, $150,000 has been spent, and 10 miles of road have been completed. What is the cost variance?
   A. $40,000
   B. $50,000
   C. −$40,000
   D. $120,000

145. A CPI value of 1.20 and an SPI value of 1.30 for a project mean which of the following?

  A. The project is making faster progress and costing less than planned.

  B. The project is making slower progress and costing more than planned.

  C. The project is making slower progress and costing less than planned.

  D. The project is making faster progress and costing more than planned.

146. The Close Project or Phase process belongs to which of the following knowledge areas?

  A. Time management

  B. Human resource management

  C. Monitoring and controlling

  D. Integration management

147. You are in the process of closing a completed project. Which of the following is not an output of the Close Project or Phase process?

  A. Lessons learned

  B. Implementation of recommended actions

  C. Transition of product

  D. Final product

148. Which of the following is not an input to the Close Project or Phase process?

  A. Product verified through the Verify Scope process

  B. Project management plan

  C. Product accepted by the customer

  D. Transition criteria

149. You have been appointed project manager for a project that is already executing. The previous project manager handed you the risk register. Which of the following do you not expect to see in this document?

  A. List of identified risks

  B. Risk probability and impact matrix

  C. List of potential responses

  D. Root causes of risks

150. Which of the following is not included in the benefit measurement methods for project selection?

     A. Scoring models
     B. Comparative approaches
     C. Dynamic programming
     D. Economic models

151. You have just been appointed the project manager of the Go Get Them project. You have started identifying the project stakeholders. Which of the following is not a true statement about the project stakeholders?

     A. Individuals and organizations directly involved in the project are the project stakeholders.
     B. All project stakeholders are supposed to be supportive of the project.
     C. Individuals and organizations that can impact the project are the project stakeholders.
     D. Individuals and organizations that will use the project product are the project stakeholders.

152. You have just received an approval for a change request made by the customer. Which process have you performed to get this change request approved?

     A. Approve Changes
     B. Control Schedule
     C. Perform Integrated Change Control
     D. Control Quality

153. Which of the following processes is included in the initiating process group?

     A. Identify Stakeholders
     B. Develop Preliminary Project Scope Statement
     C. Develop Project Management Plan
     D. Collect Requirements

154. In which of the following project process groups is a project manager assigned to the project?

     A. Monitoring and controlling
     B. Initiating
     C. Planning
     D. Human resource planning

155. You are the project manager of the Go Johnny Go project, which will generate a software product for farmers. An unpredicted risk event has happened during the executing stage of the project. You meet with the experts and determine a workaround for this risk. Which process are you performing to make this determination?

   A. Executing

   B. Plan Risk Responses

   C. Monitor and Control Risks

   D. Perform Quantitative Risk Analysis

156. Which is not a characteristic of a program?

   A. Projects in a program are related to each other.

   B. Projects in a program are managed in a coordinated fashion.

   C. A program can include work that is not part of any individual project in the program.

   D. A program is a sophisticated project that is broken into smaller projects just for the ease of executing it.

157. Which of the following is not an output of the Perform Integrated Change Control process?

   A. Approved change requests

   B. Rejected change requests

   C. Postponed change requests

   D. Implementation of changes

158. You are the project manager of Mind the Gap project, which involves providing Internet access to an underprivileged community in your city. You have to get some of the schedule activities of the project finished by an external vendor. You have written the statement of work and gathered or prepared all the documents that will be given to the bidders. You are ready to look for sellers. Which process will you perform next?

   A. Plan Procurements

   B. Request Seller Responses

   C. Conduct Procurements

   D. Request Bidders

159. You are the project manager of the Multiple Voices project, which is already executing. You have just discovered that there are differences among the stakeholders over what the project objectives are and what the stakeholders' expectations of the project are. Which of the following is true about these differences?

    A. Report the differences to the project sponsor because it is the sponsor's responsibility to resolve the differences.

    B. People are entitled to their points of view, so you should ignore the differences and honor them.

    C. You should encourage the differences because different opinions will result in the best end product.

    D. The differences about the project objectives and the different expectations of the project make the project manager's job difficult.

160. You are the project manager of a project that is executing. The project is making progress in accordance with the baseline, and the project team morale is quite high as a result. A member of the project management team who has returned from a meeting tells you that the customer is very disappointed at the poor progress the project is making and that he is planning to talk to the CEO of your organization about it. What is the first action that you will take?

    A. Talk to the CEO before the customer does.

    B. Contact the customer and find out detailed information from him.

    C. Call a project team meeting and invite the customer to the meeting.

    D. Talk to the project sponsor about this problem.

161. You are the project manager of a project that is about to be completed. You get a call from the customer to add a feature to the project product that is not part of the project scope, but without it the product will not be very useful, according to the customer. What is the first action you will take?

    A. Tell the customer that the project is almost complete and this is not the time to make any changes.

    B. Evaluate the impact of the request and process it through the integrated change control process.

    C. Ask the sponsor to allocate more funds to accommodate this change.

    D. Accept the change and use the contingency reserve funds to implement the change.

162. Which of the following is not included in the mathematical models used to select projects?

    A. Linear programming

    B. Nonlinear programming

    C. Integer programming

    D. Project-oriented programming

163. You are on the committee that makes the final selection for sellers for procurement. You have just noticed that in the procurement for a current project, the Everest Consultant Group is on the list of sellers. This company is run by your brother. What will you do?

    A. It's unnecessary to say anything; just excuse yourself from the committee.

    B. You don't need to say anything; just make sure you stay impartial in the seller selection process.

    C. Disclose this fact to the committee.

    D. Vote against this company just to stay fair.

164. You have just been appointed the project manager of the ABC project. You have started identifying the project stakeholders. You must do all of the following *except*:

    A. Identify all the stakeholders.

    B. Manage stakeholder expectations.

    C. Create conflicts among the stakeholders whenever possible in order to get a better deal for the project team.

    D. Understand stakeholders' expectations and requirements.

165. Which of the following is not expected by the PMP Code of Ethics and Professional Conduct?

    A. Satisfy the scope and objectives of your professional services.

    B. Respect the confidentiality of sensitive information obtained in the course of professional activities.

    C. Take courses to learn about ethics.

    D. Cooperate with PMI concerning ethics violations.

166. Which of the following is the document that is produced in the initiating stage of a project?

    A. The project charter

    B. The preliminary project scope statement

    C. The project management plan

    D. The project schedule

167. You are managing a project in a country foreign to you. The CEO of the performing organization asks you to write a check to a city official to get some paperwork required for the project moving forward. Such an activity in your home country would be considered bribery, which is illegal. What will you do?

    A. Investigate whether what the CEO is suggesting is legal and ethical in this country.

    B. Report the CEO to the police.

    C. Write the check to the city official because the CEO asked you to do so.

    D. Tell the CEO that he's an unethical person and you are leaving the project.

168. Which of the following processes is included in the planning process group?

    A. Identify Stakeholders

    B. Develop Project Charter

    C. Collect Requirements

    D. Acquire Project Team

169. You are the project manager of a project that has just been cancelled by the sponsor. What should you do?

    A. Write an email to the manager of the sponsor telling him how unfair it was to cancel the project.

    B. Put this project behind you and focus on the next project.

    C. Close the project following the proper processes and procedures.

    D. Schedule a meeting of the project team and invite the project sponsor to the meeting to discuss the issue.

170. Which of the following is not the purpose of the Perform Integrated Change Control process?

    A. Ensure, if possible, that no changes are made to the project scope.

    B. Influence the factors that cause change.

    C. Approve or reject a change request.

    D. Identify whether a change has occurred.

171. You are trying to put together a plan for a project. You have just prepared a list of activities. What is the next process that you should perform?

    A. Develop Schedule

    B. Control Schedule

    C. Sequence Activities

    D. Create WBS

172. Which of the following will be performed first?

    A. Qualitative risk analysis

    B. Quantitative risk analysis

    C. Directing and managing project execution

    D. Risk monitoring and control

173. You have been appointed the project manager for a project that is already being planned. The project sponsor has handed you the WBS and asked you to come up with a project schedule. Which of the following processes don't you need to perform before you can develop the project schedule?

    A. Define Activities

    B. Sequence Activities

    C. Control Schedule

    D. Estimate Activity Resources

174. You have planned your project and determined the performance baseline, which has been approved. You are all set to go for execution. The approved baseline should be changed when:

    A. You spent more than planned on a number of activities.

    B. An activity on the critical path has taken longer than scheduled.

    C. Some changes that directly or indirectly change or impact the scope, cost, or schedule have been approved.

    D. The project is running ahead of schedule.

175. Which of the following is a correct statement about project management?

    A. It guarantees maximum profit with minimum efforts.

    B. It is the application of knowledge, skills, and tools and techniques to perform project activities in order to meet project requirements.

    C. It consists of the processes determined by the functional managers in a given organization.

    D. It is only useful for very complex and large projects.

176. Which of the following is not an output of the Define Scope process?

    A. Project scope statement

    B. Product acceptance criteria

    C. List of project constraints

    D. WBS

177. You read the PMP Code of Ethics and Professional Conduct before applying for the PMP credential. The four values that make the foundation of the Code of Ethics and Professional Conduct by the PMI are the following:

    A. Fairness, charity, respect, and responsibility

    B. Fairness, honesty, respect, and responsibility

    C. Fairness, honesty, helping the environment, and responsibility

    D. Fairness, honesty, respect, and acquiring new skills

178. Bhupinder Daler, the engineering manager, sits with the engineers to explain to them their assignments in greater details. Then he backs off and encourages them to take ownership of their assignments. Most of the engineers agree that he trusts his engineers. Which management theory Bhupinder is practicing?

    A. Theory T

    B. Theory X

    C. Theory Y

    D. McClelland's Achievement Motivation Theory

179. Your supervisor often says that until the basic living needs of the employees are met, they cannot be motivated to perform better at the workplace. Which management theory does your supervisor most likely believe in?

    A. Maslow's hierarchy of needs theory

    B. Socialism

    C. Herzberg's motivation theory

    D. Theory X

180. Your project depends on two business partners: On The Fly Inc. (OTF) and The Sure Thing Inc. (ST) delivering their products to you on time. The chances are 3 out of 4 that OTF will make the delivery on time and 2 out of 3 that ST will not make the delivery on time. The probability that OTF and ST will both fail to deliver on time is equal to:

    A. 0.5

    B. 0.17

    C. 3/7

    D. 0.91

Answers and Explanations

1. Answer: D

   D is the correct answer because cost variance is not a project selection method. In fact, you will not be able to determine the cost variance until the project starts executing.

   A, B, and **C** are incorrect because these are valid project selection methods.

2. Answer: D

   D is the correct answer because operations managers and functional managers usually have a role to play in the project. The CEO and project managers are obvious stakeholders.

   A, B, and **C** are incorrect because D is a more complete answer.

3. Answer: C

   C is the correct answer because the project charter, which is an output of a process of the initiating process group, must be approved before the project can start.

   A, B, and **D** are incorrect because these are not the outputs of the processes in the initiating process group.

4. Answer: A

   A is the correct answer because the project charter approval officially starts the project.

   B is incorrect because the project scope statement determines the scope of the project, whereas the project charter must be approved before you start the project.

   C is incorrect because there is no such document as the project initiation plan document.

   D is incorrect because the project management plan is produced in the planning stage of the project, and the project does not move to the planning stage until the project charter is approved.

5. Answer: D

   D is the correct answer because the Perform Quality Control process is used to recommend corrective or preventive actions to meet quality standards.

   A is incorrect because testing is not a project management process.

   B is incorrect because quality planning is used to identify the quality standards relevant to the project and to determine how to satisfy them.

   C is incorrect because the risk response planning process is used during the planning stage for the identified risks, not during the control stage.

6. Answer: C

    C is the correct answer because the two defining characteristics of a project are that it has a beginning and an end and that it creates a unique product, service, or result.

    A, B, and **D** are incorrect because they exclude two defining characteristics of a project: It has a beginning and an end, and it creates a unique product, service, or result.

7. Answer: D

    D is the correct answer because a program is a set of related projects that are managed in a coordinated way to obtain optimal results.

    A is incorrect because a large budget does not make a project a program.

    B is incorrect because a set of processes is called a *process group.*

    C is incorrect because the projects in a program are usually related to each other by the very nature of the program.

8. Answer: B

    B is the correct answer because the Plan Procurements process is used to plan the procurements.

    A and **C** are incorrect because neither of these is a correct name for any of the project management processes.

    D is incorrect because Close Procurements belongs to the closing part of the project.

9. Answer: B

    B is the correct answer because the Conduct Procurements process is used to solicit seller responses, select sellers, and award a contract.

    A is incorrect because the tasks already mentioned in the statement of the question are performed using the Plan Procurements process.

    C is incorrect because the Administer Procurements process is performed after you already have awarded contracts.

    D is incorrect because there is no standard process called Request Seller Responses.

10. Answer: D

    D is the correct answer because the project manager has the highest level of authority in a projectized organization.

    A is incorrect because the project manager has the lowest level of authority in a functional organization.

    B is incorrect because the project manager's authority in a strong matrix organization is not higher than that in a projectized organization.

    C is incorrect because the project manager's authority in a weak matrix organization is lower than that in a projectized organization.

11. Answer: A

    A is the correct answer because the project manager has the lowest level of authority in a functional organization.

    B is incorrect because the project manager's authority in a strong matrix organization is higher than that in a functional organization.

    C is incorrect because the project manager's authority in a weak matrix organization is higher than that in a functional organization.

    D is incorrect because the project manager has the highest level of authority in a projectized organization.

12. Answer: C

    C is the correct answer because performance evaluations belong to the monitoring and controlling process group.

    A and **B** are incorrect because performance evaluations belong to the monitoring and controlling process group.

    D is incorrect because there is no project management process group named evaluating.

13. Answer: D

    D is the correct answer because it is the project manager's responsibility to manage the project stakeholders' expectations.

    A is incorrect because it is the project manager's responsibility to manage the project stakeholders' expectations.

    B and **C** are incorrect because the differences about objectives (and conflicts among the team members) must be resolved. Different expectations for the project mean that the stakeholders are not on the same page about the project scope, and that can be damaging to the project.

14. Answer: B

    B is the correct answer because the five process groups are initiating, planning, executing, monitoring and controlling, and closing. Note that monitoring and controlling is the name of one process group; it is also informally called *monitoring* or *controlling*.

    A is incorrect because monitoring and controlling is one process group.

    C and **D** are incorrect because scoping and testing are not valid names for the project management process groups.

15. Answer: A

    A is the correct answer because the project charter must make the business' case to justify the project.

    B is incorrect because the SOW is an input to the Develop Project Charter process; it will be used to develop the charter.

C is incorrect because the project scope statement is not part of the project charter.

D is incorrect because the project management plan will be developed in the planning stage after the charter has been issued.

16. Answer: B

B is the correct answer because process groups usually involve overlapping activities. For example, you monitor and control the project at the same time as you are executing it.

A and **D** are incorrect because process groups are seldom either discrete or one-time events.

C is incorrect because the level of involvement for a given process group might be different for different phases of a project; it depends upon the needs.

17. Answer: C

C is the correct answer because reviewing the initiating processes at the beginning of each phase helps keep the project focused on the business need for which the project was started.

A is incorrect because it's the wrong reason for reviewing the initiating processes.

B is incorrect because one of the purposes of reviewing the initiating processes is to determine whether the project should continue. If the business needs have changed, either the project should be cancelled or its scope should be changed.

D is incorrect because reviewing the initiating process is not a waste of time; it is a very important task.

18. Answer: A

A is the correct answer because in functional organizations, the functional managers are the bosses who assign the work to employees.

B is incorrect because employees do not report to the project managers in a functional organization.

C and **D** are incorrect because the project teams and project management teams do not make the work assignment decisions.

19. Answer: A

A is the correct answer because the initiating group is used to authorize a project or a phase of a project.

B is incorrect because there is no project management process group named phase initiating.

C and **D** are incorrect because the planning and executing process groups are not used to authorize a project.

20. Answer: B

B is the correct answer because there is no process group called designing and testing.

A and **C** are incorrect because each of these names two process groups.

D is incorrect because monitoring and controlling is a process group.

21. Answer: B and E

B and **E** are the correct answers because there are no knowledge areas recognized by PMI with the names team management and stakeholder management.

A, C, D, F, and **G** are incorrect because these are valid names for project management knowledge areas.

22. Answer: B

B is the correct answer because a Pareto diagram is used to prioritize defects by displaying the frequencies of their occurrences. It is a tool used in the Perform Quality Control process.

A is incorrect because a control chart is used to determine whether an output variable is within the control limits. It is a tool used in the Perform Quality Control process.

C is incorrect because decision tree analysis is a technique used in quantitative risk analysis to choose between alternative capital strategies, such as to build or to upgrade.

D is incorrect because variance analysis is a technique used to measure project performance by comparing the actual performance to the planned performance. The performance metrics are generally the schedule, scope, and cost. So, variance analysis can be used in cost control, scope control, and schedule control.

23. Answer: A

A is the correct answer because the quality planning process is part of the planning process group.

B and **C** are incorrect because identifying the quality standards and determining how to satisfy them is part of planning, not executing or controlling.

D is incorrect because there is no process group named the quality planning process group.

24. Answer: D

D is the correct answer because there is no process named estimate time.

A, B, and **C** are incorrect because all these processes belong to time management.

25. Answer: D

D is the correct answer because variance analysis is a technique used to measure project performance by comparing the actual performance to the planned performance in terms of scope, cost, and schedule. So, variance analysis can be used in cost control, scope control, and schedule control.

A is incorrect because a control chart is used to determine whether an output variable is within the control limits. It is a tool used in the Perform Quality Control process.

B is incorrect because a Pareto diagram is used to prioritize defects by displaying the frequencies of their occurrences. It is a tool used in the Perform Quality Control process.

C is incorrect because decision tree analysis is a technique used in the quantitative risk analysis to choose between alternative capital strategies, such as to build or to upgrade.

26. Answer: B

    B is the correct answer because the purpose of the schedule control process is to manage (monitor and control) the schedule changes and make sure the changes go through an approval system before implementation.

    A is incorrect because schedule control does not mean no change.

    C is incorrect because scope creep is an issue that belongs to scope control.

    D is incorrect because the schedule control process is to control all schedule-related changes, not just those related to the activities on the critical path.

27. Answer: A

    A is the correct answer because the scope is determined by the project scope statement, not by the project charter.

    B, C, and **D** are incorrect answers because these are the correct statements about project charter.

28. Answer: D

    D is the correct answer because the scope statement is an output of the process called Define Scope.

    A, B, and **C** are incorrect answers because these are all valid items to be included in the project scope statement.

29. Answer: B

    B is the correct answer because the project scope statement, also called the *detailed project scope statement*, is the major output of the scope definition process.

    A and **C** are incorrect because the project charter and requirement documents are input items to the Define Scope process.

    D is incorrect because you need to perform many other processes after the project definition process before you can develop the project schedule.

30. Answer: C

C is the correct answer because decision tree analysis is a technique used in quantitative risk analysis to choose between alternative capital strategies, such as to build or to upgrade.

A is incorrect because a control chart is used to determine whether an output variable is within the control limits. It is a tool used in the Perform Quality Control process.

B is incorrect because a Pareto diagram is used to prioritize defects by displaying the frequencies of their occurrences. It is a tool used in the Perform Quality Control process.

D is incorrect because variance analysis is a technique used to measure the project performance by comparing the actual performance to the planned performance in terms of scope, cost, and schedule. So, variance analysis can be used in cost control, scope control, and schedule control.

31. Answer: A

A is the correct answer because a constraint is a state of being restricted to a given course of action (or inaction). It limits the team's options. Hard deadlines and predefined budgets are examples of constraints.

B and **C** are incorrect because quality standards and activities on the critical path are not constraints.

D is incorrect because the possibility of a strike is a risk, not a constraint.

32. Answer: C

C is the correct answer because there is no standard process called Plan Scope. The scope is developed as part of the effort of developing the project management plan.

A, **B**, and **D** are incorrect answers because all these are true statements about the project scope management plan.

33. Answer: B

B is the correct answer because the requirements management plan is part of the output of the Collect Requirements process.

A is incorrect because the project scope management plan is developed as part of the effort of developing the project management plan.

C is incorrect because the project statement of work is an input to developing the project charter, which is an input to the Collect Requirements process.

D is incorrect because the WBS is created by using the process called Create WBS.

34. Answer: B

B is the correct answer because the project scope statement is an output of the Define Scope process.

A, C, and **D** are incorrect because all these are input items to the scope definition process. Scope statement templates are part of the organizational process assets, an input to the Define Scope process.

35. Answer: B

B is the correct answer because the project scope statement does not contain the scope management plan, which is created even before the scope is defined.

A, C, and **D** are incorrect answers because these items are included in the project scope statement.

36. Answer: D

D is the correct answer because when you, the project manager, anticipate or see a potential problem, you should deal with it head on.

A is incorrect because this option ignores the problem. You should not sit and let the problem happen before you act.

B and **C** are incorrect answers because these options do not deal with the problem directly.

37. Answer: B

B is the correct answer because the SOW is written by the buyer to describe the product to be procured.

A is incorrect because the SOW is not a contract.

C is incorrect because the SOW is only written for the activities or the products to be procured.

D is incorrect because the SOW is written by the buyer to describe the product to be procured.

38. Answer: A

A is the correct answer because expert judgment is part of the tools used in defining the scope.

B and **C** are incorrect because these are the tools used in collecting requirements.

D is incorrect because the project charter is an input to the Define Scope process, not a tool.

39. Answer: D

D is the correct answer because decomposition is a tool used in creating the WBS.

A, B, and **C** are incorrect answers because expert judgment, product analysis, and facilitated workshops are all tools for the project definition process.

40. Answer: A

A is the correct answer because the work breakdown structure (WBS) is a deliverable-oriented hierarchical decomposition of the project work to be performed by the project team.

B is incorrect because the hierarchy of resources is called the *resource breakdown structure* (RBS).

C is incorrect because the hierarchy of risks is called the *risk breakdown structure* (RBS).

D is incorrect because the organizational structure is called the *organizational breakdown structure* (OBS).

41. Answer: A

A is the correct answer because the WBS is a direct input to the Define Activities process; the WBS is a component of the scope baseline.

B and **D** are incorrect because the WBS is not a direct input to these processes.

C is incorrect because the scope definition process is used to develop the project scope statement, which is an input to the Create WBS process.

42. Answer: C

C is the correct answer because the WBS is created by decomposing the project deliverables into smaller components.

A and **B** are incorrect because a Pareto chart is used in quality management processes, such as the Perform Quality Control process, and analogous estimating is an estimating technique used in appropriate processes, such as cost estimating.

D is incorrect because bottom-up estimating is an estimating technique used in appropriate processes, such as activity resource estimating.

43. Answer: A

A is the correct answer because the purpose of the variance analysis is to measure the deviation of the actual project performance from the planned baseline and determine the cause of this variance.

B, C, and **D** are incorrect because these are false statements about the variance analysis.

44. Answer: D

D is the correct answer because updates to cost estimates are an output of cost controlling.

A, B, and **C** are incorrect answers because these are all valid output items for the scope control process. Cost estimates can change as a result of scope change, but the cost estimate change must go through the Control Cost process before the documents are updated.

45. Answer: B

B is the correct answer because the Create WBS process is part of the planning process group.

A and **C** are incorrect because the WBS is created by using the Create WBS process, which is part of the planning process group.

D is incorrect because there is no process group named scoping.

46. Answer: C

C is the correct answer because the critical path results from sequencing of activities and their durations.

A, B, and **D** are incorrect answers because all these affect the activity duration.

47. Answer: C

C is the correct answer because crashing is the schedule compression technique that involves analyzing a number of alternatives and choosing the one that lets you get the maximum schedule compression for the minimum cost increase.

A is incorrect because fast tracking is the schedule compression technique that involves obtaining schedule compression by executing activities (or phases) in parallel that would normally be executed in sequence.

B is incorrect because PDM (precedence diagramming method) is a technique to develop the network diagram; it's not a schedule compression technique.

D is incorrect because there is no schedule compression technique named critical path elimination.

48. Answer: D

D is the correct answer because the RBS is not an input to the project definition process.

A, B, and **C** are incorrect because the project scope statement, WBS, and WBS dictionary are all input items to the activity definition process; they are components of the scope baseline.

49. Answer: A

A is the correct answer because fast tracking is the schedule compression technique that involves obtaining schedule compression by executing activities (or phases) in parallel that would normally be executed in sequence.

B is incorrect because PDM (precedence diagramming method) is a technique to develop the network diagram; it's not a schedule compression technique.

C is incorrect because crashing is the schedule compression technique that involves analyzing a number of alternatives and choosing the one that lets you get the maximum schedule compression for the minimum cost increase.

D is incorrect because there is no schedule compression technique named critical path elimination.

50.   Answer: B

B is the correct answer because parametric estimating is a technique used in the activity duration estimating process.

A, C, and D are incorrect because parametric estimating is not used for these tasks (or processes), according to PMI.

51.   Answer: B

B is the correct answer because a project schedule network diagram is an output item of the activity sequencing process.

A, C, and D are incorrect answers because all these are input items to the activity sequencing process.

52.   Answer: C

C is the correct answer because the project scope management plan specifies how the proposed changes to the project will be managed.

A and B are incorrect because you should check the scope management plan first.

D is incorrect because project charter is not meant to contain the change management information.

53.   Answer: D

D is the correct answer because network diagrams are the output of the activity sequencing process.

A and B are incorrect because PDM (precedence diagramming method) and Pareto charts are techniques used in activity sequencing and quality control, respectively.

C is incorrect because the WBS is an output of the Create WBS process.

54.   Answer: B

B is the correct answer because once a change request is made, it is your responsibility to evaluate the impact of the change across the project.

A, C, and D are incorrect because you are taking an action without investigating.

55.   Answer: A

A is the correct answer because the resource breakdown structure is an output of the resource estimating process.

B is incorrect because the risk breakdown structure is not an output of the resource estimating process.

C is incorrect because the WBS is an output of the Create WBS process.

D is incorrect because the activity list is an input item to resource estimating.

56. Answer: D

D is the correct answer because the Delphi technique is an information-gathering technique used to solicit expert opinions anonymously by hiding the identities of the experts to prevent the domination of one expert.

A, B, and **C** are incorrect because the Delphi technique is basically an information-gathering technique.

57. Answer: C

C is the correct answer because all these processes belong to time management.

A is incorrect because the Monitor and Control Project Work process belongs to integration management.

B is incorrect because schedule compression is not a process.

D is incorrect because the Develop Project Team process belongs to human resource management.

58. Answer: A

A is the correct answer because this is the correct order of process execution; an output of the previous process is used as an input to the following process.

B is incorrect because the WBS is an input to the activity definition process, so the WBS must be created before performing the activity definition process.

C is incorrect because resource requirements are an input to the activity duration estimating process, so the activity resource estimating process must be performed before the activity duration estimating process.

D is incorrect because you need the resource requirements and the activity durations before you can develop the schedule.

 NOTE

Note that I have not used the proper formal names for the processes in this and some other questions; you should be able to identify the process even when it's referred to in an informal way.

59. Answer: B

B is the correct answer because the person or the team that will perform the work will have a more realistic understanding of what is involved and how long it will take.

A is incorrect because the project manager might not know the technical details of the work involved. Of course, the project manager will facilitate the estimate and make sure it happens in a timely fashion. It's still the responsibility of the project manager to make it happen.

C and **D** are incorrect because the project management team and senior management generally will not know the technical details of the work involved.

60. Answer: D

D is the correct answer because this is the wrong statement about the critical path.

A, **B**, and **C** are incorrect because these are the defining statements for the critical path.

61. Answer: B

B is the correct answer because the work breakdown structure (WBS) dictionary contains the description of each work package in the WBS.

A, **C**, and **D** are incorrect because these documents do not contain the work package descriptions.

62. Answer: C

C is the correct answer because the critical chain method adds duration buffers that are not work schedule activities to maintain focus on the planned activity durations.

A, **B**, and **D** are incorrect because these are not true statements about the critical chain method.

63. Answer: B

B is the correct answer because the three-point estimating technique determines the uncertainty on the activity duration, which is taken as the plain or weighted average of optimistic, most likely, and pessimistic values.

A is incorrect because the final value is the average value of the optimistic, most likely, and pessimistic values.

C and **D** are incorrect because these are false statements about the three-point estimating technique.

64. Answer: D

D is the correct answer because analogous estimating is the duration estimating technique used to determine the duration of an activity based on the duration of a similar activity in a previous project.

A, **B**, and **C** are incorrect because these are false statements about the analogous estimating technique.

65. Answer: B

B is the correct answer because the earned value technique, in its various forms, is used to measure the performance of a project.

A, **C**, and **D** are incorrect because these are false statements about the earned value technique.

66. Answer: A

A is the correct answer because rolling wave planning is a technique used in the Define Activities process. The technique is used to plan the project work at various levels of detail depending upon the availability of information.

B, **C**, and **D** are incorrect because these are false statements about the rolling wave planning technique.

67. Answer: B

B is the correct answer because parametric estimating uses historical values and other variables to estimate activity duration and cost.

A, **C**, and **D** are incorrect because these are false statements about the parametric estimating technique.

68. Answer: A

A is the correct answer because the actual cost of the completed work is not required to calculate EV according to the following equation:

$$EV = BAC \times (\text{work completed}) / (\text{total work required})$$

B, **C**, and **D** are incorrect answers because each of these items is used in calculating EV.

69. Answer: C

C is the correct answer because the cost variance is calculated as the earned value minus the actual cost.

A, **B**, and **D** are incorrect because these are wrong representations of cost variance.

70. Answer: B

B is the correct answer because CPI is calculated as the ratio of the earned value and the actual cost of the performed work.

A, **C**, and **D** are incorrect because these are wrong representations of CPI.

71. Answer: A

A is the correct answer because the activity list is an input to a number of processes, including activity sequencing, activity resource estimating, activity duration estimating, and schedule development.

B is incorrect because the activity list is an output of activity definition.

C is incorrect because the WBS is an input to the activity definition process that generates the activity list.

D is incorrect because the activity list is not there yet when you are planning the scope.

72. Answer: C

C is the correct answer because

$$ETC = BAC - EV = 300 - 90 = 210$$

A, B, and **D** are incorrect because the formula for the given values does not provide these results.

73. Answer: B

B is the correct answer because

$$ETC = BAC - EV, \text{ and}$$
$$EAC = ETC + AC = 300 - 90 + 100 = 310$$

A, C, and **D** are incorrect because the formula for the given values does not provide these results.

74. Answer: D

D is the correct answer because:

Cost performance index (CPI) = EV / AC
From the given data, 1 / CPI = AC / EV = 0.83
Therefore AC = EV × 0.85 = 120 × 0.83 = 99.6

A, B, and **C** are incorrect because the formula for the given values does not provide these results.

75. Answer: A

A is the correct answer because the activity list is an input to schedule development, but it is not an input item to schedule control.

B, C, and **D** are incorrect answers because all these items are inputs to the schedule control process. Remember that the schedule baseline and schedule management plan are parts of the project management plan.

76. Answer: C

C is the correct answer because the term "float" is synonymous with the term "slack," which is the time by which you can delay an activity without affecting the early start date of the next activity in the sequence.

A, B, and **D** are incorrect because they do not mean the same in project management as the term "float" does.

77. Answer: D

D is the correct answer because schedule development uses the leads and lags technique to adjust when the successor activity should start relative to the finish date of the predecessor activity.

A, B, and **C** are incorrect because the leads and lags technique is irrelevant to these processes.

78. Answer: A

A is the correct answer because the project scope statement is a major input item to the quality planning process called Plan Quality.

B and **C** are incorrect because quality checklists and quality metrics are the output of the quality planning process.

D is incorrect because cost of quality is a technique used in quality planning.

79. Answer: D

D is the correct answer because recommended preventive actions or change requests are usually the output of a control process, such as the Control Quality process.

A, B, and **C** are incorrect answers because all of these are valid output items for the quality planning process.

80. Answer: B

B is the correct answer because you must have a quality management plan generated by the quality planning process before you perform any other quality management process.

A is incorrect because Define Quality is not a valid name for any process recognized by PMI.

C and **D** are incorrect because quality control and quality assurance need to be performed according to the quality management plan generated by quality planning.

81. Answer: C

C is the correct answer because a Pareto chart is a technique used in the quality control process.

A, B, and **D** are incorrect answers because these are all input items to the quality control process.

82. Answer: C

C is the correct answer because quality assurance is the process used to apply the planned quality activities and standards to ensure that the project employs all processes needed to meet the project requirements.

A and **B** are incorrect because quality control is used to monitor the results to determine whether they comply with the quality standards, and quality planning is used to determine which quality standards are relevant to the project and how to meet them.

D is incorrect because there is no PMI process called Perform Testing.

83. Answer: D

    D is the correct answer because benchmarking is a technique for quality planning, not for quality control.

    A, B, and **C** are incorrect answers because all these represent techniques that can be used in quality control.

84. Answer: B

    B is the correct answer because quality metrics are the output of the quality planning process, and you are performing the quality assurance process.

    A, C, and **D** are incorrect answers because all these items are valid outputs of the quality assurance process.

85. Answer: C

    C is the correct answer because a cause and effect diagram, also called an *Ishikawa diagram*, is a tool used in the Perform Quality Control process to explore all the potential causes of a problem.

    A and **B** are incorrect because an Ishikawa diagram is a tool used in the quality control process.

    D is incorrect because auditing is a technique, not a process, used in the QA process.

86. Answer: D

    D is the correct answer because the control chart is a technique used in quality control, not in risk management.

    A, B, and **C** are incorrect answers because all these are characteristics of a control chart.

87. Answer: A

    A is the correct answer because there is no such quality control tool as a regression diagram.

    B, C, and **D** are incorrect answers because all these represent valid tools and techniques for quality control.

88. Answer: B

    B is the correct answer because benchmarking is a quality planning technique that compares practices, products, or services of a project with those of some reference projects for the purpose of learning, improving, and creating the basis for measuring performance.

    A, C, and **D** are incorrect because these are false statements about the benchmarking technique.

89. Answer: A

A is the correct answer because creating the WBS is necessary to understand and finalize the scope of the project and to determine the schedule activities.

B, C, and **D** are incorrect because creating the WBS is necessary to understand and finalize the scope of the project and to determine the schedule activities.

90. Answer: D

D is the correct answer because there is no PMI process called Procurement Quality Planning.

A, B, and **C** are incorrect answers because all these are valid processes of quality management.

91. Answer: B

B is the correct answer because the risk register is the only output of the risk identification process formally called Identify Risks.

A is incorrect because the recommended corrective actions could be the output of risk monitoring and controlling, but not of the risk identification process.

C and **D** are incorrect because these are not output items of the risk identification process.

92. Answer: D

D is the correct answer because there is no risk response strategy named audit.

A, B, and **C** are incorrect because avoid, transfer, and mitigate are the strategies to respond to negative risks (threats).

93. Answer: A

A is the correct answer because a good mitigation strategy is to take action early on to first reduce the probability of the risk happening and then plan for reducing its impact if it does occur, rather than letting it occur and then trying to reduce the impact or repair the damage.

B, C, and **D** are incorrect answers because these are correct statements about mitigation.

94. Answer: B

B is the correct answer because the risk register is the output of the risk identification process.

A, C, and **D** are incorrect because all these items are input to the risk identification process.

95. Answer: A

A is the correct answer because the processes in risk management are plan risk management, identify risks, perform qualitative risk analysis, perform quantitative risk analysis, plan risk responses, and monitor and control risks.

B is incorrect because risk evaluation is not a risk management process.

C is incorrect because risk evaluation and risk mitigation are not risk management processes.

D is incorrect because risk transference and risk assessment are not risk management processes.

96. Answer: A

A is the correct answer because work packages, the components at the lowest levels of the WBS, are decomposed into activities.

B, C, and **D** are incorrect because activities are derived from the work packages of the WBS.

97. Answer: D

D is the correct answer because risk response planning is used to develop options to maximize opportunities and minimize threats from the risks that have already been identified and analyzed.

A, B, and **C** are incorrect because the risks are identified and analyzed before you look at the options to enhance opportunities and reduce risks from them.

98. Answer: B

B is the correct answer because recommended corrective actions are an output of the risk monitoring and controlling process but not of the risk response planning process.

A, C, and **D** are incorrect answers because these items are outputs of the risk response planning process formally called Plan Risk Responses.

99. Answer: B

B is the correct answer because an acceptance strategy is used to accept the risk—that is, either take no action or take action contingent upon a condition that might become true in the future.

A, C, and **D** are incorrect because these are false interpretations of the acceptance strategy.

100. Answer: C

C is correct because performance reports are input to the risk monitoring and control process.

A, B, and **D** are incorrect answers because all these items are output of the risk monitoring and control process.

101. Answer: B

B is the correct answer because all the listed items are techniques that can be used in quantitative risk analysis.

A is incorrect because mitigation is a risk response planning strategy.

C is incorrect because checklist analysis is a technique used in the risk identification process.

D is incorrect because contingency is a risk response strategy.

102. Answer: B

B is the correct answer because risk response planning is performed in the risk response planning process.

A, C, and **D** are incorrect because these are items that can be included in the risk management plan document.

103. Answer: B

B is the correct answer because the risks are prioritized in the qualitative risk analysis.

A, C, and **D** are incorrect because the probability and impact matrix is a technique used in the qualitative risk analysis.

104. Answer: C

C is the correct answer because risk audits are used in the risk monitoring and control process.

A, B, and **D** are incorrect because all these are tools and techniques for the qualitative risk analysis process that can be used to prioritize risks.

105. Answer: D

D is the correct answer because the WBS dictionary is not part of the risk register.

A, B, and **C** are incorrect answers because all these items are part of the risk register after the updates from the risk response planning process.

106. Answer: C

C is the correct and the best answer because the project plan is developed starting from the concept and going through progressive elaboration.

A and **B** are incorrect because A is the lifecycle and B includes the project lifecycle. Progressive elaboration does not include the lifecycle of the project; its goal is to plan the project. Because the project planning may develop (or change) throughout the project lifecycle, progressive elaboration may continue through the project lifecycle, but it does not include the work of the lifecycle.

D is incorrect because it is the technique to create the WBS.

107. Answer: C

C is the correct because the project charter names the project manager and provides the project manager the authority to use organizational resources to run the project.

A is incorrect because the sponsor is not authorized by the project charter; the opposite might be true.

B is incorrect because it will be your (the project manager's) responsibility to identify all the stakeholders.

D is incorrect because the project team is not formed in the initiation phase.

108. Answer: B

B is correct because the project assumptions should be included in the project charter.

A is incorrect because assumptions by definition represent uncertainty, and as a project manager, it is your responsibility to validate the assumptions at various stages of the project.

C is incorrect because it is not the correct definition of assumption.

D is incorrect because you can start the project with the assumptions. All you have to do is validate them at various stages of the project and analyze them as part of risk management.

109. Answer: B

B is correct because the project charter is created in the initiation stage, and it is an input item to creating the project scope statement, which in turn is an input to creating the WBS.

A is incorrect because the project charter is input to the Define Scope process that creates the project scope statement.

C is incorrect because the WBS is created before schedule development, and the project charter is created before the WBS.

D is incorrect because the project scope statement is an input item to creating the WBS.

110. Answer: A

A is the correct answer because the project staff assignments are the output of the Acquire Project Team process.

B, C, and **D** are incorrect because all these items are output of the human resource planning process. These are parts of the human resource plan, a document created during human resource planning.

111.   Answer: B

B is the correct answer because the scope statement, the WBS document, and the WBS dictionary combined make the scope baseline against which all change requests will be evaluated.

A, C, and **D** are incorrect because all these are true statements about the project scope management plan.

112.   Answer: C

C is correct because, you, the project manager, create the WBS with help from the project team.

A is incorrect because the project manager creates the WBS with help from the team.

B is incorrect because the project manager creates the WBS with help from the team. The project sponsor can help as part of the team, however.

D is incorrect because the customer does not create the WBS.

113.   Answer: D

D is correct because benchmarking can be used in quality planning but not in human resource planning.

A, B, and **C** are incorrect answers because all these are tools and techniques that can be used in human resource planning.

114.   Answer: A

A is the correct answer because a risk can have a negative or a positive effect on a project.

B, C, and **D** are incorrect answers because these are true statements about project risks.

115.   Answer: C

C is the correct answer because the Manage Stakeholder Expectations process belongs to project communication management.

A, B, and **D** are incorrect answers because all these processes are part of the project human resource management.

116.   Answer: C

C is the correct answer because decision tree analysis is the technique used in quantitative risk analysis.

A, B, and **D** are incorrect answers because brainstorming, the Delphi technique, and SWOT analysis are the valid information-gathering techniques used for identifying risks.

117.   Answer: C

C is correct because secondary risks are those risks that arise as a result of risk responses.

A is incorrect because a residual risk is a risk that remains after a response has been performed.

B is incorrect because depending upon the nature of the secondary risk, it can have any priority.

D is incorrect because the risk response will depend upon the analysis results of the risk.

118.   Answer: A

A is the correct answer because an activity has external dependency when it relies on factors outside the project.

B is incorrect because an activity Y has a mandatory dependency on activity X when Y inherently depends on X.

C is incorrect because there is no such dependency called internal.

D is incorrect because we have an external dependency here.

119.   Answer: C

C is the correct answer because personal choices, such as lifestyles or political and religious beliefs, should not be considered during these assignments.

A, B, and **D** are incorrect answers because competency, availability, and salary requirements (cost) are valid factors to be considered for staff assignments.

120.   Answer: D

D is the correct answer because conflict management is a technique used in the Manage Project Team process.

A, B, and **C** are incorrect because the conflict management technique is not used in these processes.

121.   Answer: C

C is the correct answer because co-location is a technique used in the Develop Project Team process.

A, B, and **D** are incorrect because the co-location technique is not used in these processes.

122.   Answer: B

B is the correct answer because a bonus is not a tool available for project team management.

A, C, and **D** are incorrect answers because these are tools available for the Manage Project Team process.

123.   Answer: B

B is the correct answer because a virtual team is a tool for the Acquire Project Team process.

A, C, and D are incorrect answers because a virtual team is a tool for the Acquire Project Team process.

124.   Answer: C

C is the correct answer because the goal here is to develop a team that might consist of members with various levels of preparation and experience.

A, B, and D are incorrect answers because these are good characteristics for a sound reward strategy.

125.   Answer: B

B is the correct answer because collaboration provides a win/win resolution.

A is incorrect because avoidance provides a lose/lose resolution.

C is incorrect because accommodation provides a lose/win resolution.

D is incorrect because compromise provides a lose-win/lose-win resolution, and both parties might look at it as a lose/lose resolution.

126.   Answer: A

A is the correct answer because the main purpose of the activity definition process is to prepare the activity list and determine attributes for each activity.

B is incorrect because the WBS contains work packages, not activities.

C is incorrect because scope planning determines how the project scope will be defined, verified, and controlled and how the WBS will be created.

D is incorrect because the activity list is an input to schedule development.

127.   Answer: B

B is the correct answer because the main purpose of the risk identification process, formally called Identify Risks, is to create the risk register, which contains a list of risks.

A is incorrect because there is no PMI process with the name Define Risks.

C is incorrect because the risk management planning process determines how to plan and execute the risk management activities.

D is incorrect because risk response planning takes a list of risks (risk register) as input.

128. Answer: C

C is the correct answer because the quality audit is a technique for performing quality assurance.

A and B are incorrect because the quality audit is a technique for performing quality assurance.

D is incorrect because there is no such quality management process called Perform Quality Inspection.

129. Answer: B

B is the correct answer because each activity on the critical path has a zero float time, and therefore if an activity is delayed, it will delay the entire project.

A, C, and D are incorrect because these are incorrect statements about the activities on the critical path.

130. Answer: A

A is the correct answer because the selected sellers list is an output of the Conduct Procurements process.

B, C, and D are incorrect because all these items are the output of the Plan Procurements process.

131. Answer: A

A is the correct answer because there is no PMI process named Select Sellers in the *PMBOK Guide, Fourth Edition.*

B, C, and D are incorrect answers because all these processes belong to procurement management.

132. Answer: C

C is the correct answer because there is no contract type named profit shared.

A, B, and D are incorrect answers because all these are valid contract types.

133. Answer: B

B is the correct answer because fixed price (or lump sum) is the most suitable contract type for a well-defined product.

A, C, and D are incorrect because the product to be procured is well defined.

134. Answer: B

B is the correct answer because cost overrun is paid by the buyer, and the fee increases with the increase in cost as well.

A is incorrect because the firm fixed price presents risks to both buyer and seller because the fixed price might turn out to be above or below the actual cost.

C and **D** are incorrect because the fee in these cases does not rise with the rise of the actual cost.

E is incorrect because in a time and material contract, there could be a cost overrun to be paid by the buyer, but unlike a contract in the category of cost plus percentage of cost, there is no increasing fee attached to the increasing cost.

135. Answer: C

C is the correct answer because the procurement documents should be rigorous enough to ensure consistent responses from different sellers that can be fairly compared to one another and flexible enough to allow the sellers to offer suggestions on better ways to satisfy the requirements.

A is incorrect because it does not allow the sellers to be creative in offering solutions.

B is incorrect because the documents must be rigid enough that each seller understands the requirements.

D is incorrect because the requirements are set by the buyer, not by the seller.

136. Answer: C

C is the correct answer because when managed properly, differences in opinion can lead to better decisions and increased productivity.

A, B, and **D** are incorrect answers because these are true statements related to conflict management.

137. Answer: A

A is the correct answer because this is not the recommended approach toward advertising. It is a useful tool that can be used in the Request Seller Responses process.

B, C, and **D** are incorrect because all of these are true statements about advertising as a tool in the Request Seller Responses process.

138. Answer: C

C is the correct answer because approved change requests are an output of the integrated change control process and an input to the Direct and Manage Project Execution process. Remember, execution is all about implementation.

A, B, and **D** are incorrect because all these items are outputs of the Direct and Manage Project Execution process.

139. Answer: B

B is the correct answer because the Manage Project Team process belongs to the project human resource management.

A, C, and **D** are incorrect because all these processes are part of project integration management.

140. Answer: B

B is the correct answer because you might need to negotiate with functional managers to acquire project team members.

A, C, and **D** are incorrect because negotiation is not one of the tools used in these processes, according to PMI.

In real life, though, remember that negotiation is a very useful tool that can be used in countless situations.

141. Answer: C

C is the correct answer because the administrative part of the project closure must be performed whenever the project closure is performed at the end of a project or at the end of each phase of a project.

A, B, and **D** are incorrect because these are false statements about administrative closure.

142. Answer: C

C is the correct answer because releasing resources is part of the Close Project process. Remember, the formal name of the process is Close Project or Phase.

A and **B** are incorrect because there are no PMI processes named Release Resources and Administrative Closure. Administrative closure is a procedure that is an output of the Close Project process.

D is incorrect because resources are released during the Close Project or Phase process.

143. Answer: A

A is the correct answer because a Pareto diagram is a tool used in the Perform Quality Control process to rank errors based on the frequency of occurrences.

B and **C** are incorrect because a Pareto diagram is a tool used to rank defects in the quality control process. Caution: Quality control tools can also be used in quality assurance. Pay attention to what a tool is being used for.

D is incorrect because auditing is a technique used in the QA process.

144. Answer: B

B is the correct answer because the formula for cost variance is:

EV = BAC × (work completed / total work required)

which means

EV = $600,000 × (10 miles / 30 miles) = $200,000
CV = EV − AC

which means

CV = $200,000 − $150,000 = $50, 000

A, C, and **D** are incorrect because if the correct formula is applied, these results will not be achieved.

145. Answer: A

A is the correct answer because a CPI value greater than 1 means the cost performance of the project is better than planned, and an SPI value of greater than 1 means the schedule performance of the project is better than planned.

B, C, and **D** are incorrect because a CPI value greater than 1 means the cost performance of the project is better than planned, and an SPI value of greater than 1 means the schedule performance of the project is better than planned.

146. Answer: D

D is the correct answer because the Close Project or Phase process is part of project integration management.

A and **B** are incorrect because the Close Project or Phase process is part of project integration management.

C is incorrect because monitoring and controlling is a process group, not a knowledge area.

147. Answer: B

B is the correct answer because implementation of recommended actions can be the output of the Direct and Manage Project Execution process.

A, C, and **D** are incorrect because all these items are the output of the Close Project or Phase process.

148. Answer: C

C is the correct answer because the product accepted by the customer is an output of the Close Project or Phase process.

A, B, and **D** are incorrect because all these items are valid input to the Close Project or Phase process.

149. Answer: B

B is the correct answer because the risk probability and impact matrix is a tool for qualitative risk analysis.

A, **C**, and **D** are incorrect because all these items are included in the risk register.

150. Answer: C

C is the correct answer because dynamic programming is a mathematical model, not a benefit measurement method.

A, **B**, and **D** are incorrect because these are the valid project selection methods included in the category of benefit measurement methods.

151. Answer: B

B is the correct answer because a project can have positive as well as negative stakeholders.

A, **C**, and **D** are incorrect because these are true statements.

152. Answer: C

C is the correct answer because change requests are approved or rejected by processing them through the integrated change control process.

A is incorrect because there is no PMI process named Approve Changes.

B and **D** are incorrect because schedule control and quality control can generate recommendations for actions and requests for changes, but those actions and changes must be approved through the change control process.

153. Answer: A

A is the correct answer because the initiating process group contains two processes: Develop Project Charter and Identify Stakeholders.

B is incorrect because there is no standard process named Develop Preliminary Project Scope Statement.

C and **D** are incorrect because these processes belong to the planning process group.

154. Answer: B

B is the correct answer because a project manager is assigned to the project in the project charter, which is an output of the Develop Project Charter process in the initiating process group.

A and **C** are incorrect because a project cannot start until the project charter is approved and the project charter names the project manager.

D is incorrect because human resource planning is a knowledge area and not a process group.

155. Answer: C

C is the correct answer because the risk was discovered during execution and was not identified during planning.

A is incorrect because executing is a process group and not a process.

B is incorrect because the risk was discovered during execution and was not identified during planning.

D is incorrect because quantitative risk analysis is performed during the planning stage.

156. Answer: D

D is the correct answer because it is a wrong statement about a program. A program is a set of related projects that can produce independent products for different customers.

A, B, and **C** are incorrect answers because these are characteristics of a program.

157. Answer: D

D is the correct answer because changes are implemented by using the Direct and Manage Project Execution process.

A, B, and **C** are incorrect answers because all these items are outputs of the integrated change control process.

158. Answer: C

C is the correct answer because you have already done the planning procurements work, as stated in the definition of the question.

A is incorrect because you have just finished the plan procurements work.

B and **D** are is incorrect because there are no standard processes with these names.

159. Answer: D

D is the correct answer because it is the project manager's responsibility to manage the project stakeholders' expectations and keep them on the same page about the project objectives.

A is incorrect because it is the project manager's responsibility to manage the project stakeholders' expectations.

B and **C** are incorrect because the differences about objectives (and conflicts among the team members) must be resolved. Different expectations from the project mean that the stakeholders are not on the same page about the project scope, and that can be damaging to the project.

160. Answer: B

B is the correct answer because it deals with the problem head-on in a professional manner with the intention of solving it.

A, **C**, and **D** are incorrect because by choosing any one of these options, you are not dealing with the problem directly and effectively.

161. Answer: B

B is the correct answer because the first thing you should do about a change request is study its effects and process it through the change control process.

A, **C**, and **D** are incorrect answers because the change first must go through the change control process.

162. Answer: D

D is the correct answer because there is no such method as project-oriented programming used for project selection.

A, **B**, and **C** are incorrect because these are valid project selection methods included in the category of mathematical models. Another method included in this model is dynamic programming.

163. Answer: C

C is the correct answer because the code of conduct clearly states that any situation that can be looked upon as conflict of interest should be disclosed.

A, **B**, and **D** are incorrect because you are not being upfront and open.

164. Answer: C

C is the correct answer because your job is to understand and resolve conflicts, not to create them.

A, **B**, and **D** are incorrect because these are true statements.

165. Answer: C

C is the correct answer because this is not part of the PMP Code of Ethics and Professional Conduct.

A, **B**, and **D** are all incorrect because these activities are included in the PMP Code of Professional Conduct.

166. Answer: A

A is the correct answer because project charter is produced in the initiating stage.

B is incorrect because there is no standard document called the preliminary project scope statement in the *PMBOK Guide, Fourth Edition.*

C and **D** are incorrect because the project management plan and project schedule are produced in the planning stage of the project.

167. Answer: A

A is the correct answer because if in a foreign land you are asked to do something that is unethical and illegal in your home country, you are supposed to investigate whether it is illegal and unethical there as well.

B and D are incorrect because you don't know yet whether the sponsor is asking you to do something illegal.

C is incorrect because you think it is unethical and illegal, so you must investigate it.

168. Answer: C

C is the correct answer because the Collect Requirements process belongs to the planning process group.

A and B are incorrect because these processes belong to the initiating process group.

D is incorrect because the Acquire Project Team process belongs to the executing process group.

169. Answer: C

C is the correct answer because if the project sponsor has cancelled the project, it's the end of the story, but you still need to close the project using the Close Project or Phase process.

A, B, and D are incorrect because these are not the appropriate actions to take.

170. Answer: A

A is the correct answer because the purpose of change control is to manage the changes, not necessarily oppose them.

B, C, and D are incorrect because all these are valid purposes of the integrated change control process.

171. Answer: C

C is the correct answer because once you have a list of activities, you can sequence them.

A is incorrect because there are a number of processes that must be performed after preparing the list of activities and before scheduling the activities.

B is incorrect because you must have a schedule before you can control it.

D is incorrect because you must have a WBS before you can create a list of activities.

172. Answer: A

A is the correct answer because qualitative risk analysis is performed before quantitative risk analysis, and planning is performed before executing.

B is incorrect because qualitative risk analysis is performed before quantitative risk analysis.

C is incorrect because planning is performed before executing.

D is incorrect because you must identify and analyze risks before you can control them.

173. Answer: C

    C is the correct answer because you cannot control a schedule unless you have a schedule; it's common sense. (Remember Thomas Paine?)

    A, **B**, and **D** are incorrect answers because all these processes need to be performed before you can develop the project schedule.

174. Answer: C

    C is the correct answer because the baseline should only be changed due to the approved changes in the factors that define or impact the baseline.

    A, **B**, and **D** are incorrect because these are not reasons to change the baseline.

175. Answer: B

    B is the correct answer because project management involves performing processes belonging to knowledge areas, and you use your experience and skills to perform those processes.

    A is incorrect because this is not the defining characteristic of project management.

    C is incorrect because project management is a discipline that exists independent of functional managers.

    D is incorrect because the size of the project is not a criterion for using project management. Each project needs to be managed for efficient execution.

176. Answer: D

    D is the correct answer because the WBS is an output of the Create WBS process.

    A is incorrect because the project scope statement is a major output of the Define Scope process.

    B and **C** are incorrect because these items are parts of the project scope statement.

177. Answer: B

    B is the correct answer because fairness, honesty, respect, and responsibility are the four fundamental values in the Code of Ethics and Professional Conduct by the PMI.

    A, **C**, and **D** are incorrect because one fundamental value is missing from each of these options.

178. Answer: C

C is the correct answer because Theory Y managers trust their employees.

A is incorrect because there is no standard management theory called Theory T.

B is incorrect because Theory X managers think that employees dislike their work and will try to avoid it.

D is incorrect because McClellands's theory states that the need for achievement, affiliation, and power motivates the employees. C is the more appropriate answer in this case.

179. Answer: A

A is the correct answer because your supervisor's comments are consistent with Maslow's hierarchy of needs theory.

B is incorrect because socialism is not a management theory; it's an economic system theory, like capitalism.

C and D are incorrect because these theories do not apply to the comments made by your supervisor.

180. Answer: B

B is the correct answer because:

The probability that OTF will not deliver is $1 - 3/4 = 1/4$

The probability that ST will not deliver is $2/3$

The probability that both will not deliver is $1/4 \times 2/3 = 2/12 = 1/6 = 0.17$

A, C, and D are incorrect answers because these are based either on miscalculations or on calculations based on incorrect understanding of probability.

Appendix D

Glossary

360-degree survey. A form of feedback from all around the entity being evaluated.

abusive manner. Conduct that hurts another person either physically or emotionally, such as creating feelings of exploitation, manipulation, fear, or humiliation.

activity. A component of project work.

activity definition. The process of identifying the specific schedule activities that need to be performed to produce the project deliverables.

activity duration. The time measured in calendar units between the start and finish of a schedule activity.

activity duration estimating. The process of estimating the time in work periods individually for each schedule activity required for its completion. A work period is a measurement of time when the work is in progress; it is measured in hours, days, or months depending upon the size of the activity.

activity resource estimating. The process of estimating the types and amounts of resources that will be required to perform each schedule activity.

activity sequencing. The process of identifying and documenting the dependencies among schedule activities.

actual cost (AC). The total cost actually incurred until a specific point on the timescale in performing the work for a project or a project activity.

alternatives identification. A technique used to apply nonstandard approaches, such as brainstorming and lateral thinking, to perform project work.

analogous estimating. A technique used to estimate the duration of an activity based on the duration of a similar activity in a previous project.

assumption. A factor that you consider to be true without any proof or verification. Assumptions can appear in both the input and the output of various processes.

assumptions analysis. A technique used to examine the validity of an assumption and thereby identify the risk resulting from the inaccuracy, inconsistency, or incompleteness of each assumption.

asynchronous communication. A communication in which the two communicating entities do not have to be present on both ends of the communication line at the same time. E-mail is an example of asynchronous communication because when the sender of the e-mail pushes the send button, the intended recipient of the e-mail message does not have to be logged on to the e-mail server.

baseline. A reference plan for components, such as schedule, scope, and cost, against which performance deviations are measured. The reference plan can be the original or the modified plan.

benchmarking. Comparing practices, products, or services of a project with those of some reference projects for the purposes of learning, improvement, and creating the basis for measuring performance.

brainstorming. A creative technique generally used in a group environment to gather ideas as candidates for a solution to a problem or an issue without any immediate evaluation of these ideas. The evaluation and analysis of these ideas happens later.

budget. Aggregation of cost estimates with a timeline assigned to it.

budget at completion (BAC). The total budget authorized for performing the project work. This is the planned budget for the project, the cost that you originally estimated for the project.

cause and effect diagram. A diagram used to explore all the potential causes (inputs) that result in a single effect (output), such as a problem or a defect.

change control board. A formal group of stakeholders with the authority to process change requests, which includes reviewing, approving, rejecting, and delaying change requests.

change control system. A collection of formal documented procedures that specifies how the project deliverables and documents will be changed, controlled, and approved.

change request. A request for deviating from the project plan or related policies or procedures, such as modifying scope, schedule, or cost. Change requests may include recommendations for corrective and preventive actions.

claim. An assertion, demand, or request made by a buyer against the seller or vice versa for consideration or compensation under the terms of a legal contract.

close procurements. The process used to complete and settle each contract, which includes resolving any open item and closing each contract applicable to the project.

close project or phase. A process used to finalize all activities across all of the process groups to formally close the project or a phase of it. It's also used to establish the procedures for administrative and contract closures.

code of accounts. A numbering system used to uniquely identify each component of a WBS.

communication management plan. A document that describes the communications needs and expectations of the project and how these needs and expectations will be met.

confidence level. A statistical term that refers to the certainty attached to an estimate and is often represented in percentage form, such as a 95% confidence level.

configuration management. Refers to controlling the characteristics of a product, a service, or a result of a project. It includes documenting the features of a product or a service, controlling and documenting changes to the features, and providing support for auditing the products for conformance to requirements.

constraint. A restriction (or a limitation) that can affect the performance of the project. Assumptions can appear in both the input and the output of various processes.

contingency. A future event or condition that is possible but cannot be predicted with certainty. In this case, an action will be contingent upon the condition—that is, the action will be executed only if the condition happens.

contingency reserve. Funds or time reserved in addition to the calculated estimates to deal with the uncertainties in the duration used in the schedule and the cost used in the budget and to deal with overruns of the project objectives to meet the stakeholder expectations.

contract. A mutually binding agreement between a buyer and a seller that obligates the seller to provide the specified product, service, or result and obligates the buyer to make the payment for it.

control. To analyze the performance and make and implement recommendations for corrective actions or other changes to bring the project back on track.

control account. A node in the WBS that acts as a management control point where scope, schedule, and actual cost are integrated and compared to the earned value to measure the project performance.

control chart. A chart or diagram used to monitor whether the variance of a specified variable is within the acceptable limits dictated by quality control.

COQ. Cost of quality; the total cost of quality-related efforts throughout the product lifecycle.

corrective actions. Actions recommended for execution in the future in order to bring project performance back in line with the project management plan.

cost baseline. The planned budget for the project over a time period, used as a basis against which to monitor, control, and measure the cost performance of the project. The cost performance is measured by comparing the actual cost to the planned cost over a time period.

cost performance index (CPI). A measure of the cost efficiency of a project calculated by dividing earned value (EV) by actual cost (AC).

cost variance (CV). A measure of cost performance obtained by subtracting actual value (AC) from earned value (EV). A positive result indicates good performance, whereas a negative result indicates bad performance.

CPFF. Cost plus fixed fee; a contract type.

CPIF. Cost plus incentive fee; a contract type.

CPPC. Cost plus percentage of cost; a contract type.

crashing. A project schedule compression technique used to decrease the project duration with minimal additional cost. A number of alternatives are analyzed, including the assignment of additional resources.

critical path. The longest path (sequence of activities) in a project schedule network diagram. Because it is the longest path, it determines the duration of the project.

critical path method (CPM). A schedule network analysis technique used to identify the schedule flexibility and the critical path of the project schedule network diagram.

decision tree analysis. A technique that uses a decision tree diagram to choose from different options available; each option is represented by a branch of the tree. EMV analysis is done along each branch, which helps to make a decision about which option to choose.

decode. To convert the received message from the media back into useful ideas and thoughts.

decomposition. A planning technique to subdivide the project scope, including deliverables, into smaller, manageable tasks called *work packages*.

defect. An imperfection or deficiency that keeps a component from meeting its requirements or specifications. A defect is caused by an error (problem) and can be repaired by fixing the error.

deliverable. A unique and verifiable product, a capability to provide a service, or a result that must be produced to complete a project or a process or phase of the project.

Delphi technique. An information-gathering technique used for experts to reach a consensus while sharing their ideas and preferences anonymously.

distribute information. The process of making information available to stakeholders according to the project management plan.

earned value (EV) or budgeted cost of work performed (BCWP). The value of the actually performed work expressed in terms of the approved budget for a project or a project activity for a given time period.

earned value management (EVM) or earned value technique (EVT). A management methodology and a technique to measure project progress by comparing integrated measures of scope, schedule, and cost with the planned performance baseline.

encode. To convert thoughts and ideas into a message that could be transmitted through the media.

enterprise environmental factors. Factors internal or external to the performing organization that can influence the project's success, such as the organization's culture, infrastructure, existing skill set, market conditions, and project management software. These are input to both the project charter and the preliminary project scope statement.

estimate at completion (EAC) at budgeted rate. The estimate from the current point in time of how much it will cost to complete the entire project or an entire project activity for which the BAC is given. The value of EAC is obtained by adding the value of ETC at the budgeted rate to AC.

estimate at completion (EAC) at current CPI. The estimate from the current point in time of how much it will cost to complete the entire project or an entire project activity for which the BAC is given. The value of EAC is obtained by adding the value of ETC at the current CPI to AC.

estimate to complete (ETC) at budgeted rate. The expected cost, estimated by assuming the future performance will be at the budgeted rate, to complete the remaining work for the project or for a project activity.

estimate to complete (ETC) at present CPI. The expected cost, estimated by assuming the future performance will be at the current CPI, to complete the remaining work for the project or for a project activity.

Expected Monetary Value (EMV) analysis. A statistical technique used to calculate the expected outcome when there are multiple possible outcome values with probabilities assigned to them.

experiment design. A statistical method that can be used to identify the factors that can influence a set of specific variables of a product or a process under development or in production.

fairness. An act of making decisions and behaving impartially and objectively, free from favoritism, competing self-interest, and prejudice.

fast tracking. A project schedule compression technique used to decrease the project duration by performing project phases or some schedule activities within a phase simultaneously, when they would normally be performed in sequence.

float time. The positive difference between the late start date and the early start date of a schedule activity.

flowchart. A diagram that depicts inputs, actions, and outputs of one or more processes in a system.

FP. Fixed price; a contract type.

histogram. A bar chart that shows a distribution of variables.

honesty. The policy of understanding the truth based on facts and acting in a truthful manner both in communication and in conduct.

human resource plan. A document that describes roles and responsibilities, reporting relationships among the roles, and staffing management.

initiating process group. A process group that contains two processes: develop project charter and develop preliminary project scope statement.

inspection. A technique to examine whether an activity, component, product, service, or result conforms to specific requirements.

issue. An item or a matter that is under discussion or dispute and for which there are most likely opposing views and disagreements among the stakeholders.

issue log. A tool used to manage issues that includes opening, modifying, tracking, documenting, and resolving issues.

knowledge area. A knowledge area in project management is defined by its knowledge requirements related to managing a specific aspect of a project, such as cost, by using a set of processes. PMI recognizes a total of nine knowledge areas, such as cost management and human resource management.

lag. A technique to modify a dependency relationship by delaying the successor activity. For example, a lag of five days in a finish-to-start relationship means the successor activity cannot start until five days after the predecessor activity has ended.

lateral thinking. Thinking outside the box, beyond the realm of your experience, to search for new solutions and methods, rather than only better uses of the current solutions and methods.

lead. A technique to modify a dependency relationship by accelerating the successor activity. For example, a lead of five days in a finish-to-start relationship means the successor activity can start up until five days before the finish date of the predecessor activity.

logical relationship. A dependency between two project schedule activities or between a schedule activity and a schedule milestone.

managing stakeholder expectations. A process used for communicating and working with stakeholders to stay on the same page with them on the project requirements by addressing their needs and issues as they arise.

methodology. A system of procedures and techniques practiced in a discipline to accomplish a task. For example, risk management methodology is used in the discipline of project management to determine how risk management processes will be performed.

milestone. A significant point (or event) in the life of a project.

mitigation. The process of taking actions to reduce or prevent the impact of a disaster that is expected to occur.

model. A set of rules to describe how something works, which takes input and makes predictions as output.

monitor. To collect project performance information/data as planned, convert the information to performance measurements, and report the performance.

monitor and control risks. To track identified risks, identify new risks, monitor residual risks, implement risk response plans, and evaluate risk management processes.

Monte Carlo simulation. An analysis technique that randomly generates values for uncertain elements (that is, variables) and takes them as input to a model to generate output. In other words, it simulates a model by feeding randomly selected input values.

organization. A group of individuals organized to work for some purpose or mission.

organizational process assets. The processes and process-related assets of the organizations participating in the project that can be used to perform the project successfully, such as templates, guidelines, knowledge base, and policies and procedures.

parametric estimating. A quantitative technique used to calculate the activity duration when the productivity rate of the resource performing the activity is available.

Pareto diagram. A diagram used to rank the importance of each error (problem) based on the frequency of its occurrence over time in the form of defects.

perform quality assurance. A process used for ensuring that quality requirements are met.

performance measurement baseline. An approved integrated plan for the project specifying some parameters to be included in the performance measurements, such as scope, schedule, and cost. The performance of the project is measured against this baseline. Some technical and quality parameters can also become part of this baseline.

performance report. A document or a presentation that presents the project progress in terms of some parameters, such as earned value management parameters, based on the analysis of performance information/data.

performing organization. The organization that is performing the project.

planning component. A WBS component at the bottom level of a branch of the WBS hierarchy for which some planning can be performed.

planning package. A WBS component that is below the control account that has a well-defined work content but does not yet have a detailed schedule.

portfolio. A set of projects, programs, and related work that is managed in a coordinated fashion to obtain business objectives in the strategic plan of the organization.

portfolio management. The centralized management of one or more portfolios, which includes identifying, authorizing, prioritizing, managing, and controlling projects, programs, and other related work in order to obtain specific business objectives in the strategic plan of the organization.

precedence diagramming method (PDM). A technique used to construct a project schedule network diagram in which a node (a box) represents an activity and an arrow represents the dependency relationship.

preventive actions. Directions to perform an activity that will reduce the probability of negative consequences associated with project risks. These preventive actions are recommended by the QA process during process analysis.

process. A set of interrelated activities performed to obtain a specified set of products, results, or services.

process analysis. A technique used to identify the needed improvements in a process by following the steps outlined in the process improvement plan.

process improvement. An iterative method for improving the quality of all processes.

procurement. Refers to obtaining (purchasing or renting) products, services, or results from outside the project team to complete the project.

procurements. Purchases and acquisitions that are needed to complete the project but that cannot be produced by the in-house project team.

procurement audit. A structured review of the procurement process with the purpose of identifying successes and failures from the planning through the executing stage of the project.

procurement management. An execution of a set of processes used to obtain products, services, or results from outside the project team to complete the project.

procurement management plan. A document that describes how procurements will be managed.

product scope. Features and functions that characterize a product, service, or result to be delivered by the project.

program. A set of related projects managed in a coordinated fashion to improve overall efficiency and effectiveness that may not be obtained by managing the projects individually.

program management. The centralized coordinated management of a specific program to achieve its strategic goals, objectives, and benefits.

program management office (PMO). An entity in an organization that is responsible for providing centralized coordinated support to the program managers managing programs and unrelated projects.

progressive elaboration. A technique used to continuously improving a plan by working out more details and better accuracy as more detailed and specific information becomes available as the project progresses.

project calendar. A calendar of working days or shifts used to establish when a schedule activity can be performed. A calendar typically specifies holidays and weekends when a schedule activity cannot be performed.

project charter. A document that states the initial requirements to satisfy the stakeholders' needs and expectations and also formally authorizes the project.

project interfaces. The formal and informal boundaries and relationships among team members, departments, organizations, or functions. An example might be how the development department and the QA department interact with each other while working on the same project.

Project Management Information System (PMIS). An information system that consists of tools used to store, integrate, and retrieve the outputs of the project management processes. This can be used to support all stages of the project from initiating to closing.

project management plan. An approved document that describes how the project will be executed, monitored and controlled, and closed.

project management practitioner. Any individual who, as part of the project management profession, participates in an activity that contributes to the management of a project, program, or portfolio.

project performance. Measure of actual project progress against planned progress.

project/product transition. Handing over of the project output to the appropriate party.

project schedule. A schedule that consists of planned dates for performing schedule activities and meeting schedule milestones.

project schedule network diagram. A schematic display of logical relationships among the project schedule activities. The time flow in these diagrams is from left to right.

project scope. The work that must be performed (and only that work) to deliver products, services, or results with specified features that were promised by the project. The project scope draws the boundaries around the project—what is included and what is not.

project scope creep. Changes applied to the project scope without going through the approval process, such as the integrated change control process.

project scope statement. A document that defines the scope of a project by stating what needs to be accomplished by the project.

qualitative risk analysis. A process used to prioritize risks by estimating the probability of their occurrence and their impact on the project.

quality. The degree to which a set of characteristics of project deliverables and objectives fulfills the project requirements.

quality audit. A structured and independent review to determine whether project activities comply with the policies, processes, and procedures of the project and the performing organization. It verifies the implementation of approved change requests, corrective actions, defect repairs, and preventive actions.

quality baseline. A criterion that specifies the quality objectives for the project and thereby makes the basis for measuring and reporting the quality performance.

quality control. Monitoring results of executing quality-related activities and recommending necessary changes and actions to conform with the quality plans.

quality management plan. A management plan that describes how the project management team will implement the quality policy of the performing organization for the specific project.

quality metrics. An operational criterion that defines in specific terms what something (such as a characteristic or a feature) is and how the quality control process measures it.

quality planning. The process of identifying the quality standards relevant to the project at hand and determining how to satisfy these standards.

quality policy. Overall intentions and high-level direction of an organization with respect to quality, established by management at the executive level.

quantitative risk analysis. A process used to perform numerical analysis to estimate the effect of each identified risk on the overall project objectives and deliverables.

RAM. Responsibility assignment matrix; a matrix used to specify the relationships between schedule activities, roles to perform those activities, and team members assigned to the roles.

requirement. A condition, characteristic, or capability that a specific outcome of the project must have.

residual risk. A risk that remains after the risk response has been performed.

resource breakdown structure (RBS). A hierarchical structure of resource types required to complete the schedule activities of a project.

respect. A behavior of showing high regard for yourself, the people you are dealing with, and the resources entrusted to you.

responsibility. An act of taking ownership for the decisions you make or fail to make, the actions you take or fail to take, and the consequences that result.

risk. An uncertain event or condition that, if it occurs, has a positive or negative effect on meeting the project objectives.

risk breakdown structure (RBS). A hierarchical structure that breaks down the identified risk categories into subcategories. In developing this structure, you will end up identifying various areas and causes of potential risks.

risk identification. A process used to identify the risks for a given project and record their characteristics in a document called the *risk register*.

risk management plan. A document that describes how risk management will be structured and performed for the project at hand. It becomes part of the project management plan.

risk management planning. A process used to determine how to approach, plan, and execute risk management activities for a given project. This process produces the risk management plan.

risk register. A document that contains the results of risk analysis and risk response planning.

risk trigger. An alert that indicates a risk event has occurred or is about to occur.

role. A defined function that contains a set of responsibilities to be performed by a team member, such as a programmer or a tester.

rolling wave planning. A case of progressive elaboration in which the deliverables about which full information is available are decomposed to the lowest level, whereas the deliverables for which full information is not available are left at higher levels until the information becomes available.

run chart. A chart that shows the history and pattern of variations.

scatter diagram. A diagram used to show the pattern of the relationship between two variables—an independent variable and another variable that depends on the independent variable.

schedule activity. A scheduled task (component of work) performed during the lifecycle of a project.

schedule baseline. A specific version of the project schedule developed from the schedule network analysis and the schedule model data. This is the approved version of the schedule with a start date and an end date, and it is used as a basis against which the project schedule performance is measured.

schedule development. The process of creating the project schedule by analyzing schedule activity sequences, schedule activity durations, resource requirements, and schedule constraints.

schedule milestone. A significant event in the project schedule, such as the completion of a major deliverable.

schedule network analysis. A technique used to generate a project schedule by identifying the early and late start and finish dates for the project.

schedule performance index (SPI). A measure of the schedule efficiency of a project calculated by dividing earned value (EV) by planned value (PV).

schedule revision. An update to the project schedule that includes changing the project start date, end date, or both.

scope baseline. The approved project scope, which includes the approved project scope statement, the WBS based on the approved project scope statement, and the corresponding WBS dictionary.

scope definition. The process used to develop the detailed project scope statement.

scope planning. The process of developing the project scope management plan.

secondary risk. A risk that arises as a result of implementing a risk response.

simulation. Any analytical method used to imitate a real-life system.

SOX compliance. Compliance with the Sarbanes-Oxley Act of 2002, also called the Public Company Accounting Reform and Investor Protection Act of 2002.

staff management plan. A document that describes when and how human resource requirements for a project will be met.

stakeholder management strategy. The approach developed to deal with the stakeholders in the best interests of the project.

stakeholder register. A document that identifies the project stakeholders and the relevant information about them.

statement of work (SOW). A document that describes the products or services to be delivered by the project. It is an input to developing the project charter and the preliminary project scope statement.

statistical sampling. Randomly selecting a part of the population for study.

strengths, weaknesses, opportunities, and threats (SWOT) analysis. A technique used to gather information for risk identification by examining a given project from the perspectives of its strengths, weaknesses, opportunities, and threats.

subprojects. Parts of the main projects that are independent enough that each can be performed by separate project teams.

synchronous communication. Communication in which both the sender and the receiver have to be present at the same time, such as face-to-face project meetings and teleconferencing.

T&M. Time and material; a contract type.

variance. A measurable deviation in the value of a project variable, such as cost from a known baseline or expected value.

variance analysis. A technique used to assess the magnitude of variation in the value of a variable (such as cost from the baseline or expected value), determine the cause of the variance, and decide whether a corrective action is required.

verify scope. The process of formally accepting the completed project deliverables.

virtual team. A team of members working on the same project with few or no face-to-face meetings. Various technologies, such as e-mail, video conferencing, and the World Wide Web, are used to facilitate communication among team members.

war room. A conference room used for project team meetings.

work breakdown structure (WBS). A deliverable-oriented hierarchical structure that displays the decomposition of deliverables into work, which must be performed to accomplish the project objectives and create the project deliverables.

work package. A deliverable or a task at the lowest level of each branch of the WBS.

workaround. A response to a negative risk that has occurred. A workaround is based on a quick solution and is not planned in advance of the risk occurrence event.

Bibliography

Primary Reference

Project Management Institute. *A Guide to the Project Management Body of Knowledge (PMBOK Guide)*. Fourth Edition. Newtown Square, PA: Project Management Institute, 2008.

Secondary References

Project Management Institute. *The Standard for Program Management*. Second Edition. Newtown Square, PA: Project Management Institute, 2008.

Project Management Institute. *The Standard for Portfolio Management*. Second Edition. Newtown Square, PA: Project Management Institute, 2008.

Sanghera, Paul. *90 Days to Success as a Project Manager*. Boston: Course Technology PTR, 2009.

Sanghera, Paul. *PgMP: Program Management Professional Exam Study Guide*. Indianapolis: Wiley Publishing, Inc., 2007.

Sanghera, Paul. *PgMP: Fundamentals of Effective Program Management*. Fort Lauderdale: J. Ross Publishing, 2008.

Verma, V. K. *Human Resource Skills for the Project Manager*. Vol. 2. Newtown Square, PA: Project Management Institute, 1996.

Index